# THE
# PROMISES
# OF GOD

DAILY DEVOTIONALS

# THE
# PROMISES
# OF GOD

DAILY DEVOTIONALS

## H.M.S. RICHARDS

REVIEW AND HERALD® PUBLISHING ASSOCIATION
HAGERSTOWN, MD 21740

This book was
Copyedited by Jocelyn Fay and Delma Miller
Cover design by Palimor Studios
Cover photo by Voice of Prophecy
Interior design by Candy Harvey
Electronic makeup by Shirley M. Bolivar
Typeset: 11.5/13 Bembo

PRINTED IN THE U.S.A. (Reprinted 2004)

06  05  04          5  4  3  2

**R&H Cataloging Service**
Richards, H. M. S.
    The promises of God.

    1. Devotional calendar—Seventh-day Adventists.
I.  II. Title

ISBN: 0-8280-1793-X

# FOREWORD

Sawdust and shotguns. Boxing gloves and poetry. Oxymorons? Hardly. These expressions awkwardly describe the giant footprint of H.M.S. Richards, "Dean of Adventist Preachers." His life profoundly influenced so many lives.

I'm so pleased that after all these years his book *The Promises of God* is being placed back into print as a devotional book for adults. This classic first came out in 1956. That's precisely the year I remember my godly parents gathering our family of five little boys around the battery-operated tube radio each Sunday morning as we shivered on the cold prairies of Saskatchewan to hear Richards' broadcast, *The Voice of Prophecy,* wafting over CFQC-Saskatoon.

My young life was deeply affected by Elder H.M.S. Richards. I recall with pleasure the time our family traveled from Bermuda to Glendale, California, in 1961 and presented a Melashenko Family Singers musical worship at broadcast headquarters one morning. I was probably 14; my brothers' ages were 13, 12, 11, and 10. We sheepishly stood before the entire broadcast staff who was gathered for worship, including Elder Richards, Del Delker, and the King's Heralds out there in the audience—and we were entertaining *them!* Talk about role reversals! But there sat Elder Richards near the front row, tapping his foot and smiling broadly from ear to ear, chuckling softly as he listened to *his* big Russian basso-profundo friend Joe (formerly a King's Heralds bass member) lift up Jesus through music with his family of seven. I'll never forget seeing him wipe a tear from his eye as we finished our program by singing "Faith of Our Fathers" at the tops of our lungs.

In college Elder Richards visited my class of theology majors. I still remember some of the books he recommended we read, such as *Fifty Years in the Church of Rome,* by Charles Chiniquy.

In 1966 Elder Richards graciously received my college quartet into his private study. We rudely dropped in unannounced to visit and sing for him at his home on Bywood Street. The audacity! But he acted as if we were celebrities and he had all the time in the world for us. We were overwhelmed that he would take time with us "kids" to talk about his joy in ministry through music and the spoken word.

I remember something else. My first church assignment as a young pastor was the brand-new Camarillo church near Los Angeles. We had finished building it in 1975 and planned a special opening day service. We invited Elder Richards to come and speak, and announced a double-header service to accommodate all the guests. Sure enough, both services were packed, with standing room only. Trouble was, he preached two different sermons, so people weren't willing to go home and give up their seats for either service! I recall noticing that he placed a $5 bill in the offering plate at both services, and wondered how he could afford to do that. Later I learned from his wife, Mabel, that he always placed $5 in the offering. That was his custom throughout his entire ministry. (Five dollars was a lot of money in those days. Still is.)

Flavia Weedn once wrote that "some people come into our lives and leave footprints on our hearts, and we are never ever the same."

That was H.M.S. Richards. For me, a living legend. Consummate ambassador for Jesus. Preacher of the Living Word.

—E. Lonnie Melashenko
Director-Speaker
Voice of Prophecy
Moorpark, California

# JANUARY 1

*And I will put enmity between thee and the woman, and between thy seed and her seed; it shall bruise thy head, and thou shalt bruise his heel (Gen. 3:15).*

Our text for New Year's Day is appropriate, for it is the first promise of God to fallen humanity. It is the first revelation of God's covenant of grace, the first gospel sermon, the first prophecy of redemption. It is the first promise of our Lord Jesus Christ to every believer—not only of a Savior, but also of a Lord. When He was bruised at His crucifixion, the power of the serpent seemed supreme, but our Savior said: "Now is the judgment of this world: now shall the prince of this world be cast out. And I, if I be lifted up from the earth, will draw all men unto me" (John 12:31, 32).

Terrible was the bruising that our Lord endured, but even in the hour of apparent defeat He was victor. Soon the promise and prophecy of Genesis 3:15 will meet its complete fulfillment at our Lord's second coming and the final judgment.

During the year that we enter today, we may suffer much from the serpent and his seed, but we are not to despair. Jesus our Savior is our defender. We may be happy, too, as we trust in His strength. The psalmist exhorts, "Let all those that put their trust in thee rejoice: let them ever shout for joy, because thou defendest them" (Ps. 5:11).

We may be wounded at times and limp in our afflictions, but our Lord has set His foot on the serpent's head, and by faith we may have victory here and now, and at last reign with Christ Jesus, the Seed of the woman.

> Have faith in God, and in the virgin's Seed;
> Have faith in God, His promise meets our need;
> Have faith in God, from sin and Satan freed;
> Have faith, dear friend, in God.

MEDITATION PRAYER: *"Arise for our help, and redeem us for thy mercies' sake" (Ps. 44:26).*

# JANUARY 2

*And she shall bring forth a son, and thou shalt call his name JESUS: for he shall save his people from their sins (Matt. 1:21).*

As he was nearing death Thomas D. Talmage, the great evangelist, was asked by his son, "What do you really believe now, Father?"

Quickly the answer came: "Well, son, when I started to preach at twenty-five years of age, I held to one hundred doctrines; at thirty-five, I had fifty; at fifty, only twenty-five; later on, there were but ten; and now as I am facing eternity I hold only this one: I am a great sinner, but Jesus Christ is a great Savior."

The word "Jesus" means "Savior." It is our Lord's personal name and was given to Him at birth by angelic command. The word "Christ" means "the Anointed," or "Messiah" (John 1:41). It was at His baptism in the Jordan River that Jesus was anointed by the Holy Ghost (Acts 10:38) and publicly proclaimed by the voice of God to be His Son (Matt. 3:16, 17). By His resurrection and ascension He was finally proved to be Christ in the full sense of the word. "Therefore let all the house of Israel know assuredly, that God hath made that same Jesus, whom ye have crucified, both Lord and Christ" (Acts 2:36). His name reveals three things about His salvation:

First, He and He alone can save. "Neither is there salvation in any other: for there is none other name under heaven given among men, whereby we must be saved" (Acts 4:12).

Second, He will save only "his people," the saved of all nations. (Compare 1 Peter 2:9; Titus 2:14; Acts 15:14.)

Third, His name shows the breadth and depth of His salvation. He saves not only from the consequences of sin but from the sin itself, showing that He is the source not only of justification but also of sanctification. His name is really the contents table of the whole Bible. Are we among His people? Is He our Savior now?

MEDITATION PRAYER: *"Salvation belongeth unto the Lord: thy blessing is upon thy people" (Ps. 3:8).*

# JANUARY 3

*And the God of peace shall bruise Satan under your feet shortly. The grace of our Lord Jesus Christ be with you (Rom. 16:20).*

When Lord Nelson sent home to England his dispatches following the Battle of the Nile, he wrote, *"Victory* is not a name strong enough for such a scene as this." What will it be when the promise of our text is completely fulfilled? The word "victory" will not be strong enough for such a scene, such glory. This promise follows well on our text for January 1. Believers have the promise not only that the Seed of the woman will bruise the serpent's head but that he will be bruised under their feet. Victory will not come to God's children by their own power. It is God who will bruise Satan.

In His conflicts with Satan our Savior left us an example. He used "the sword of the Spirit, which is the word of God" (Eph. 6:17). In His three great temptations our Lord relied on the sword of the Scripture, and the enemy was not able to match its power. The Savior had only the Old Testament, but today we have the New Testament also to draw upon. Let us use this heavenly weapon, which is "sharper than any twoedged sword" (Heb. 4:12). So let us "keep looking up, going forward in faith," for the promise is that "God . . . shall bruise Satan under your feet *shortly."* Until then we may have victory every day. Let us often think of that word "shortly." What a joy to hear it! Soon, quickly, shortly, the victory will be ours, and Satan's head will be bruised. For this we must trust the God of peace. "And this is the victory that overcometh the world, even our faith" (1 John 5:4).

> Have faith in God, His victory brings release;
> Have faith in God, each day thy joy increase;
> Have faith in God, soon comes His rest and peace;
> Have faith, dear friend, in God.

MEDITATION PRAYER: *"But thou, O Lord, art a shield for me; my glory, and the lifter up of mine head" (Ps. 3:3).*

# JANUARY 4

*While the earth remaineth, seedtime and harvest, and cold and heat, and summer and winter, and day and night shall not cease (Gen. 8:22).*

One morning after a terrific thunderstorm a little child came downstairs and asked, "Daddy, what was God doing last night? Was He making the morning?" The father replied, "Yes, dear, I guess He was."

This is the promise of God: Day and night, the seasons one after another, will come. The earth had just been devastated by the Flood, the routine of life destroyed. Noah looked upon the scene of desolation and then turned to God in worship. Soon the smoke of his sacrifice ascended, and his faith was shown by his works. The great curse of the Flood was gone, and the Lord promised new blessings. The seasons and the succession of day and night are to continue as long as the earth endures. Sunset and sunrise, sunrise and sunset, is the record of history and astronomy. God's promise has not failed, nor will it fail. Whenever we see the sunrise, let us remember God's promise.

"Seedtime and harvest" make life possible. "Summer and winter, and day and night" are His fulfilled promises. The God of Noah is the God of nature, the God of fulfilled and fulfilling promises.

Over a fireplace in Princeton University is a motto written by Albert Einstein, which reads, "God is a scientist, not a magician." God's ways of upholding the universe we call the laws of nature; they are not erratic; they are dependable because they are based upon His promises. Modern science would be impossible if they were not.

Let us learn from Noah to make God first in our lives.

> Have faith in God, nor day nor night shall cease;
> Have faith in God, the seasons' due increase;
> Have faith in God, from Him our life and peace;
> Have faith, dear friend, in God.

MEDITATION PRAYER: *"And the heavens shall praise thy wonders, O Lord: thy faithfulness also in the congregation of the saints" (Ps. 89:5).*

# JANUARY 5

*And it shall come to pass, when I bring a cloud over the earth, that the bow shall be seen in the cloud: and I will remember my covenant, which is between me and you and every living creature of all flesh; and the waters shall no more become a flood to destroy all flesh (Gen. 9:14, 15).*

The waters of Noah will not return. The rainbow is a teacher from generation to generation. Children ask its meaning, and reverent parents explain it to them: There will not be another universal flood.

God's covenant with Noah still stands fast. Someday it will be completed in the eternal redemption of His people. So why should we worry about the clouds of trouble that darken the world? We never see the rainbow until a cloud arises. It has been said, "The soul would have no rainbow had the eyes no tears." How often we fail to think of God's promises until we find ourselves in one of life's cloudy days. Then we search the memory and God's Holy Book for them. When the sky is dark, God's precious promises shine like a rainbow above our troubles.

There is a rainbow about His throne (Rev. 4:2, 3). He always sees it there and remembers His promise. Our Savior, who pleads His blood for our sins, points to the bow as a token of God's peace with the human race. It was the prophet Ezekiel who saw that "as the appearance of the bow that is in the cloud in the day of rain, so was the appearance of the brightness round about" (Eze. 1:28). The more we know of God, the more we shall trust His rainbow promise of peace and love.

> There's a rainbow in the sky;
> We cannot see it, yet it's true;
> Arching where the storm unfurls,
> Like God's promise to the world,
> There's a rainbow in the sky—
> For you!

MEDITATION PRAYER: *"Thy faithfulness is unto all generations: thou hast established the earth, and it abideth" (Ps. 119:90).*

# JANUARY 6

*But he answered and said, It is written, Man shall not live by bread alone, but by every word that proceedeth out of the mouth of God (Matt. 4:4).*

Bread, the staff of life, represents food and everything that humanity needs for physical life—even the land on which the food grows. Leo Tolstoy tells of a land-hungry man who went to a distant country where, for a thousand rubles, he was offered all the land he could walk around in a day. He was to put his money down on a certain spot and then walk until sunset. When he returned to the money, all the land enclosed by his footsteps would be his. So the man started walking fast; then he ran, hurrying with all his strength. After great exertion he returned to the point of departure just as the sun was setting, but the task had been too great for him. He fell dead where he had started. Then all he could claim was a plot of ground six by three feet.

Our heavenly Father knows that we have need of bread. He knows also that we cannot "live by bread alone." We have a spiritual hunger that can never be satisfied with material things. Jesus said, "A man's life consisteth not in the abundance of the things which he possesseth" (Luke 12:15). He also said, "I am the bread of life" (John 6:35). "Give us this day our daily bread" is a prayer to be daily prayed and daily answered. "Thy words were found, and I did eat them; and thy word was unto me the joy and rejoicing of mine heart" (Jer. 15:16).

> Break Thou the bread of life,
>     Dear Lord, to me,
> As Thou didst break the loaves
>     Beside the sea;
> Beyond the sacred page
>     I seek Thee, Lord;
> My spirit pants for Thee,
>     O living Word!
>         —Mary A. Lathbury

MEDITATION PRAYER: *"Thy word is very pure: therefore thy servant loveth it"* (Ps. 119:140).

# JANUARY 7

*And he shall be like a tree planted by the rivers of water, that bringeth forth his fruit in his season; his leaf also shall not wither; and whatsoever he doeth shall prosper (Ps. 1:3).*

A tree keeps on growing as long as it lives; so should the true believer. Like a tree, he or she grows stronger day by day and year by year. The age of a tree can usually be determined by its annual growth rings. In dry years they are narrow; in seasons of plentiful rain they are wide. But the tree always grows *some*. Sometimes the growth is rapid, sometimes slow, but it is growth. The law of a tree is "grow or die." So it is with individuals who delight in the law of the Lord. They grow spiritually—in easy times and hard, in prosperity and adversity—sometimes rapidly, at other times slowly; but they grow.

Few people forget their first view of the great sequoia trees of California. Many look in silent awe at the General Sherman Tree, probably the oldest living thing on earth today. We are told that it was a large tree when David wrote the first psalm, which contains our text for today. It was a great tree when Jesus walked by Galilee, a monarch in the days of the Reformation, and now a world wonder. Empires have risen and fallen, but that great tree lives and is still growing. The child of God is to be like a tree, a tree planted by the rivers of water, always growing.

Looking down from a high mountain, I once gazed across the Arizona desert. Across its sun-scorched face ran a green line to the far horizon. It was the strange, upside-down Hassayampa River. The waters flowing sometimes unseen beneath its sandy bed nourish the luxuriant trees that mark its course across the desert. "Like a tree planted by the rivers of water," the child of God lives, grows, and bears fruit in the desert of this world. This is God's promise: "He shall be like a tree."

MEDITATION PRAYER: *"For thou hast made him a little lower than the angels, and hast crowned him with glory and honour" (Ps. 8:5).*

13

# JANUARY 8

*Come now, and let us reason together, saith the Lord: though your sins be as scarlet, they shall be as white as snow: though they be red like crimson, they shall be as wool (Isa. 1:18).*

Sir James Simpson, the celebrated Scottish surgeon and scientist who was one of the pioneers in the medical use of anesthetics, was once asked by a young man what he considered his greatest discovery. His simple reply was "My greatest discovery was that I am a sinner, but that Jesus is a great Savior."

God wants to reason with us about our sins, and this He does in today's promise—God's promise to everybody, for "all have sinned" (Rom. 3:23). It is a matter of life and death, "for the wages of sin is death" (Rom. 6:23).

Here is God's promise that when we meet the conditions, our sins "as scarlet . . . shall be as white as snow." That means forgiveness, cleansing, a new life out of death. But we must admit our need by coming to Christ. He came to do the will and work of God on earth, and He says: "All that the Father giveth me shall come to me; and him that cometh to me I will in no wise cast out" (John 6:37). These are His wonderful words to us. Shall we not come to Him? You see, that is our part of it. We must make the decision. Why not come to Him now? He says *now*—"Come now." Tomorrow never comes. Anything that we ever do will be done now. We live in the path of a point, and that point is *now*. "Now is the accepted time; behold, now is the day of salvation" (2 Cor. 6:2).

It is said that if one looks at a red rose through a piece of scarlet glass, the rose will look white. When God looks at our sins, "red like crimson," through the atoning sacrifice of the cross, they appear "as white as snow." And this is the reason: "Christ died for our sins" (1 Cor. 15:3).

MEDITATION PRAYER: *"Thou hast forgiven the iniquity of thy people, thou hast covered all their sin" (Ps. 85:2).*

# JANUARY 9

*And as Moses lifted up the serpent in the wilderness, even so must the Son of man be lifted up: that <u>whosoever believeth</u> in him should not perish, but have eternal life (John 3:14, 15).*

Because of their sins the children of Israel were attacked by "fiery serpents" in their wilderness journey (Num. 21). Thousands died. By divine instruction Moses made a serpent of brass and erected it upon a pole. <u>Then all who looked upon it were healed. This was an enacted prophecy of Christ and His death for our sins.</u>

An ill man came to his pharmacist and said, "Can you give me something for a bad cold?"

"Have you brought your prescription with you?" asked the pharmacist.

"No," was the answer, "but I brought my cold with me to be cured."

Often those seeking a cure for the sin disease try to bring their prescription to the Lord, but all He asks is that the sinner say:

> Just as I am, without one plea
> But that Thy blood was shed for me.
> —Charlotte Elliott

Notice, the Son of man *must* be lifted up, must die, if we are to live. At the cross His bitter enemies said, "He saved others; himself he cannot save" (Matt. 27:42). They never told a greater truth. To save humanity, He had to die. That's why He came to this world—"to give his life a ransom for many" (Matt. 20:28). <u>And notice this:</u> God used death, the terrible wages of sin, to destroy sin and death and to bring eternal life to all believers. A look at the brass serpent healed the serpent's bite. <u>At last it will be seen that our Savior's death upon the cross was really the death of death.</u>

Read today's promise text again, and emphasize the word "<u>whosoever.</u>" <u>That includes all of us if we will believe.</u>

MEDITATION PRAYER: *"Turn us again, O God of hosts, and cause thy face to shine; and we shall be saved" (Ps. 80:7).*

# JANUARY 10

*And he brought him forth abroad, and said, Look now toward heaven,*
*and tell the stars, if thou be able to number them: and he said unto*
*him, So shall thy seed be. And he believed in the Lord;*
*and he counted it to him for righteousness (Gen. 15:5, 6).*

On his deathbed King Philip II of Spain sent this word to his confessor: "Father Confessor, . . . I protest to you that I will do everything you shall say to be necessary for my being saved, so that what I admit doing will be placed to your account, as I am ready to acquit myself of all that shall be ordered to me." And one writer says, "He did everything he could for salvation."

Our promise text for today shows God's answer, the only answer, to earth's great problem—how to be righteous, how to be good. This is never accomplished by human effort. It is the gift of God, and faith is the hand by which we accept it. "The just shall live by faith" (Gal. 3:11). Sinners are made righteous by faith, not by works.

Notice here the law of first mention. In our text three great salvation words—"believed," "counted," "righteousness"—are found for the first time in the Bible, and all together. Abraham believed in the Lord, and God did the rest. Surely we can believe God when in His Word He promises to forgive our sins and count us righteous through Christ's atoning sacrifice. "Even the righteousness of God which is by faith of Jesus Christ unto all and upon all them that believe: for there is no difference: for all have sinned, and come short of the glory of God; being justified freely by his grace through the redemption that is in Christ Jesus" (Rom. 3:22-24). Will you believe in the Lord?

> Let not conscience make you linger,
> Nor of fitness fondly dream;
> All the fitness He requireth
> Is to feel your need of Him.
>
> —Joseph Hart

MEDITATION PRAYER: *"Lead me, O Lord, in thy righteousness" (Ps. 5:8).*

# JANUARY 11

*Behold my servant, whom I uphold; mine elect,*
*in whom my soul delighteth; I have put my spirit upon him:*
*he shall bring forth judgment to the Gentiles (Isa. 42:1).*

This is a prophecy of Christ. How wonderful it is in the mouth of Isaiah, spoken seven long centuries before Jesus was cradled in the Bethlehem manger. "Behold My servant," said the Lord. "Look upon Him. I uphold Him. He is My elect. I delight in Him. I have put My Spirit upon Him. He shall bring forth judgment and righteousness to the nations." Who could this be but Jesus?

In Isaiah's day the Israelites sought to confine the blessings of God to their own nation, but the coming Savior is for everyone. His gospel is to go forth to all and bring righteousness to them. The command of God here is really "Look to Jesus." In Hebrews 3:1 we have almost the same words: "Consider . . . Christ Jesus." Of those who crucified Jesus it was prophesied in Zechariah 12:10, "They shall look upon me whom they have pierced." And all His followers today are uged by the apostle to "look for the Savior" (Phil. 3:20). We should all be "looking unto Jesus the author and finisher of our faith; who for the joy that was set before him endured the cross, despising the shame, and is set down at the right hand of the throne of God" (Heb. 12:2). Where are we looking? At Christ, or at some of the failings of His followers?

Once when Mr. Astor was fording the Susquehanna River on horseback, he became dizzy and almost lost his balance from looking at the swirling waters below. A hunter traveling with him struck him on the chin and shouted, "Look up!" He did so and recovered his equilibrium. From the dizzy world that swirls about us, we need to look up to Christ. In Him is God's Spirit; in Him is our righteousness; in Him is life.

MEDITATION PRAYER: *"Rejoice the soul of thy servant: for unto thee, O Lord, do I lift up my soul" (Ps. 86:4).*

# JANUARY 12

*And he said, Certainly I will be with thee; and this shall be a token unto thee, that I have sent thee: When thou hast brought forth the people out of Egypt, ye shall serve God upon this mountain (Ex. 3:12).*

"Tell me," said one of Martin Luther's enemies, "when the whole world turns against you—church, state, princes, people—where will you be then?"

"Why, then as now," cried Luther, "in the hands of Almighty God."

God was sending Moses to confront the most powerful ruler in the world. No wonder he was afraid. But would God send a man alone to reprove a king and defeat an empire? Of course not! "Certainly I will be with thee." What more than that promise did Moses need?

As John Wesley lay dying, his preachers gathered round his bed. Suddenly he roused from unconsciousness, a smile broke over his face, and he said, "The best of all is God is with us." To us today, as to Moses and Wesley, that is the best of all. When God sent heaven's richest treasure, His Son and our Savior, to redeem humanity, the inspired promise declared, "They shall call his name Emmanuel, which being interpreted is, God with us" (Matt. 1:23). When we go on God's errands, He is with us, so we cannot fail. Then let us go, not timidly, halfheartedly, carelessly, or presumptuously, but realizing the very presence of God.

> O let me walk with Thee, my God,
> As Enoch walked in days of old.
> —Mrs. L. D. Avery Stuttle

What sort of persons ought we to be today, walking with God! If He is with us, we must succeed.

MEDITATION PRAYER: *"Though I walk in the midst of trouble, thou wilt revive me: thou shalt stretch forth thine hand . . . , and thy right hand shall save me" (Ps. 138:7).*

# JANUARY 13

*As truly as I live, all the earth shall be*
*filled with the glory of the Lord (Num. 14:21).*

The older I grow," said Thomas Carlyle, "and now as I stand upon the brink of eternity, the more comes back to me this sentence from the catechism that I learned as a child, and the fuller and deeper its meaning becomes: 'What is the chief end of man? To glorify God and enjoy Him forever.'"

The children of Israel had refused to glorify God by listening to His voice. They believed the majority report of the committee of spies and planned to appoint a pro-Egyptian leader to take them back to the land of bondage. There were giants in the Land of Promise, and the Israelites were afraid of giants. The official report of the committee said, "We were in our own sight as grasshoppers" (Num. 13:33). They had the grasshopper complex, and one is never so much like a grasshopper as when he or she feels like one.

Now, what about the march to the Promised Land? It seemed that the grasshopper people had ruined everything. God was about to destroy them, but Moses interceded for the backsliders. He reminded the Lord that all the unbelieving world was looking on and would say that God did not bring them into Canaan because He could not, that He was a limited God. And the Lord answered him, "I have pardoned according to thy word: but as truly as I live, all the earth shall be filled with the glory of the Lord" (Num. 14:20, 21).

So, friend, we may fail God, but God's glory will not fail. Egypt, the desert, the hunger, the thirst, the endless marching, the Amalekites, the mixed multitude, the fiery serpents, the subversive report, the grasshopper people—yes, all of that and more! But the glory will come; the earth will be filled with it. Let us march on to the Land of Promise.

MEDITATION PRAYER: *"Shew thy marvellous lovingkindness, O thou that savest by thy right hand them which put their trust in thee" (Ps. 17:7).*

# JANUARY 14

*Blessed are they which do hunger and thirst after righteousness: for they shall be filled (Matt. 5:6).*

Have you ever seen anyone really hungry? In some parts of this earth such people may be seen every day. Millions of them have been hungry all their lives and are hungry at this very moment. Hollow-eyed, they hold out their hands in earnest appeal for something to eat.

We must continually eat and drink, or die. Too much hunger or too much thirst is a terrible thing, but a certain amount is good. God created people and animals with hunger as part of their nature, and a wise provision it was, too. Without the urge of hunger, food would not be taken, and death by starvation would ensue. Even intelligent life would soon vanish from the earth. Human beings eat what they like and because they are hungry. And so by nature they eat, in general, that which sustains life. By and large, hunger and thirst are good. They drive people to eat and drink, and so to live.

But notice our promise text: "Blessed are they which do hunger and thirst after righteousness: for they shall be filled." Here is a real blessing, a spiritual blessing. Without a spiritual hunger and thirst no one will ever be filled. It is blessed to have this divine hunger. Jesus said, "No man can come to me, except the Father which hath sent me draw him" (John 6:44). Then, speaking of this God-implanted thirst for God and righteousness, He continues, "If any man thirst, let him come unto me, and drink" (John 7:37).

What does this promise mean to you, to me? The real question is Are we hungry? Are we thirsty? If we are, we shall be filled.

> Are you hungry? Come and eat,
>     The Bread of Heaven see;
> Are you thirsty? Come and drink,
>     The Word of God is free.

MEDITATION PRAYER: *"Oh that men would praise the Lord. . . . For he satisfieth the longing soul, and filleth the hungry soul with goodness" (Ps. 107:8, 9).*

# JANUARY 15

*Be strong and of a good courage, fear not, nor be afraid of them:*
*for the Lord thy God, he it is that doth go with thee;*
*he will not fail thee, nor forsake thee (Deut. 31:6).*

Between St. Giles Cathedral and the Parliament House in Edinburgh is a stone with the letters "J. K." on it, marking the spot where the dust of the great Reformer John Knox reposes. Knox was fully worthy of the verdict of the Regent Morton, who, as he saw him laid in the grave, exclaimed, "There lies he who never feared the face of man." Why was John Knox so fearless before people? Because by faith he had looked upon the face of God.

In any warfare what a wonderful promise is our text! Israel was about to cross over Jordan and meet seven enemy nations. They would need courage, and more than that, they would need the help of the Lord. This was promised to them and gloriously fulfilled. We need to be strong and of good courage. Why should we ever be afraid while obeying God's Word?

Notice, there is a threefold promise in this text: (1) The Lord will go with us; (2) He will not fail us; (3) He will not forsake us. Jesus knew that His Father was with Him. "I am not alone," He said, "because the Father is with me" (John 16:32). No one will be lonely or afraid when they realize that God is with them.

Last, and most important of all, He will not forsake us. Human helpers may forsake us in a crisis or leave us through extreme weariness. But never God! He is "the Lord *thy* God." He is the ever-present helper who never fails, never forsakes. "Trust ye in the Lord for ever: for in the Lord Jehovah is everlasting strength" (Isa. 26:4).

> Courage, brother, courage!
>   Turn not back, nor fear;
> God will not forsake us,
>   He is ever near.

MEDITATION PRAYER: *"I will love thee, O Lord, my strength"*
*(Ps. 18:1).*

# JANUARY 16

*He will keep the feet of his saints, and the wicked shall be silent in darkness; for by strength shall no man prevail (1 Sam. 2:9).*

A distinguished artist, speaking to some students on artistic composition, declared it to be wrong pictorially to paint a woods or forest without a path leading out of it. When a true artist paints such a landscape, they put in some suggestion of a path to carry the eye out of the picture. Otherwise the tangle of trees and undergrowth would suffocate us, or the wide, trackless spaces dismay us. So God provides a way of escape for His children.

The way of life is often rough, but the Lord will keep our feet. If we surrender all our ways to Him, He will be our guard and guide. Not only will He give His angels charge to keep us (Ps. 91:11), but He Himself will preserve our goings; He will keep our feet from falling. He will pluck our feet out of the net set by crafty foes (Ps. 25:15) and set them on the solid rock of faith. "He brought me up also . . . out of the miry clay, and set my feet upon a rock, and established my goings" (Ps. 40:2). He will not suffer our feet to be moved from the way of life (Ps. 66:9). He will guide our feet by His Word. "Thy word is a lamp unto my feet, and a light unto my path" (Ps. 119:105). He will make our feet like hinds' feet so that we can run the way of His commandments (Ps. 18:33). He will make beautiful the feet of those who bring good tidings (Isa. 52:7), for they are "shod with the preparation of the gospel of peace" (Eph. 6:15). And He will keep the feet of His saints in many other ways. God will lead us in "the way everlasting" (Ps. 139:24).

> I must have the Savior with me,
>> For I dare not walk alone;
> I must feel His presence near me,
>> And His arm around me thrown.
>> —Lizzie Edwards

MEDITATION PRAYER: *"Make thy way straight before my face" (Ps. 5:8).*

# JANUARY 17

*For thou art my lamp, O Lord: and the Lord
will lighten my darkness (2 Sam. 22:29).*

John Henry Jowett used to tell of a farmer who gave him a lantern when he had to meet a train on a stormy night, saying, "Just to help you see where you are going and keep you out of the ditch." Then the farmer added: "You see that glimmer of light yonder? That is Saddleworth station. Make for it." The lantern gave him a light for each step, and the glimmer in the distance showed him the appointed course.

"In thy light shall we see light" (Ps. 36:9). "Light is sown for the righteous" (Ps. 97:11). And in 1 John 1:5 it is written that "God is light." This light shines from His Word (Ps. 119:105), and we are to hold it forth as a torch in a dark night (Phil. 2:15, 16). But our light is from God's lamp; we merely reflect it. We are to "walk in the light *of the Lord*" (Isa. 2:5).

Are we in the dark? Let us be of good cheer—a brighter day is coming soon. Things will change. It may even become darker for a while, but the morning *will* come. When we cannot find one ray of light in ourselves, in our friends, or in the whole world, "then shall thy light rise in obscurity, and thy darkness be as the noon day" (Isa. 58:10). The Lord who said, "Let there be light," will speak us into sunshine. Look by faith to Jesus, and you will see the light of God.

> The Lord is my light; though clouds may arise,
> Faith, stronger than sight, looks up to the skies
> Where Jesus forever in glory doth reign:
> Then how can I ever in darkness remain?
> The Lord is my light, my joy, and my song;
> By day and by night He leads me along.
> —James Nicholson

MEDITATION PRAYER: *"For thou wilt light my candle: the Lord my God will enlighten my darkness" (Ps. 18:28).*

# JANUARY 18

*For our light affliction, which is but for a moment, worketh for us a far more exceeding and eternal weight of glory (2 Cor. 4:17).*

Edward L. Branham tells us that while he was in an airplane high over an island in the South Seas a fellow passenger told him to look down. There, following the plane, was a huge rainbow—a complete circle instead of the usual arc. Inside the gorgeous circle was a dark cross, the shadow of the plane. Wherever the cross went, the rainbow went. So each of our afflictions is a cross, but each cross is surrounded with the rainbow of God's promise.

Afflictions are afflictions. They do afflict us, pain us, try us, test us. Call affliction by any other name, and it is still something hard to endure. But notice the contrast between the *light* affliction and the *weight* of glory. With the believer, all things are to be weighed in the scales of eternity, not in the short balances of time.

The ancient king could look at the motto on his signet ring, "This, too, shall pass away," and know that every troubled hour would end at last. But we can know that our afflictions will end in glory—exceeding glory. In the school of adversity the child of faith is prepared for the day of glory. He or she learns to compare the light affliction with the weight of glory—the moment with eternal ages.

> Life is not a cloudless journey,
>     Storms and darkness oft oppress,
> But the Father's changeless mercy
>     Comes to cheer the heart's distress;
> Heavy clouds may darkly hover,
>     Hiding all faith's view above,
> But across the thickest darkness
>     Shines the rainbow of His love.
>             —Flora Kirkland

MEDITATION PRAYER: *"For thou wilt save the afflicted people; but wilt bring down high looks"* (Ps. 18:27).

# JANUARY 19

*The Lord is with you, while ye be with him; and if*
*ye seek him, he will be found of you; but if ye forsake*
*him, he will forsake you (2 Chron. 15:2).*

These three pronouncements are really one. In other words, it is strictly up to us. The Lord is with us as long as we are with Him. If we seek Him, He will be found. If we forsake Him, He will forsake us. Our relationship to God depends upon us. We may enjoy His presence if we desire it.

When discouraged, we sometimes complain, "The Lord has forsaken me!" Should we not look closely and honestly into our own hearts? Possibly we have forsaken the Lord. How? By failing to keep the candle of faith aflame. We stop feeding upon the Word of God. We neglect prayer. Soon the witness of the Spirit is gone, and we feel that God has forsaken us, whereas we have forsaken Him. This forsaking of God on our part is not often a defiant avowal of unbelief, but the easy drift of the tide, the current of the spirit of the age. We need not remain as spiritual orphans, however, for it is written, "Ye shall seek me, and find me, when ye shall search for me with all your heart" (Jer. 29:13).

This is not the time to forsake God. This is the day to seek Him, to find Him, and to walk with Him to the end.

> I would be, dear Savior, wholly Thine;
>    Teach me how, teach me how;
> I would do Thy will, O Lord, not mine;
>    Help me, help me now.
> —F. E. Belden

Repentance, confession, faith—faith that comes by feeding on the Word (Rom. 10:17)—doing the first works, will bring us again the presence of the Lord, to accompany us day by day.

MEDITATION PRAYER: *"Leave me not, neither forsake me, O God of my salvation"* (Ps. 27:9).

# JANUARY 20

*The Lord also will be a refuge for the oppressed,*
*a refuge in times of trouble (Ps. 9:9).*

A Christian worker from New York City, visiting the well-known Eliada Orphanage, told the children how in that great city there were signs reading "Safety First" put up everywhere to keep people from danger. One little fellow said, "But down here we have 'God First.'" How true it is that the greater includes the lesser. The individuals who put God first in their life are assured of safety. The Most High becomes their habitation, and no evil will befall them (Ps. 91:9, 10). Whatever comes, God will care for them, and they will have a place of refuge.

Every soul needs a refuge. Sooner or later we all must find a place of safety, an impregnable fortress. Sometimes the world is too much for us, and we must flee to that "place of quiet rest, near to the heart of God." Our Lord Jesus Christ said to His weary disciples, "Come ye . . . apart . . . and rest a while" (Mark 6:31).

Our great enemy, the devil, is a merciless oppressor. His service is cruel bondage. But the Lord offers freedom to the oppressed. He has proclaimed "liberty throughout all the land unto all the inhabitants thereof" (Lev. 25:10). He offers pardon, hope, and peace to sinners. "God was in Christ, reconciling the world unto himself" (2 Cor. 5:19). But let us remember that our text promises a refuge to earnest Christians. In every time of trouble the Lord is their refuge. "God is our refuge and strength, a very present help in trouble" (Ps. 46:1). And He pleads, "Turn you to the strong hold, ye prisoners of hope" (Zech. 9:12).

> The Lord's our Rock, in Him we hide,
> A shelter in the time of storm;
> Secure whatever may betide,
> A shelter in the time of storm.
> —Vernon J. Charlesworth

MEDITATION PRAYER: *"The Lord is my rock, and my fortress, and my deliverer; my God, my strength, in whom I will trust" (Ps. 18:2).*

# JANUARY 21

*If a man die, shall he live again? all the days of my appointed time will I wait, till my change come. Thou shalt call, and I will answer thee: thou wilt have a desire to the work of thine hands (Job 14:14, 15).*

Is there life after death? Our hearts find no sure answer in science or philosophy. This question regarding the nature of humanity must be answered by God, who made us. Only the Creator knows the future of the race. Our text voices the age-old question "If a man die, shall he live again?" Then comes the answer by divine inspiration: "Thou shalt call, and I will answer thee: thou wilt have a desire to the work of thine hands."

Jesus stood at the tomb of His friend and cried, "Lazarus, come forth," and he that had been dead came forth. He did not *walk* forth, for he was bound with graveclothes, which had to be loosened before he could move. He *came* forth by the power of God. Not one of God's children will be forgotten. They will all hear the call of the Life-giver.

On his seventieth birthday Victor Hugo wrote: "Winter is on my head, but eternal spring is in my heart. The nearer I approach the end, the plainer I hear around me the immortal symphonies of the worlds which invite me." True Christians always have eternal spring in their hearts, because the nearer they get to the end of this life, the nearer they approach the beginning of another—an immortal life, which is the gift of God. Our Savior said: "I am the resurrection, and the life: he that believeth in me, though he were dead, yet shall he live: and whosoever liveth and believeth in me shall never die" (John 11:25, 26).

The Holy Scriptures answer the question Will human beings live again? Yes, they will live. But when? Our answer, as far as God's people are concerned, is found in John 6:40: "And this is the will of him that sent me, that every one which seeth the Son, and believeth on him, may have everlasting life: and I will raise him up at the last day."

MEDITATION PRAYER: *"I shall be satisfied, when I awake, with thy likeness" (Ps. 17:15).*

# JANUARY 22

*Thou wilt shew me the path of life: in thy presence is fulness of joy; at thy right hand there are pleasures for evermore (Ps. 16:11).*

A father in Watford, England, was greatly troubled about his son who had gone wrong. The boy was far away, ill, and despondent. He wrote his father, fearfully asking whether there was any hope of a reconciliation. The father sent him a telegram of just one word, "Home," and it was signed "Father." The gospel of Jesus Christ is God's telegram to a sinful world. It is summed up in one word, "Home," and is signed by one word, "Father"—even *our* Father in heaven.

God alone knows the path of life. Human beings have traced many paths, and millions have plodded their sad miles for thousands of years, finding at the end that all their "yesterdays have lighted fools the way to dusty death." He who is the living God, and He alone, knows and shows the path of life. "In him was life; and the life was the light of men" (John 1:4). "As the Father hath life in himself; so hath he given to the Son to have life in himself" (John 5:26). The path of life is revealed in the words of Christ: "The words that I speak unto you, . . . they are life" (John 6:63).

Are you acquainted with "fulness of joy"? God's path of life leads to joy here and now—joy in His service, joy even in suffering and disappointment. "Count it all joy when ye fall into divers temptations [or trials]" (James 1:2; see 1 Peter 1:6-8). "For the kingdom of God is . . . joy in the Holy Ghost" (Rom. 14:17). This joy of believers cannot be explained; it is a "joy unspeakable and full of glory" (1 Peter 1:8). And the path of life leads on to the very right hand of God above, where we enter into the joy of the Lord (Matt. 25:21) and find in His presence "pleasures for evermore."

In His Word God has clearly shown us the path of life. Let us follow it today, for "the path of the just is as the shining light, that shineth more and more unto the perfect day" (Prov. 4:18).

MEDITATION PRAYER: *"My heart shall rejoice in thy salvation" (Ps. 13:5).*

# JANUARY 23

*But ye shall receive power, after that the Holy Ghost is come upon you: and ye shall be witnesses unto me both in Jerusalem, and in all Judaea, and in Samaria, and unto the uttermost part of the earth (Acts 1:8).*

At a large open-air meeting in Liverpool, England, a skeptic gave a strong address against Christianity. At the close he said, "If any person here can say a single word in favor of Jesus Christ, let them come out and say it." Not a soul spoke, and the silence became oppressive. Then two young girls arose and walked hand in hand up to the speaker and said, "We can't speak, but we can sing for Christ." Immediately they began: "'Stand up! stand up for Jesus!'" When that song ceased, the vast throng was deeply moved, many sobbing. The crowd melted and quietly went away. The promise of power for witnessing is one of the greatest promises ever made to God's servants.

The Holy Spirit was promised by our Savior just before He returned to His Father after fulfilling His atoning sacrifice on earth. On the day of Pentecost, not long afterward, the promise was fulfilled; and the waiting, praying disciples were "endued with power from on high" (Luke 24:49; see Acts 2). The outpouring of the Holy Spirit was the divine signal that Christ's sacrifice was accepted of God.

With this witness and this power these humble disciples went forth into a hostile and unbelieving world and shook it to its foundations. Notice, the power of Pentecost was power for witnessing. The gift of tongues enabled them to preach the gospel to thousands. "Ye shall receive power, . . . and ye shall be witnesses unto me." The power of the Holy Spirit is not for personal glory or selfish enjoyment; it is an enabling to witness for Christ. It is for witnessing and for witnesses only. If we have no certainty, no evidence, no witness of Christ, we shall receive no power. The promised power and presence of the Holy Spirit are for us as we go witnessing for Christ.

MEDITATION PRAYER: *"My tongue also shall talk of thy righteousness all the day long" (Ps. 71:24).*

29

# JANUARY 24

*Trust in the Lord with all thine heart; and lean not
unto thine own understanding. In all thy ways
acknowledge him, and he shall direct thy paths (Prov. 3:5, 6).*

William T. Stead, who went down on the *Titanic,* was asked to
become editor of the *Pall Mall Gazette* in London. He consulted his friend Dean Church about it, and after their interview Mr.
Stead expressed his assurance that he would be divinely guided. The
dean was astonished at his certainty. "I should feel swindled," said Mr.
Stead, "if I were not so led."

"Why so?" asked the dean.

"Why? I read in the book of Proverbs: 'In all thy ways acknowledge him, and he shall direct thy paths.' I have acknowledged Him, and
I know that I shall be directed."

One of the hardest lessons to learn in this life is to trust God fully.
It is so easy, so natural, to lean on our own understanding. "Be not
afraid, only believe" (Mark 5:36) is the medicine we need. The real test
is the Lord's demand for "*all* thine heart." The same divine requirement is repeated in the last verse of our text: "In *all* thy ways acknowledge him." If God is not in *all* our ways, He is not in our ways *at all.*
In little things, as well as the large, we are privileged to acknowledge
God. He is interested in us 24 hours a day, 60 minutes of the hour, 60
seconds of the minute.

He watches over all our life's journey, from the first uncertain step
of babyhood to the last uncertain step of old age. He knows all about
us, gives us all blessings, and leads us all through life if we desire and
permit Him to do so. Why then should we not acknowledge Him? "O
Lord, I know that the way of man is not in himself: it is not in man that
walketh to direct his steps" (Jer. 10:23). Then let us ask the Lord to direct them. "A man's heart deviseth his way: but the Lord directeth his
steps" (Prov. 16:9).

MEDITATION PRAYER: *"Hold up my goings in thy paths, that
my footsteps slip not" (Ps. 17:5).*

# JANUARY 25

*Cast thy bread upon the waters:*
*for thou shalt find it after many days (Eccl. 11:1).*

In 1855 a Bible colporteur went to Toulon, France, and sold copies of the New Testament to the soldiers embarking for the Crimean War. One soldier asked him what the book might be. "The Word of God," he said.

"Let me have it" was the reply. Then he added with a laugh, "Now it will do very well to light my pipe."

The colporteur was sorry and thought his efforts wasted. A year later he was working in central France and sought lodging at an inn. The family in charge were in great distress at the death of their son, who had been wounded in the Crimea and had come home to die. "But we have much consolation," said the mother, "because he was so peaceful and happy."

"How was that?" asked the colporteur.

"He said he found all his comfort in one little book that he always carried with him."

The colporteur asked to see it, and was brought a copy of the New Testament. The last 20 pages had been torn out, but on the inside of the cover were these words: "Received at Toulon [with the date]; despised, neglected, read, believed, and found salvation." The place and date were recognized by the colporteur.

All your acts, words, and thoughts will return to you sometime, somewhere. The great river of time may seem to carry away all the precious fruit of your hard labor, but do not despair or cease to cast your bread upon the rolling waters. Somewhere it will feed the hungry.

Put your heart into the Lord's service; give your energy, your enthusiasm, your time, your treasure, your love, to Him. "Cast thy bread upon the waters." God will watch over it, and the day will come when you will find it again on some far shore or near at hand.

MEDITATION PRAYER: *"Let my cry come near before thee, O Lord: give me understanding according to thy word" (Ps. 119:169).*

# JANUARY 26

*For I am not ashamed of the gospel of Christ: for it is the power of God unto salvation to every one that believeth; to the Jew first, and also to the Greek. For therein is the righteousness of God revealed from faith to faith: as it is written, The just shall live by faith (Rom. 1:16, 17).*

A little church in a mining town of Bolivia was being dedicated. It was constructed of such material as the people had on hand. The floor and some of the furniture were made of shipping boxes for explosives used in the mines. When the preacher stepped behind the pulpit, he saw the words *explosivos peligrosos* ("dangerous explosives").

The gospel is "the power of God unto salvation." The apostle Paul here uses the word for "power," from which our word "dynamite" is derived. The true gospel is the mighty power of God unto salvation to everyone who believes, and the apostle was not ashamed of it, because he experienced its power in his own life and saw its transforming action in others.

The pagan world, with all its culture and degradation, could not resist the gospel. Hatred, persecution, ridicule, argument—nothing could destroy it. The gospel alone could meet the need of the sinful human heart. It was built on humanity's weakness and God's power. It was, and is, the answer to earth's great problem—how to find righteousness. "For therein is the righteousness of God revealed . . . , The just shall live by faith." To be just is to be righteous, and this is no human attainment. "Not by works of righteousness which we have done, but according to his mercy he saved us" (Titus 3:5).

Righteousness is always and only and forever by faith (Rom. 10:10). It is imputed to us (Rom. 4:22). It is imparted to us (Phil. 3:9). It is the righteousness demanded by the law of God, but not given by it. It bears the fruit of obedience (Rom. 8:3, 4; cf. James 2:17, 18). You will never be ashamed of the gospel of Christ if you accept it as God's power for your life.

MEDITATION PRAYER: *"For thou, Lord, wilt bless the righteous; with favour wilt thou compass him as with a shield" (Ps. 5:12).*

# JANUARY 27

*I know that, whatsoever God doeth, it shall be for ever:*
*nothing can be put to it, nor any thing taken from it:*
*and God doeth it, that men should fear before him (Eccl. 3:14).*

Every confession of faith must begin, as does the famous Apostles' Creed, with the pronoun "I." Real faith is a personal experience. "Live by faith until you have faith," Peter Boehler admonished John Wesley.

> Nothing before, nothing behind;
> The steps of Faith
> Fall on the seeming void, and find
> The Rock beneath.
> —John Greenleaf Whittier

Millions of people today are spiritually adrift. They have no sure haven for their souls. They have no solid anchor of truth, no clear conviction of right and wrong, of yes and no, of white and black—only a hopeless gray of indecision. It is not always popular to be positive.

The unhappiness of modern people comes directly from their lack of faith. Every one of us needs a refuge from the storms of life, and that refuge is faith in God. For peace of soul we must be able to say "I know." The writer of today's text knew something. He knew that what God does He does for eternity. The things that God is doing now will reach fulfillment despite opposing forces. When we see God at work in the world, we should take courage and "fear before him." We are too greatly influenced by the spirit of the age, by time. Humanity's ideas, ways, doings, are as changeable as the weather, but through daily study of God's Word and prayer we may keep in step with the Eternal on His march through the ages.

> Changeless in a world of change,
> Thy Word reveals the way,
> Shining all along the path
> From darkness unto day.

MEDITATION PRAYER: *"In the Lord put I my trust" (Ps. 11:1).*

# JANUARY 28

*Be not afraid of their faces: for I am*
*with thee to deliver thee, saith the Lord (Jer. 1:8).*

The visitor to Westminster Abbey sees many memorials to great people, but there is no nobler tribute than that inscribed on the monument to Lord Lawrence—simply his name, the date of his death, and these words: "He feared man so little because he feared God so much."

Be afraid to be afraid! Conceit and pride are to be dreaded, but so is cowardice. Severe punishment is given to soldiers guilty of "cowardice in the face of the enemy." Fear is one of Satan's chief weapons, and when it enters the heart, we are in danger of falling into sin. The apostle Peter was overcome with fear and denied that he had ever known his Lord (Matt. 26:69-75).

Do they threaten you? Then it is time for boldness. "And now, Lord, behold their threatenings: and grant unto thy servants, that with all boldness they may speak thy word" (Acts 4:29).

Should we ever "be afraid of a man that shall die" (Isa. 51:12)? Are you afraid of losing your position? God will never suffer His servants to "want any good thing" (Ps. 34:10).

Do they ridicule you? Scorn and ridicule never killed God's servants of old (Job 16:20). Remember, Daniel stood alone in the lions' den when it would have been easier to go along with the crowd. The three young men on the plain of Dura stood for a conviction when it meant discord with the public orchestra.

So let us fear to fear. God said to Jeremiah, "Be not dismayed at their faces, lest I confound thee before them" (Jer. 1:17).

And what reason we have for bravery! "I am with thee to deliver thee, saith the Lord." So let us fall on our knees and cry for help. Then, armed with this promise, we can rise up saying, "I will fear no evil: for thou art with me" (Ps. 23:4).

MEDITATION PRAYER: *"O Lord my God, in thee do I put my trust: save me from all them that persecute me, and deliver me" (Ps. 7:1).*

# JANUARY 29

*If any man defile the temple of God, him shall God destroy;*
*for the temple of God is holy, which temple ye are (1 Cor. 3:17).*

It is the will of God that every man, woman, and child should be His living temple. In view of this, our text for today is a double promise—a warning and an encouragement. First the warning: Destruction is ahead for those who desecrate God's temple. In all lands temples are places to be entered with reverence. In Western lands a man removes his hat in sacred places; in Eastern lands an individual removes his or her shoes. Any act of sacrilege would be punished by the authorities, or more directly by the worshipers present.

But notice our text—God Himself will punish those who defile His temple. This is as certain as it is serious. God will destroy them. Why? Because "the temple of God is holy." When holiness is ignored, there is danger ahead. Nadab and Abihu "offered strange fire before the Lord, which he commanded them not. And there went out fire from the Lord, and devoured them" (Lev. 10:1, 2). Uzzah profaned the holy ark and died "by the ark" (2 Sam. 6:7). Uzziah defiled the Temple, and leprosy rose up in the forehead of the angry king "beside the incense altar" (2 Chron. 26:19).

Now the encouragement: "The temple of God is holy, which temple ye are." We are not our own. "For ye are bought with a price: therefore glorify God in your body, and in your spirit, which are God's" (1 Cor. 6:20).

Yes, we are to glorify God in our bodies—in our eating, drinking, exercising, breathing, doing. We are to glorify God in our spirits—in our thinking, planning, meditating, praying. "Be not conformed to this world: but be ye transformed by the renewing of your mind, that ye may prove what is that good, and acceptable, and perfect, will of God" (Rom. 12:2).

MEDITATION PRAYER: *"O Lord our Lord, how excellent is thy name in all the earth! who hast set thy glory above the heavens" (Ps. 8:1).*

# JANUARY 30

*For the Lord will not cast off for ever: but though he cause grief,*
*yet will he have compassion according to the multitude*
*of his mercies (Lam. 3:31, 32).*

Kagawa of Japan, once threatened with blindness, lay for months in the dark with scorching pain in his eyes. He wrote: "Health is gone. Sight is gone. But as I lie forsaken in this dark room, God still gives light. At the center of things there is a heart."

Do you think the Lord has cast you off, that He has actually forgotten you? If so, read this promise again: "The Lord will not cast off for ever." He may cast away for a time, when He sees reason for it, but not forever. When it seems that your prayers are not answered, do not despair or cease to pray or to have faith in God. Job went through such an experience. His battle with Satan was more desperate than most of us ever wage, yet he was in God's keeping all the time. In his darkest hour of loss and grief he said of God, "Though he slay me, yet will I trust in him" (Job 13:15).

In the Scripture God is sometimes said to cause what He permits. "Though he cause grief," we read, "yet will he have compassion according to the multitude of his mercies." Sometimes God causes grief *because* He has compassion. Some lessons can be learned only in the school of tears. Then we turn to God in earnest. His Word becomes real to us, and its promises most precious. Then we see God's sunshine through the rain. Even of Christ in His humanity it is written, "Though he were a Son, yet learned he obedience by the things which he suffered" (Heb. 5:8).

Do you think you are cut off? No, never! "God hath not cast away his people which he foreknew" (Rom. 11:2). He loves you. Of Jesus and His disciples it is written, "Having loved his own which were in the world, he loved them unto the end" (John 13:1). He still loves you, so be of good cheer!

MEDITATION PRAYER: *"Keep me as the apple of the eye, hide me under the shadow of thy wings" (Ps. 17:8).*

*For he that soweth to his flesh shall of the flesh
reap corruption: but he that soweth to the Spirit
shall of the Spirit reap life everlasting (Gal. 6:8).*

Yes, the harvest is coming. We shall all reap, but what—corruption or life everlasting? Sowing looks like a losing business, for we put seed into the ground and never see it again. Sowing "to the Spirit" seems like such a strange, intangible thing. We deny ourselves, and it may appear that we get nothing for it. Yet if we sow to the Spirit by living for God, studying to obey His commandments, and seeking to promote His honor in the world, we shall not sow in vain. The harvest will come at last, and it will be life—yes, everlasting life!

One Saturday night an old Scottish minister who had once been a missionary to India was feeling very low because he had seen little success in his work. Just then a messenger brought the monthly parcel of magazines from Edinburgh, and the first thing he read was an account of a revival in a certain district in India, produced by a tract. The writer of the article said that no one knew by whom the tract had been translated into the dialect of that district, but the old minister knew—and his heart rejoiced.

We must not stop sowing because the harvest seems delayed or because others deride us or hinder us. The very next verse after our text for today brings a very important *if*. "Let us not be weary in well doing: for in due season we shall reap, *if* we faint not."

And what is the full harvest? Corruption, if we sow to the flesh—incompleteness, frustration, dissatisfaction, a sorrow unto death. But if we sow to the Spirit, we have life, the knowledge of God, communion with God, the enjoyment of God. And life will flow on like a widening, deepening river until at last it flows into the infinite ocean of eternity, where the life of God is our "life everlasting" forever.

MEDITATION PRAYER: *"Thou wilt shew me the path of life: in thy presence is fulness of joy; at thy right hand there are pleasures for evermore"* (Ps. 16:11).

# FEBRUARY 1

*Blessed are they that do his commandments, that they*
*may have right to the tree of life, and may enter*
*in through the gates into the city (Rev. 22:14).*

Revelation 22:14 is the last blessing in the Bible, and it is our first promise for this month. What a wonderful experience it will be actually to enter the New Jerusalem through one of those gates of pearl and then to walk with the redeemed multitude to the river of life, reach our hands up among the leaves of the tree of life, pluck its fruit, and know that we have a right to it! Yes, the wonder of it has held us in meditation many a day in the past and will do so many a time in the days to come if the Lord tarries.

But what about those first words? What gives us the right to the tree of life and to the Holy City itself? What brings these blessings? Let us read it again: "Blessed are they that do his commandments, that they may have right . . ."

> They with joy may enter the city,
> Free from sin, from sorrow and strife,
> Sanctified, glorified, now and forever,
> They may have right to the tree of life.
> —P. P. Bliss

Some prefer the translation "Blessed are those who wash their robes" (RSV). Those who wash their robes from the stain of sin do keep God's commandments, and all that they do is really done by the Lord Himself, as we read in Philippians 2:12, 13: "Work out your own salvation with fear and trembling. For it is God which worketh in you both to will and to do of his good pleasure." So you see, God both wills it and does it. Our obedience is His obedience, and it is ours by "faith which worketh by love" (Gal. 5:6). So the final blessing of the redeemed in glory is through the grace of God.

MEDITATION PRAYER: *"Make me to go in the path of thy commandments; for therein do I delight" (Ps. 119:35).*

# FEBRUARY 2

*The law of his God is in his heart;*
*none of his steps shall slide (Ps. 37:31).*

This promise is a double-exposure picture of the true follower of God. This person walks rightly (the exterior life) because the law of God is in the heart (the interior life). When the law of God is in the heart, the whole life is right. That is where God intends His law to be, for there it lies, like the tables of stone in the golden ark, in the place intended for it (Deut. 10:2). As Spurgeon said of the law of God: "In the head it puzzles, on the back it burdens, in the heart it upholds."

Notice the choice of words in our text—"the law of *his* God." When we know the Lord as *our* God, His law becomes liberty to us. "I will walk at liberty: for I seek thy precepts" (Ps. 119:45). In James 1:25 God's law is called "the perfect law of liberty." Believers are the children of God; therefore the will and word and law of their Father are their delight.

Then, because "the law of his God is in his heart, none of his steps shall slide." This is a guarantee that the obedient-hearted believer will be sustained in every step he or she takes, doing what is right, and therefore what is wise. Righteous action is always the most prudent and safe, though it may not seem so at the time. When we keep to the path of God's law, we are walking on the royal highway of God's providence and grace. The law of God, written by the Holy Spirit in the believer's heart, is the new-covenant road map to heaven. "Behold, the days come, saith the Lord, when I will make a new covenant. . . . I will put my laws into their mind, and write them in their hearts" (Heb. 8:8-10).

He who walks righteously walks safely.

MEDITATION PRAYER: *"Thou hast enlarged my steps under me, that my feet did not slip" (Ps. 18:36).*

# FEBRUARY 3

*And he said, Thy name shall be called no more Jacob,*
*but Israel: for as a prince hast thou power with*
*God and with men, and hast prevailed (Gen. 32:28).*

In Bible times names were often indicative of character. So it was with Jacob, the supplanter. Jacob was his name, and Jacob he was. But now the greatest experience of his life had just taken place—the dark night of wrestling by the ford Jabbok. He was on his way back from the far country to the Promised Land. He was coming back to God's land, and this night he came back to God. He ceased his own striving, attempting everything in his own human wisdom and strength, and clung to God.

Jacob was fearful. His company had gone on over the brook. Esau, his brother, no doubt filled with the old anger and revenge, was coming to meet him with 400 armed men. His only defense was in the Lord as darkness came down upon the earth and upon his soul. He was alone in prayer when suddenly an unseen stranger grappled with him. All night the terrible contest continued. At daybreak his strong antagonist touched his thigh, and instantly it was out of joint. Then he must have recognized that he was wrestling with a divine being, who said, "Let me go, for the day breaketh. And he [Jacob] said, I will not let thee go, except thou bless me" (Gen. 32:26). Then he received his new name, Israel, "a prince of God," "an overcomer."

At his last public service the aged John Wesley gave out his brother's hymn "Wrestling Jacob," and realizing how he himself was left alone—his brother and most of his friends having preceded him in death—he broke down and wept.

Like Jacob, we may have a new experience and the new name, Israel.

MEDITATION PRAYER: *"For thou hast maintained my right and my cause" (Ps. 9:4).*

# FEBRUARY 4

*Honour thy father and thy mother: that thy days may be long upon the land which the Lord thy God giveth thee (Ex. 20:12).*

The fifth commandment is "the first commandment with promise" (Eph. 6:2). It is the commandment with a promise of long life upon the earth. Do you love life? Then look well to this commandment, which is widely disobeyed today. Fathers and mothers are human, with faults and failings; but every son and daughter—and that means all of us—should show gratitude for the care our parents have given us. That is just common gratitude, all too often uncommon.

How much more than others should Christians honor their father and mother—those who gave them life and love in babyhood, who sacrificed for them in youth, and who now need their love and care. Let it never be said of us as Christians that we ignore this promise-illuminated word of the Ten Commandments.

Think of the wonderful example of Jesus. He had no home, no money, but He had a friend; and from the cross itself He willed His widowed mother to John as a precious legacy. "Now there stood by the cross of Jesus his mother. . . . When Jesus therefore saw his mother, and the disciple standing by, whom he loved, he saith unto his mother, Woman, behold thy son! Then saith he to the disciple, Behold thy mother! And from that hour that disciple took her unto his own home" (John 19:25-27).

Disobedience, which is dishonor to parents, is a mark of the last perilous age of the world (2 Tim. 3:1, 2). Let us bring the home circle closer together as earthly night closes down, and God will give light and love wherever children honor and love father and mother. Never forget or neglect them. Write the letter, say the loving word, bring the help needed—for time is short!

MEDITATION PRAYER: *"Remove from me reproach and contempt; for I have kept thy testimonies" (Ps. 119:22).*

41

# FEBRUARY 5

*For if ye forgive men their trespasses, your heavenly Father will also forgive you: but if ye forgive not men their trespasses, neither will your Father forgive your trespasses (Matt. 6:14, 15).*

The one who will not forgive is unforgivable. Some people say, "God may forgive you, but I never will." That is understandable at times, and human—but it is wrong. We pray, "Forgive us our debts, as we forgive our debtors" (Matt. 6:12). Do we mean it? It is as clear as the Word of the Lord can make it that our forgiveness of others is necessary if the heavenly Father is to forgive us. And surely we need His forgiving mercy every day.

In one of the parables that Jesus told, the man who had been forgiven a great debt of 10,000 talents, which he had owed to his king, would not forgive someone else a debt of 100 pence, but "took him by the throat, saying, Pay me that thou owest" (Matt. 18:28). Because of his unforgiving spirit the king at once placed him back under the terrible unpayable debt of 10,000 talents. "His lord commanded him to be sold, and his wife, and children, and all that he had, and payment to be made" (verse 25). This is the law of the King: Forgive, and be forgiven; forgive others, and God forgives you.

Our forgiveness of others must be real. Two farmers whose land joined had been at enmity for years. One was bitten by a rattlesnake and given up to die. He called for his neighbor, confessed that he was guilty of wrong in their years-long dispute, and asked him to forgive him. The neighbor very graciously forgave him. Then the dying man added, "But remember, if I get well, the old grudge still stands!"

God reads the heart. If we forgive, He forgives; and how wonderful is His forgiveness!

MEDITATION PRAYER: *"Have mercy upon me, O God, according to thy lovingkindness: according unto the multitude of thy tender mercies blot out my transgressions" (Ps. 51:1).*

# FEBRUARY 6

*And Jesus said unto them, Come ye after me,*
*and I will make you to become fishers of men (Mark 1:17).*

This is our Lord's call to His disciples. He calls all to work for Him. It is only by coming after Him that we can successfully work for others. All who try to do spiritual work without that first requisite and preparation will fail miserably and be miserable while failing. No drudgery is worse than doing God's work with humanity's tools. No life is more unsatisfying than the life that God desires to use in His service, but that we will not surrender to Him. No work is more discouraging than to fish all night and catch nothing. Well it is for us in such a case if, like weary Peter, we say to the Master, "We have toiled all the night, and have taken nothing: nevertheless at thy word I will let down the net" (Luke 5:5).

When we obey the word of Christ, and fish on the right side of the ship, we enclose "a great multitude of fishes." This is the reward of obedience. The Lord's methods bring the Lord's results. Oh, how we long to be successful fishers for Christ! But we are tempted to use methods that He would never use. We may splash the water and wear our lives out in labor but never take a fish. If perchance we catch a few small ones, they slip away into the sea again.

We must follow after Jesus if we are to succeed. Sensationalism, entertainment, philosophy, etc.—in these things we are not coming after Jesus. Can we imagine the Lord Jesus gathering a crowd by these fleshly methods? We must keep to our fishing as our Master did. We must preach our Lord's doctrine, proclaim a full and free gospel, for this is the net in which souls are taken. We must preach with His boldness, gentleness, and love. We must work with the power of the Holy Spirit. We must come after Him—not run before Him, nor aside from Him—and then He will make us fishers of men.

MEDITATION PRAYER: *"Lord, thou hast heard the desire of the humble: thou wilt prepare their heart" (Ps. 10:17).*

# FEBRUARY 7

*But if ye will not do so, behold, ye have sinned against*
*the Lord: and be sure your sin will find you out (Num. 32:23).*

Moses was leading the 12 tribes of Israel to the Promised Land. Just before they crossed the Jordan, soon to take possession of Canaan and contend with its fierce inhabitants, the tribes of Reuben and Gad and half the tribe of Manasseh decided to claim the land where Israel was then encamped. It looked like insurrection. Should they refuse to cross Jordan with the other tribes, the armies of Israel would be weakened just when every person was needed in the ranks. But they proposed to build houses for their families and shelters for their cattle in the land of Gilead and then go "ready armed before the children of Israel. . . . We will not return unto our houses, until the children of Israel have inherited every man his inheritance" (Num. 32:17, 18).

Moses, as God's spokesperson, agreed to this plan and said, "If ye will do this thing, . . . then afterward ye shall return, and be guiltless before the Lord, and before Israel. . . . But if ye will not do so, behold, ye have sinned against the Lord: and be sure your sin will find you out" (verses 20-23). This is a warning of evil in case of disobedience. Should the contract be broken, then they would be declared sinners against God and God's people. And their sin would find them out, would follow them and be a curse upon them.

Is sin any less evil today? Can we break faith just because we do not like to carry out our promised agreements? Let us remember this: "To obey is better than sacrifice, and to hearken than the fat of rams" (1 Sam. 15:22), as the prophet said to King Saul. For the defiant, unrepentant, or unheeding soul there is no escape, no refuge—their own sin will find them out. But for the repentant one there is a certain hiding place. "The blood of Jesus Christ his Son cleanseth us from all sin" (1 John 1:7).

MEDITATION PRAYER: *"Keep back thy servant also from presumptuous sins; let them not have dominion over me" (Ps. 19:13).*

44

# FEBRUARY 8

*Have not I commanded thee? Be strong and of a good courage:*
*be not afraid, neither be thou dismayed: for the Lord thy God*
*is with thee whithersoever thou goest (Joshua 1:9).*

Joshua must have been a timid man by nature, but we picture him as a strong, brave general as we see him with his foot on the neck of heathen kings and leading the armies of Israel to victory over mighty multitudes of the enemy. These instructions from the Lord urged him again and again to be strong and of good courage—"Be not afraid, be not discouraged!" Why was this? Joshua was timid, but God knew that he would be a great leader if only he had courage. Timid people make good leaders if their faith is strong. They know their own weakness and realize that all their strength and courage and fearlessness must come from God.

So it was with Joshua. Had he shown fear and dismay before the mighty armies that outnumbered Israel, the whole army would have fallen into panic. Leaders must lead. So the Lord gave this great promise: "For the Lord thy God is with thee whithersoever thou goest." This brought Joshua the courage he needed. The very next verses say: "Then Joshua commanded the officers of the people, saying, Pass through the host, and command the people, saying, Prepare you victuals; for within three days ye shall pass over this Jordan, to go in to possess the land, which the Lord your God giveth you to possess it."

The Lord's promise to be with Joshua filled him with fearless zeal to go forward, the spirit of advance and victory. Before the cities "walled up to heaven," before the great warriors, before vast hosts like the sand of the sea, he knew that the Lord his God was with him; and that was victory.

When we go on God's orders, we have God's presence.

MEDITATION PRAYER: *"Thou hast subdued under me those that rose up against me" (Ps. 18:39).*

45

# FEBRUARY 9

*For he will not lay upon man
more than right (Job 34:23).*

The book of Job records the sufferings of a good man who could not understand why these terrible losses and troubles should come to him. His three special friends came to comfort him, but only made matters worse. Their comfort consisted largely of accusing Job of sin and urging him to confess it. Their idea of justifying the ways of God to human beings was Do good, and you will be wealthy and healthy; do evil, and you will be poor and sick. These three men have many spiritual descendants today. Job said, "Miserable comforters are ye all" (Job 16:2), and so they were.

It is true that evil tends to death, and good to life, even in this world; but that is not all the truth. Thousands of God's children are great sufferers, and trouble often develops superior character. "We glory in tribulations also: knowing that tribulation worketh patience; and patience, experience; and experience, hope: and hope maketh not ashamed; because the love of God is shed abroad in our hearts by the Holy Ghost which is given unto us" (Rom. 5:3-5).

After the three miserable men had finished making others miserable, young Elihu came as the Lord's spokesperson and assured the sufferer that God "will not lay upon man more than right." This is a truth hard—sometimes impossible—to understand when we are in trouble. But we can believe it, for the Lord "knoweth our frame; he remembereth that we are dust" (Ps. 103:14).

Job was the center of a conflict larger than his personal affairs. He did not know it, but he could say, "God is greater than man" (Job 33:12). Once we accept this fundamental fact, we can resign all trouble into His hands and say with the New Testament disciples, "The will of the Lord be done" (Acts 21:14), and with Abraham, the friend of God, "Shall not the Judge of all the earth do right?" (Gen. 18:25).

MEDITATION PRAYER: *"Give us help from trouble: for vain is the help of man" (Ps. 60:11).*

46

# FEBRUARY 10

*Let your conversation be without covetousness; and be content with such things as ye have: for he hath said, I will never leave thee, nor forsake thee (Heb. 13:5).*

This promise is repeated again and again in the Bible. The Lord says this time after time so that we will be absolutely certain and never forget it. We are never to doubt God's care for us. In the Greek this promise, "I will never leave thee, nor forsake thee," has an extra negative, shutting out any possibility of the Lord's ever leaving one of His children so that they can justly feel forsaken of God. He will not—no, no, never! This is a priceless promise, and the child of God may rest upon it.

We may be called to travel over strange ways, but we shall always have good company, for "the Lord of hosts is with us" (Ps. 46:7). Today's text is no promise of exemption from trouble, but it secures us against desertion. We may walk through dark valleys, but "the darkness and the light are both alike" to the Lord (Ps. 139:12). We may be poor in this world's goods, but we shall always have our Lord's company, provision, and assistance. In the midst of our enemies He is our "shield, and . . . exceeding great reward" (Gen. 15:1). We may grow old and feeble, but God will not forsake us. "Even to your old age," He says, "and even to hoar hairs will I carry you: I have made, and I will bear; even I will carry, and will deliver you" (Isa. 46:4).

We may travel far and fast in this age of speed, but God will not be left behind, for no human being can measure footsteps with the eternal God. In childhood, maturity, and old age His promise holds and grows richer every day: "I will never leave thee, nor forsake thee." So let us go on without fear.

MEDITATION PRAYER: *"But mine eyes are unto thee, O God the Lord: in thee is my trust; leave not my soul destitute" (Ps. 141:8).*

# FEBRUARY 11

*If any of you lack wisdom, let him ask of God, that giveth to all men liberally, and upbraideth not; and it shall be given him (James 1:5).*

If any of you lack wisdom . . ." There is no *if* about it, for we all lack wisdom. What do we really know, after all? Very little indeed. How can we direct our own ways? "O Lord, I know that the way of man is not in himself: it is not in man that walketh to direct his steps" (Jer. 10:23). How much less do we know about directing others. Each of us might truly say, "Lord, I excel in ignorance and folly, and wisdom I have none." How often the pompous pronouncements of past ages have become confessions of ignorance in later days!

Even in scientific affairs the Word of God has antedated some fundamental discoveries. For centuries the thinkers proclaimed the earth flat, square, or oblong, while all the time the Bible said that it is a circle, or sphere (Isa. 40:22). For more than a thousand years the best scientific brains declared the earth to be the center of the visible universe, about which moved our sun, the planets, and the stars. The Bible declared that "it is turned as clay to the seal" (Job 38:14). In physical science, archaeology, astronomy, physiology, and other fields of knowledge the Word of God has proved itself ahead of the age in which it was written.

Our text says, "Let him ask of God." That is the only requirement. If we request it, the needed wisdom is ours. Let us pray for it now—wisdom for today's need, for its seeming simplicities and complexities. Let us pray in faith for this liberal education, for the wisdom from above, the wisdom "which God ordained before the world unto our glory: which none of the princes of this world knew: for had they known it, they would not have crucified the Lord of glory" (1 Cor. 2:7, 8).

MEDITATION PRAYER: *"Lead me in thy truth, and teach me"* (Ps. 25:5).

48

# FEBRUARY 12

*As for me, I will behold thy face in righteousness: I shall be satisfied, when I awake, with thy likeness (Ps. 17:15).*

My maternal grandmother fell asleep in Christ at the age of 94, leaving a request that I preach her memorial sermon from this text. Since that day this promise has meant much to me. Those of this world have their interest in this world alone, but those of the world to come look for more.

As Christians we have a treasure that is twofold: God's presence here and His likeness hereafter. By faith we behold His face in righteousness now, for we are justified in the Lord Jesus (1 Cor. 6:11). It is the "glory of God in the face of Jesus Christ" (2 Cor. 4:6) that shines in our hearts now. This is our heaven below, and it will be our heaven above also.

But seeing is not the end, only the beginning. Even here we are changed by looking. "But we all, with open face beholding as in a glass the glory of the Lord, are changed into the same image from glory to glory even as by the Spirit of the Lord" (2 Cor. 3:18). We may sleep awhile and then wake up, "changed, in a moment," to His likeness. "We know that, when he shall appear, we shall be like him; for we shall see him as he is" (1 John 3:2).

There is much in the best life here on earth that is unsatisfying. The fullest life here is incomplete, but when we awake with His likeness, we shall be satisfied at last.

A great Welsh preacher left carved on his tombstone his name, followed by these words: "who was satisfied in Jesus." That was his testimony in the Lord's service here. But what will it be to be there in the presence of the Lord!

MEDITATION PRAYER: *"For thou wilt not leave my soul in hell; neither wilt thou suffer thine Holy One to see corruption" (Ps. 16:10).*

# FEBRUARY 13

*Behold, I will send you Elijah the prophet before the coming of the great and dreadful day of the Lord: and he shall turn the heart of the fathers to the children, and the heart of the children to their fathers, lest I come and smite the earth with a curse (Mal. 4:5, 6).*

Think of the great work of Elijah in a time of apostasy in Israel—his conflict with Ahab and Jezebel, his being fed by ravens at the brook Cherith, his victory over the priests of Baal at Mount Carmel, his flight to the mountain of God, his conviction that he alone was left of the worshipers of Jehovah, his surprise that there were 7,000 others who had not bowed the knee to Baal and were true to God!

It was Elijah's work to turn Israel back to the commandments of God. He seems to be a type of the church in the wilderness (Rev. 12:6, 14). During three and a half years of terrible famine he kept the light of truth burning in desolate places while Jezebel, through her husband, Ahab, ruled the land and persecuted the prophets of God, just as the ecclesiastical power ruled in the Dark Ages and persecuted all dissenters.

Elijah was a type of John the Baptist, who prepared the way for the first advent of our Savior (Matt. 11:11, 14; 17:10-12). John the Baptist was not Elijah in person, reincarnated (John 1:21), but he came "in the spirit and power of Elias, to turn the hearts of the fathers to the children, and the disobedient to the wisdom of the just; to make ready a people prepared for the Lord" (Luke 1:17).

Elijah is also a type of God's people and their work in the days of apostasy just before the second coming of our Lord. In such a time families should be drawn closer together. Let us seek the salvation of our loved ones in this time of the Elijah message.

MEDITATION PRAYER: *"Wilt thou not revive us again: that thy people may rejoice in thee?" (Ps. 85:6).*

# FEBRUARY 14

*The grass withereth, the flower fadeth: but the word of our God shall stand for ever (Isa. 40:8).*

We see evidence every day of the mutability of earthly things. Whole generations pass off the stage in a few years. At the time of my writing this, only seven men are left of the great armies in blue and gray that fought in America from 1861 to 1865. Even in our day empires, kingdoms, and republics that seemed as solid as a rock have vanished. Systems of philosophy, ways of thinking and living, religious customs, fade into the forgotten past. Scientific theories and hypotheses that were announced as absolute truth have in the past few years been completely demolished. A book on physics 25 years old is now hopelessly out of date. Like the grass, like the flowers, human ideas, human works, human beings themselves, fade away. There is nothing in human experience that is changeless except change.

> Our little systems have their day;
> They have their day and cease to be;
> They are but broken lights of Thee,
> And Thou, O Lord, art more than they.
> —Alfred, Lord Tennyson

In a world of change and flux, where everything earthly bears the seeds of decay, this promise comes to us: "The word of our God shall stand for ever." We may build our hope upon the impregnable rock of Holy Scripture. The Word of God is like Him, eternal. "I am the Lord, I change not" (Mal. 3:6).

And God's Word not only stands; it abides as His memorial and monument and reminder through all the years and months and days to come. "The word of the Lord endureth for ever. And this is the word which by the gospel is preached unto you" (1 Peter 1:25).

MEDITATION PRAYER: *"I trust in thy word" (Ps. 119:42).*

# FEBRUARY 15

*For we are made partakers of Christ, if we hold the
beginning of our confidence stedfast unto the end (Heb. 3:14).*

This promise is found in the middle of a dissertation regarding the
Israelites in their wilderness wandering. They had been blessed
and led of God toward the Land of Promise, but many of them drew
back in their hearts to the land of bondage. They provoked God by
their unbelief and sins. For 40 years they had seen His mighty works,
yet because of their attitude of rebellion the Lord said of them, "They
do alway err in their heart; and they have not known my ways" (Heb.
3:10). They departed from the living God; therefore He departed from
them, and they died in the wilderness. But their children, who did not
rebel against God, went into Canaan.

Today God is leading His people to their heavenly rest, and they
are to learn from the failures of the ancient wanderers. We are warned
against "an evil heart of unbelief" (verse 12). We are urged to "exhort
one another daily, while it is called Today," and are reminded of the
"deceitfulness of sin" (verse 13).

Our Christian experience is not like a coat to be put on today and
taken off tomorrow. If our confidence, our faith, is genuine, it is a part
of us. As the songwriter puts it: "It's in my heart." Confidence is trust.
We are to trust the Lord as long as we live. Then we shall be strong in
Him to meet all life's trials. "In quietness and in confidence shall be
your strength" (Isa. 30:15). To be partakers of Christ here and hereafter, we must have faith, which is "the substance ["confidence," mar-
gin] of things hoped for, the evidence of things not seen" (Heb. 11:1).

"Cast not away therefore your confidence, which hath great recompence of reward. For ye have need of patience, that, after ye have
done the will of God, ye might receive the promise" (Heb. 10:35, 36).

MEDITATION PRAYER: *"Our fathers trusted in thee: they
trusted, and thou didst deliver them" (Ps. 22:4).*

# FEBRUARY 16

*For God so loved the world, that he gave his only*
*begotten Son, that whosoever believeth in him*
*should not perish, but have everlasting life (John 3:16).*

Should we awake tomorrow morning and find all the Bibles in the world turned to blank pages except for this one text, there would still be salvation enough for the whole world.

Of all the stars in the sky the North Star, or polestar, is the most useful to mariners sailing north of the equator. This text is the polestar of the Scriptures, for no doubt it has guided more souls to salvation than any other. Like the Great Bear among the constellations of the sky, so is this promise among the promises of the Bible. It is the one great promise of promises that can be repeated by almost everyone who has read the Scriptures at all.

Here we have *God's love* with a "so" in it, making it shine out with measureless light.

Next we have *God's gift,* in which heaven's infinite treasure is offered for humanity's need. And this is *God's Son,* the gift of God's love, which could never be fully known until the heavenly Father's Only Begotten came to live and die for all.

Then there is the clear requirement of believing, pointing to God's gracious way of salvation for all guilty sinners, rich and poor.

Next we notice that widest of all words, "whosoever," and know that there is room for us all.

Last comes the great promise that believers in Jesus shall not perish, but have everlasting life. This is the gospel in essence, much in little, great salvation in few words. It is not an intricate theology or involved philosophy. It is easy to understand and easy to receive—if we will. It is wonderfully simple, and simply wonderful. If we believe, we have eternal life.

MEDITATION PRAYER: *"He asked life of thee, and thou gavest it him, even length of days for ever and ever" (Ps. 21:4).*

# FEBRUARY 17

*He shall cover thee with his feathers, and under his wings shalt
thou trust: his truth shall be thy shield and buckler (Ps. 91:4).*

Have you not seen little chicks peeping out from their mother's
feathers? Remember their little whispers of contented joy? How
warm and safe they were! In this figure the Lord shows His care for His
own. Just as a hen spreads her wings over her brood and allows them to
nestle there in safety, so the Lord will protect His people and encourage
them to hide in Him. We may shelter ourselves in God and feel the deep
comforting peace that comes from the knowledge that He is guarding us.
We may sleep, for He is awake protecting us. We trust while He covers
us. God Himself becomes our house and home and refuge and rest.

> Under his wings I am safely abiding;
>     Though the night deepens and tempests are wild,
> Still I can trust Him; I know He will keep me;
>     He has redeemed me, and I am His child.
>                     —Rev. W. O. Cushing

From this place of safety we go out to war in the Lord's name and
cause, and His care follows us in that, too. We need protection from all
the fiery darts of the enemy. When we trust God implicitly, we find
that His truth is our shield and buckler.

We are protected *in* His truth and *by* His truth. God cannot lie. His
Word "is true from the beginning" to the end (Ps. 119:160). His
promises never fail; they must stand forever. His sure truth is all the
shield we need. How important it is, then, to receive it, to read it, to
hold it in our hearts.

Come, friend, let us hide under those great wings until earth's
calamities be overpassed.

MEDITATION PRAYER: *"They that know thy name will put
their trust in thee: for thou, Lord, hast not forsaken them that seek thee"*
*(Ps. 9:10).*

# FEBRUARY 18

*For sin shall not have dominion over you: for ye
are not under the law, but under grace (Rom. 6:14).*

Here in this life the punishment of sin is that it brings a person
under its power. Sin will reign anywhere it can, but it is not satisfied with any authority less than the throne of the heart. For that reason the apostle warns, "Let not sin therefore reign in your mortal body,
that ye should obey it in the lusts thereof" (verse 12).

We are to reckon ourselves dead unto sin since God has reckoned
us righteous through faith in Christ (Rom. 4:9). Sin is the transgression
of God's law (1 John 3:4), and sin is a universal curse, because "all have
sinned, and come short of the glory of God" (Rom. 3:23). Therefore,
all the world is under the condemnation of the law and thus guilty before God (Rom. 3:19). But now, believing in Jesus Christ as the atoning sacrifice for our sins, we are justified by faith (Gal. 3:8), and the law
cannot condemn us.

"For by grace are ye saved through faith; and that not of yourselves:
it is the gift of God: not of works, lest any man should boast" (Eph. 2:8,
9). Now, therefore, "being justified freely by his grace through the redemption that is in Christ Jesus" (Rom. 3:24), we are to live for God.
No longer are we to yield to sin. The old nature, the former life as a
slave under the power of sin, is dead, and we are risen to "walk in newness of life" (Rom. 6:4).

God's grace, greater than all our sins, makes us free from the condemnation of past sin and enables us to live victoriously day by day. It
is when sin has dominion over us that we are "under the law" in the
meaning of this text. But when that tyrannous dominion is broken by
the grace of God in Christ Jesus, we are no longer under the law, but
under grace. May God give us this victory forever and ever!

MEDITATION PRAYER: *"For thy name's sake, O Lord, pardon mine iniquity; for it is great" (Ps. 25:11).*

# FEBRUARY 19

*Let the wicked forsake his way, and the unrighteous man his thoughts:
and let him return unto the Lord, and he will have mercy upon him;
and to our God, for he will abundantly pardon (Isa. 55:7).*

Isaiah is the gospel prophet, and here he preaches the gospel with power. What a mighty appeal is this to sinners: "Let the wicked forsake his way." It is something they can do, or God would not command them to do it. The Lord does not demand something that sinners cannot do. Let them forsake their way; but they cannot unless their thoughts are changed. So the sentence continues with "and the unrighteous man his thoughts." "For as he thinketh in his heart, so is he" (Prov. 23:7).

One reason for much backsliding is that sinners try to reform their ways without a change of heart or mind. The heart must be converted, changed, or turned around before the ways can be God's ways. But they must not only turn away from their ways and thoughts; they must return unto the Lord. It is not in human beings to direct their own ways (Jer. 10:23). If they do not come to the Lord when they turn from sin, their last state will be worse than their first (Matt. 12:45). Do not hold back because you are afraid that God will not accept you. There is no doubt about it—"He *will* have mercy" upon you is the promise of our text.

> There is welcome for the sinner,
>     And more graces for the good;
> There is mercy with the Savior;
>     There is healing in His blood.
>                     —Frederick W. Faber

God will pardon—and not only pardon, but *"abundantly* pardon." So come to the Lord, and come today!

MEDITATION PRAYER: *"Turn thou me, and I shall be turned; for thou art the Lord my God"* (Jer. 31:18).

# FEBRUARY 20

*Lying lips are abomination to the Lord:*
*but they that deal truly are his delight (Prov. 12:22).*

The Lord is "the God of truth" (Isa. 65:16). All His works are truth (Dan. 4:37). The Holy Word of God is the "scripture of truth" (Dan. 10:21). His Holy Spirit is called "the Spirit of truth" (John 16:13). All the true children of God in this world are "of the truth" (1 John 3:19) and bear witness to the truth (John 18:37). In praying for His disciples, our Lord said, "Sanctify them through thy truth: thy word is truth" (John 17:17).

All this being true, it is no wonder that lying lips are an abomination to the Lord. God's character is truth, and falsehood is the direct opposite. The lie represents the character of the devil. He was the world's first liar, and it is quite plain that he was heaven's first liar too, since he was cast out of heaven (Luke 10:18).

Jesus said to certain important people: "Ye are of your father the devil, and the lusts of your father ye will do. He was a murderer from the beginning, and abode not in the truth, because there is no truth in him. When he speaketh a lie, he speaketh of his own: for he is a liar, and the father of it" (John 8:44).

Of all true Christians it can be said that their word is as good as their bond. If their words and acts are not truth itself, they do not represent Christ, who was the living truth itself. We are to walk in the truth (3 John 3). We are to speak the truth with our neighbors (Eph. 4:25), but always in love (verse 15). Someday lying lips will be put to silence (Ps. 31:18). May God keep the door of our lips (Ps. 141:3)!

MEDITATION PRAYER: *"Behold, thou desirest truth in the inward parts: and in the hidden part thou shalt make me to know wisdom" (Ps. 51:6).*

# FEBRUARY 21

*Therefore be ye also ready: for in such an hour*
*as ye think not the Son of man cometh (Matt. 24:44).*

These words of promise urge preparedness. We are not only to get ready, but to be ready to stay ready. The coming of the Son of man will surprise even believers. "In such an hour as ye think not the Son of man cometh."

The war was over. The men were coming home. One little girl, anxious to meet her brother who had been gone for three years, asked her mother what dress she should wear. "Your white dress," said the mother. "I'll meet Bob at the dock. You wait for us here at home."

It seemed like a long wait. In warming some chocolate to drink, Mary spilled it all over her dress. Just then her mother and long-awaited brother came up the steps. Frantically Mary ran and hid in the closet. Her brother just must not see her in that soiled dress. "Mary, Mary, where are you?" she heard him call. But she just crept farther back into the closet. "Mary, dear, where are you? Here's Bob." It was her mother's voice this time.

Finally they found her, sobbing as though her heart would break.

"What are you doing in here?" her brother asked.

"Oh, Bob, I'm so ashamed. My dress is all ruined. I wanted to be clean and pretty when you came home."

Our Lord warns us that He will come in such an hour as we think not. We shall have no time to get ready then. We must be ready. "And now, little children, abide in him; that, when he shall appear, we may have confidence, and not be ashamed before him at his coming" (1 John 2:28). "But of that day and hour knoweth no man, no, not the angels of heaven, but my Father only." "Watch therefore: for ye know not what hour your Lord doth come" (Matt. 24:36, 42).

MEDITATION PRAYER: *"Return, O Lord, deliver my soul: oh save me for thy mercies' sake" (Ps. 6:4).*

# FEBRUARY 22

*And they that be wise shall shine as the brightness*
*of the firmament; and they that turn many to*
*righteousness as the stars for ever and ever (Dan. 12:3).*

To be wise with the wisdom that God bestows and to be a winner of souls—what more glorious attainment? Does my service for God, my testimony, actually win people to Christ? Is it effective?

When Sir Astley Cooper, the famous British surgeon, was asked by another surgeon how many times he had performed a certain wonderful feat of surgery, he replied, "Thirteen times."

"But, sir, I have done that operation 160 times."

"I saved 11 of the 13," said Sir Astley. "How many of your 160 did you save?"

"Ah, sir, I lost them all; but the operation was very brilliant."

Of how many popular ministers might the same be said. Souls are not saved, but the preaching is very brilliant. People who try to shine here are not apt to shine hereafter. The wisdom of God in a human life leads to the salvation of souls. "God does not accept the most splendid service unless self is laid upon the altar, a living, consuming sacrifice. . . . While worldly ambitions, worldly projects, and the greatest plans and purposes of men will perish like the grass, 'they that be wise shall shine as the brightness of the firmament; and they that turn many to righteousness as the stars forever and ever'" (*Gospel Workers*, p. 371).

Not only like a star, but like *the* stars—the whole firmament itself. Look up at the clear sky tonight, and think of this wonderful promise. Think of the magnitude of the stars, their distance, their unchanging glory! In their brightness, majesty, and inconceivable antiquity they remind us of their Creator, the Ancient of days. They proclaim the glory of God forever and ever, and so also will those who win souls for Christ.

MEDITATION PRAYER: *"So teach us to number our days, that we may apply our hearts unto wisdom"* (Ps. 90:12).

# FEBRUARY 23

*The liberal soul shall be made fat: and he that watereth shall be watered also himself (Prov. 11:25).*

There need be no fear of overweight here. It is the liberal soul that shall be made fat. If we help others, we shall be helped. If I consider the poor, the Lord will consider me. If I feed His flock, He will feed me. "Give, and it shall be given unto you; good measure, pressed down, and shaken together, and running over, shall men give into your bosom. For with the same measure that ye mete withal it shall be measured to you again" (Luke 6:38).

A traveler was seeking a new community in which to live. He met an old man by the wayside and said: "Good morning, sir. I should like to settle in this community. What kind of people live here? I hope better than in the place I left."

"What kind of people were they?"

"Terrible—cheats, gossips, never gave anyone a chance."

"Don't stop here," said the old man. "The people here are no different from those you left."

Later in the day another traveler greeted the same old man. "Good afternoon," he said. "I am looking for a good community where I may live in quiet. What is it like here?"

"How were the people you left?"

"They were the finest I have known—always willing to help in trouble. Like all human beings, of course, they made mistakes; but they were so honest and sincere I hated to leave them."

"Well, then," said the old man, "this is the place for you. These people are no different from those you left."

As we give, it shall be given. As we do, it shall be done to us. This is the law and the prophets, the golden rule, the facts of life, and the promise of our Lord Himself.

MEDITATION PRAYER: *"With the merciful thou wilt shew thyself merciful; with an upright man thou wilt shew thyself upright" (Ps. 18:25).*

# FEBRUARY 24

*In that day there shall be a fountain opened to the
house of David and to the inhabitants of
Jerusalem for sin and for uncleanness (Zech. 13:1).*

Was this fountain opened in due time? "For I delivered unto
you first of all that which I also received, how that Christ died
for our sins according to the scriptures" (1 Cor. 15:3).

"But one of the soldiers with a spear pierced his side, and forthwith
came there out blood and water" (John 19:34). "Being . . . justified by
his blood" (Rom. 5:9). "In whom we have redemption through his
blood" (Eph. 1:7). We have "peace through the blood of . . . [the] cross"
(Col. 1:20). We "enter into the holiest by the blood of Jesus" (Heb.
10:19). "The blood of Jesus Christ his Son cleanseth us from all sin"
(1 John 1:7). He has redeemed us by His blood from every nation (Rev.
5:9). We are washed "white in the blood of the Lamb" (Rev. 7:14).

And so the blessed fountain flows on forever and for all. Dr.
Plummer, of Philadelphia, preaching before Congress, took as his text,
"Though your sins be as scarlet, they shall be as white as snow; though
they be red like crimson, they shall be as wool" (Isa. 1:18). He said,
"Some weeks ago I used this text as the basis for a sermon in an Eastern
penitentiary, and I see no reason for not using it here."

This fountain is to cleanse sin and uncleanness in high and in low
alike. The atoning sacrifice of Jesus upon the cross is the one and only
sacrifice, made once and for all. This cleansing fountain in the house of
David is Christ and His redemption.

> There is a fountain filled with blood,
>   Drawn from Immanuel's veins;
> And sinners plunged beneath that flood,
>   Lose all their guilty stains.
> —William Cowper

MEDITATION PRAYER: *"Shew us thy mercy, O Lord, and
grant us thy salvation" (Ps. 85:7).*

# FEBRUARY 25

*Above all, take the shield of faith, wherewith ye shall be able to quench all the fiery darts of the wicked (Eph. 6:16).*

The apostle Paul is describing the spiritual equipment of the Christian warrior. Then, "above all," or over all the other armament, he says, take "the shield of faith."

We know that our adversary is always seeking to destroy us, so we are to be sober and vigilant, and to resist him. "Whom resist stedfast in the faith" (1 Peter 5:9). The shield of faith is absolutely necessary to this resistance. "This is the victory that overcometh the world, even our faith" (1 John 5:4). In overcoming the world, we overcome the prince of this world (verse 18).

Martin Luther said, "The only faith which makes a Christian is that which casts itself on God for life or death." How shall we get this shield of faith? Where shall we find it? Listen to the Word of God: "So then faith cometh by hearing, and hearing by the word of God" (Rom. 10:17). Let us open the door of Holy Scripture, and there we shall find the shield hanging on the wall.

Dwight L. Moody once said: "I suppose if all the times I have prayed for faith were put together, it would amount to months. I thought that someday faith would come down and strike me like lightning. But faith did not seem to come. One day I read in the tenth chapter of Romans, 'Faith cometh by hearing, and hearing by the word of God.' I had closed my Bible and prayed for faith. I now opened my Bible and began to study, and faith has been growing ever since." We are not only to pray for faith but to seek for it in the Holy Scriptures.

Our enemy is likely to attack at any time, so let us not forget the shield.

MEDITATION PRAYER: *"Thou hast also given me the shield of thy salvation" (Ps. 18:35).*

# FEBRUARY 26

*He that overcometh shall inherit all things; and I*
*will be his God, and he shall be my son (Rev. 21:7).*

Continual victory is the privilege of God's children. Let us remember the words of the apostle Paul: "Thanks be unto God, which always causeth us to triumph in Christ" (2 Cor. 2:14). This is not an up-and-down experience, but a day-by-day victory and triumph.

Our Savior "knew that the life of His trusting disciples would be like His, a series of uninterrupted victories, not seen to be such here, but recognized as such in the great hereafter" (*The Desire of Ages,* p. 679).

What will overcomers inherit? "All things." Some of the things to be inherited are mentioned in this same twenty-first chapter of Revelation: free access to the water of life; complete separation from unbelief, from the unclean, from deception, from idolatry, from falsehood, from crime and murder; the gift of a painless world, a sorrowless world, a deathless world, a tearless world.

The reward is great because the victory is great. Victories that are worth having are the result of hard battles. After the decisive victory on Lake Erie in the War of 1812, Commodore Perry announced the result to General Harrison in these words: "We have met the enemy, and they are ours." So Christ could have said; and soon all of His followers will be able to say the same.

Notice, the overcomer does not *earn* all things; he *inherits* all things. The servant earns; the son inherits. "Behold, what manner of love the Father hath bestowed upon us, that we should be called the sons of God" (1 John 3:1). Through faith we are born again, become the sons and daughters of God, and inherit all things by right of birth.

Can we all be overcomers? Yes. How? By the blood of the Lamb and by the word of our testimony (Rev. 12:11). If we reign with Christ there, we must stand up for Him here.

MEDITATION PRAYER: *"Thou God of my salvation: . . . my tongue shall sing aloud of thy righteousness" (Ps. 51:14).*

# FEBRUARY 27

*Wait on the Lord: be of good courage, and he shall strengthen thine heart: wait, I say, on the Lord (Ps. 27:14).*

With many people it is harder to wait than to move on to something else. Rudyard Kipling wrote, "If you can wait and not be tired by waiting." Often waiting is a greater test of strength and faith than the performing of some task.

A Chinese emperor, passing through his dominions, was entertained at a home in which the master, his wife, children, grandchildren, great-grandchildren, and servants all lived together in perfect harmony. The emperor was profoundly impressed with what he saw, and asked the head of the house what means he used to preserve harmony among such a large number and variety of persons. Taking out his pencil, the old man wrote three words: "Patience, patience, patience!"

Moses waited in the wilderness of Midian 40 years. Paul waited in Arabia for three years. When our Savior went away to heaven, He left His disciples waiting. Even when there was so much to do, a perishing world to be warned, He commanded them to tarry in Jerusalem and "wait for the promise of the Father" (Acts 1:4).

"Wait on the Lord . . . , and he shall strengthen thine heart." When the heart is strong, it labors and rests, labors and rests. The heart needs calming and cheering. "Keep thy heart with all diligence; for out of it are the issues of life" (Prov. 4:23). Is your heart weak? Wait on the Lord—trust Him—"and he shall strengthen thine heart." This is true physically as well as spiritually. Every heartbeat comes from Him. He who pens these lines can say as did God's servant of old, "Wait, I say, on the Lord." And I do say it most earnestly, for I know it is true— "He shall strengthen thine heart: wait, I say, on the Lord."

MEDITATION PRAYER: *"Let none that wait on thee be ashamed" (Ps. 25:3).*

64

# FEBRUARY 28

*For the Lord God is a sun and shield: the Lord*
*will give grace and glory: no good thing will he*
*withhold from them that walk uprightly (Ps. 84:11).*

The greatest question of our day," says Will Durant, the philosopher, "is not Communism versus individualism, not Europe versus America, not even the East versus the West. It is whether a man can
bear to live without God."

To every believer the Lord God is a sun and shield, light and protection. And what a wonderful promise is the next part of the verse:
"The Lord will give grace and glory." God may not give us money, but
He will give grace. He may not give us health, but He will give grace.
He may not give us friends, but He will give grace. He may send us
trial, but He will give grace enough to meet it. We may have to labor,
we may have to suffer, but God's grace will be ours.

And notice that next word, "and"—"grace *and* glory." We are not
ready for the glory yet; we are not fit for it. But when the Savior shall
appear and we shall see Him as He is, we shall be like Him (1 John 3:2).
Then we shall enter the glory. First the bread of grace, then the wine
of glory. We must go through the holy place of grace before we can
enter the most holy place of glory.

No matter what happens, remember this: The Lord will not withhold any good thing from us if we walk uprightly. He may withhold
many pleasing things, but no good thing, and He is the righteous judge
of what is good and best for us. Speaking right to the hearts of fathers,
He said: "If ye then, being evil, know how to give good gifts unto your
children, how much more shall your Father which is in heaven give
good things to them that ask him?" (Matt. 7:11).

MEDITATION PRAYER: *"There be many that say, Who will*
*shew us any good? Lord, lift thou up the light of thy countenance upon us"*
*(Ps. 4:6).*

# MARCH 1

*But the path of the just is as the shining light,*
*that shineth more and more unto the perfect day (Prov. 4:18).*

The path of the just may be rough, steep, and hard to follow, but there is light there, and the light keeps growing. Notice, it is the path of the just. The righteous do not stand still; they do not wait for something to happen; they do not stay in the same position. They keep moving onward, ever onward. There is progress in the spiritual life, and that progress is always toward more light, more truth, more spiritual satisfaction.

It is the path of obedience—yes, of willing obedience. Jesus said, "If any man will do his will, he shall know of the doctrine, whether it be of God, or whether I speak of myself" (John 7:17). When we desire, when we will in our inmost hearts, to do the will of God as it is revealed to us, then whatever truth we need will be ours. We shall know. That is why the path of the just gets brighter all the time. The obedient child of God is moving toward the light, and the light grows. "I do not know how the loving Father will bring out light at last," affirmed David Livingstone, "but He knows, and He will do it."

God's children are light bearers. Wherever they go, the light shines forth. Under the picture of Peter Milne in the little church that he founded on the island of Nguna, in the New Hebrides, are these words: "When he came there was no light; when he died there was no darkness."

How about the path we are traveling? Is it like "the *dawning* light, that shineth more and more unto the perfect day" (ARV)? Is our path of life like that? It may be, and it will be if on us "the Sun of righteousness arise with healing in his wings ["beams," margin, ARV]" (Mal. 4:2).

MEDITATION PRAYER: *"Thy word is a lamp unto my feet, and a light unto my path" (Ps. 119:105).*

# MARCH 2

*Humble yourselves therefore under the mighty hand*
*of God, that he may exalt you in due time (1 Peter 5:6).*

Pride is the chief doctrine of the devil; humility, the mark of the saint. When a man boasted in the presence of Joseph Parker, the preacher, that he was a self-made man, Parker commented, "Well, sir, that relieves the Lord of a great responsibility."

In serving God we stoop to conquer; we bow down in order to be lifted up, for submission is the way to exaltation. It is in the plan of God to put down the proud sooner or later. "The Lord will destroy the house of the proud" (Prov. 15:25). The apostle Peter says, "God resisteth the proud, and giveth grace to the humble" (1 Peter 5:5).

True humility comes from a true knowledge of ourselves and of God. As Phillips Brooks put it: "The true way to be humble is not to stoop until you are smaller than yourself, but to stand at your real height against some higher nature that will show you what the real smallness of your greatness is." And that is true. We do not know our littleness until we begin to realize God's greatness. As the old adage puts it: "A mountain shames a molehill until they are both humbled by the stars." It is under the mighty hand of God that we are to humble ourselves. When the Lord smites us, it is our duty and privilege to accept it with profound submission and thankfulness. It is a hard school, but it teaches precious lessons.

Notice that the Lord's exaltation of us is "in due time," and God is the only judge of the day and hour for that exaltation. We have not reached true humility until we can say, "Not only have Thine own way, Lord, but have Thine own time, Lord. Thy will be done!"

MEDITATION PRAYER: *"Lord, thou hast heard the desire of the humble" (Ps. 10:17).*

# MARCH 3

*Casting all your care upon him;*
*for he careth for you (1 Peter 5:7).*

This text is really a promise. It is the same as "Cast thy burden upon the Lord, and he shall sustain thee" (Ps. 55:22). Many of us are unhappy in our Christian experience because we do not really trust the Lord. We give Him some of our problems, but not all of them. We are not willing to let them go. I think of the old man carrying a heavy burden on his back and trudging along a country road in the Deep South. A passerby with a horse and wagon invited him to get in and ride. The old man laboriously climbed in, but kept the heavy burden on his back. After a while the driver said, "Uncle, why don't you put that big sack down in the wagon box and take it easy?"

"Oh," the old man said, "you have been so good to give me a ride. I wouldn't think of making you tote my bundle too."

Foolish? Yes, but so are Christians who do not cast all their care upon the Lord.

Some years ago on a farm in South Dakota there lived two boys. One day their father asked them to take a piece of machinery over to a neighbor. The boys tied a rope around it, ran a long pole through the rope, and placed the farm implement in the middle of the pole. Then each lifted his end of the pole to his shoulder, and they started out. They had not gone far before the younger boy became very tired, and they had to stop and rest. When they started again, the older brother moved the machinery nearer his end of the pole so he would be carrying most of the weight. *Thank you Ginny! "my wife"*

How like our Lord Jesus Christ! We are loaded down with the burdens of life, but He says, "Come unto me, all ye that labour and are heavy laden, and I will give you rest" (Matt. 11:28). He gives us rest by taking our burdens.

MEDITATION PRAYER: *"Let me not be ashamed; for I put my trust in thee" (Ps. 25:20).*

# MARCH 4

*Then shalt thou call, and the Lord shall answer;*
*thou shalt cry, and he shall say, Here I am (Isa. 58:9).*

For the basis of this wonderful promise, read the four preceding verses. In brief: "Make your life a blessing, do good to others, and I will do good to you." Multitudes can testify that they have called upon the Lord in their distress, and He has answered.

Sometimes the Lord answers in most unexpected ways. A Christian woman's husband died, leaving her little with which to provide for her and her little daughter's needs. Her only possession of value was her husband's carpentry tools. Shortly after the funeral she was presented with a bill for labor, which a neighbor said was due him. Not only was the bill beyond the widow's means to pay, but she was certain that it had already been paid, although she had no receipt. The man offered to settle for the carpentry tools. In great distress she went to her room to pray for guidance. Soon her little girl, who had been playing in the garage, came in with a stack of papers. They were receipted bills, and the very top one was the answer to her problem. She could say with one of old, "I sought the Lord, and he heard me, and delivered me from all my fears" (Ps. 34:4).

God hears prayer, and He answers. "O thou that hearest prayer, unto thee shall all flesh come" (Ps. 65:2). Many of us are so busy talking to God that, as Savonarola said, we have no time to listen to what He has to say to us. "Prayer at its highest is a two-way conversation," wrote Frank Laubach, "and for me the most important part is listening—to God's replies."

On the boisterous sea the disciples cried out when they saw what they thought was an apparition, and a voice, tender, loving, reassuring, came, "It is I; be not afraid" (Matt. 14:27). The greatest answer to our prayers is the presence of God.

MEDITATION PRAYER: *"I have called upon thee, for thou wilt hear me, O God" (Ps. 17:6).*

69

# MARCH 5

*And ye shall seek me, and find me, when ye*
*shall search for me with all your heart (Jer. 29:13).*

To know God, we must seek for Him. If we do seek, we shall find Him in His works, in His Word, and in our hearts. But it must be our vocation and not our avocation. We shall not find God by a glance here and there, by a careless flipping of pages, a thoughtless prayer now and then, a wandering mind. We must search as though our life depended upon it, as indeed it does. We are to search with all our heart.

God demands earnestness and sincerity. Even skeptics respect that. When David Hume, the agnostic, was criticized for listening to John Brown, a Scottish minister, he replied, "I don't believe all that he says, but *he* does, and once a week I like to hear a man who believes what he says."

God says, "Then shall ye call upon me, and ye shall go and pray unto me, and I will hearken unto you" (Jer. 29:12). When? When will He hearken? When will He listen? "When ye shall search for me with all your heart." Jesus said, "Ye cannot serve God and mammon" (Matt. 6:24). We cannot hold on to God with one hand and the world with the other. If we try it, we will wind up by being wholehearted for the world and fainthearted for God. The apostle said, "This one thing I do" (Phil. 3:13).

When Matthew, sitting at the receipt of customs, was called by Jesus, he got up and left all the money on the table and followed Him. At the Lake of Galilee the disciples had just made the most successful haul of fish in all their experience, but when they got to shore, they forsook all and followed Jesus. They were in dead earnest, and that is why they will live forever. They found God in Christ because they were wholehearted.

MEDITATION PRAYER: *"Hear the right, O Lord, attend unto my cry, give ear unto my prayer, that goeth not out of feigned lips" (Ps. 17:1).*

# MARCH 6

*Thus saith the Lord, Stand ye in the ways, and see,*
*and ask for the old paths, where is the good way,*
*and walk therein, and ye shall find rest for your souls (Jer. 6:16).*

Here the prophet is talking about spiritual things, because the rest found is soul rest.

D. J. Evans tells of his experience in a deep coal mine where he once worked. All his companions had left him. Suddenly his lamp fell and went out. He was in utter darkness, and his only hope was in finding some sure guide to the shaft. As he groped in the dark his feet struck the rails on which the coal cars ran. Cautiously, but with many a stumble, he hobbled along, keeping one foot sliding on the rail. He could see nothing, but he could feel the rail. At long last he reached the foot of the shaft and sent up a signal for a cage. Soon he was lifted to the surface and walked out into the glorious sunlight, which showed him the road home. Trusting those tracks in the darkness, he found the lighted way at last.

God has laid down spiritual, moral guides for us to follow, and these guides, like the rails in the mine, lead to the light. Even in the darkness they bring soul rest, for we know that we are on the right way. Our Savior said, "I am the way, the truth, and the life" (John 14:6). The Holy Scriptures reveal the Lord Jesus as the true, eternal way of righteousness. He was before all time, "whose goings forth have been from of old, from everlasting" (Micah 5:2). When we seek the old way, the original way, we seek the true way, the truth itself as it is in Jesus. The good way, the true way, the old way, may lead through darkness, but it always leads upward at last to the light. But seeing the good way, recognizing it, knowing it, even loving it, is not enough. We must "walk therein." Obedience is the response of faith.

MEDITATION PRAYER: *"Teach me thy way, O Lord, and lead me in a plain path, because of mine enemies" (Ps. 27:11).*

# MARCH 7

*But thou, O Daniel, shut up the words, and seal
the book, even to the time of the end: many shall run
to and fro, and knowledge shall be increased (Dan. 12:4).*

Today's promise is especially for us who live in the time of the end,
a period of time just before the end and leading up to it, in which
many lines of prophecy focus and find their fulfillment. It seems quite
clear that specifically this time of the end began about the beginning of
the nineteenth century, when a great interest was aroused in the
prophetic "times" of Daniel. Knowledge of Bible prophecy was greatly
increased and spread abroad, and in every line of human endeavor a
new day dawned. The isolation of nations ended, and increasingly the
world has become one world. Communication has been revolutionized
through the printing press, the telephone and telegraph, radio and television. By means of the railroad, steamship, and airplane, many have
been able to "run to and fro," and knowledge has been increased.

Since we live in an age of greater light and knowledge, we share
greater responsibility. The apostle said, "To him that knoweth to do
good, and doeth it not, to him it is sin" (James 4:17). To the people of
His day Jesus said, "If ye were blind, ye should have no sin: but now
ye say, We see; therefore your sin remaineth" (John 9:41). We live in
an age of light. Think of it—the Holy Scriptures, in whole or in part,
are now translated into more than 2,000 languages. Religious freedom
is widespread in the world. What excuse can we offer if we fail to obey
the truth?

But there is still more in our text for today: Not only will the light
come, not only will knowledge come, not only will people run to and
fro in Bible study throughout the world, but the background of the
whole promise is that it is the time of the end. The Word of God says
to our hearts, "Be ready!"

MEDITATION PRAYER: *"I will delight myself in thy statutes:
I will not forget thy word" (Ps. 119:16).*

# MARCH 8

*Behold, the days come, saith the Lord God, that I*
*will send a famine in the land, not a famine of bread, nor*
*a thirst for water, but of hearing the words of the Lord (Amos 8:11).*

Famine is a terrible thing. We read in the Bible of the famine in the land of Egypt and how God saved the people through Joseph, His servant. We read also of a famine in Samaria, where the people were reduced to the greatest extremities, eating the most disgusting things at high prices. We have heard of terrible famines in various parts of the world in which human beings even resorted to cannibalism. Hunger is one of the most beneficent, yet terrible, instincts, the very fire of life underlying all impulses to labor, and driving human beings to noble activities. Have you ever been really hungry or thirsty?

But the great coming famine is "not a famine of bread, nor a thirst for water." It is a spiritual famine, "a famine . . . of hearing the words of the Lord." Those who have had a taste of the Word of God and have neglected it will suddenly desire it but will not be able to find it. Their souls will hunger for it as they have never hungered for anything else in their lives.

"And they shall wander from sea to sea, and from the north even to the east, they shall run to and fro to seek the word of the Lord, and shall not find it" (Amos 8:12). Yes, cars will rush along the great highways. Airplanes will dart through the sky from one end of the earth to the other. "Where is that person of God who tried to teach me the truth? Where is Mother's open Bible? Where is that river of life that flows from the throne of God?" But they shall not find it.

What does this promise bring us to? To just one word—*now!*

MEDITATION PRAYER: *"Jesus said . . . , I am the bread of life." "Said they unto him, Lord, evermore give us this bread" (John 6:35, 34).*

# MARCH 9

*Blessed are the poor in spirit:*
*for theirs is the kingdom of heaven (Matt. 5:3).*

Two men were praying in God's temple. One said, "God, I thank thee, that I am not as other men are." The other would not even look up toward heaven, but said, "God be merciful to me a sinner" (Luke 18:11, 13). When Peter saw the divine power and purity of Jesus Christ, he fell at His feet exclaiming, "Depart from me; for I am a sinful man, O Lord" (Luke 5:8).

The Romans sometimes worshiped the god Janus Bifrons, who had two faces—one looking outward toward the enemy, the other backward toward home. How like the truly penitent heart! It not only repents for the sins of the past, but takes heed to the future. It is like a ship's lights—one at the bow, the other at the stern. It looks not only at the track that has been made but to the path ahead.

"Whom Christ pardons, He first makes penitent, and it is the office of the Holy Spirit to convince of sin" (*Thoughts From the Mount of Blessing,* p. 7). Those who in the presence of Christ's purity feel that they are "wretched, and miserable, and poor, and blind, and naked" (Rev. 3:17) are the ones who long for "the grace of God that bringeth salvation" (Titus 2:11).

There is forgiveness for the truly penitent, for Christ is "the Lamb of God, which taketh away the sin of the world" (John 1:29). God's promise is "Though your sins be as scarlet, they shall be as white as snow" (Isa. 1:18). And again: "A new heart also will I give you" (Eze. 36:26). The truly penitent are blessed. They are the poor in spirit of whom Jesus says, "Theirs is the kingdom of heaven." Those who have a sense of their real poverty will be made rich. In this beatitude of the poor in spirit we may all share.

MEDITATION PRAYER: *"Arise, O Lord; O God, lift up thine hand: forget not the humble" (Ps. 10:12).*

# MARCH 10

*The righteous also shall hold on his way, and he that*
*hath clean hands shall be stronger and stronger (Job 17:9).*

Something strange had happened in the house. The little boy was
washing his hands again. Mother had always had a struggle with
him on the subject of clean hands, but for the past week it seemed that
he had been washing them almost constantly. At last she asked, "Son,
why are you washing your hands again?" The boy hung his head and
said, "You know, Johnny Smith has been mean to me, and I want to
be so strong that he can't touch me."

"What do you mean, son?"

"Well, Mother, you know the memory verse we had in Sabbath
school says, 'He that hath clean hands shall be stronger and stronger.'"

You may smile at this child's simplicity, but have you ever thought
of the great promise in this text? God wants us to hold on our way, the
way He has appointed for us. We are not to deviate from it, because it
is the way of life. Sometimes this road to the city of God runs over bot-
tomless bogs, and again over terrifying mountains. Obstructions have to
be cleared away; sometimes the road itself must be repaired. But "he that
hath clean hands shall be stronger and stronger." Hands are the symbol
of the acts of life, the doings of the heart. What the heart is, the hands
display in their deeds. Clean hands mean a clean heart. How may the
heart be cleansed? Tennyson puts into the mouth of Sir Galahad these
words: "My strength is as the strength of ten, because my heart is pure."

How do we get this clean heart? It is God's gift. "Then will I sprin-
kle clean water upon you, and ye shall be clean: from all your filthiness,
and from all your idols, will I cleanse you. A new heart also will I give
you, and a new spirit will I put within you" (Eze. 36:25, 26).

MEDITATION PRAYER: *"Purge me with hyssop, and I shall be*
*clean: wash me, and I shall be whiter than snow" (Ps. 51:7).*

# MARCH 11

*And the Lord, he it is that doth go before thee; he will
be with thee, he will not fail thee, neither forsake thee:
fear not, neither be dismayed (Deut. 31:8).*

While living in Ottawa, Canada, I heard Sir Ernest Shackleton report on his antarctic explorations. He spoke of his consciousness of the presence of God while penetrating lands never visited before by a human being, and said: "Bending above the oars, struggling through the snow, battling across the ranges, always there was with us Another. He made the difference between triumph and disaster. He brought us through."

Do you face some tremendous task? Is a great battle before you? This is your text. Buckle on the armor and attack. If God goes before us, it is safe for us to follow. Any path is possible if God goes before us. He is not only before us, but with us. "Above, beneath, around, within is the Omnipotent, Omnipresent One" (C. H. Spurgeon, *Faith's Checkbook,* Nov. 30). Through every minute and hour of time, and on into eternity, God is with us. How can we fail?

And being with us, He will not, He cannot, fail us; and He will never forsake us. The apostolic writer records the promise "I will never leave thee, nor forsake thee" (Heb. 13:5). Promise

Our little son was walking with me one night along a dark path beneath the live oak trees. He was quiet and said nothing for a long time. Then, as the path grew darker, suddenly he clutched my hand and said, "Daddy, we are not afraid, are we?" You see, as long as I was not afraid, he was not afraid.

The Lord goes before us; He is with us. He will not fail us; He will not forsake us. Therefore, "fear not, neither be dismayed."

MEDITATION PRAYER: *"Let all those that put their trust in thee rejoice: let them ever shout for joy, because thou defendest them" (Ps. 5:11).*

# MARCH 12

*It is vain for you to rise up early, to sit up late, to eat the bread of sorrows: for so he giveth his beloved sleep (Ps. 127:2).*

Tension! That is another name for life today as lived by millions. Tension, tension! Worry, worry! First thing up in the morning, planning, conniving, seeking, desiring; sitting up late at night planning, conniving, seeking, desiring; but always unsatisfied. Books on how to relax, how to sleep, how to live with oneself, how to have mind peace, soul peace, are published by the dozen and have a wide circle of readers. But the tension grows and will continue to grow until people learn to trust in God.

The consumption of sedatives increases as tension increases, but the greatest sedative of all is calm, simple faith in the goodness of God. That will do more than anything out of a bottle to bring about wholesome, healthful rest and relaxation at night.

When Martin Luther's enemies were plotting to put him to death, he was seized by his friends, who hid him in Wartburg Castle, whose mighty stone walls were strong and impenetrable. There, safe from his physical enemies, Luther began struggling with himself. He learned that even strong castles cannot protect a person's soul. It is said that at one time he picked up an inkstand and threw it at a vision of the devil. Then he turned to God for help and found the strength needed—trust. He found relaxation in faith. He found calmness.

And so may we all trust God and rest in Him, for "the Lord of hosts is with us; the God of Jacob is our refuge" (Ps. 46:7). He knows all about us. Therefore, let us go to bed at the proper hour, read a bit of His Word, put ourselves in His care, and go to sleep. We do not need to lie awake and worry, for He "giveth his beloved sleep."

MEDITATION PRAYER: *"I will both lay me down in peace, and sleep: for thou, Lord, only makest me dwell in safety" (Ps. 4:8).*

# MARCH 13

*And the blood shall be to you for a token upon the houses where ye are: and when I see the blood, I will pass over you, and the plague shall not be upon you to destroy you, when I smite the land of Egypt (Ex. 12:13).*

The sign of the blood on the door meant safety to those within the houses of Israel on that dark Passover night so long ago. The first-born in the blood-marked houses were safe when the angel of death passed over.

Traveling in an Eastern country just after terrible riots and massacres had taken place between representatives of opposing religious groups, in which Christians were not involved, I noticed crude red crosses scrawled on buildings and walls. The few Christians living there had placed this symbol of their faith upon their doors, and they were safe within.

"When I see the blood, I will pass over you" were the words of God. The apostle says, "Christ our passover is sacrificed for us" (1 Cor. 5:7). And again, "Christ died for our sins according to the scriptures" (1 Cor. 15:3). It has been said that there are 13 different theories of the atonement, but the truth in all of them is not enough to express fully the wonder and glory of our salvation through the precious blood of our Redeemer. We can never fully understand it, and it will be the subject of our study through the endless ages of eternity. We cannot see the blood in all its meaning, but what we do see is for our comfort. The Lord's sight of it secures our safety—"When *I* see the blood, I will pass over you."

We are justified by the blood, and when God sees that we are under its protection He will, He must, pass over us, because "he . . . spared not his own Son, but delivered him up for us all" (Rom. 8:32). That is our surety.

MEDITATION PRAYER: *"I will rejoice in thy salvation" (Ps. 9:14).*

# MARCH 14

*Lay up for yourselves treasures in heaven, where neither moth nor rust doth corrupt, and where thieves do not break through nor steal: for where your treasure is, there will your heart be also (Matt. 6:20, 21).*

Security! What a magic word today! J. B. Priestley tells of a city clerk who seemed to be happy, but deep inside there was a haunting fear of losing his job. This fear was always in the circumference of his mind. The trouble was that he had nothing in his heart to beat back the fear. He lived in a world from which God had been banished, but not the devil. Without God, fear will dwell in the heart. It is impossible to build a fortress strong enough to keep out the enemy of fear. The secret of security is a heart fixed on God.

Treasure here slips through our fingers. Thieves steal it; it is lost; it just disappears. The only treasure that is eternally safe is the treasure deposited in the bank of heaven. Our greatest treasures are not money, but hope, trust, faith, friendship, love. Even these treasures are evanescent and passing if kept in the treasury of earth. They must, by God's grace, be laid up in heaven.

Our Savior told the rich young ruler to sell what he had and give to the poor, and he would have treasure in heaven. That is one way to transfer our treasure to a safe place. Some heap treasure together for the last days (James 5:2); others heap treasure together for eternity.

In His story of the rich farmer, Jesus showed that the man was poor because he had laid up treasure for himself and was not rich toward God (Luke 12:21). Where our treasure is, there is our heart. That's the important fact, for out of the heart are the issues of life (Prov. 4:23). When all we have and are is surrendered to God, we have real security.

MEDITATION PRAYER: *"Thou hast proved mine heart" (Ps. 17:3).*

# MARCH 15

*And I say also unto thee, That thou art Peter,*
*and upon this rock I will build my church; and the gates*
*of hell shall not prevail against it (Matt. 16:18).*

A man once asked Charles H. Spurgeon if his church was a pure church, since he was looking for a pure church to join. The great preacher said that he was not sure about his church. He knew there were many good people in it and some truly Christian people, but he added that there might be a Judas in it, as there was in Christ's first church. There might be some deceivers and idolaters, those who walk unruly, as there were in the churches of Rome, Corinth, Galatia, Ephesus, Colosse, Philippi, and Thessalonica, and all the others to which the New Testament Epistles were written. Spurgeon said he didn't think that his church, on the whole, was the one the man was looking for. In fact, he did not know that there had been a perfect church in all history. "But," he added, "if you should happen to find such a church, I beg of you not to join it, for you would spoil it."

Christ's church may not be perfect, but it is still the object of His supreme regard (*The Acts of the Apostles,* p. 12). Wars, conquests, changing civilizations, have rolled over the world, but the church still stands. Why? Because its foundation is immovable. "For other foundation can no man lay than that is laid, which is Jesus Christ" (1 Cor. 3:11).

Is the church important? If it were not, Christ never would have founded it. He promised that the gates of hell should never prevail against it. Remember, the Lord added to the church such as were being saved (Acts 2:47). "The New Testament knows nothing of unattached Christians," said Archibald M. Hunter.

MEDITATION PRAYER: *"But as for me, I will come into thy house in the multitude of thy mercy" (Ps. 5:7).*

# MARCH 16

*Jesus said unto him, If thou canst believe,*
*all things are possible to him that believeth (Mark 9:23).*

Afather was pleading with Jesus for the healing of his boy. He described his terrible affliction, then said, "If thou canst do any thing, have compassion on us, and help us" (Mark 9:22). Jesus said unto him, "If thou canst believe, all things are possible."

Our unbelief is our greatest hindrance in spiritual life. In fact, there is no other real difficulty in our way. The Lord can do all things that need to be done for us, but He makes it a rule that "according to your faith be it unto you" (Matt. 9:29).

August Hermann Francke, the seventeenth-century theologian, said, "A grain of living faith is worth more than a pound of historic knowledge; and a drop of love, than an ocean of science."

I rather like the small boy's version of the hymn "Trust and Obey." He said that they sang "Trust and OK" at his Sabbath school. And everything must be OK when we really trust in God.

Why can we not believe God and His promises? He is always true. He is faithful to His word. When we are in the right state of mind, it is as easy for us to believe in God as it is for a child to trust their father. It seems that we can believe in God as far as the past is concerned, and for the distant future; but it is our present trial that tests our faith. How foolish this is! Let us trust God here and now, and the future will take care of itself. When we reach the future, it will be the present, and Christ will be there.

> 'Tis so sweet to trust in Jesus,
>     Just to take Him at His word;
> Just to rest upon His promise,
>     Just to know, "Thus saith the Lord."
>                 —Louisa M. R. Stead

MEDITATION PRAYER: *"But be not thou far from me, O Lord: O my strength, haste thee to help me" (Ps. 22:19).*

# MARCH 17

*Verily, verily, I say unto you, He that believeth on me, the works that I do shall he do also; and greater works than these shall he do; because I go unto my Father (John 14:12).*

It is by the power of the Holy Spirit that the disciples of Christ were to do, and are to do, greater works than Christ did. This is because He went unto the Father. What had that to do with it? Everything, because we read in John 16:7: "It is expedient for you that I go away: for if I go not away, the Comforter will not come unto you; but if I depart, I will send him unto you."

It was by the power of the Holy Spirit that the mighty apostolic deeds were done. "But when the Comforter is come," Jesus said, "whom I will send unto you from the Father, even the Spirit of truth, which proceedeth from the Father, he shall testify of me: and ye also shall bear witness, because ye have been with me from the beginning" (John 15:26, 27). These words were gloriously fulfilled after the descent of the Holy Spirit on the day of Pentecost. The disciples were filled with power and went forth, testifying of the resurrection of Jesus Christ and bearing witness to their faith. They spoke in the power of the Spirit, so that thousands were converted in a day. Our Savior did not mean that the disciples would put forth greater effort than He had, nor that they would perform more miraculous deeds, but that their work would have greater magnitude.

And so it was, and so it is today. The Savior's ministry was limited to a small country 150 miles long and 50 miles wide, yet thousands heard Him. But when the apostles went forth, millions heard, and hundreds of thousands accepted the gospel as the Holy Spirit bore witness to their hearts. It is our privilege to work for Christ in the same way today.

MEDITATION PRAYER: *"O God, thou art terrible out of thy holy places: the God of Israel is he that giveth strength and power unto his people" (Ps. 68:35).*

# MARCH 18

*Blessed is he that readeth, and they that hear the words of this prophecy, and keep those things which are written therein: for the time is at hand (Rev. 1:3).*

Where else do we find so direct a blessing pronounced upon the hearing, reading, and observance of any part of God's Word? Surely, with this blessing in connection with the prophecies of the book of Revelation, we ought to study them earnestly. Every passing year makes them more important. Every fulfillment in history makes more urgent the need of study, not only of this book, but of the entire volume of Sacred Scripture.

Uriah Smith reminds us that "every fulfillment of prophecy brings its duties. There are things in the Revelation to be observed, or performed. Practical duties are to be fulfilled as the result of an understanding and accomplishment of the prophecy" (*Daniel and the Revelation* [1944], p. 341).

An example of this is seen in Revelation 14:12: "Here are they that keep the commandments of God, and the faith of Jesus." God, who sees the future, sees things that we do not see. He has revealed some things to us in divine prophecy. But we are to obey Him, to keep those things that He has commanded, whether or not we understand everything.

Archibald Rutledge tells the story of a turpentine worker whose faithful dog had died in a great forest fire because he would not desert his master's dinner pail, which he had been told to watch. With tears running down his face, the old man said, "I always had to be careful what I told that dog to do, 'cause I knew he'd do it." Are we always as faithful?

Let us study the book of Revelation, not only with interest, but with obedience, "for the time is at hand."

MEDITATION PRAYER: *"Moreover by them [God's commandments] is thy servant warned: and in keeping of them there is great reward" (Ps. 19:11).*

# MARCH 19

*Therefore by the deeds of the law there shall
no flesh be justified in his sight: for by the law
is the knowledge of sin (Rom. 3:20).*

A man who had never been to sea before was crossing the Bay of Biscay and saw what he thought to be an approaching hurricane. Trembling with fear, he said to one of the experienced sailors, "Do you think we will be able to live through it?" "Through what?" asked the sailor. "Through that fast-approaching storm." The sailor smiled and said: "You need have no fear of that storm. It will never touch us. It has passed already."

So it is with believers. Judgment for their sin is passed already. Christ has been tried, condemned, and executed on the cross in their stead. He died for our sins (1 Cor. 15:3). As the apostle Paul puts it: "Being justified by faith, we have peace with God through our Lord Jesus Christ" (Rom. 5:1). God's law "could not justify man, because in his sinful nature he could not keep the law" (*Patriarchs and Prophets*, p. 373).

"The law reveals to man his sins, but it provides no remedy. While it promises life to the obedient, it declares that death is the portion of the transgressor. The gospel of Christ alone can free him from the condemnation or the defilement of sin. He must exercise repentance toward God, whose law has been transgressed; and faith in Christ, his atoning sacrifice" (*The Great Controversy*, pp. 467, 468).

Our text emphasizes a negative promise—by the deeds of the law no flesh shall be justified in God's sight. We need to remember this. It is not by our works that we are to be saved. It is only by the works of Christ that we are made just or righteous before God.

Jesus died for us, and we have accepted His sacrifice. Therefore God looks upon Him and sees His righteousness in place of sin.

MEDITATION PRAYER: *"Hear me when I call, O God of my righteousness" (Ps. 4:1).*

# MARCH 20

*And we know that all things work together*
*for good to them that love God, to them who*
*are the called according to his purpose (Rom. 8:28).*

A skilled surgeon, about to perform a delicate operation on the ear, said reassuringly to the patient, "I may hurt you, but I will not injure you." How often God speaks to us in the same way! More abundant health and life, even eternal life, are His only purpose; but it is often hard for us to see it in the hour of trial, temptation, and suffering.

"All things work together for good to them that love God," but all things are not necessarily good in themselves. The good and the evil, and the good and evil together, work for good to them that love God and are in His providence. The good may be immediate or far off, but it is God's good in God's own time.

We find this lesson in the old story about the gravel walk and the mignonette. "How fragrant you are this morning," said the gravel walk.

"Yes," said the mignonette, "I have been trodden upon and bruised, and it has brought forth all my sweetness."

"But," said the gravel walk, "I am trodden on every day, and I only grow harder."

Two characteristics of believers are given here: one, their feelings toward God; the other, God's feelings toward them.

To those who love God, all things work together for good. It must be so, for love works no evil (Rom. 13:10). And "to them who are the called according to his purpose," all things find some way, often unknown to us, of working together for our good. It must be so, for He of whom and through whom and to whom are all things (Rom. 11:36) would never suffer His eternal purpose to be thwarted by anything really adverse to us.

MEDITATION PRAYER: *"I will be glad and rejoice in thee"* *(Ps. 9:2).*

# MARCH 21

*There hath no temptation taken you but such as is common*
*to man: but God is faithful, who will not suffer you to be*
*tempted above that ye are able; but will with the temptation also*
*make a way to escape, that ye may be able to bear it (1 Cor. 10:13).*

We are not to walk unbidden into temptation, nor are we to give up to despondency when temptation comes upon us. We are to know that no temptation will be too much for us through the grace God gives us. There will be a way of escape prepared by God.

Temptations are great teachers. "My temptations," said Martin Luther, "have been my masters in divinity." Some try to overcome temptation by fleeing from organized society, but they cannot get away from themselves. God promises help to win the internal battle against self.

Sometimes the bravest thing to do with temptation is to flee from it. We think of the storekeeper who said to the boy who had been lingering too long near a tempting display of fruit, "What are you doing—trying to steal one of those apples?" "No," said the boy, "trying not to." In such a case it is a good thing for the boy to remove the temptation by removing himself.

Temptation as enticement to sin never comes from God. "God cannot be tempted with evil, and he himself tempteth no man" (James 1:13, ARV). The only safeguard against temptation is the indwelling Christ in the heart, and He will never abandon the soul for whom He has died. "Live in contact with the living Christ, and He will hold you firmly by a hand that will never let go" (*Thoughts From the Mount of Blessing,* p. 119). And remember: "The name of the Lord is a strong tower: the righteous runneth into it, and is safe" (Prov. 18:10).

MEDITATION PRAYER: *"Lead us not into temptation, but deliver us from evil" (Matt. 6:13).*

# MARCH 22

*Come, and let us return unto the Lord:*
*for he hath torn, and he will heal us;*
*he hath smitten, and he will bind us up (Hosea 6:1).*

The greatest short story ever written is called the story of the prodigal son, but it's really the story of the forgiving father. He had two prodigal sons—one stayed home, the other went away; but the father was there to forgive. When he saw the long-lost boy a great way off, he was moved with compassion and ran and fell on his neck and kissed him, replaced his rags with the best robe, put the ring of sonship on his finger and shoes of peace upon his feet, and provided the feast of reconciliation. "For," he said, "this my son was dead, and is alive again; he was lost, and is found."

Read the entire wonderful story again for yourself. In it we hear the voice of the Holy Spirit saying, "Come, and let us return unto the Lord." Have you wandered away from Him? Come back, for "he hath torn, and he will heal us." That is God's way. By the pain of our affliction when we wander away from Him, He makes us realize our need of healing.

Remember, the diagnosis of the law comes before the healing of the gospel. "Come unto me," He says, "all ye that labour and are heavy laden, and I will give you rest" (Matt. 11:28). Only the weary seek rest, only the ill seek healing, only the wounded seek help, only the lost desire to be found. And although we may wander in some far country, our heavenly Father says to every one of us, "Return unto me; for I have redeemed thee" (Isa. 44:22).

> Come, ye sinners, poor and needy,
> Weak and wounded, sick and sore,
> Jesus ready stands to save you,
> Full of pity, love and power.
>
> —Joseph Hart

MEDITATION PRAYER: *"The troubles of my heart are enlarged: O bring thou me out of my distresses" (Ps. 25:17).*

# MARCH 23

*And what agreement hath the temple of God with idols?*
*for ye are the temple of the living God; as God hath said,*
*I will dwell in them, and walk in them; and I will*
*be their God, and they shall be my people (2 Cor. 6:16).*

In His high-priestly prayer Jesus requested for His followers "that they all may be one; as thou, Father, art in me, and I in thee, that they also may be one in us: . . . I in them, and thou in me, that they may be made perfect in one" (John 17:21-23). Each believer is a living temple. There is no place in any consecrated life for idols. Notice three things here:

First, a mutual interest—each belongs to each. God is the portion of His people, and they are His portion.

Second, a mutual consideration. God will always think of His people, and they will always think of Him. God says that His thoughts toward us are thoughts of peace, and not of evil, to give us an expected end (Jer. 29:11). What do we think of Him and of His work?

Third, a mutual fellowship. God dwells in us as believers, and we dwell in God. Such a great thought makes life sacred in all its experiences. God dwells with us—yes, in us. We are His people. In a special way was this fellowship true of Jesus, for "God was in Christ, reconciling the world unto himself" (2 Cor. 5:19). In our sphere we are to be like Him. As He was in the world, so are we to be in the world (1 John 4:17). We are to be like Him.

> God be in my head, and in my understanding;
> God be in my eyes, and in my looking;
> God be in my mouth, and in my speaking;
> God be in my heart, and in my thinking;
> God be at my end, and at my departing.
> —Sarum Primer

MEDITATION PRAYER: *"Search me, O God, and know my heart: try me, and know my thoughts" (Ps. 139:23).*

# MARCH 24

*Yea, and all that will live godly in Christ*
*Jesus shall suffer persecution (2 Tim. 3:12).*

During the Diocletian persecutions, when the meeting places, sacred books, and homes of Christians were burned, and they themselves were deprived of all civil rights and honors, the emperor struck a coin with this inscription: "The Christian name extinguished." The Christian church was born in persecution, and it will never be entirely free of persecution until the end of time.

A godly life here on earth is a constant challenge to the ungodly. Righteousness holds the mirror up to unrighteousness. Those who do right are a constant irritation to those who do wrong. Jesus said to His disciples, "If they have persecuted me, they will also persecute you" (John 15:20).

In our Savior's prophecy of Matthew 24 He speaks of certain times of persecution as signs—first, of the fall of Jerusalem; second, of the end of the world. "And ye shall be hated of all men for my name's sake: but he that endureth to the end shall be saved" (Matt. 10:22).

Suffering for evildoing is not persecution "for righteousness' sake," but if we are persecuted for doing good, there is blessing in it. Among six men turned out of Oxford University for praying were John and Charles Wesley and George Whitefield. Evil persecutes good, but good never persecutes evil. Cain persecuted Abel, the Scripture says, "because his own works were evil, and his brother's righteous" (1 John 3:12). In Old Testament days the prophets were persecuted and put to death by the very people they tried to help. Most of the apostles also suffered martyrdom for their faith. Jesus, the greatest apostle, prophet, and priest, was persecuted from city to city, spit upon, denied, derided, and finally crucified as a common criminal; yet He was the King of love.

MEDITATION PRAYER: *"Arise, O Lord, . . . deliver my soul from the wicked" (Ps. 17:13).*

# MARCH 25

*There remaineth therefore a rest to the people of God.*
*For he that is entered into his rest, he also hath ceased*
*from his own works, as God did from his (Heb. 4:9, 10).*

It was God's plan to give spiritual rest to His people, but they entered not into it because of unbelief. Joshua could not give it to them; the land of Canaan could not yield it. David sang of this rest and declared it would be another day that would be offered to the people of the world. So this rest of blessing remains for believers. Even our works for God, which might be called "very good," give us no confidence. We are not saved by works, but by grace through faith, and that not of ourselves, for it is the gift of God (Eph. 2:8). Everything has been done. Christ has finished His work. "This is the work of God, that ye believe on him whom he hath sent" (John 6:29). Let us cease from our works as God did from His.

All God's providential matters, all His work for people's souls, we must leave in His hands. We must cast these burdens upon the Lord, and He will sustain us. By faith we are to labor to enter into this rest. In the endless confusion and tension of the world, we may find our rest in Christ.

Dr. James Rendel Harris was once staying with friends in the state of Delaware. In the room where he slept, the bed coverlet was made of brown linen spun in the old days by a godly grandmother. On it she had embroidered Mrs. Browning's lines:

> God's greatness flowed around our incompleteness—
> Round our restlessness, His rest.

When asked in the morning how he had slept, Dr. Harris replied, "How could I have slept other than well with such a text as that over me?"

MEDITATION PRAYER: *"Oh that I had wings, like a dove! for then would I fly away, and be at rest"* (Ps. 55:6).

# MARCH 26

*Jesus Christ the same yesterday,*
*and to day, and for ever (Heb. 13:8).*

Jesus Christ is still the Son of God, still the Great Unique.

When proofreaders find what they think is a mistake, they cross it out. If later they discover that what they thought was a mistake is correct, they write the word "stet" over against their marking. This means that their change was wrong: "Let the original stand." So Pilate might have written over against Christ, "Stet—I was wrong; let the original stand."

We can depend on Jesus. He does not change with the weather, with the regime, with the economic situation or the political wind. He is the Son of God, the Savior, the Redeemer, the Lord our righteousness, "whose goings forth have been . . . from everlasting," as we read in Micah 5:2. Those who knew Him best said, "Thou art the Son of God; thou art the King of Israel" (John 1:49). Our Savior will be the same tomorrow, for "he shall reign . . . for ever; and of his kingdom there shall be no end" (Luke 1:33). People have condemned Him, repudiated Him, neglected Him, rejected Him, but they have not changed Him or His power to save.

Those who try to forget Jesus, and just hope that when they look around again He will not be there, will be disappointed. He will be there. You may have rejected Him and considered the case closed, but it will be opened again. "Because he hath appointed a day, in the which he will judge the world in righteousness by that man whom he hath ordained" (Acts 17:31).

Yes, the case will be reopened. Jesus Christ is always the same—yesterday, today, tomorrow, and forever. As revealed to us in the Holy Scripture, the original must stand, "that Jesus Christ is Lord, to the glory of God the Father" (Phil. 2:11).

MEDITATION PRAYER: *"But thou art the same, and thy years shall have no end" (Ps. 102:27).*

# MARCH 27

*And the prayer of faith shall save the sick, and*
*the Lord shall raise him up; and if he have*
*committed sins, they shall be forgiven him (James 5:15).*

Today He is the same compassionate physician that He was while on this earth. We should let the afflicted understand that in Him there is healing balm for every disease, restoring power for every infirmity. His disciples in this time are to pray for the sick as verily as His disciples of old prayed. And recoveries will follow, for 'the prayer of faith shall save the sick'" (*Counsels on Health,* p. 210).

Sickness is a hard school, but it teaches us precious lessons. It brings us nearer to God, and we see ourselves more nearly as God sees us. We find forgiveness for sin, and often a renewal of health is a part of God's will for us. It is "the prayer of faith" that saves the sick. It is not God's plan to give immortal bodies to His people until the second coming of our Lord and the resurrection of the dead. But many of the sick are healed and raised up to health and faithful service. "I am the Lord that healeth thee" are the words of God in Exodus 15:26.

In Psalm 103:3 the Lord is said to be the one who forgives all our iniquities and heals all our diseases. Jesus Himself was the Great Physician, "who went about doing good, and healing all that were oppressed of the devil" (Acts 10:38).

I personally know a very successful eye surgeon who always prays with his patients. But it is no denial of faith to cooperate with God in the laws of our being by making the proper use of diet, exercise, sunlight, water, and rest—all of which are conducive to health. Faith and works go together, and it is our blessed privilege to pray for the sick that they may be healed.

MEDITATION PRAYER: *"Look upon mine affliction and my pain; and forgive all my sins" (Ps. 25:18).*

# MARCH 28

*But the word of the Lord endureth for ever. And this is the word which by the gospel is preached unto you (1 Peter 1:25).*

In the village of Newbury, England, after the bombing during World War II, there stood fragments of the walls of an old church amid a heap of stone and debris. On one side were the ruins of a home for the aged; on the other the wreckage of a schoolhouse. Such bombing seemed an attempt to wipe out religion, education, and mercy; or, to put it in other words, an attempt to do away with faith, hope, and charity.

But these three are the very heart of the Word of God, and "the word of the Lord endureth for ever." All the wars of ages past and of days to come cannot destroy it. All human teachings and all human teachers pass away as the grass of the field, but we are told here that the Word of the Lord is different. It will endure forever. This is the Word; that is preached to us, and how thankful we should be! It is a divine gospel; it is the Word of the Lord; it is an ever-living gospel.

This Word of God will convince and convert and regenerate and sustain and comfort every heart that receives it. It is an unchanging Word; not green grass today and dry straw tomorrow, but always the living Word of the living God. It is a Word to make us happy, because it is "for ever."

Ah, friend, make use of it. Accept it as the very bread of heaven, and feed upon it every day of your life. "Of making many books there is no end" (Eccl. 12:12), and God's Book is endless.

> O Word of God Incarnate,
>      O Wisdom from on high,
> O Truth unchanged, unchanging,
>      O Light of our dark sky,
> We praise Thee for the radiance
>      That from the hallowed page,
> A lantern to our footsteps,
>      Shines on from age to age.
>                    —William Walsham How

MEDITATION PRAYER: *"Thy word have I hid in mine heart, that I might not sin against thee" (Ps. 119:11).*

93

# MARCH 29

*The Lord is nigh unto all them that call upon him,*
*to all that call upon him in truth (Ps. 145:18).*

During a fatal illness a hopeless unbeliever in his despairing bitterness commanded his little girl to print a placard with the words "God is nowhere," and to hang it on the wall at the foot of his bed, where he could see it constantly. She obeyed, but in her excitement she disarranged the letters so that the motto read "God is now here." With the father's surprise at these unexpected words the Holy Spirit brought faith to his heart.

God is "not far from every one of us: for in him we live, and move, and have our being" (Acts 17:27, 28). The poet said, He is "nearer than hands and feet." By His Holy Spirit God is everywhere. He is "the high and lofty One that inhabiteth eternity," and he dwells "with him also that is of a contrite . . . spirit" (Isa. 57:15). Those who call upon Him, those who honestly seek Him, recognize His presence.

Electricity was always in the world, but nobody knew it until scientists discovered it. So God may be near us, but we will never really know it until we call upon Him, until we truly seek Him. The greatest need of humanity today is to know that God is always near at hand and that He is in charge of the world.

Bishop William A. Quayle went to bed one night overburdened with the problems of the world, which he could not solve. Then he seemed to hear the voice of God say, "Quayle, you go to sleep; I'll sit up the rest of the night."

> Still, still with Thee, when purple morning breaketh,
> When the bird waketh, and the shadows flee;
> Fairer than morning, lovelier than the daylight,
> Dawns the sweet consciousness, I am with Thee!
> —Harriet Beecher Stowe

MEDITATION PRAYER: *"Be not far from me; for trouble is near; for there is none to help"* (Ps. 22:11).

# MARCH 30

*My sheep hear my voice, and I know them, and they follow me:*
*and I give unto them eternal life; and they shall never perish,*
*neither shall any man pluck them out of my hand (John 10:27, 28).*

A traveler in the Near East asserted to a shepherd that the sheep knew their master by his dress, not his voice. To prove his point, the stranger changed clothes with the shepherd and went among the sheep, calling them and trying to lead them. Not knowing his voice, the sheep wouldn't move. But when the shepherd called, they ran at once to him, although he was wearing strange clothing. "A stranger," said Jesus, "they will not follow" (John 10:5). Not only do the sheep know the voice of their master, but Jesus, as the Good Shepherd, says, "I know them." Are you not glad, friend, that Christ knows you, the sheep of His pasture?

Notice the threefold blessing of being His sheep: First, He gives eternal life; second, they shall never perish; third, no man shall pluck them out of His hand. Eternal life is God's gift in Christ. "To them who by patient continuance in well doing seek for glory and honour and immortality," He gives "eternal life" (Rom. 2:7). It is given to those who seek it by faith, "for God so loved the world, that he gave his only begotten Son, that whosoever believeth in him should not perish, but have everlasting life" (John 3:16). We are safe in His nail-pierced hand, and no one can pluck us from that hand.

> And so through all the length of days
> Thy goodness faileth never;
> Good Shepherd! I would sing Thy praise
> Within Thy house forever.
> —H. W. Baker

MEDITATION PRAYER: *"Yea, though I walk through the valley of the shadow of death, I will fear no evil: for thou art with me; thy rod and thy staff they comfort me" (Ps. 23:4).*

# MARCH 31

*The Lord shall preserve thee from all evil: he shall preserve thy soul. The Lord shall preserve thy going out and thy coming in from this time forth, and even for evermore (Ps. 121:7, 8).*

George MacDonald, in his book *Robert Falconer,* wrote: "This is a sane, wholesome, practical, working faith: First, that it is a man's business to do the will of God; second, that God takes on Himself the special care of that man; and third, that therefore that man ought never to be afraid of anything."

Not afraid of anything! That is just what today's promise means. The Lord preserves from all evil—not only from without but from within, because "he shall preserve thy soul," is the promise. He shall preserve our going out. God guides us when we come in contact with the world—our business, our work, our pleasures; and in our coming in—back home again. God preserves the inner life, and how we do need His preservation there! We need His preservation in our intimate contacts with others, and especially in our personal life with ourselves. This promise isn't just for Sabbaths or weekends, but for every day, "even for evermore."

The Pilgrims on the *Mayflower* began their famous Compact with the words "In the name of God, amen." Daniel Webster called this the first clause of the American Constitution. These adventurers in faith knew that the preservation of a new civilization in the New World depended upon God.

> Lead us, heavenly Father, lead us
> O'er the world's tempestuous sea;
> Guard us, guide us, keep us, feed us,
> For we have no help but Thee.
> —James Edmeston

MEDITATION PRAYER: *"Preserve me, O God: for in thee do I put my trust"* (Ps. 16:1).

# APRIL 1

*Behold, I shew you a mystery; We shall not all sleep, but we*
*shall all be changed, in a moment, in the twinkling of an eye,*
*at the last trump: for the trumpet shall sound, and the dead shall*
*be raised incorruptible, and we shall be changed (1 Cor. 15:51, 52).*

One day while in London we visited Bunhill Fields cemetery, the resting place of many of God's children. There lie John Bunyan, Isaac Watts, Dr. John Conder, and others. On the latter's tomb are these words: "I have sinned, I have repented; I have trusted, I have loved; I rest, I shall rise; and through the grace of Christ, however unworthy, I shall reign." Love demands a future life. Even Hume's skepticism disintegrated as he pathetically confessed that whenever he thought of his mother he believed in immortality.

The poet Browning's last words were "Never say that I am dead." To the believer death is a sleep. Jesus said of Lazarus, "Our friend Lazarus sleepeth; but I go, that I may awake him out of sleep" (John 11:11). Death is an anomaly, a disharmony in God's universe. Someday it will be unknown. "The last enemy that shall be destroyed is death" (1 Cor. 15:26). The day of life is coming, and then we shall understand this mystery that we shall not all sleep but we shall all be changed.

"For the Lord himself shall descend from heaven with a shout, with the voice of the archangel, and with the trump of God: and the dead in Christ shall rise first: then we which are alive and remain shall be caught up together with them in the clouds, to meet the Lord in the air: and so shall we ever be with the Lord. Wherefore comfort one another with these words" (1 Thess. 4:16–18).

> Surely He cometh! then the end of sickness,
> Death, and heartache in a world deranged;
> This is the end and this is the beginning,
> This the beginning, for we shall be changed.

MEDITATION PRAYER: *"As for me, I will behold thy face in righteousness" (Ps. 17:15).*

# APRIL 2

*If ye keep my commandments, ye shall abide
in my love; even as I have kept my Father's
commandments, and abide in his love (John 15:10).*

These things cannot be separated—abiding in obedience and abiding in the love of Christ.

Travelers in the Alps tell us that they come to have a very peculiar feeling toward their mountain guides. It is not alone companionship, friendship, or fellowship, but really a combination of all three. They learn to obey the guide in everything as they have never obeyed anyone else.

Our Guide once said, "If ye keep my commandments, ye shall abide in my love." Obedience will produce a fellowship, a heart association, a nearness, that could never be produced by all the zeal and fervor in the world without obedience. Someone has said: "Obedience is the key that unlocks the door into the dwelling of the indwelling Christ." Do we have faith in Christ? Obedience is the test. "By their fruits ye shall know them" (Matt. 7:20).

> Trust and obey, for there's no other way
> To be happy in Jesus, but to trust and obey.
> —Rev. J. H. Sammis

We have our Savior's example. He was obedient to His Father's commandment, and so abode in His love. Our Savior said, "If ye love me, keep my commandments" (John 14:15). Everything goes back to love, after all. "Love is the fulfilling of the law" (Rom. 13:10), not its breaking, denial, or neglect.

When asked if she always came when her mother called, a little girl said, "Yes, but sometimes I go so far away I can't hear her call." Is that our trouble? Let us come close to Jesus and be obedient.

MEDITATION PRAYER: *"Teach me, O Lord, the way of thy statutes; and I shall keep it unto the end" (Ps. 119:33).*

# APRIL 3

*For whosoever will save his life shall lose it;*
*but whosoever shall lose his life for my sake*
*and the gospel's, the same shall save it (Mark 8:35).*

This is Christ's challenge: "Fling away life to keep it."

Fra Angelico renounced wealth, ease, and luxury, and by fasting wasted to a shadow, kneeling as he painted. John Howard renounced his patrician position in society in favor of the poor. The apostle Paul turned from national leadership and honor to poverty and persecution for the love of Christ. And our Savior "made himself of no reputation" and came to earth as a Son of man, and was made subject unto death, "even the death of the cross," for our sakes. "Wherefore God also hath highly exalted him, and given him a name which is above every name" (Phil. 2:7-9).

All the heroes, martyrs, and reformers of the past, and multitudes of missionaries and everyday Christians of the present, have left lands, houses, homes, dear ones, ambitions, and have gone forth to sacrificial service for God. Losing life, they found it. It is by denying self and taking up their cross that the disciples of Jesus truly follow Him, and so, losing their life, find it.

What could be more foolish than for people to make first things last; to gain all this world, and yet lose their soul—themselves? "What shall a man give in exchange for his soul?" (Mark 8:37). So, in language the weightiest because it is the simplest, our Lord urges full surrender and promises a full reward.

> Take my will and make it Thine;
> It shall be no longer mine;
> Take my heart, it is Thine own!
> It shall be Thy royal throne.
> —Frances R. Havergal

MEDITATION PRAYER: *"I will praise thee, O Lord, with my whole heart; I will shew forth all thy marvellous works" (Ps. 9:1).*

# APRIL 4

*And the world passeth away,*
*and the lust thereof: but he that doeth*
*the will of God abideth for ever (1 John 2:17).*

With this text sacred memories of childhood overcome me. Sweet worship on Sabbath eve in our home, the reading from the great family Bible as only Father could read it—or Mother, when he was away—the prayers all around, and then the song "Abide With Me." Especially impressive was the second verse:

> Swift to its close ebbs out life's little day;
> Earth's joys grow dim, its glories pass away;
> Change and decay in all around I see;
> O Thou, who changest not, abide with me!
> —Henry F. Lyte

Everything human changes, fades, passes away. We return to the old home and find only strangers. A few more years, and "he shall return no more to his house, neither shall his place know him any more" (Job 7:10).

There is a text that infidels as well as Christians believe. It is Psalm 103:15, 16: "As for man, his days are as grass: as a flower of the field, so he flourisheth. For the wind passeth over it, and it is gone; and the place thereof shall know it no more."

Truly the world with its desires is a passing show, "but"—what a word of promise that is here—"but he that doeth the will of God abideth for ever." And the will of God is love.

The earth itself may change, but God is eternal and so is His love. "For the mountains shall depart, and the hills be removed; but my kindness shall not depart from thee, neither shall the covenant of my peace be removed, saith the Lord that hath mercy on thee" (Isa. 54:10). So, amid the changing scenes about us, we may say, "Now *abideth* faith, hope, love" (1 Cor. 13:13, ARV).

MEDITATION PRAYER: *"Thy name, O Lord, endureth for ever; and thy memorial, O Lord, throughout all generations" (Ps. 135:13).*

# APRIL 5

*And whatsoever we ask, we receive of him,*
*because we keep his commandments, and do those*
*things that are pleasing in his sight (1 John 3:22).*

In harmony with this promise are the words of our Savior in Matthew 7:7, 8: "Ask, and it shall be given you; seek, and ye shall find; knock, and it shall be opened unto you: for every one that asketh receiveth; and he that seeketh findeth; and to him that knocketh it shall be opened." Believers ask according to God's will. And should they ask what He wills not, they bow to God's will; so He gives them their request or something better. We are heard, not because our works merit a hearing, but because our works of faith are the fruit of God's Spirit and so are "pleasing in his sight." Then our prayers, being the voice of the same Spirit (Rom. 8:26), are answered. "Then shall ye call upon me, . . . and I will hearken unto you" (Jer. 29:12).

A host, on leaving the room to which she had just escorted a guest, pointed to a bracket containing a candle and matches, and said, "This is the emergency light. We once had a serious emergency in the night, when the electric lights failed. Now we always keep a candle here in case of need."

Prayer is the believer's emergency candle within easy reach, and always ready to give light. It requires no machinery to keep it in order. It is not affected by droughts, coal strikes, or hurricanes. All it needs is the match of faith to light it.

Yes, prayer is a light for times of special need—and for every day, too, and every time of day. "Evening, and morning, and at noon, will I pray, and cry aloud: and he shall hear my voice" (Ps. 55:17).

My soul needs light, Thy light, O Lord, to share;
Give me the faith to light the lamp of prayer.

MEDITATION PRAYER: *"Let my prayer be set forth before thee as incense; and the lifting up of my hands as the evening sacrifice"* (Ps. 141:2).

# APRIL 6

*But seek ye first the kingdom of God, and his righteousness;*
*and all these things shall be added unto you (Matt. 6:33).*

Every day our lives should open just as the Bible opens—"In the beginning God." What we seek first will be first to us.

D. L. Moody tells of a man who came to him one day weeping and told a strange story. This man had left his hometown and gone to another town to seek success, but had found none. He went to church, and the sermon was from this text: "Seek ye first the kingdom of God." He felt that it was preached just to him, but he did not want to be a Christian yet; he wanted to get rich first.

He moved to another village, and still another, with always the same experience—the first sermon he heard in each place was "Seek ye first the kingdom of God." The last time he heard this sermon it was as an arrow to his heart, but he wanted to own a farm at least before becoming a Christian, so he delayed.

"Now," he said to Mr. Moody, "I am rich. I go to church every week, but no sermon ever touches my heart. It is as hard as stone."

It's the biggest mistake possible not to make first things first. Solomon sought God's glory first, and God gave him earthly glory. The widow of Zarephath made the first cake for the prophet; after that her meal barrel was never empty. "I have been young, and now am old," said David, "yet have I not seen the righteous forsaken, nor his seed begging bread" (Ps. 37:25). The promise of Jesus is that those who give up house, siblings, parents, and children for the sake of the gospel shall receive an hundredfold in this life, and in the world to come, eternal life (Mark 10:29, 30). The kingdom of God and His righteousness are the goal of life. Then God adds the clothing, food, drink, homes, and friends. If we seek Him, He will look after the "things" we need.

MEDITATION PRAYER: *"When thou saidst, Seek ye my face; my heart said unto thee, Thy face, Lord, will I seek" (Ps. 27:8).*

# APRIL 7

*The Lord is well pleased for his righteousness' sake;*
*he will magnify the law, and make it honourable (Isa. 42:21).*

The law of God was spoken with audible voice from Mount Sinai. Again it was repeated by Jesus Christ in its spiritual principles in His sermon on the mount. Our Lord, in His own life, was the Word made flesh, which "dwelt among us, (and we beheld his glory, the glory as of the only begotten of the Father,) full of grace and truth" (John 1:14). Jesus appeared among men as God's "righteous servant" (Isa. 53:11). He revealed God's law as a law of love.

The first table of the Ten Commandments reveals love to God, the second reveals love to other people. "Love is the fulfilling of the law" (Rom. 13:10), and Jesus Christ is incarnate love. He put the magnifying glass of His holy righteousness, as it were, over the law, and it became "exceeding broad" (Ps. 119:96). The commandment said, "Thou shalt not kill" (Ex. 20:13). Through Christ the commandment includes all hatred, and therefore its scope is greatly magnified. The seventh commandment forbids adultery, unfaithfulness in marriage; but, through the magnifying glass of Christ's holy teaching, it includes even the lustful look or thought.

So the entire law of God is magnified through His life and reaches every heart and every human life. And since the transgression of the law is sin, and Jesus died for our sins upon the cross, His atoning sacrifice shows the holy nature and eternal character of God's law.

Notice that this prophetic promise pointed to Him who said, "I am not come to destroy, but to fulfil" (Matt. 5:17).

> O that the Lord would guide my ways
> To keep His statutes still!
> O that my God would grant me grace
> To know and do His will!
> —Isaac Watts

MEDITATION PRAYER: *"Open thou mine eyes, that I may behold wondrous things out of thy law" (Ps. 119:18).*

# APRIL 8

*For God shall bring every work into judgment, with every secret thing, whether it be good, or whether it be evil (Eccl. 12:14).*

William Thackeray tells of a visit to the Naples museum, where he saw a piece of wall from Herculaneum, which had been covered by the great volcanic eruption of Mount Vesuvius in A.D. 79. On that wall he saw a picture scratched with a nail. It was the figure of a soldier, and was evidently the work of a child. You could almost imagine the child turning around and smiling after finishing the etching.

Nearly all of us who have come to the years of accountability have had our Pompeii, our Herculaneum. Deep under the ashes of life lies the past—careless deeds, careless words, sins, and sorrows. Every time we open a box of old letters and look at our own childish scrawls or our mother's letters to us while we were away at school, we excavate our hearts and walk through the streets and rooms of the buried city, the city of memory.

But someday God will "bring every work into judgment," and then He "will render to every man according to his deeds" (Rom. 2:6). We have all "sinned, and come short of the glory of God" (Rom. 3:23). Will we not all, then, be terrified at the thought of judgment? There is only one way to be saved from such fear, and that is to know that the Judge Himself has already died for us, has paid our penalty, and will appear before the court as our advocate. "For the Father . . . hath committed all judgment unto the Son" (John 5:22). And "we have an advocate with the Father, Jesus Christ the righteous" (1 John 2:1). Those who have repented, and forsaken their sins, and put their case in the hands of Christ need have no fear of the judgment. "He that heareth my word, and believeth on him that sent me, hath everlasting life, and shall not come into condemnation; but is passed from death unto life" (John 5:24).

MEDITATION PRAYER: *"Judge me, O Lord; for I have walked in mine integrity: I have trusted also in the Lord" (Ps. 26:1).*

# APRIL 9

*And the times of this ignorance God winked at; but now commandeth all men every where to repent: because he hath appointed a day, in the which he will judge the world in righteousness by that man whom he hath ordained; whereof he hath given assurance unto all men, in that he hath raised him from the dead (Acts 17:30, 31).*

Repent! the message of John the Baptist. *Repent!* the message of Jesus. *Repent!* the message of the apostles. *Repent!* the message of every true minister of Christ. *Repent!* the most unpopular subject with all sinners.

Visiting St. Michan's church, built by the Danes outside the walls of Dublin about the eleventh century, I noticed a chair near the pulpit facing the congregation. I was told that it was the chair of repentance. In the old Scottish churches such a chair was called a cutty stool. It was a low stool on which open sinners who were repentant were made to sit for public rebuke. In *Roget's Thesaurus* the cutty stool is used as a synonym for stool of repentance. "Sackcloth and ashes" is another phrase meaning the same, or to "eat humble pie."

God actually commands all people everywhere to repent. Why the command? Because the day of judgment is already appointed. That judgment will be in righteousness, and it is "by that man whom he [that is, God] hath ordained," and that man is Jesus Christ.

Not only is it good for sinners to repent, not only must repentance precede forgiveness, but God has given us assurance of Christ as judge, "in that he hath raised him from the dead." Did you ever think of it that way before? The resurrection of Christ should bring us seriously face to face with the coming judgment and the necessity of repentance. It is true, for God "hath committed all judgment unto the Son" (John 5:22). The command of God is ringing in our ears, Repent, repent! "Repent ye therefore, and be converted, that your sins may be blotted out" (Acts 3:19).

MEDITATION PRAYER: *"I acknowledge my sin unto thee, and mine iniquity have I not hid" (Ps. 32:5).*

# APRIL 10

*If ye abide in me, and my words abide in you, ye shall*
*ask what ye will, and it shall be done unto you (John 15:7).*

But what shall we ask? There is a story of an old Bible woman in Leicester, England, whose custom it was to carry flowers to the hospital and to talk with the patients, the nurses, and even the doctors about religion, about the Lord and His work. One day one of the doctors asked her, "Do you believe God really hears our prayers? I'm hard up. If I asked Him, would He send me five pounds?"

The old saint answered, "If you were introduced to the prince of Wales, would you immediately put your hand into his pocket?"

"No," replied the doctor, "not until I knew him better."

Then the Bible woman said, "You will need to be a great deal better acquainted with God before you can expect such an answer as you wish."

Notice the promise is that *if we abide in Christ,* we may ask what we will. This promise is taken from our Savior's description of the believer as a branch abiding in Him, the True Vine. If we are abiding in the Vine and partaking of His nourishment and life, then we shall pray according to His will, and whatsoever we ask shall be done unto us. We are to abide in Christ's love as Christ abides in the Father's love (John 15:10).

This abiding in Christ is not only a glorious privilege but an apostolic command. "And now, little children, abide in him; that, when he shall appear, we may have confidence, and not be ashamed before him at his coming" (1 John 2:28). We abide in Him when His words abide in us. Those who are "in Christ" feed upon the Word of Christ. Their prayers are according to His will; therefore, they are answered. Let us seek to abide in Him. Let us seek His Word; let us seek His will. Then we shall know better how to pray, "Thy will be done in earth, as it is in heaven" (Matt. 6:10).

MEDITATION PRAYER: *"Thou hast given him his heart's desire, and hast not withholden the request of his lips" (Ps. 21:2).*

# APRIL 11

*Behold, the righteous shall be recompensed in the earth: much more the wicked and the sinner (Prov. 11:31).*

On some docks in great seaport cities you may see a sign reading "Stowaways prosecuted on the other side." Two months' imprisonment is the usual penalty. A stowaway is one who sneaks aboard ship and hides to steal a passage.

Is it not true that those who leave our mortal shores unrepentant will indeed be prosecuted on the other side? Our promise text refers not only to the wicked but also to the righteous. "The righteous shall be recompensed in the earth," but certainly not in the earth as it is now. God does send many blessings to His people here. Of those who serve Him fully, Jesus said: "There is no man that hath left house, or brethren, or sisters, or father, or mother, or wife, or children, or lands, for my sake, and the gospel's, but he shall receive an hundredfold now in this time, houses, and brethren, and sisters, and mothers, and children, and lands, with persecutions; and in the world to come eternal life" (Mark 10:29, 30).

But notice, the full reward is in the world to come, the new earth, redeemed after our Lord's second coming and the judgment of the great white throne. "Blessed are the meek: for they shall inherit the earth," our Lord declared in His sermon on the mount (Matt. 5:5). Right here on this earth, where the Son of God was crucified when He came to seek and to save that which was lost, the righteous whom He died to redeem will receive their eternal reward. For God created the earth "not in vain, he formed it to be inhabited" (Isa. 45:18).

As the righteous are to be rewarded here, so also are the wicked. Here where they have sinned, they will meet their final reward. They will rise in the second resurrection, be judged guilty, and receive their punishment when fire comes down from God out of heaven and devours them (Rev. 20:9). This will be the end of sin and sinners.

MEDITATION PRAYER: *"The judgments of the Lord are true and righteous altogether" (Ps. 19:9).*

# APRIL 12

*Nevertheless we, according to his promise,
look for new heavens and a new earth,
wherein dwelleth righteousness (2 Peter 3:13).*

When Albert Einstein died, one wrote of him in a great magazine: "His only instruments were a pencil and a scratch pad on which he would jot down rows of mathematical symbols. Out of these obscure symbols came the most explosive ideas of the century." Do you fully understand his famous equation $E = mc^2$? Neither do I. But the bomb exploded just the same. He died before his unified-field theory was proved, but we remember he said, "I cannot believe that God plays dice with the cosmos."

In the third chapter of Second Peter we find an inspired picture of heavens exploding, and elements melting with fervent heat (verse 12). Then comes our promise: "Nevertheless"—that is, in spite of all this, in spite of a universe dissolved not only into atoms but into neutrons, deutrons, positrons, mesons, et cetera, ad infinitum—"Nevertheless we, according to his promise, look for new heavens and a new earth, wherein dwelleth righteousness." God's promise is stronger than the crash of electrons, and God will guide the redeemed to their appointed places in the new earth, surrounded by its new heavens.

And the new heavens and new earth will endure forever. That is the definite plan of God. "For as the new heavens and the new earth, which I will make, shall remain before me, saith the Lord, so shall your seed and your name remain. And it shall come to pass, that from one new moon to another, and from one sabbath to another, shall all flesh come to worship before me, saith the Lord" (Isa. 66:22, 23).

MEDITATION PRAYER: *"They shall be abundantly satisfied with the fatness of thy house; and thou shalt make them drink of the river of thy pleasures" (Ps. 36:8).*

# APRIL 13

*Blessed is he that considereth the poor: the Lord will deliver him in time of trouble. The Lord will preserve him, and keep him alive; and he shall be blessed upon the earth: and thou wilt not deliver him unto the will of his enemies (Ps. 41:1, 2).*

It is incredible," said Lucian, the pagan jeerer and skeptic, "to see the ardor with which those Christians help each other in their wants. They spare nothing. Their first Legislator has put into their heads that they are all brothers, and Julian the Apostate said, 'These Galileans nourish not only their own poor but ours as well.'"

The poor are really Christ's representatives, and it is a Christian's duty to help those in need. Jesus said, "The poor always ye have with you" (John 12:8). We cannot put our offering into the actual hands of Jesus, for He is in heaven, but we can help the needy here on earth. We can do more by care than by cash, and more still by both. Those who help others will themselves be helped. The Lord will deliver them in time of trouble; He will preserve those who are liberal—keep them alive, bless them upon the earth, and they will not be delivered to the will of their enemies. "The liberal soul shall be made fat," reads the Scripture (Prov. 11:25). We might add, "The body too, if it needs it."

"Give, and it shall be given unto you; good measure, pressed down, and shaken together, and running over, shall men give into your bosom. For with the same measure that ye mete withal it shall be measured to you again" (Luke 6:38). However generous we may be, we shall have a time of trouble. But if we consider the poor, we may put in a special claim for God's deliverance. Many people will help only themselves, but the Lord will help those who help others.

MEDITATION PRAYER: *"Lord, who is like unto thee, which deliverest the poor from him that is too strong for him, yea, the poor and the needy from him that spoileth him?" (Ps. 35:10).*

# APRIL 14

*For thus saith the Lord God of Israel, The barrel of meal shall not waste, neither shall the cruse of oil fail, until the day that the Lord sendeth rain upon the earth (1 Kings 17:14).*

Mother, I think God always hears when we scrape the bottom of the barrel," said a little boy to his mother one day. They were very poor and often found themselves in real need. Many times they used the last stick of wood and the last bit of bread before they knew where the next supply was coming from. But they had often been provided for unexpectedly and in providential ways just when they were most in need.

The little boy seemed to think that when his mother scraped the bottom of the barrel, God always heard and knew then that they were in special need. That was his way of saying what Abraham had said so beautifully thousands of years before, when he called a place where God had delivered him Jehovah-jireh, "the Lord will provide."

Our heavenly Father knows what we need before we ask Him (Matt. 6:8), and He has promised that in the days of famine we shall be satisfied (Ps. 37:19).

The words of our promise text today were spoken by the prophet Elijah to the widow of Zarephath, and these words were fulfilled. The widow, her son, and the prophet were fed from the unfailing meal barrel and oil cruse for a year, in spite of the famine all around them. God does not promise needless luxuries, but He does say that our bread and our water shall be sure (Isa. 33:16).

Without God's blessing we could not earn our daily bread. We could not live at all; our hearts would not beat. We need to remember that it is He who, in the last analysis, "giveth food to all flesh" (Ps. 136:25). Let our prayer ascend to Him, "Give us this day our daily bread" (Matt. 6:11).

MEDITATION PRAYER: *"Bless the Lord, O my soul . . . ; who satisfieth thy mouth with good things; so that thy youth is renewed like the eagle's" (Ps. 103:2-5).*

# APRIL 15

*And Jesus said unto them, I am the bread of life:*
*he that cometh to me shall never hunger; and he that*
*believeth on me shall never thirst (John 6:35).*

Bread has been called the staff of life. It represents or symbolizes all food necessary for human existence. It is said that the primitive Greeks subsisted upon acorns, but after they learned the art of wheat culture and bread making they discarded their former food and considered it fit only for swine.

Those who have once tasted the true Bread of Life will have no more desire for the fleshpots of Egypt, but will always pray, "Lord, evermore give us this bread" (John 6:34). It's a sad day when Christians who have eaten the Bread of Life lose their hunger for it. Christ is the Bread of Life and the Water of Life, our spiritual food and drink.

Jesus was born at Bethlehem, which means "house of bread." He is called not only the Bread of Life, but the Bread of God, the True Bread, the Bread from heaven (John 6:32, 33).

Like the good corn bruised and broken, and fine flour baked, He gave His flesh for the life of the world. As one old writer well says of our need of Him, "Without bread, there is no feast; with bread, there need be no famine."

The Lord's Supper—the feast of commemoration, communion, and love—represents all this (1 Cor. 10:16, 17). Believers eat and drink of Christ's bounty (Isa. 55:1, 2). They taste of the Lord's goodness (Ps. 34:8). They feed as His sheep in green pastures (Ps. 23:2). They sit down as His guests at the banqueting house (S. of Sol. 2:4). They are "abundantly satisfied" with the good things of the Lord's house while they "drink of the river of . . . [His] pleasures" (Ps. 36:8).

MEDITATION PRAYER: *"Thou preparest a table before me in the presence of mine enemies: thou anointest my head with oil; my cup runneth over" (Ps. 23:5).*

# APRIL 16

*But thou, when thou prayest, enter into thy closet, and when thou hast shut thy door, pray to thy Father which is in secret; and thy Father which seeth in secret shall reward thee openly (Matt. 6:6).*

The traffic light on the corner had just turned red. A father was watching the minute hand of the great clock on the First National Bank. "Three minutes to three!" he muttered. "By the time I have parked the car the bank will be closed."

Then from the back seat a voice spoke up: "Daddy, why don't banks stay open as long as the stores and shops? They seem to work only a little time, about five hours a day."

"Well, son," the father explained, "most of the employees at the bank do a great deal of their work after the doors are closed, sometimes way into the night. Much of their work must be done without interruption, behind closed doors."

And so it is with the Christian's prayer life. A great deal of it must be done behind closed doors. Surely we are to pray in public, in church, in the family circle, with our friends; but our own spiritual communion with God is to be done alone. "It is only at the altar of God that we can kindle our tapers with divine fire" (*Gospel Workers*, p. 255).

Secret prayer is the secret of spiritual life. "God's messengers must tarry long with Him, if they would have success in their work. The story is told of an old Lancashire woman who was listening to the reasons that her neighbors gave for their minister's success. They spoke of his gifts, of his style of address, of his manners. 'Nay,' said the old woman, 'I will tell you what it is. Your man is very thick with the Almighty'" (*ibid*). You see, his public power came from personal communion with God.

MEDITATION PRAYER: *"Hearken unto the voice of my cry, my King, and my God: for unto thee will I pray. My voice shalt thou hear in the morning, O Lord; in the morning will I direct my prayer unto thee, and will look up" (Ps. 5:2, 3).*

# APRIL 17

*Now therefore go, and I will be with thy mouth,*
*and teach thee what thou shalt say (Ex. 4:12).*

Moses had to distrust his own ability before he could be God's messenger. He had to bow at the burning bush before he could speak burning words. It is sometimes good for witnesses to be "slow of speech," for then their words have more weight.

When we obey, when we "go for God," He will teach us what and when to speak. "Then the Lord put forth his hand, and touched my mouth," said the prophet Jeremiah. "And the Lord said unto me, Behold, I have put my words in thy mouth" (Jer. 1:9). And Jesus promised His disciples that when they would be called to testify before their persecutors He would give them "a mouth and wisdom, which all your adversaries shall not be able to gainsay nor resist" (Luke 21:15). If our speaking were by God's teaching, there would be less evil and more peace in the world. When we go for God we can speak for God.

> I spoke a word, and no one heard;
> I wrote a word, and no one cared,
> Or seemed to heed; but after half a score of years
> It blossomed in a fragrant deed.
>
> Preachers and teachers all are we—
> Sowers of seed unconsciously.
> Our hearers are beyond our ken,
> Yet all we give may come again
> With usury of joy or pain. We never know
> To what a little word may grow.
> See to it then that all your seeds
> Be such as bring forth noble deeds.
> —John Oxenham

MEDITATION PRAYER: *"Let the words of my mouth, and the meditation of my heart, be acceptable in thy sight, O Lord, my strength, and my redeemer" (Ps. 19:14).*

# APRIL 18

*I say unto you, that likewise joy shall be in heaven over one sinner that repenteth, more than over ninety and nine just persons, which need no repentance (Luke 15:7).*

Nothing is more lost than a lost sheep. Traveling over the high desert, one may come upon a lost sheep. It bleats piteously and is afraid of every sound. It rushes here and there calling companions, trying to recover a trace of the path. Unless someone finds it in time, it will perish in the solitude. The shepherd, having missed his sheep, goes in search of it. He sees it from a distance, hastens toward it, raises it on his shoulders, and bears it home rejoicing.

This is a true picture of the lost sinner. In the verses preceding our text Jesus has just told about the 99 sheep safe in the fold, the one lost on the desert mountain, the shepherd's search for it, his success in finding it, and his jubilant return.

My friend, the Good Shepherd is seeking you, but He cannot save you unless you repent. When you repent, you become one of His sheep, and He will seek you until He finds you. Then there will be joy in heaven, joy over you and your salvation; and you will share that joy here and hereafter. You may have wandered a long way into the dark mountains of sin, but if you repent, the Good Shepherd will find you and bring you home. "Repent ye therefore, and be converted, that your sins may be blotted out" (Acts 3:19).

> But all through the mountains, thunder-riven,
>     And up from the rocky steep,
> There rose a cry to the gate of heaven,
>     "Rejoice, I have found My sheep!"
> And the angels sang around the throne,
>     "Rejoice, for the Lord brings back His own!"
>     —Elizabeth C. Clephane

MEDITATION PRAYER: *"So we thy people and sheep of thy pasture will give thee thanks for ever" (Ps. 79:13).*

# APRIL 19

*The angel of the Lord encampeth round about*
*them that fear him, and delivereth them (Ps. 34:7).*

During pioneer days in the Midwest many scattered settlements suffered from Indian raids. One stormy night a war party crossed the Wabash River into Indiana. The chief quietly opened the door of a cabin and saw a family upon their knees, the open Bible before them. The enemy closed the door as silently as he had opened it and told his warriors not to molest those people, for, he said, "They are talking to the Great Spirit, who would be angry." In the morning the family saw the houses of the neighbors in ashes and could not understand why they had been spared.

We do not know the dangers surrounding us, but we do know that "the angel of the Lord encampeth round about" us to deliver us. Notice, the angels do not come and go; they encamp about God's children. It is a permanent protection.

There is more written about angels in the Bible than there is about baptism, more about angels than about heaven, more about angels than about the Sabbath and many other important subjects in the Bible; yet how few sermons we hear on this most interesting and important subject. The angels excel in strength and keep the commandments of God (Ps. 103:20). They are ministering spirits to those who shall be the heirs of salvation (Heb. 1:14). They appear and disappear at will. They are the sentinel guards of those who fear God. They are sent for our deliverance.

Do we fear God? If so, we have the fellowship and protection of these "ministers of his, that do his pleasure" (Ps. 103:21). This promised angel guardianship reveals the importance of all Christ's disciples, even "these little ones; for I say unto you, That in heaven their angels do always behold the face of my Father" (Matt. 18:10).

MEDITATION PRAYER: *"For thou hast been a shelter for me, and a strong tower from the enemy" (Ps. 61:3).*

# APRIL 20

*And now, brethren, I commend you to God, and to the*
*word of his grace, which is able to build you up, and to give*
*you an inheritance among all them which are sanctified (Acts 20:32).*

What a commendation is this, commended to God! When asked which was his favorite language, Emperor Charles IV said that in the daily affairs of the home he spoke German; in business, English; in diplomacy, French; but when he prayed, he used Spanish. In that beautiful language the word of farewell is adios ("unto God").

So the apostle commends his friends not only to God but to the word of God's grace, which is able to build them up; and it is able to build us up too.

Over the fireplace of a clubhouse belonging to a group of Alcoholics Anonymous is a plaque bearing this inscription: "But for the grace of God." We may have no other support on earth, but if God's grace is ours we shall have an inheritance, and the right kind of inheritance too—"among all them which are sanctified." "For by grace are ye saved through faith; and that not of yourselves: it is the gift of God" (Eph. 2:8).

The word of God's grace is our teacher, "for the grace of God that bringeth salvation hath appeared to all men, teaching us that, denying ungodliness and worldly lusts, we should live soberly, righteously, and godly, in this present world" (Titus 2:11, 12).

In the days of Moses God proclaimed His name, and in truly Christian lives today we are to proclaim the name of the Lord—"the Lord God, merciful and gracious, longsuffering, and abundant in goodness and truth" (Ex. 34:6).

MEDITATION PRAYER: *"Oh how great is thy goodness, which thou hast laid up for them that fear thee; which thou hast wrought for them that trust in thee before the sons of men!" (Ps. 31:19).*

# APRIL 21

*Now is the judgment of this world: now shall the prince of this world be cast out. And I, if I be lifted up from the earth, will draw all men unto me. This he said, signifying what death he should die (John 12:31-33).*

Dominating the city of Rio de Janeiro and atop Mount Corcovado, rising nearly 2,500 feet above the sea, stands the enormous statue of Christ the Redeemer. Its outstretched arms, 92 feet from fingertip to fingertip, form a cross. Because of its great size and its location, it can be seen for many miles by land, sea, and air. Seeing this colossal figure against the sky, one is led to think of the words of Scripture: "And I, if I be lifted up from the earth, will draw all men unto me."

Jesus spoke these words in view of the cross. He was looking forward to His death, and His sacrifice on Calvary was indeed the "judgment," or crisis, of this world. At last the whole universe saw the true character of the devil—that "he was a murderer from the beginning" (John 8:44). From that moment to this, the magnetism of the cross has been drawing the hearts of people everywhere. His cross is the center of everything.

The apostle says that "as in Adam all die, even so in Christ shall all be made alive" (1 Cor. 15:22).

If we are drawn to religion by anything except Christ and Him crucified, we shall soon be drawn away from it. Music will not draw people to Jesus, eloquence will not draw them, logic will not draw them, ceremony will not draw them, noise will not draw them. Jesus Himself must draw them to Himself. This is the secret of real gospel work. Try preaching the crucified, risen, ascended, and soon-coming Savior. This is the greatest drawing power ever known on earth.

MEDITATION PRAYER: *"Be thou exalted, O God, above the heavens: let thy glory be above all the earth" (Ps. 57:11).*

# APRIL 22

*And they said, Believe on the Lord Jesus Christ,*
*and thou shalt be saved, and thy house (Acts 16:31).*

This gospel for a man with a sword at his throat ought to be good enough for us. It is simple enough for one to understand without taking a course in systematic theology. We are to look away from self and sin and all personal merit, and trust the Lord Jesus as our Savior. We are to believe in Him, rest in Him, and accept Him as our all in all.

A high school boy drove a much dilapidated old automobile to school. Seeing it one day, a teacher asked, "What kind of car do you have here?"

"RFD" was the answer.

"RFD? I have never heard of that make of car."

"Yes," said the boy, "Rescued From Dump!"

We Christians are RFD people. We have been rescued from the dump of life through the blood of Christ. To believe on the Lord Jesus Christ means to trust Him, to accept all He says, to obey all His commandments; to believe, repent, confess, and walk in all the light He brings to us, for He is "the true Light, which lighteth every man that cometh into the world" (John 1:9).

Let us not forget the last words of this promise, for they apply to our house also. Let us in our prayers every day mention the names of our brothers and sisters, parents, children, friends, relatives, those who work with us and for us, and give the Lord no rest until His promise, "and thy house," is fulfilled.

> 'Tis simply to receive Him,
> The holy One and just,
> 'Tis only to believe Him,
> It is not Try, but Trust.
>
> —E. G. Taylor

MEDITATION PRAYER: *"They cried unto thee, and were delivered: they trusted in thee, and were not confounded"* (Ps. 22:5).

# APRIL 23

*Neither is there salvation in any other: for there is none other name under heaven given among men, whereby we must be saved (Acts 4:12).*

A visitor to the Copenhagen Cathedral saw Thorvaldsen's *Kristus*. The story of the famous statue is this: When the sculptor had finished molding the soft clay of the model, he left it to dry and went home. A dense fog rolled in, and when Thorvaldsen returned the next morning he thought his masterpiece was ruined. The hands that had been uplifted to bless were now stretched out invitingly, and the regal head was bowed low. But as he gazed he saw a new Christ, different from his previous conception. This was a Christ to worship.

There is none other to save us. Let us bow before Him. His name was angel announced: "Thou shalt call his name Jesus: for he shall save his people from their sins" (Matt. 1:21). His name means "Savior." There may be truth and beauty in art and philosophy and many other things, but in Jesus Christ there is salvation.

In Calcutta a young Brahman came to the home of a Christian teacher for an interview. He said, "Many things that Christianity contains, I find in Hinduism; but Christianity has one thing that Hinduism has not."

"What is that?" the teacher asked.

The reply was striking: "A Savior."

In this, Jesus is the Great Unique. "For there is one God, and one mediator between God and men, the man Christ Jesus; who gave himself a ransom for all" (1 Tim. 2:5, 6). Being both Son of God and Son of man, He came "to seek and to save that which was lost" (Luke 19:10). "To him give all the prophets witness, that through his name whosoever believeth in him shall receive remission of sins" (Acts 10:43). We need to be saved, and He is the Savior; so why do we wait? Let us come to Him.

MEDITATION PRAYER: *"Say unto my soul, I am thy salvation" (Ps. 35:3).*

# APRIL 24

*Go ye therefore, and teach all nations, baptizing them in the name of the Father, and of the Son, and of the Holy Ghost: teaching them to observe all things whatsoever I have commanded you: and, lo, I am with you alway, even unto the end of the world (Matt. 28:19, 20).*

Someone asked the duke of Wellington if he thought Christians ought to attempt to go into all the world with the gospel. His answer was "What are your marching orders?" In our text today we find the Christian's marching order. But may this not be difficult, even dangerous? Yes, but we are to go, nevertheless.

We think of the story of Captain Pat Etheridge of the Cape Hatteras station of the United States Coast Guard. One night in a howling hurricane he saw the distress signal of a ship that had gone aground on the dangerous Diamond Shoal about 10 miles at sea. The rescue ships could be launched, but getting them back again was the problem. Captain Etheridge ordered the boats rolled out. One of the lifeguards protested, "Captain Pat, we can get out there, but we can never get back." "Boys," came the reply, "we don't have to come back!"

Our Captain has not promised that we will come back safely to our homeland when we go out in His service, but He has commanded us to go. But notice the wonderful promise that goes with His command: "Lo, I am with you alway, even unto the end of the world."

His promised presence, unfailing in all emergencies of life, underlies the faithfulness of His servants, even unto death. The presence of Jesus was very real to Stephen as the cruel stones rained down upon him. It was real to John Bunyan as he dreamed his immortal dream in Bedford jail and to uncounted multitudes of men and women who have obeyed the command of Jesus, "Go ye." His promised presence was not merely a theory, a fancy, but a wonderful fact.

MEDITATION PRAYER: *"I will praise thee, O Lord, among the people: I will sing unto thee among the nations" (Ps. 57:9).*

# APRIL 25

*For whosoever shall call upon the name*
*of the Lord shall be saved (Rom. 10:13).*

The wind was high, the sea boisterous. In fact, it was a real storm on Galilee. The disciples saw what they thought was a phantom walking on the water, but their fears were calmed by the familiar voice of Jesus, "It is I; be not afraid." Then Peter said, "Lord, if it be thou, bid me come unto thee on the water." Jesus said, "Come." Peter began to walk toward Him on the water; but when he saw the raging billows, fear entered his heart and he began to sink. Then he prayed the shortest prayer on record, "Lord, save me." Jesus reached forth His hand and took him. (Matt. 14:26-31.) This is an illustration of calling on the Lord, crying out to Him as a child might cry to its mother or father in time of danger or fear.

Jesus came to seek and save the lost. He was born of the blessed virgin that He might "save his people from their sins" (Matt. 1:21). That's why His name is Jesus, the Savior. But only those who call upon the name of the Lord, only those who cry out for help, find His salvation and are helped. True enough, we are saved by grace through faith, and not of ourselves. "It is the gift of God" (Eph. 2:8). But in another sense we are saved by prayer. "Whosoever shall call . . . shall be saved." This is one prayer that will always be answered in the affirmative. The sincere cry to God for salvation will be heard. The promise distinctly says "Whosoever." But no one will call upon God for salvation until they realize that they are lost. Friend, if you need help, pray, and pray now.

Prayer changes things for you and me.
　　　Whatever be the care,
　Just bring it to the throne of grace
　　　And wait for answered prayer.

MEDITATION PRAYER: *"For this shall every one that is godly pray unto thee in a time when thou mayest be found: surely in the floods of great waters they shall not come nigh unto him" (Ps. 32:6).*

# APRIL 26

*Then Peter said unto them, Repent, and be baptized every one of you in the name of Jesus Christ for the remission of sins, and ye shall receive the gift of the Holy Ghost (Acts 2:38).*

True repentance means sorrow for sin and the forsaking of it. Samuel Johnson's father, who was a book merchant, had a stall in various towns on market days. Being ill one day, he asked young Samuel to take his place in the market at Uttoxeter. The lad was proud and clever and refused to go. The poor old man, ill as he was, had to go himself. When the father returned that night very tired and worn, he said not a word to his son; but the boy's heart smote him.

Fifty years later, after Samuel Johnson had become famous throughout England, he went to Uttoxeter on market day and stood bareheaded for hours close to the spot where his father's bookstall had been. People stared at the burly man standing there in the wind and rain without a hat on his head. But the brave man, remembering his old unkindness to his father, was showing his repentance.

In his great Pentecostal sermon Peter mentions baptism as a step to be taken by those who have believed and repented of their sins. Baptism is an act of faith. It is a reenaction of the death, burial, and resurrection of Jesus Christ (Rom. 6:1-6). It shows the believer's death to sin, the burial of the old self, and the resurrection to walk "in newness of life." It is an act of obedience, and Jesus is the "author of eternal salvation unto all them that obey him" (Heb. 5:9).

The disciples at Pentecost and afterward were endued with the ordinary and extraordinary gifts of the Spirit. They were filled with wisdom, faith, and power (Acts 6:3, 8). D. L. Moody said, "The Holy Spirit is God at work."

Have you repented? Have you been baptized in the name of Jesus Christ for the remission of sins? Have you received the gift of the Holy Ghost? Let us walk in the path of obedience.

MEDITATION PRAYER: *"Cast me not away from thy presence; and take not thy holy spirit from me" (Ps. 51:11).*

# APRIL 27

*Howbeit when he, the Spirit of truth, is come, he will guide you into all truth: for he shall not speak of himself; but whatsoever he shall hear, that shall he speak: and he will shew you things to come. He shall glorify me: for he shall receive of mine, and shall shew it unto you (John 16:13, 14).*

An American, with an Englishman, was viewing Niagara Falls. Taking his friend to the foot of the gigantic cataract, he exclaimed, "There is the greatest unused power in the world!"

"Ah, no, my brother; you are mistaken" was the quick reply. "The greatest unused power in the world is the Holy Spirit of the living God." Is the Holy Spirit using us, guiding us? The Holy Spirit is the Spirit of truth, and He will guide us into all truth.

We were visiting the great Carlsbad Caverns in New Mexico. How beautiful and wonderful they were—one marvel after another as we threaded our way through twisting and turning passageways, galleries, rooms, grottoes, on past the Rock of Ages to the great Throne Room itself. However, we could never have found our way through the labyrinthine ways without our guide, who led us step by step to reveal the marvels and glories to us.

The truth is like that—like a vast cavern. But we must have a guide or we shall lose our way. The Spirit of truth leads us step by step, room by room, passageway by passageway; and He always takes us by the Rock of Ages, the Lord Jesus, into the great Throne Room of the final revelation of God. The Holy Spirit inspired the Holy Scriptures, for "holy men of God spake as they were moved by the Holy Ghost" (2 Peter 1:21). Therefore all that He speaks directly to the heart is in harmony with what is written in the Holy Book. He guides us into "all truth," so that we shall not be one-sided and out of balance. The Holy Spirit glorifies Jesus. How? By receiving the things of Christ and showing them to us. The Holy Spirit is the one who makes real in me what Jesus did for me.

MEDITATION PRAYER: *"Shew me thy ways, O Lord; teach me thy paths" (Ps. 25:4).*

# APRIL 28

*He that spared not his own Son, but delivered*
*him up for us all, how shall he not with him*
*also freely give us all things? (Rom. 8:32).*

If not a promise in form, this is certainly a promise in fact. It is a mighty sea of promises.

William Spurgeon of Wales was lecturing in Scotland, and after the lecture an old man approached him and said, "Dr. Spurgeon, I'm glad to meet you. I'm the father of Henry Drummond."

"Oh, then," said Spurgeon, "I already know you, for I know your son so well."

If you wish to know what God is like, look at Jesus, for "God was in Christ, reconciling the world unto himself" (2 Cor. 5:19). Our unsparing God "spared not his own Son, but delivered him up for us all." All things belong to Him, and when God gave Jesus to us, with this gift He gave us all things.

One who has ever heard J. Wilbur Chapman preach will never forget it. In his service one night a man rose and gave this remarkable testimony: "I got off the train at the Pennsylvania Station as a tramp, and for a year I begged in the streets for a living. One night I touched a man on the shoulder and said, 'Please, mister, give me a dime.' As soon as I saw his face I recognized my own father. 'Father, don't you know me?' I asked. Throwing his arms around me, he cried: 'I have found you! I have found you! All I have is yours.' Just think of it—I, a tramp, stood begging my father for 10 cents, when for 18 years he had been looking for me to give me all he possessed."

We do not have to beg God or urge Him frantically to give us what we need. In Christ He has given us not only salvation but "all things to enjoy" (1 Tim. 6:17), and has given them freely. Our text today is really a checkbook of faith.

MEDITATION PRAYER: *"Many, O Lord my God, are thy wonderful works which thou hast done, and thy thoughts which are to usward: . . . they are more than can be numbered" (Ps. 40:5).*

# APRIL 29

*For I am persuaded, that neither death, nor life, nor angels, nor principalities, nor powers, nor things present, nor things to come, nor height, nor depth, nor any other creature, shall be able to separate us from the love of God, which is in Christ Jesus our Lord (Rom. 8:38, 39).*

The apostle knew it. The love of God is greater than the measure of a human being's mind. It is higher, deeper, broader, than all things and all thinking; and nothing can separate us from it, ever.

A starry-eyed young woman, having written a number of poems, went to an editor and told him she wished to have her poems published in his magazine. "What are they about?" asked the editor. "All about love" was the prompt reply. "Well, what is love?" questioned the editor. "Love," said the young woman, "is gazing upon a lily pond at night, with the shimmering moonbeams, when the lilies are in full bloom, and—" "Stop, stop!" cried the editor, sternly. "You are all wrong. I'll tell you what love is. It's getting up cheerfully at 2:00 in the morning to fill the hot-water bottle for a sick child. That's real love. I'm sorry, but I don't think I can use your poems." The editor was right. Real love is doing something for somebody who needs our help no matter how hard it is for us to give it. And "God *so* loved."

Nothing that happens in life, not even death itself, can separate us from the love of God revealed in Christ Jesus. The inspired apostle John beheld the height, the depth, the breadth, of the Father's love toward us. Failing to find suitable language to express it, he called upon the world to behold it. "Behold, what manner of love the Father hath bestowed upon us, that we should be called the sons of God" (1 John 3:1).

"God is love" is written on every opening bud, on every blushing flower, on all the beauties of nature. It is written in the heart of a mother; but clearest of all, upon the cross.

MEDITATION PRAYER: *"Let thy lovingkindness and thy truth continually preserve me" (Ps. 40:11).*

# APRIL 30

*In my Father's house are many mansions: if it were not so,*
*I would have told you. I go to prepare a place for you. And if I*
*go and prepare a place for you, I will come again, and receive you unto*
*myself; that where I am, there ye may be also (John 14:2, 3).*

God fits heaven for the redeemed, and the redeemed for heaven. This is really His promise, a prepared place for us if we are prepared. He is preparing for us. Are we preparing for Him? And, after all, our great reward is not so much the *place* as the Savior Himself. We are to be with Him.

A traveler who had just returned from a trip to Jerusalem was visiting with Humboldt, the great naturalist and statesman, and discovered that he was as thoroughly acquainted with the streets and buildings of Jerusalem as was he himself. So he asked the aged statesman how long it had been since he visited Jerusalem. He replied, "I have never been there, but I intended to visit the Holy City 60 years ago, so I prepared myself."

If we are to be at home in the heavenly land, we must begin to prepare ourselves for it now. We must study the city. We must have contact with the King of that land.

The King is coming to receive His own. There is no doubt about it. His word has never been broken (John 10:35). "I am preparing; I will come again," He says. "I will receive you unto myself." And we can only answer, "Even so, come, Lord Jesus" (Rev. 22:20).

> Could we but climb where Moses stood,
> And view the landscape o'er
> Not all this world's pretended good
> Could ever charm us more.
> —Isaac Watts

MEDITATION PRAYER: *"Lord, thou hast been our dwelling place in all generations. Before the mountains were brought forth, or ever thou hadst formed the earth and the world, even from everlasting to everlasting, thou art God" (Ps. 90:1, 2).*

# MAY 1

*And he said unto me, It is done. I am Alpha and Omega,*
*the beginning and the end. I will give unto him that is athirst*
*of the fountain of the water of life freely (Rev. 21:6).*

The dark shadow of sin has then forever vanished. The wicked, root and branch (Mal. 4:1), are destroyed out of the land of the living, and the universal anthem of praise and thanksgiving (Rev. 5:13) goes up from a redeemed world and a clean universe to a covenant-keeping God" (Uriah Smith, *Daniel and the Revelation,* p. 759). Then may this sublime sentence be uttered, "It is done."

Georgia Harkness, writing of her undergraduate days at Cornell University, says that one of her deepest impressions was the inscription over the entrance to the main hall of the College of Arts and Sciences, "Above all nations is humanity." But to this conviction, which is accepted by an increasing number of thoughtful people today, there must be added another, "Above all humanity is God."

The plan of God will at last be accomplished. He who Himself is the whole alphabet of existence, the Alpha and Omega, the A and the Z, will bring it to pass. There in that city "never built with hands nor hoary with the years of time," the pilgrims of earth will see Him whom having not seen they loved (1 Peter 1:8). And when the glorious New Jerusalem comes down from God out of heaven we shall indeed have heaven on earth, and God Himself shall dwell with us and be our God (Rev. 21:3). Here the river of life will flow forever from the throne of God.

By faith we may drink of the water of life now. As Jesus said to the woman at the well: "Whosoever drinketh of the water that I shall give him shall never thirst; but the water that I shall give him shall be in him a well of water springing up into everlasting life" (John 4:14). Let us ask of Him that we may drink now, freely, for it is the gift of God.

MEDITATION PRAYER: *"As the hart panteth after the water brooks, so panteth my soul after thee, O God" (Ps. 42:1).*

# MAY 2

*So then every one of us shall give*
*account of himself to God (Rom. 14:12).*

Did you ever make out an income tax report? Did you have any trouble with it? Were you afraid that the sharp-eyed government auditors would find some flaw in it? It is quite a task for many people to make out a simple and accurate statement of their financial affairs, but it would be still more difficult for them to make out a complete report of their lives—thoughts, words, and actions—that would pass the scrutiny of a holy and righteous and divine judge.

Notice the word in this promise is not *may, could,* or *should,* but *shall.* "Every one of us shall give account of himself to God." If we must go to judgment, we need a lawyer, an advocate, someone to represent us at court. Let me recommend an advocate who has never lost a case. "We have an advocate with the Father, Jesus Christ the righteous" (1 John 2:1). He appeared in Pilate's judgment hall, and from there He went to the cross. Then He appeared in the presence of God to make intercession for us. Last of all, to those who look for Him He shall "appear the second time without sin [that is, not dealing with sin] unto salvation" (Heb. 9:28).

A woman of prominence once needed legal counsel and was advised to consult an eminent attorney. She kept putting it off until finally she could wait no longer, for the court was about to convene. She went to the attorney and began to state her case, but he stopped her, saying: "Madam, you're too late. Yesterday I would have been glad to take your case and appear before the court as your advocate, but now I cannot, for I have just been appointed to be your judge."

"God hath committed all judgment unto the Son" because He is the Son of God (John 5:22). Let us hasten to put ourselves and all our interests in His hands so that He may represent us before God.

MEDITATION PRAYER: *"Thou dost establish equity, thou executest judgment and righteousness in Jacob" (Ps. 99:4).*

# MAY 3

*David said moreover, The Lord that delivered me out of
the paw of the lion, and out of the paw of the bear, he will
deliver me out of the hand of this Philistine (1 Sam. 17:37).*

This is a promise in anticipation. David spoke the word, and God endorsed it and so made it true. Because of past deliverances David argued that God would help him in a new danger, and we can argue on the same basis. In Jesus Christ all the promises of Holy Scripture are "yea, and . . . Amen, unto the glory of God" (2 Cor. 1:20).

Our Lord has said, "I will never leave thee, nor forsake thee" (Heb. 13:5). So why should we fear? David *ran* to meet the giant Philistine. Why? He was thinking of the dead bear and lion. He had known God's presence in the past, so he trusted Him for the present and for the future. Our Lord is "the same yesterday, and to day, and for ever" (verse 8).

At a dark time during the American Civil War, Governor Richard Yates of Illinois wrote a despairing letter to Abraham Lincoln. The president's brief reply was "Dick, stand still and see the salvation of the Lord." The man in the White House had known troubles before, but he also knew that God was a God of deliverance.

In the fifty-fifth psalm we read the words of David: "I will call upon God; and the Lord shall save me" (verse 16). What gave him this faith? Notice the eighteenth verse: "He hath delivered my soul in peace from the battle that was against me." Let us never forget God's deliverances in the past, the deliverances of others as well as our own.

> In all my ways Thy hand I own,
>     Thy ruling providence I see;
> Assist me still my course to run,
>     And still direct my paths to Thee.
>                         —Charles Wesley

MEDITATION PRAYER: *"When I cry unto thee, then shall mine enemies turn back: this I know; for God is for me" (Ps. 56:9).*

# MAY 4

*But whoso looketh into the perfect law of liberty,*
*and continueth therein, he being not a forgetful hearer, but a*
*doer of the work, this man shall be blessed in his deed (James 1:25).*

The whole of this great passage may be summed up in little—there is blessing in obedience.

A missionary, attempting to learn the language of the people for whom he was laboring, was trying to find a word for *obedience,* a virtue that was seldom, if ever, practiced in that land. One day as he returned home from the village his dog stayed behind. But when he whistled, the dog came running at top speed. An old man sitting by the roadside said with admiration, *"Mui aden delejan ge,"* a free translation of which would be "Your dog is all ear." That was it! The missionary had found his word for obedience, and a beautiful one it was. We should indeed be "all ear" to our Lord. If God really has our ear, He will have our heart, too. True hearing is obeying. Forgetful hearers are disobedient.

We are to be not only hearers but *lookers.* We are to look into the perfect law of liberty and continue therein; that is, continue our looking and walking in that way.

As boys on the farm, my brother and I used to see who could plow the straightest furrow. We would fix our eye on some distant object at the far end of the field and keep looking at it as we plowed toward it. We had to continue therein. The person who continues looking at God's perfect law continues listening to His perfect words. That person is obedient. And such a one is "blessed in his deed."

> Jesus calls us! By Thy mercies,
>     Savior, may we hear Thy call,
> Give our hearts to Thy obedience,
>     Serve and love Thee best of all.
>                        —Frances Alexander

MEDITATION PRAYER: *"I delight to do thy will, O my God: yea, thy law is within my heart"* (Ps. 40:8).

# MAY 5

*And in the days of these kings shall the God of heaven*
*set up a kingdom, which shall never be destroyed: and the kingdom*
*shall not be left to other people, but it shall break in pieces and*
*consume all these kingdoms, and it shall stand for ever (Dan. 2:44).*

In his monumental work *A Study of History* Arnold J. Toynbee describes the rise and fall of 20 civilizations down to our own time, and says: "Having explored the extension of our Western society in space, we have to consider its extension in time; though we are at once confronted with the fact that we cannot know its future."

To the world's most brilliant minds the future of our civilization is an absolute blank, but to the eye of faith it is revealed in such great promise prophecies as our text today. "In the days of these kings"—that is, in the days of the kingdoms of modern Europe—the God of heaven shall set up a kingdom. In other words, heaven on earth.

We read the entire second chapter of the book of Daniel and see that the image of prophecy has become the image of history—the head of gold, Babylon; breast of silver, Medo-Persia; belly and sides, Grecia; legs of iron, Rome; feet part of iron and part of clay, the broken fragments of the Roman Empire, partly strong, partly brittle. Then the mystery stone, cut out without human hands, smites the image on its feet and grows to be a mighty mountain and fills the whole earth. It is the fifth kingdom, God's kingdom, the kingdom of Christ, the "stone which the builders rejected" (Luke 20:17). And it is to be in the days of these kingdoms, these modern kingdoms that we know.

The kingdom of grace is ours now, the kingdom that is within you (Luke 17:21). The kingdom of glory is surely coming. Behind the changing kaleidoscope of civilizations, behind the confusion and chaos of sin, this world is God's world; and the glory is coming—soon.

MEDITATION PRAYER: *"Be thou exalted, O God, above the heavens; let thy glory be above all the earth" (Ps. 57:5).*

# MAY 6

*Repent ye therefore, and be converted, that your sins may be blotted out, when the times of refreshing shall come from the presence of the Lord; and he shall send Jesus Christ, which before has preached unto you (Acts 3:19, 20).*

We really have four great promises in our text today: that we shall be converted, that our sins will be blotted out, that times of refreshing will come, and above all, that Jesus Christ Himself will be sent to this world. But repentance is the key to it all. Jesus said, "Except ye repent, ye shall all . . . perish" (Luke 13:3).

When the people at Wittenberg showed Luther their licenses to sin, his answer was "Unless you repent you will all perish." And when he first heard of Tetzel's selling these indulgences, he said, "Please, God, I'll make a hole in his drum."

Without repentance there can be no conversion or blotting out of sins, no time of refreshing from the presence of the Lord. God is looking for "twice-born men," as Harold Begbie called them, people who are converted, "born again" (John 3:3). True conversion is evidenced by a change in the life.

A janitor in an Episcopal chapel became converted. When asked for evidence of her change of heart, she said, "I now take up the big mat at the entrance and sweep under it, while before I just swept around it." To those who truly repent and are converted come the words "I have blotted out, as a thick cloud, . . . thy sins" (Isa. 44:22).

The gift of the Holy Spirit is given to all who believe (Acts 2:38), but the fullness of the promised refreshing will come in the latter rain.

First the showers from the presence of the Lord, then our Lord Himself.

MEDITATION PRAYER: *"For I acknowledge my transgressions: and my sin is ever before me" (Ps. 51:3).*

# MAY 7

*A new heart also will I give you, and a new spirit will I put within you: and I will take away the stony heart out of your flesh, and I will give you an heart of flesh (Eze. 36:26).*

Years ago an American Indian chief, Tedyuskung, of the Delawares, was sitting at the fireside of a devout Quaker. Both were silently looking into the fire, enjoying each other's company. Suddenly the Quaker said, "I will tell thee what I have been thinking about. It is of a rule given by the Author of the Christian religion, which from its excellence we call the golden rule."

"Stop," said the chief. "Don't praise it to me. Tell me what it is."

"It is for one to do to another as he would have the other do to him."

"That is impossible. It cannot be done," replied Tedyuskung. Silence again reigned. The chief arose and walked nervously about the room. Stopping before his friend, he said, "Brother, I have been thoughtful of what you told me. If the Great Spirit that made man would give him a new heart, he could do as you say, but not else." And Tedyuskung was right. Only the regenerated heart can please God. More often we should hear the prayer and pray the prayer "Create in me a clean heart, O God; and renew a right spirit within me" (Ps. 51:10).

"I feel like a contemptible fine lady—all outside and no inside," said Elizabeth Fry before she was converted. It is the heart, the mind, the inside, that must be changed and can be changed only by the power of God.

> I come in faith to Thee,
>     For all my sins atone.
> A new heart give to me
>     For this, my heart of stone.

MEDITATION PRAYER: *"The sacrifices of God are a broken spirit: a broken and a contrite heart, O God, thou wilt not despise" (Ps. 51:17).*

# MAY 8

*Return, ye backsliding children, and I will*
*heal your backslidings. Behold, we come unto thee;*
*for thou art the Lord our God (Jer. 3:22).*

God loves backsliders? Here is the proof of it. "Return," He says, "and I will heal your backslidings." God Himself is the only physician who can do that. A backslider is only a Christian grown cold.

In a great bronze foundry, lying side by side, were two heads made of metal. One was perfect, with all the features of a noble, manly face clear and distinct. In the other, hardly a feature was discernible. The reason for this was that the metal had been allowed to grow a little too cool. And that's the way it is in the Christian life. Many a believer who might be stamped with the image and superscription of their Creator grows cold, the image is marred, the likeness blurred.

How about it, friend; is the metal growing cold? Return—return to God. Sit down and read the fifteenth chapter of Luke, which was written especially for you. It has been called the greatest short story ever written, the story of the prodigal son and the forgiving father. When that boy "came to himself" he said, "I will arise and go to my father." Friend, haven't you come to yourself today? Won't you arise and come back home? "Return," God says, "and I will heal your backslidings." Won't you make part of our text your response to Him, "Behold, we come unto thee"?

The symptoms of backsliding are like those attending a physical decline: loss of appetite, disrelish for food. When you find yourself not enjoying prayer and the reading of the Bible, beware! Begin to pray as never before, feed on the Word of God, exercise in Christian work. Return to the Lord, the Great Physician, and He will heal you.

MEDITATION PRAYER: *"O Lord my God, I cried unto thee, and thou hast healed me" (Ps. 30:2).*

# MAY 9

*Can a woman forget her sucking child, that she
should not have compassion on the son of her womb?
yea, they may forget, yet will I not forget thee (Isa. 49:15).*

C an a woman forget her child? She may, but it's unnatural. A little girl was told by her busy mother to go and play with her
dolls, but the child complained, "I just love them and love them, but
they never love me back." And so God keeps loving us and loving us,
but often we do not love Him back. Yet He does not forget us, even
as a mother does not forget her wandering son, but remembers him as
her baby.

"If I am thy child, O God," said Augustine at the time of his conversion, "it is because thou didst give me such a mother." And surely
many of us may say that.

Of the daughter of Pharaoh it is written, "She saw the child: and,
behold, the babe wept" (Ex. 2:6). A true woman may resist many
things, but no woman with a mother's heart can resist the cry of her
own child. How many thousands of mothers have sacrificed their lives
for their babies! The story is as old as the world and as sweet as heaven.
God uses it to picture His love to us. "Mother is the name for God in
the lips and hearts of little children."

A true mother never forgets, never forsakes. She follows her babe
through childhood, adulthood, and down to the end of the darkest path
the world has ever known. She never forgets.

From the great father-mother heart of God comes the promise
"Yea, they may forget, yet will I not forget thee." He will not forget,
because He loves and cares.

MEDITATION PRAYER: *"Remember, O Lord, thy tender mer-
cies and thy lovingkindnesses; for they have been ever of old" (Ps. 25:6).*

# MAY 10

*And Babylon, the glory of kingdoms, the beauty
of the Chaldees' excellency, shall be as when God
overthrew Sodom and Gomorrah (Isa. 13:19).*

This is a promise of prophecy, a prediction, to be fulfilled in history. I was walking over the ruins of Babylon. There they were, the foundations of the ancient palaces, the hanging gardens, the impregnable walls, the great temple, or ziggurat, the great avenues of victory. But they were all a great ruin.

I found exactly what Isaiah had prophesied. Babylon, "the golden city of a golden age," lay in vast disorder with no human inhabitant within its ancient walls. Its worldwide commerce was gone, its terrible armies vanished into the mists of time.

King Nebuchadnezzar had looked out over his world capital and said, "Is not this great Babylon, that I have built for the house of the kingdom by the might of my power, and for the honour of my majesty?" (Dan. 4:30). But now it is only a memory and a name. The history of this world is really "a tale of two cities," Babylon and Jerusalem. Ancient Babylon declared war against God's people and God's city, Jerusalem. But Babylon collapsed and is forgotten in its grave of the past, from which no Gabriel of future history will ever call it forth to pleasant memories. It is indeed like Sodom and Gomorrah. Any nation, any city, any man, that forgets God and opposes God's plan for this world is on the road to ruin.

> Great Pharaoh's hosts with tossing plumes,
> Like echoes now in empty rooms.
> All Assyria's marching death,
> But a memory and a breath.
> Babylon and her golden strand,
> The place, the name, and drifting sand.

MEDITATION PRAYER: *"But thou, O God, shalt bring them down into the pit of destruction: bloody and deceitful men shall not live out half their days; but I will trust in thee" (Ps. 55:23).*

# MAY 11

*Train up a child in the way he should go: and when*
*he is old, he will not depart from it (Prov. 22:6).*

W e smiled," said Hazel M. Woodruff, "when a young mother
took her 3-week-old son to church, 'so that he would always
be in the habit of going to church.' Forty years later, when we saw him
assisting in the Communion, we remembered his mother's words."

When a thoughtful child was asked why a certain tree in the garden was crooked, he answered, "I s'pose somebody must have stepped
on it when it was a little fellow." We need to be careful about stepping
on little fellows. It is claimed that training is a greater factor than heredity in character development. However that may be, it is a primary
parental duty. Someday God will ask us, "Where is the flock that was
given thee, thy beautiful flock?" (Jer. 13:20).

In a meeting in London years ago Lord Shaftesbury stated that he
had learned from personal observation that nearly all the adult male
criminals of that city had fallen into crime between the ages of 8 and
16; that if a young man lived an honest life up to the age of 20, he had
49 chances to 1 of living an honorable life.

A governor of Massachusetts once declared that the average age of
600 of the 700 inmates of the state prison was less than 21. "These," he
said, "are not good men fallen after good training, but mostly young
men who never were trained."

The apostolic command is "Bring them [your children] up in the
nurture and admonition of the Lord" (Eph. 6:4). Things of God are to
be taught "diligently" to our children. We are to talk of them in the
house, out of doors, and everywhere (Deut. 6:7-9). In order to train a
child aright, we must ask God, "How shall we order the child, and how
shall we do unto him?" (Judges 13:12). *as a dad I failed.*

MEDITATION PRAYER: *"O God, thou hast taught me from*
*my youth: and hitherto have I declared thy wondrous works" (Ps. 71:17).*

# MAY 12

*Pride goeth before destruction, and an
haughty spirit before a fall (Prov. 16:18).*

Pride is a sort of atheism. It puts the glory of the creature above the Creator. Of Lucifer we are told that his "heart was lifted up" because of his beauty (Eze. 28:17), and the testimony of Jesus is "I beheld Satan as lightning fall from heaven" (Luke 10:18).

Of the mighty empire of Egypt, God said, "The pride of her power shall come down" (Eze. 30:6). That's the direction of pride and haughtiness—downward, always downward. The mighty power of the Philistines was cut off because of pride (Zech. 9:6), and the pride of Assyria was brought low (Zech. 10:11). In the fullness of his pride, Nebuchadnezzar viewed the mighty city of Babylon and said, "Is not this great Babylon, that I have built for . . . the honour of my majesty?" (Dan. 4:30). The words were no more than out of his mouth when his reason was taken from him and he was reduced to the mentality of a beast, and he fed on grass until he learned "that the most High ruleth in the kingdom of men" (verse 17). Of mighty Babylon itself God said, "I am against thee, O thou most proud ["pride," margin]" (Jer. 50:31).

Why should we have false pride? We have nothing that was not given to us. "If you want to realize your own importance," said Robert Burdette, "put your finger into a bowl of water, then take it out and look at the hole."

When Albert Schweitzer—doctor, philosopher, musician, and missionary—was building his hospital in French Equatorial Africa, a local man was asked to help. He refused, saying that he was an intellectual. "I once thought I was an intellectual," Schweitzer said as he returned to his work. The greater the man, the greater his true humility. "Oh, why should the spirit of mortal be proud?"

MEDITATION PRAYER: *"Behold, thou hast made my days as an handbreadth; and mine age is as nothing before thee: verily every man at his best state is altogether vanity" (Ps. 39:5).*

# MAY 13

*God is our refuge and strength, a very present help in trouble. Therefore will not we fear, though the earth be removed, and though the mountains be carried into the midst of the sea (Ps. 46:1, 2).*

This is the song of God's people in every time of trouble.

With the key of science human beings have unlocked a few of the secrets of the universe, and as a result terrible fear is now gripping the world—fear of the universe itself, fear of a nuclear cloud. But God is our refuge; therefore we will not fear.

A minister attended a lecture on astronomy, the wonders of God's great creation. He heard of a universe a million light-years away, a universe so vast that our minds sink in contemplation of it. At the close of the lecture a friend said to him, "I feel pretty small tonight."

The minister replied, "I don't. I feel larger than ever." Then he explained that, great as is the universe, God is greater.

Dwight L. Moody's favorite text was Isaiah 12:2: "I will trust, and not be afraid: for the Lord Jehovah is my strength." He used to say that you can travel first class or second class to heaven. Second class is "What time I am afraid, I will trust in thee" (Ps. 56:3). First class is "I will trust, and not be afraid," and that's the better way.

Let us learn to sing this song of trust, for truly "the eternal God is thy refuge, and underneath are the everlasting arms" (Deut. 33:27).

> Other refuge have I none,
>   Hangs my helpless soul on Thee;
> Leave, O leave me not alone!
>   Still support and comfort me.
> —Charles Wesley

MEDITATION PRAYER: *"How excellent is thy lovingkindness, O God! therefore the children of men put their trust under the shadow of thy wings" (Ps. 36:7).*

# MAY 14

*If I regard iniquity in my heart,*
*the Lord will not hear me (Ps. 66:18).*

This is a sort of negative promise, but we know that the opposite of it is true: If we do not regard iniquity in our hearts, the Lord will hear us. This text does not refer primarily to some sin that has surprised a person, into which they have fallen by unexpected temptation, but to sin that is regarded, loved, cherished in the heart. This sort of sin blocks the prayer line to heaven.

In Coleridge's "Rime of the Ancient Mariner" we have a picture of how sin hinders prayer. Unrepentant, but in distress, the ancient mariner tried to pray, but could not.

> "I looked to heaven, and tried to pray;
> But or ever a prayer had gusht,
> A wicked whisper came, and made
> My heart as dry as dust."

It was only after he repented that he found himself able to pray.

The prophet Isaiah records the warning of God, "When ye spread forth your hands, I will hide mine eyes from you: yea, when ye make many prayers, I will not hear: your hands are full of blood" (Isa. 1:15).

The prayers of those who plan to go on sinning will not be heard, because they "ask amiss" (James 4:3). "We know that God heareth not sinners" were the words of the healed blind man (John 9:31). An unconfessed sin is like a bullet in the body. There can be no help until it is removed. Humans call sin an accident; God calls it an abomination. Sin is a disconnection in the telephone line to glory; it is static in the radio of prayer. Repentance, and repentance alone, will restore communications when the sinner prays the publican's prayer, "God be merciful to me a sinner" (Luke 18:13).

MEDITATION PRAYER: *"Wash me throughly from mine iniquity, and cleanse me from my sin" (Ps. 51:2).*

140

# MAY 15

*The wicked shall be turned into hell,*
*and all the nations that forget God (Ps. 9:17).*

This life is not the end, though many people wish it were. According to Holy Scripture, there is heaven to win and hell to shun.

One day an elector of Cologne, who was also archbishop, used profane words in the presence of a farmer, who could not conceal his astonishment. "Why do you look so surprised?" he was asked. "Because an archbishop can be so profane." Quickly the answer came, "I do not swear as an archbishop, but as a prince." "But, Your Highness," asked the farmer, "when the prince goes to hell, what will become of the archbishop?" The reply was not recorded.

It is plain from Scripture that the wicked are not in hell now, for we read in 2 Peter 2:9: "The Lord knoweth how to deliver the godly out of temptations, and to reserve the unjust unto the day of judgment to be punished." The final hell, or "lake of fire," which is the "perdition of ungodly men" (2 Peter 3:7), is illustrated by the fire that destroyed the cities of Sodom and Gomorrah, turning them into ashes, "making them an ensample unto those that after should live ungodly" (2 Peter 2:6). For they suffered "the vengeance of eternal fire" (Jude 7). This is everlasting punishment "prepared for the devil and his angels" (Matt. 25:41). The wicked shall "go away into everlasting punishment: but the righteous into life eternal" (verse 46). What is this everlasting punishment? It is this: "Everlasting destruction from the presence of the Lord" (2 Thess. 1:9). "The wages of sin is death" (Rom. 6:23), and this will be the final reward of the wicked—destruction in hell, the lake of fire. It is for us to see that we are not among the wicked, that we do not forget God. "For God so loved the world, that . . . whosoever believeth in him should not perish, but have everlasting life" (John 3:16).

MEDITATION PRAYER: *"Lord, make me to know mine end, and the measure of my days, what it is" (Ps. 39:4).*

# MAY 16

*Acquaint now thyself with him, and be at peace: thereby good shall come unto thee (Job 22:21).*

Unless acquainted with God, the human heart is never at peace with itself or with others. An English psychiatrist has written: "With peace in his soul, a man can face the most terrifying experiences. But without peace in his soul, he cannot manage even as simple a task as writing a letter."

How shall we know God and be at peace with Him? Here is our answer: "Being justified by faith, we have peace with God" (Rom. 5:1). When we come to Him in faith as our Father in heaven, He will be no stranger to us, and we shall find that peace, "sweet peace, the gift of God's love." If we were really acquainted with God, if we knew His love, His mercy, His kindness, His power, His watchfulness over us, we would have peace.

Standing on top of the Cheviot Hills, with his little son's hand clasped in his own, a father taught his child a lesson of the measureless love of God. Pointing north over Scotland, south over England, east over the North Sea, west over the hills toward the Atlantic, he said, "Johnny, my boy, God's love is as big as all that."

"Why, Father," the boy cheerily replied with sparkling eyes, "then we must be right in the middle of it."

Yes, right in the middle of God's love today and forever, we shall be at peace. "Now the Lord of peace himself give you peace always by all means" (2 Thess. 3:16).

> When peace, like a river, attendeth my way,
> When sorrows like sea billows roll;
> Whatever my lot, Thou hast taught me to say,
> "It is well, it is well with my soul."
> —Horatio G. Spafford

MEDITATION PRAYER: *"But I will sing of thy power; yea, I will sing aloud of thy mercy in the morning: for thou hast been my defence and refuge in the day of my trouble" (Ps. 59:16).*

# MAY 17

*For whatsoever is born of God overcometh
the world: and this is the victory that overcometh
the world, even our faith (1 John 5:4).*

"I'm tired," said the little girl to her father, who was swimming in the ocean with her and her little brother. And then the little brother announced, "I'm awfully tired too."

"All right," the father said. "Sister, you are the older and stronger. You can float while I carry little brother to shore. Then I'll come back for you." When the father returned, his little daughter was nowhere in sight. Very much alarmed, he hastened back to shore for help. Then, in a small boat, the men searched up and down the coast until at last they saw the child floating, obviously unafraid. When someone asked her how she managed to stay afloat so long and keep up her courage, she replied, "My father told me that I could, and I believed him."

We must never lose faith in what our Father tells us we can do. In Christ, He has really said to us, "I believe in you." "All things are possible to him that believeth" (Mark 9:23).

"A simple childlike faith in a Divine Friend solves all the problems that come to us by land or sea," said Helen Keller. But our victory is by faith, and even that faith is not of ourselves; "it is the gift of God" (Eph. 2:8). And this faith of ours may be strengthened, it may grow, and will grow if we feed upon the Word of God, for "faith cometh by hearing, and hearing by the word of God" (Rom. 10:17). Our victory comes through—

> A faith that shines more bright and clear
> When tempests rage without;
> That when in danger knows no fear,
> In darkness feels no doubt.
> —William H. Bathurst

MEDITATION PRAYER: *"O my God, I trust in thee: let me not be ashamed" (Ps. 25:2).*

# MAY 18

*Be ye strong therefore, and let not your*
*hands be weak: for your work*
*shall be rewarded (2 Chron. 15:7).*

If the service of God is worth anything, it is worth everything. We are to do it with determined diligence. In a time of great stress I received from my father an encouraging letter with this motto for my desk: "'Know that your labour is not in vain in the Lord'" (1 Cor. 15:58). Indeed, earnest labor for God is not in vain; it "shall be rewarded."

God had done great things for King Asa and for Judah, but they needed encouragement. They were hesitating and feeble and had to be warned and instructed that the Lord would be with them while they were with Him. And so the sequel proved. Great blessing came upon the king and upon the whole nation, and there was a wonderful spiritual revival. So it will be with us; we shall find our best reward in the Lord's cause when we throw our whole soul into it. Then will come prosperity to the work of God and in our own experience.

> O for that flame of living fire
> 　Which shone so bright in saints of old;
> Which bade their souls to heaven aspire,
> 　Calm in distress, in danger bold!
> 　　　　　—William H. Bathurst

Let us remember the words of the apostle Paul in 1 Corinthians 16:13: "Watch ye, stand fast in the faith, quit you like men, be strong." And again, his exhortation in Ephesians 6:10: "Finally, my brethren, be strong in the Lord, and in the power of his might." That is always our privilege, and may it be our experience.

MEDITATION PRAYER: *"I have not hid thy righteousness within my heart; I have declared thy faithfulness and thy salvation: I have not concealed thy lovingkindness and thy truth from the great congregation" (Ps. 40:10).*

# MAY 19

*Be ye also patient; stablish your hearts:*
*for the coming of the Lord draweth nigh (James 5:8).*

P*atience* means the readiness to await God's time without doubting God's truth. God does things in His own way and in His own time. We are to "rest in the Lord, and wait patiently for him" (Ps. 37:7), and not to fret ourselves because of the prosperity of the wicked and the apparent languishing of God's work in the world. We must remember that "those that wait upon the Lord, they shall inherit the earth" (verse 9). Patience is really a form of faith. It says, "God is working; I will leave things in His hands." It is in our patience that we possess our souls (Luke 21:19).

Bishop Wilberforce and Thomas Carlyle were once talking together about the deep things of life. Carlyle asked, "My lord, have you a creed?"

"Yes," replied the bishop, "and the older I grow, the firmer that creed becomes under my feet. There is only one thing that staggers me."

"What is that?"

"The slow progress that that creed seems to make in the world."

After a moment of silence, Carlyle made this wise remark: "Yes, but if you have a creed, you can afford to wait."

The last appeal in the Song of Solomon (8:14) is "Make haste, my beloved." And the last prayer in the Bible is "Even so, come, Lord Jesus." And to this the Savior replies, "Surely I come quickly" (Rev. 22:20). Are we growing weary because we do not always see the harvest of our seed sowing? This glorious truth cries to us: "Be patient." Do temptations strike at us, pain and disappointment worry us? Our text preaches to us: "Stablish your hearts." The King is coming, and only those who have such a hope can afford to wait.

MEDITATION PRAYER: *"My soul, wait thou only upon God; for my expectation is from him" (Ps. 62:5).*

# MAY 20

*And it shall be, if thou do at all forget the Lord thy God,*
*and walk after other gods, and serve them, and worship them,*
*I testify against you this day that ye shall surely perish (Deut. 8:19).*

Years ago a famous child specialist said, "When it comes to a serious illness, the child who has been taught to obey stands four times the chance of recovery that the spoiled and undisciplined child does." That child has been taught that one of the Ten Commandments is for children to obey their parents. Has it ever entered your mind that the question of obedience might mean the saving of your child's life?

God chose Israel as His people. In Exodus 4:22 He says, "Israel is my son, even my firstborn." That nation's obedience to God was not only a matter of blessing, but a matter of life and death. Did this warning of God meet its fulfillment? The history of His chosen people proves that God spoke the truth. In spite of His blessings they did go after other gods (Deut. 31:18). God sent His holy prophets to warn them, "but they mocked the messengers of God, and despised his words, and misused his prophets, until the wrath of the Lord arose against his people, till there was no remedy" (2 Chron. 36:16). Then the king of Babylon came and carried them into captivity for 70 years. The Temple of God was thrown down, the city of Jerusalem burned. Under Ezra and Nehemiah many returned from captivity. The nation with its worship was reestablished, the Temple and city were rebuilt, and the nation never did fall into idolatry again.

Five hundred years passed, and as a people they rejected the greatest prophet of all, the Lord Jesus Christ, the long-expected Messiah. He said unto them, "Behold, your house is left unto you desolate" (Matt. 23:38). He foresaw and predicted the fall of the city and the dispersal of the nation. This all took place in the year A.D. 70.

MEDITATION PRAYER: *"Do good in thy good pleasure unto Zion: build thou the walls of Jerusalem" (Ps. 51:18).*

# MAY 21

*For every one that exalteth himself shall be abased;*
*and he that humbleth himself shall be exalted (Luke 18:14).*

Neither God nor another person will seek to lift up people who lift up themselves, but both God and others will unite to honor honest, modest worth. John Bunyan put it this way:

> He that is down needs fear no fall;
>     He that is low, no pride;
> He that is humble ever shall
>     Have God to be his guide.

One of the last messages of G. Fred Bergen, director of the orphan homes founded by George Müller, was "Tell my younger brethren that they may be too big for God to use them, but they cannot be too small." If we exalt ourselves, it is almost certain that some other human being will humble us sooner or later; but if we humble ourselves, the Lord will surely exalt us in due time. God took Saul when he was little in his own eyes and exalted him to be king; but when he began to follow his own ideas instead of the commands of God, he lost his kingship.

Sir Isaac Newton was one of this world's greatest thinkers, yet he was a very humble Christian man. He said, "I do not know how I appear to the world, but to myself I seem to have been only like a boy playing on the seashore, and diverting myself by now and then finding a smooth pebble or a prettier shell than ordinary, while the great ocean of truth lay all undiscovered before me." The scripture "Before honour is humility" (Prov. 15:33) was fulfilled in his outstanding life.

"A Christian is like the ripening corn," said Thomas Guthrie. "The riper he grows, the more lowly he bows his head." If we take care of our humility, God will take care of our exaltation.

MEDITATION PRAYER: *"Thy right hand hath holden me up, and thy gentleness hath made me great" (Ps. 18:35).*

# MAY 22

**_And I will walk among you, and will be your
God, and ye shall be my people (Lev. 26:12)._**

We have the same promise in the New Testament, in 2
Corinthians 6:16: "I will dwell in them, and walk in them; and
I will be their God, and they shall be my people." Our text was a
promise to Israel in the Promised Land, and it is a promise to God's children in every land, in every age, even today. God promises to be with
us. He said, "I will never leave thee, nor forsake thee" (Heb. 13:5).

Where does God walk? Among His people, where they live. In
church on the Sabbath day? Yes. Where else? Toyohiko Kagawa reminds us that God sits on the dust heap, among the prison convicts,
with the juvenile delinquents. He stands at the door begging bread. He
is among the sick. He stands in line with the unemployed. If we would
meet God, we must visit the prison cells, the hospital wards. We must
meet the beggar at the door, we must visit the young man or woman
who needs help, if we would meet God. Not only is He the God of the
universe, the God of Israel as a nation; but He is our God, and we are
His people.

"Lord," prayed Augustine, "Thou madest us for Thyself, and we
can find no rest until we find rest in Thee."

Remember this: God never forsakes anyone unless that person has
first forsaken Him.

> O God, our help in ages past,
> Our hope for years to come,
> Our shelter from the stormy blast,
> And our eternal home!
>
> —Isaac Watts

MEDITATION PRAYER: _"Unto thee, O my strength, will I
sing: for God is my defence, and the God of my mercy" (Ps. 59:17)._

# MAY 23

*And the Lord said unto Moses, Whosoever hath sinned against me, him will I blot out of my book (Ex. 32:33).*

This promise is a warning. It is God's answer to Moses' prayer. The children of Israel had lapsed into idolatry and were worshipping the golden calf. Moses loved these people so much that he asked God, if He could not forgive them, to blot his name out of the book of life. Then came these words of warning promise, which show that some whose names are in the book of life will be blotted out of that book.

> Is my name written there,
> On the page white and fair?
> In the book of Thy kingdom,
> Is my name written there?
> —Mrs. M. A. Kidder

May it not be well to pray these words once in a while? Sin against God must be very terrible if it causes our names to be blotted from His book. Sin is not only important; it is deadly. When H. M. Stanley was pressing his way through the forests in the heart of Africa, his most formidable foes, those who caused most loss of life to his caravan, were not the giant tribes, but the small Wambutti. Those little men had little bows and arrows that looked like children's playthings, but upon those tiny arrows was a small drop of poison that would kill an elephant or a human.

Sin may seem little, but it is not unimportant. Unless forsaken, it will bring us to eternal loss.

Jesus said to His disciples, "Rejoice, because your names are written in heaven" (Luke 10:20). How did they know they were there? Because they had forsaken their sins. The promise is: "I have blotted out, as a thick cloud, thy transgressions, and, as a cloud, thy sins" (Isa. 44:22). Let us confess and forsake every sin today.

MEDITATION PRAYER: *"I will declare mine iniquity; I will be sorry for my sin" (Ps. 38:18).*

# MAY 24

*For yet a little while, and he that shall come will come, and will not tarry (Heb. 10:37).*

The world is filled with a vast impatience, which sometimes seems to seep into the hearts of God's children. There is an amusing story of a Chinese farmer who, to make his truck garden produce faster, pulled the plants up a little higher out of the ground each morning. That, he thought, would put him ahead of the other gardeners who just waited for their plants to grow. One day he discovered that every plant had died. "Extremely foolish," we say; yet no more so than our complaints because our prayers are not answered immediately.

From the doubt manifested by Christian workers, it might seem as though the work of God would never be finished. It appears that "the times are out of joint," and some even go to the extreme of believing that God has "forsaken the earth" (Eze. 8:12). But God is patient with us, and we must learn to be patient with life. It is not always for us "to know the times or the seasons, which the Father hath put in his own power" (Acts 1:7).

Temptation to impatience will grow as we draw nearer to the fulfillment of the promise of our Lord's return, for is it not commanded us, "Be ye also patient; . . . for the coming of the Lord draweth nigh" (James 5:8)? The verse preceding today's text is: "For ye have need of patience, that, after ye have done the will of God, ye might receive the promise."

Obedience to the Word of God, then patience to make the promise sure in its fulfillment—that is what we need. To the patient heart the waiting is just a little while and then the Lord will come, and will not tarry. May it be said of all of us, "Here is the patience of the saints" (Rev. 14:12), and then all the "little while" will be bright.

MEDITATION PRAYER: *"Let integrity and uprightness preserve me; for I wait on thee" (Ps. 25:21).*

# MAY 25

*And, behold, I come quickly; and my reward is with me, to give every man according as his work shall be (Rev. 22:12).*

Christ's life here on earth assures us of His kinship with us on earth, and His ascension to heaven enables us to feel our kinship with Him in heaven. He is coming back to receive us unto Himself, that where He is, there we may be also (John 14:3).

The eleventh verse of Revelation 22 marks the close of probation. Then the irrevocable decree goes forth. How long it will be before Christ comes, we are not told; but it is "quickly." He comes quickly, and He comes with rewards. In His coming every human being has an interest, for He will give to "every man according as his work shall be." What have we done with the precious gift of life? How have we used it? In that day the deeds of many professed Christians will speak louder than their words.

A dying mother called her 13-year-old daughter, the eldest of seven children, to her and said: "Mary, you must be mother now to the children. Keep them together. Be patient with Father. He is kind to us when he doesn't drink." And then she was gone. Mary entered bravely upon her holy commission. Two years later a severe fever brought her low. To the deaconess who was ministering to her, she said: "I haven't gone to church because I have had no fit clothes, and I have been too tired at night to say my prayers properly. What can I say to Jesus when I see Him?" The wise deaconess took the small hands, hardened with toil for others, and said, "Don't say anything, Mary; just show Him your hands."

What has our work been? Our work represents our life. What has our life been? How have we used it? Let us think of these things today, "for we shall all stand before the judgment seat of Christ" (Rom. 14:10).

MEDITATION PRAYER: *"The Lord shall judge the people: judge me, O Lord, according to my righteousness, and according to mine integrity" (Ps. 7:8).*

# MAY 26

*Surely the Lord God will do nothing,*
*but he revealeth his secret unto his*
*servants the prophets (Amos 3:7).*

The holy prophets of God brought His divine revelation to humanity. They set forth His message and foretold the future. God reveals Himself to people in various ways—through the Holy Scripture, through the great book of nature, through His providences, and through direct contact with the human spirit. And all His revelations are in harmony, for God Himself is their author. Whatever is necessary for God's people to know concerning their welfare will be revealed through His servants the prophets.

The prophets of the Old Testament foretold the coming of Jesus Christ, the greatest prophet of all. They foretold events still in the future. Every year that goes by strengthens prophecy, and its events offer absolute proof of the divine inspiration of the Scriptures. Jesus said, "I have told you before it come to pass, that, when it is come to pass, ye might believe" (John 14:29).

In the ancient torch races one runner passed the torch on to the next. So the flaming torch of prophecy, passed down from hand to hand across the centuries, when held aloft, changes the gloomy path of history to the lighted way.

A traveler in a stagecoach once attempted to divert the company and display his hostility to the Scriptures by ridiculing them. "As to the prophecies," he said, "they were all written after the events took place." A minister, who had previously been silent, replied, "Sir, I must beg leave to mention one remarkable prophecy as an exception: 'Knowing this first, that there shall come in the last days scoffers' [2 Peter 3:3]."

The prophecies of the Bible are really promises, and "the Lord is not slack concerning his promise" (verse 9). Let us study and believe the prophecies, and we shall receive a great spiritual revival.

MEDITATION PRAYER: *"The entrance of thy words giveth light; it giveth understanding unto the simple" (Ps. 119:130).*

# MAY 27

*But thou, Bethlehem Ephratah, though thou be little among the thousands of Judah, yet out of thee shall he come forth unto me that is to be ruler of Israel; whose goings forth have been from of old, from everlasting (Micah 5:2).*

Jesus Christ was the only man whose biography was written before he was born, and this is a part of it. The very place of His birth was recorded 700 years before the angel announced to the shepherds on the starlit hills of Judea, "Unto you is born this day in the city of David a Saviour, which is Christ the Lord" (Luke 2:11). Bethlehem was the city of David, and on His human side Jesus was a descendant of David. He is called the Son of David (Matt. 1:1). And the promise was made that He should sit on "the throne of his father David" (Luke 1:32).

But who is this Jesus of Nazareth, born in Bethlehem? He is not only a man of the house of David, but He is divine, because His "goings forth have been from of old, from everlasting," or, as the margin says, "the days of eternity." Here His preexistence is declared. That same theme is taken up by the apostle John: "In the beginning was the Word, and the Word was with God, and the Word was God. The same was in the beginning with God. All things were made by him" (John 1:1-3). This creating Word was Jesus Christ, for we read in verse 14: "The Word was made flesh, and dwelt among us, (and we beheld his glory, the glory as of the only begotten of the Father,) full of grace and truth." The "only begotten" is Jesus, for "God so loved the world, that he gave his only begotten Son" (John 3:16). He had been going forth as Creator from the days of eternity. Now He had come forth as the Redeemer of the lost.

Bethlehem—what a name it is!—"house of bread"; and He who came from this little town is the Bread of Life.

MEDITATION PRAYER: *"Make haste to help me, O Lord my salvation" (Ps. 38:22).*

# MAY 28

*And one shall say unto him, What are these wounds
in thine hands? Then he shall answer, Those with which
I was wounded in the house of my friends (Zech. 13:6).*

This is the story of redemption told in glory by the Lord Himself. To the questioner He explains how "he came unto his own, and his own received him not" (John 1:11). Redemption necessitated wounds, suffering, death; and our Savior will carry the scars of those wounds throughout the ages. The pride of human beings does not like wounds. The apostle speaks of the "offence of the cross" in his day (Gal. 5:11), and it is still in the world. The proud unbelief that rejected the wounds of the cross in the apostle's day still rejects them in our day.

One of the most precious art possessions in the world is a rude drawing—a graffito, it is called—found in the guard room of the Palatine, now in a museum in Rome. It is a picture of the reaction of sinful people in the first and second centuries to the wounds of the cross. This rude drawing made on the plaster of the wall represents an ass upon a cross. Underneath it the soldier who drew it has scribbled the name of his fellow soldier whose faith he mocks—"Alexamines," he says, "worships his God." This shows the scorn and contempt for the cross in those days. It reveals the enormous odds of hate and slander against which believers had to make their way.

Jesus is not merely a great teacher among other great teachers in the world. He is the world's Redeemer. "We preach Christ crucified," declares the apostle Paul (1 Cor. 1:23). The Savior's wounds of old were received where He should have received kindness, acceptance, and love. Let us today see that He is not wounded again in the house of His friends—in *our* house.

MEDITATION PRAYER: *"Let such as love thy salvation say continually, The Lord be magnified" (Ps. 40:16).*

# MAY 29

*Behold, I stand at the door, and knock: if any man hear my voice, and open the door, I will come in to him, and will sup with him, and he with me (Rev. 3:20).*

If we hear His knock and open the door, He will come in and be our guest—that's the promise. We think of Holman Hunt's great painting in St. Paul's Cathedral in London. The Savior stands before the door with a lantern in His hand while the shadows of night are pressing in. He knocks at the door, He listens, He waits; but there is no sign of movement from within. One critic called the artist's attention to the missing latch, and was told that it was on the inside of the door. The door represents a person's heart, which, when Christ knocks, must be opened by that person.

A small boy, viewing this great picture, *The Light of the World,* asked his father, "Daddy, why don't they let Jesus in?" The father answered, "I don't know." A moment later the little fellow said, "I know why they don't let Him in. They live in the basement and can't hear Him knock." Could that be the trouble with any of us? Do we live below the level of recognition in spiritual things? If, when we read this promise, we feel our need, let us throw wide the portals of the heart to Him. We do not have to urge Him to come in. He says, "I will come in to him." Shall we not let Him in just now?

> Yes, I'll open this proud heart's door,
>     Yes, I'll let Him in.
> Gladly I'll welcome Him evermore;
>     O, yes, I'll let Him in.
> Blessed Savior, abide with me,
>     Cares and trials will lighter be;
> I am safe if I'm only with Thee,
>     O, blessed Lord, come in!
>                     —Horatio R. Palmer

MEDITATION PRAYER: *"And now, Lord, what wait I for? my hope is in thee" (Ps. 39:7).*

# MAY 30

*For it is written, As I live, saith the Lord,*
*every knee shall bow to me, and every tongue*
*shall confess to God (Rom. 14:11).*

The time will come when every voice in the universe, angelic and human, will acknowledge the righteousness and justice of God. Every knee, both of pride and of humility, will bow before Him. Here the apostle has just declared that "we shall all stand before the judgment seat of Christ" (Rom. 14:10); and to sustain this statement he quotes from Isaiah 45:23, "For it is written, . . . every tongue shall confess to God."

Christ is the Son of God the Father, who "hath committed all judgment unto the Son" (John 5:22). Therefore, He is the absolute master of us all—to rule, to judge our works, words, and thoughts, and to dispose of our eternal destiny. We do not see all the ways of God now, but someday we shall. "Now we see through a glass, darkly; but then face to face" (1 Cor. 13:12).

"Because sentence against an evil work is not executed speedily, therefore the heart of the sons of men is fully set in them to do evil" (Eccl. 8:11). But the Lord's righteous sentence will someday be executed, and everyone will acknowledge that it is righteous.

The time will come when the word will go forth: "Just and true are thy ways, thou King of saints. . . . For all nations shall come and worship before thee; for thy judgments are made manifest" (Rev. 15:3, 4). God's justice will be manifest to all. To some it will be a cry of despair like that of Judas, "I have betrayed the innocent blood" (Matt. 27:4); or like the demon who recognized the deity of our Savior and said, "I know thee who thou art, the Holy One of God" (Mark 1:24). But to us may it be the cry of admiration and love: "O come, let us worship and bow down: let us kneel before the Lord our maker" (Ps. 95:6).

MEDITATION PRAYER: *"I will praise thee with uprightness of heart, when I shall have learned thy righteous judgments" (Ps. 119:7).*

# MAY 31

*For the Lamb which is in the midst of the throne shall feed them, and shall lead them unto living fountains of waters: and God shall wipe away all tears from their eyes (Rev. 7:17).*

What a beautiful picture of the heavenly Shepherd with His sheep is portrayed in our text! He is a shepherd-king, for He has a throne. He leads His own in green pastures by fountains of living waters, and God Himself shall wipe away their tears by showing them the great design behind the tangled web of life and how all things, even for them, have worked together for good (Rom. 8:28).

The home eternal is for the redeemed, for it is the Lamb who leads them, "the Lamb for sinners slain." Because He is there, "they shall hunger no more, neither thirst any more" (Rev. 7:16). Because God is there, they shall sorrow no more, for "God is love" (1 John 4:16).

Savonarola, in his Florentine dungeon the night before he was burned at the stake, was seen by the jailer to smile. "What is it?" the guard asked. Savonarola replied, "I hear the sound of falling chains, and their clang is like sweet music to my ears." He was looking forward to the resurrection land. As Jeremy Taylor puts it: "Days without nights, joys without sorrows, sanctity without sin, charity without stain, possession without fear, society without envying, communion of joys without lessening; and they shall dwell in a blessed country where an enemy never entered and from whence a friend never went away." That beautiful promise is for us, too.

> O sweet and blessed country,
>     The home of God's elect!
> O sweet and blessed country,
>     That eager hearts expect!
> Jesus, in mercy bring us
>     To that dear land of rest;
> Who art, with God the Father,
>     And Spirit, ever blest.
>
> —Bernard of Cluny

MEDITATION PRAYER: *"Thou hast turned for me my mourning into dancing: thou hast put off my sackcloth, and girded me with gladness" (Ps. 30:11).*

# JUNE 1

*And they shall fight against thee; but they shall
not prevail against thee; for I am with thee,
saith the Lord, to deliver thee (Jer. 1:19).*

This is not a promise of no trouble, but a promise of God's presence in trouble; not a promise of no battle, but a promise of victory in battle; and, above all, a promise that the Lord will be with us. Daniel was not kept out of the den of lions, but the angel of the Lord was with him there. Joseph was righteous, but he went to prison just the same. Was it worth it? Yes. The Scriptures say, "The Lord was with Joseph" (Gen. 39:21). Where? In the prison. The three Hebrew heroes were not kept out of the fiery furnace, but with them in the fire was "the form of the fourth . . . like the Son of God" (Dan. 3:25).

The enemies may roar like lions and be fierce as ravening wolves, but we are not to be "afraid of their faces" (Jer. 1:8). God has promised to be with us; therefore, with the apostolic writer we may boldly say, "The Lord is my helper, and I will not fear what man shall do unto me" (Heb. 13:6).

> God has not promised skies always blue,
> Flower-strewn pathways all our lives through;
> God hath not promised sun without rain,
> Joy without sorrow, peace without pain.
> But God hath promised strength for the day,
> Rest from the labour, light for the way,
> Grace for the trials, help from above,
> Unfailing sympathy, undying love.
> —Annie Johnson Flint

Reproduced by permission. Evangelical Publishers, Toronto, Canada.

MEDITATION PRAYER: *"Draw nigh unto my soul, and redeem it: deliver me because of mine enemies" (Ps. 69:18).*

# JUNE 2

*For he doth not afflict willingly nor*
*grieve the children of men (Lam. 3:33).*

This is really a promise, though not found in the form of a promise; and a wonderful promise it is, too. We find it right in the middle of the book of Lamentations, the book of sorrows, written by a man who had many sorrows. Jeremiah warned the people of Jerusalem of coming calamities because of their disobedience to God. He pleaded with them to turn from their evil ways. Though he himself was blamed for their troubles, falsely accused, and thrown into prison, still he loved his people, his city, his nation. He lived in a time of trouble, and he was a man of trouble. Once he cried out, "Behold, and see if there be any sorrow like unto my sorrow" (Lam. 1:12); but he never accused God of bringing afflictions upon the people for no purpose. He made it clear that it was because the people had transgressed and the Lord desired to bring their hearts back to Him. He said that the Lord was his "refuge in the day of affliction" (Jer. 16:19), and truly He was.

It may be that in our afflictions, sorrows, and troubles, God is trying to teach us some lesson that we will not otherwise learn. When I was a child my mother and father had to chasten me often for my wrongdoing, but I never resented it, because I knew they loved me. Always I saw a tear glistening or felt a hand trembling on my head. Remember, friend, God loves us, every one.

> O Joy that seekest me through pain,
>     I cannot close my heart to Thee;
> I trace the rainbow through the rain,
> And feel the promise is not vain
>     That morn shall tearless be.
>                 —George Matheson

MEDITATION PRAYER: *"I know, O Lord, that thy judgments are right, and that thou in faithfulness hast afflicted me"* (Ps. 119:75).

# JUNE 3

*Thou wilt keep him in perfect peace, whose mind is stayed on thee: because he trusteth in thee. Trust ye in the Lord for ever: for in the Lord Jehovah is everlasting strength (Isa. 26:3, 4).*

Dozens of books have been written during late years on the subject of soul peace and how to have it, but here is the real secret—trust in God. Robert Louis Stevenson tells the story of a ship caught in a storm off a rocky coast. When the terror of the people was at its highest, one man braver than the rest made his perilous way to the pilothouse. There he saw the pilot lashed to his post with his hands on the wheel and a smile on his face. The passenger rushed back to the deck below shouting, "All is well. We shall be saved. I saw the pilot and he smiled at me." That smiling face averted panic and converted despair into hope.

So if by faith we see the face of the Pilot of Galilee, the despair of life disappears, and the soul is filled with peace and hope. To see God's face in Christ brings peace to us. Our Savior is the "Prince of Peace" (Isa. 9:6), and He says to all who trust in Him, "Peace I leave with you, my peace I give unto you: not as the world giveth, give I unto you. Let not your heart be troubled, neither let it be afraid" (John 14:27). Do we have His peace?

The ancients used to inscribe by the tombs of their dead, *"Non est* [He is not]." The difference that Jesus makes is found in John Bunyan's sweet words: "The Pilgrim they laid in a . . . chamber, whose window opened toward the sun-rising; the name of the chamber was Peace, where he slept till break of day."

When the mind is stayed on God, there is everlasting strength, and therefore peace. As Herbert Hoover said, "Peace is not made in documents, but in the hearts of men." This inner peace comes to us when we really trust in God, who will fill us "with all joy and peace in believing" (Rom. 15:13).

MEDITATION PRAYER: *"Great peace have they which love thy law: and nothing shall offend them" (Ps. 119:165).*

# JUNE 4

*But if the wicked will turn from all his sins that he hath committed, and keep all my statutes, and do that which is lawful and right, he shall surely live, he shall not die (Eze. 18:21).*

According to our text today the wicked are those who have sinned. The Scriptures declare that "all have sinned" (Rom. 3:23), so this promise is to all. Death has passed upon all humanity, because all have sinned (Rom. 5:12); but "if the wicked will turn from all his sins . . . , and do that which is . . . right, he shall surely live." This is a universal promise to fill a universal need.

We have all sinned, and except we repent we "shall all likewise perish" (Luke 13:3). There are two kinds of repentance. One is that of Judas, the other that of Peter. One is the ice broken; the other, the ice melted. Judas was sorry for the results of his sin; Peter was sorry for his sin. After his repentance Judas went and hanged himself; but Peter, after his repentance, went to Pentecost. Real repentance is to turn from our sins and to walk in the ways of obedience; in other words, to "do that which is lawful and right." The thought here is Obey and live; disobey and perish. The truth of this is seen in the history of civilizations, of nations, of individuals. But even obedience is a gift from God, for it is of Him and through Him and by Him that we both will and do His good pleasure (Phil. 2:13).

"There is no worse imprisonment," says George Albert Coe, "than inability to repent." The time to turn from our sins is now, before the groove of habit becomes so deep that we shall never care, or be able, to get out of it. The only difference between a groove and a grave is in depth. Let us turn from sin today, repent today, begin to walk in the path of obedience today; and we shall have God's promise of life, eternal life. "The Lord is . . . not willing that any should perish, but that all should come to repentance" (2 Peter 3:9).

MEDITATION PRAYER: *"I said, I will confess my transgressions unto the Lord; and thou forgavest the iniquity of my sin" (Ps. 32:5).*

# JUNE 5

*And the kingdom and dominion, and the greatness of the kingdom under the whole heaven, shall be given to the people of the saints of the most High, whose kingdom is an everlasting kingdom, and all dominions shall serve and obey him (Dan. 7:27).*

There is a longing today for a world of peace and righteousness. Millions of people are praying, "Thy kingdom come. Thy will be done in earth, as it is in heaven" (Matt. 6:10). It is easy to pray such a prayer, but do we really desire it to come to pass? There are multitudes who seek the kingdom of God, but many do not seek it *first*. Jesus said, "Seek ye first the kingdom of God" (Matt. 6:33). Remember, it is already founded in the hearts of His people, for when our Savior was here He said, "The kingdom of God is within you," or "among you," as the margin says (Luke 17:21). Someday it will burst in glory and power upon the world. This kingdom is an everlasting kingdom, and it will include all the earth.

The promise of the angel to the blessed virgin Mary was "Thou shalt . . . bring forth a son, and shalt call his name Jesus. He shall be great, and shall be called the Son of the Highest: and the Lord God shall give unto him the throne of his father David: . . . and of his kingdom there shall be no end" (Luke 1:31-33). His kingdom of grace was founded in His sufferings, but His coming kingdom of world dominion is the glory that shall follow (1 Peter 1:11). In Daniel's great prophecy of the second chapter, the prophetic metal-and-clay image symbolizes the course of earthly dominions from Babylon the great to the broken Roman Empire of our day. In verse 44 we are told that in the days of our present modern kingdoms the God of heaven shall set up a kingdom.

This fifth world kingdom, God's kingdom, is given to the people of the Most High. Are we His people? Do we have citizenship in His kingdom now? Are we looking for the glory day?

MEDITATION PRAYER: *"Thy kingdom is an everlasting kingdom, and thy dominion endureth throughout all generations" (Ps. 145:13).*

# JUNE 6

*Let the brother of low degree rejoice in that he is exalted:*
*but the rich, in that he is made low: because as the flower*
*of the grass he shall pass away (James 1:9, 10).*

This is a promise that we need always to remember and never to forget. The demotions and exaltations of this world are transitory. They really mean little, but may have great results. If we seek worldly approval, or even indulge in religious or spiritual pride, or seek to exalt ourselves, we need to remember this promise, which will surely come to pass: "As the flower of the grass . . . [we] shall pass away." Not merely the glory, but we ourselves. Life is short, but it is long enough for the purposes that God has in mind for us. Let us not become exalted when things go well; nor discouraged, downhearted, even despairing, when things go ill. It is all but for a moment when measured with the endless cycles of eternity.

One of George Frederick Watts's most suggestive pictures is in the Tate Gallery in London. It is entitled *Sic Transit,* and is a theme of great simplicity. Lying upon a bier there rests a shrouded figure. Life is over. What does it all mean? Around the deceased lie certain things that show what was his station in life—a plumed helmet, a spear, a shield. He was a warrior. "He was loved," says the rose. "He traveled," says the scallop shell. He was not without culture, for on the ground lie the musician's lute and the book of the scholar. A golden cup proclaims that he has drunk of the rich wine of life. But now he is dead. What is the sum of life? What remains of all the years spent in living? The artist sums it all up in three lines written upon the canvas:

> What I spent I had;
> What I saved I lost;
> What I gave I have.

MEDITATION PRAYER: *"In thy name shall they rejoice all the day: and in thy righteousness shall they be exalted" (Ps. 89:16).*

# JUNE 7

*Who art thou, O great mountain? before Zerubbabel thou
shalt become a plain: and he shall bring forth the headstone
thereof with shoutings, crying, Grace, grace unto it (Zech. 4:7).*

W. M. Clayton once met an old Swiss who had been a profes-
sional mountain guide, and one thing he said was never forgotten. They were talking about the heights of mountains in Asia and
North and South America compared with those of his native
Switzerland, when he remarked, "Remember this, young man, a
mountain is never so high as from the bottom." Then he explained:
"When you stand at the base of a mountain that you have never
climbed and look up to its heights, contemplating the dangers and difficulties plainly to be seen while calculating the hidden ones, that
mountain looks high; but when you have actually climbed it and overcome all the difficulties and look down, it doesn't seem so high after all.
You may know its height in feet, but you are not so impressed as you
were at its base."

Zerubbabel was attempting to climb an unscalable mountain; he
was trying to build the Temple of God against great difficulties and danger. Then came this promise from the Lord: The great mountain will
vanish; it will actually become a plain. And it did. So with us—our
mountains of difficulty, distress, and necessity may have no path over
them, through them, or around them. Then faith comes, and the
mountain disappears and becomes a plain. But before this happens, our
faith must claim the Lord's word, "Not by might, nor by power, but
by my spirit" (Zech. 4:6).

We can never solve the tremendous problem that faces us. It is "not
by might." Our difficulties cannot be removed by others. It is "not by
power." It may be a great mountain, but when faith lays hold upon the
mighty arm of God, it becomes a plain.

MEDITATION PRAYER: *"I will be glad and rejoice in thy
mercy: for thou hast considered my trouble; thou hast known my soul in adver-
sities" (Ps. 31:7).*

# JUNE 8

*For the vision is yet for an appointed time, but at the end it shall speak, and not lie: though it tarry, wait for it; because it will surely come, it will not tarry (Hab. 2:3).*

We can depend upon God's prophetic word. Many prophecies, especially those of Daniel and the apostle John, were revealed through visions. Bible prophecies are really Bible promises. Some began to be fulfilled immediately after they were recorded in Scripture; others came to pass ages later. Some are still to be fulfilled. But not one has failed. At the "appointed time" they always have spoken, and they always will speak. True, they sometimes tarry, but we are to wait. It may seem like a long time, and often it is long from our standpoint; but not with God, with whom "one day is . . . as a thousand years, and a thousand years as one day" (2 Peter 3:8). The point is that the prophecy will surely come to pass; it will not be too slow, neither will it be too fast.

In a certain city of Europe there is a great tower noted for its clock. Tourists come from many lands to see it, and they are always there at the noon hour. Suddenly, just as the great clock strikes the hour, a little door opens and out on the platform appears the form of Emperor Charles V with his court. The courtiers bow before him at every stroke of the clock, and with the twelfth they disappear and the door closes.

So it is with the prophecies of God's Word. The hour for their fulfillment strikes; the dramatis personae appear upon the stage of human history and do their work according to the prophetic picture at that appointed time. The fulfilled prophecies prove the Word of God to be inspired. They also help to prepare God's people for coming events and give them courage and hope in the midst of tribulation. Let us be of good courage, "for yet a little while, and he that shall come will come, and will not tarry" (Heb. 10:37).

MEDITATION PRAYER: *"I wait for the Lord, my soul doth wait, and in his word do I hope" (Ps. 130:5).*

# JUNE 9

*Bring ye all the tithes into the storehouse, that there may be meat*
*in mine house, and prove me now herewith, saith the Lord of hosts,*
*if I will not open you the windows of heaven, and pour you out a*
*blessing, that there shall not be room enough to receive it (Mal. 3:10).*

Including the tithe, or tenth, the ancient Israelites gave offerings amounting, some say, to at least one fourth of their income. Can the Christian believer in this age of grace do less? Centuries before the Jewish economy, Abraham paid tithes to the priest of the Most High God, and Jacob said to God on the night of his dream, "I will surely give the tenth unto thee" (Gen. 28:22). Our Lord said to some of the religious leaders of His day who were careful in tithing but careless in other things, "These ought ye to have done, and not to leave the other undone" (Matt. 23:23).

Seriously, friends, we cannot expect heaven to be opened in blessing unless we pay our dues unto God and His cause.

A widow taught her boys to lay aside for the Lord's work 10 cents of each dollar they earned. Charley became restless and went to the Far West of those days and fell into sin. Still the habit of tithing was so strong that he continued to return unto God His own. One day as he held a shining 10-cent piece before him, he exclaimed: "This is all foolishness. I'll go and buy a drink with this dime and end this nonsense forever." He rushed to the bar, threw the coin on the counter, and ordered a drink. But before it reached him, his silver seemed to turn into an accusing spirit that cried, "You are using God's money to buy a curse." He picked up the dime, rushed out the door and far into the country, threw himself upon the ground, and pleaded for mercy. After hours of conflict he arose a child of the King. The tithe had led him to his Redeemer.

MEDITATION PRAYER: *"The heavens are thine, the earth also is thine: as for the world and the fulness thereof, thou hast founded them" (Ps. 89:11).*

# JUNE 10

*Remembering the former things of old: for I am God, and there is none else; I am God, and there is none like me, declaring the end from the beginning, and from ancient times the things that are not yet done, saying, My counsel shall stand, and I will do all my pleasure (Isa. 46:9, 10).*

This is God's challenge to unbelief. In ancient days God challenged false religious systems, saying, "Declare us things for to come. Shew the things that are to come hereafter, that we may know that ye are gods" (Isa. 41:22, 23). The idols of the nations were silent, for they were no gods. Only the living God can foresee and foretell the future, and in this way He has borne witness to Himself through the ages. "I have spoken it," He declares. "I will also bring it to pass; I have purposed it, I will also do it" (Isa. 46:11). The fulfillment of prophecy in history is a fascinating story. Sometimes it is fulfilled after long waiting, but it never fails. History proves that God spoke the truth. Let us study the prophecies of Daniel and the Revelation, the prophecies of the apostle Paul, and above all, the prophecies of Jesus.

Dr. Edward Young, author of *Night Thoughts,* was visited by a friend a few days before his death. Their conversation concerned the prophecies. Dr. Young closed the conversation with these words: "My friend, there are three considerations upon which my faith in Christ is built as upon a rock: the fall of man, the redemption of man, and the resurrection of man. These three cardinal articles of our religion are such as human ingenuity could never have invented. Therefore, they must be divine. The other argument is this: If the prophecies have been fulfilled, of which there is abundant demonstration, the Scripture must be the Word of God. And if the Scripture is the Word of God, Christianity must be true."

The apostle Peter exhorts us to study the prophecies.

MEDITATION PRAYER: *"For ever, O Lord, thy word is settled in heaven" (Ps. 119:89).*

# JUNE 11

*Thou shalt not be afraid for the terror by night; nor for the arrow that flieth by day; nor for the pestilence that walketh in darkness; nor for the destruction that wasteth at noonday. A thousand shall fall at thy side, and ten thousand at thy right hand; but it shall not come nigh thee (Ps. 91:5-7).*

In the early days of the reign of Alexander I, Bible reading and devotion were held in contempt among the upper classes in Russia. Prince Galitzin was appointed one of the official rulers of the church, and he purchased a Bible secretly in order to acquaint himself with the first principles of Christianity. It changed his whole life. Then Napoleon Bonaparte invaded Russia, and all St. Petersburg prepared either to fight or to flee. Galitzin alone remained unmoved and continued work on his palace as though his country were in the midst of profound peace. In astonishment the czar asked, "How is it that you go on building when everyone else prepares to flee?"

"The Lord is my defense, sire," replied Galitzin. "I'm as safe here as anywhere." Then he showed him his Bible, the first Bible Alexander had ever seen. The prince opened it to the ninety-first psalm: "He that dwelleth in the secret place of the most High shall abide under the shadow of the Almighty." The czar was profoundly impressed and went to the cathedral for worship before leaving for his campaign. The pastor began to read this same psalm. "Did Galitzin tell you to select that psalm?" asked the czar after the service. "No, I prayed the Lord to be guided in my choice."

The czar went a day's march with his army. In the evening, feeling anxious, he ordered his chaplain to read to him, and he began, " 'He that dwelleth in the secret place of the most High—' "

"Stop," cried the czar. "Did Galitzin tell you to read that to me?"

"Certainly not," said the chaplain. "I asked God to direct me."

From that time on, Alexander read the Bible secretly every day.

MEDITATION PRAYER: *"What time I am afraid, I will trust in thee" (Ps. 56:3).*

# JUNE 12

*Say to them that are of a fearful heart, Be strong,*
*fear not: behold, your God will come with vengeance, even*
*God with a recompence; he will come and save you (Isa. 35:4).*

This is a promise for us when we are troubled, afraid, or worried. Notice this command of God: "Be strong, fear not." God would not command this if it were not possible. Our deliverance from fear and worry is based on faith. And the promise is: "Your God will come with vengeance, even God with a recompence; he will come and save you."

We need to study the whole plan of God and to see the end from the beginning. Full rewards are not given in this life, but there is a judgment day coming. In Hebrews 2:2 we read that every transgression will receive "a just recompence of reward." And God's people may know that their confidence has "great recompence of reward" (Heb. 10:35). But the greatest reason we should never worry or be troubled is that the Lord Himself promises to come and save us. He will come to us in Christ at His second coming, but He comes to us now by His Spirit. In fact, He is never far from any one of us, as the great apostle Paul tells us in Acts 17:27.

Years ago I heard Bishop William Alfred Quayle preach, and I shall never forget the words of that great Cornishman. He told about sitting alone in his study at night worrying about some torturing anxiety. About midnight it seemed that God came to him and said, "Quayle, you go to bed. I'll sit up the rest of the night." The Lord had not forsaken him. He was there and knew what to do. He will come and save us, too, if we will let Him. If we believe, we shall cease our worrying and begin to trust. Let us "rest in the Lord, and wait patiently for him" (Ps. 37:7).

MEDITATION PRAYER: *"O keep my soul, and deliver me: . . . for I put my trust in thee" (Ps. 25:20).*

# JUNE 13

*Behold, he cometh with clouds; and every eye shall
see him, and they also which pierced him: and all
kindreds of the earth shall wail because of him (Rev. 1:7).*

Jesus is coming, and "every eye shall see him." Once He came in
weakness as the Babe of Bethlehem; now He comes in glory in the
clouds of heaven (Acts 1:9-11). His coming is visible. He comes with
the splendor of the lightning (Matt. 24:27). He comes with the "sound
of a trumpet," "and the dead in Christ shall rise first" (Matt. 24:31;
1 Thess. 4:16). He comes to the wicked as a thief, unexpectedly (Luke
12:39, 40).

Our Savior declared that those who condemned Him and took part
in the tragedy of His death would see Him "sitting on the right hand
of power, and coming in the clouds of heaven" (Mark 14:62). "They
also which pierced him," in addition to "every eye," will see Him
come. How can they? Only by a resurrection. This seems to be clearly
indicated in Daniel 12:1, 2: "Many . . . [not all] that sleep . . . shall
awake," some of the righteous, not all of them, will rise to everlasting
life, and "some [not all of the wicked] to shame and everlasting contempt." The coming of our Lord will be a scene of terror to the
wicked, because they are unprepared for it, but to God's people it will
bring joy and triumph. "When the world's distress comes, then the
saints' rest comes."

Someone has imagined the convalescent traveler sitting in the door-
way of the inn to which the good Samaritan had taken him, looking up
the road waiting for the return of his deliverer. He might say, "He
promised to come back, and I know he will keep his word; but I want
to be waiting and watching for him." And so it should be with
Christians who await the return of their Lord from heaven.

Let us live in expectation of our Lord's return. The last prayer in
the Bible is "Even so, come, Lord Jesus" (Rev. 22:20).

MEDITATION PRAYER: *"Thou art the God of my salvation;
on thee do I wait all the day"* (Ps. 25:5).

# JUNE 14

*For the Lord knoweth the way of the righteous:*
*but the way of the ungodly shall perish (Ps. 1:6).*

The way of the righteous may at times seem to be a long hard way, but God knows it, and He is watching over His children. Just as certainly, "the way of the ungodly shall perish." It may seem like a very wonderful, interesting, and successful way, but in the end that way of life will perish. This promise of judgment for the wicked is just as certain as God's promise of reward for His people.

When David looked at the prosperity of the wicked, he said, "My steps had well nigh slipped" (Ps. 73:2). He almost lost his faith when he saw evil in prosperity, and good often suffering the world's frown and even persecution. But then he added, "Until I went into the sanctuary of God; then understood I their end" (verse 17). In the light of God's sanctuary we see the justice, truth, and eternal righteousness of Heaven, and everything looks different. We may not see it now, but someday we shall see it as God sees it.

It is as sure as God's Word is sure that "the wages of sin is death; but the gift of God is eternal life through Jesus Christ our Lord" (Rom. 6:23). Unless we are on the heavenly way, we are on the way that shall perish. In entire agreement with this are the words of John 3:16. Those who believe will have everlasting life; others will perish. It is not the will of God "that any should perish, but that all should come to repentance" (2 Peter 3:9).

Remember this: The ungodly are those without God. They may not oppose Him, fight Him, blaspheme Him, argue against His existence. They may not even be among the atheists or infidels. They are simply ungodly and live as though there were no God. They neglect Him, and their end is destruction. God knows this, and He wants us to know it. Let us not walk in the way that shall perish, but with Him who is "the way, the truth, and the life" (John 14:6).

MEDITATION PRAYER: *"Teach me thy way, O Lord; I will walk in thy truth: unite my heart to fear thy name" (Ps. 86:11).*

# JUNE 15

*The Lord hath heard my supplication;*
*the Lord will receive my prayer (Ps. 6:9).*

Others may not hear me, but the Lord will. Abraham Lincoln said, "I have been driven many times to my knees by the overwhelming conviction that I had nowhere else to go." This promise, which lies sleeping in the psalmist's believing, may be ours by faith. One of the attributes of the true and living God is that He hears prayer. "O thou that hearest prayer, unto thee shall all flesh come" (Ps. 65:2).

Billy Sunday once told of a little girl who was obliged to have an operation. Just before receiving the anesthetic, she asked the doctor, "What are you going to do to me?"

"My dear, we are going to operate, and then you will be well again."

"But," she persisted, "what is going to happen now?"

"Why, we are going to put you to sleep so you will not feel any pain."

Then the child said, "But before going to sleep I always say my prayers." And there in the presence of the interns, physicians, and nurses, the little girl climbed down, got on her knees, and said aloud:

Now I lay me down to sleep,
I pray the Lord my soul to keep;
If I should die before I wake,
I pray the Lord my soul to take.

That little girl prayed with the simple faith of a child. In the simplicity of prayer, may we all be as little children. Let us do as did David, who said, "What time I am afraid, I will trust in thee" (Ps. 56:3), and then we shall be afraid no more.

Let us pray in simple faith, for "the Lord will receive my prayer."

MEDITATION PRAYER: *"Thou answeredst them, O Lord our God: thou wast a God that forgavest them" (Ps. 99:8).*

# JUNE 16

*Thou shalt be hid from the scourge of the tongue: neither shalt thou be afraid of destruction when it cometh (Job 5:21).*

Although "the tongue of the wise is health" (Prov. 12:18) and "a wholesome tongue is a tree of life" (Prov. 15:4), it is certainly true that a slanderous tongue is sharpened like that of a serpent (Ps. 140:3). It is spoken of in Psalm 57:4 as a sharp sword. There are many people who hide wickedness under their tongues (Job 20:12).

It is true that the day will come when "every tongue shall confess to God" (Rom. 14:11). But there are those who do not now bridle their tongues (James 1:26), and in such cases "the tongue is a fire, a world of iniquity" (James 3:6). It separates chief friends (Prov. 16:28), breaks up churches, destroys peace of mind. It is a direct cause of tears, heartbreak, ill health, and death. But in spite of all this, and with all our philosophy, it is humanly impossible to tame the tongue (James 3:8).

A mother once told her children to divide all people into two classes, friends and strangers. "Friends we love too much to gossip about; strangers we know too little," she said. George Meredith said that a gossip is a beast of prey who does not even wait for the death of the victim he devours. Almost everyone at some time suffers "the scourge of the tongue." But God promises that His children will be hid from it, protected from it. The tongue can be a scourge by flattery as well as by slander. William Cowper quoted Proverbs 29:5, "A man that flattereth his neighbour spreadeth a net for his feet," and then added: "He that slanders me paints me blacker than I am, and he that flatters me, whiter. They both daub me, and when I look into the glass of conscience I see myself disguised by both." God is our protection from both. Let us flee to Him. And remember: "A lying tongue is but for a moment" (Prov. 12:19).

MEDITATION PRAYER: *"Thou shalt hide them in the secret of thy presence . . . : thou shalt keep them secretly . . . from the strife of tongues" (Ps. 31:20).*

# JUNE 17

*After these things the word of the Lord came unto*
*Abram in a vision, saying, Fear not, Abram: I am*
*thy shield, and thy exceeding great reward (Gen. 15:1).*

God's friend had just been delivered in a great battle against four
kings, but he was to face other dangers just ahead. He needed a
shield, and he had the very best, for God said to him, "I am thy shield."

In our travels among the Arabs we discovered that they do not call
their ancestor Abram or Abraham, but "The Friend." Why was he
called the friend of God? For our answer we read James 2:23:
"Abraham believed God . . . : and he was called the Friend of God."

God becomes "a shield unto them that put their trust in him"
(Prov. 30:5). In ancient times the man without a shield was soon done
to death in battle by the weapons of his enemy. In those days there was
the small shield and the great shield. God is the great shield to all who
put their trust in Him, as did Abraham. There are many missiles of the
enemy of souls that cannot be dodged, so our only protection is a
shield; and God is that shield. His protecting providences are our shield
here and our reward here and hereafter.

When Felix of Nola was hotly pursued by desperate murderers, he
took refuge in a cave, and almost instantly spiders wove their webs over
its entrance. Seeing this, the murderers who came along a few minutes
later passed by. Afterward this man of God said, "Where God is not, a
wall is but a spider's web. Where God is, a spider's web is a wall."

It was true in Abraham's day, and it is true now, that God "is a
shield unto them that put their trust in him."

MEDITATION PRAYER: *"The Lord is my rock, . . . in him will*
*I trust: he is my shield, and the horn of my salvation, my high tower, and my*
*refuge, my savior; thou savest me from violence" (2 Sam. 22:2, 3).*

# JUNE 18

*All the ends of the world shall remember and*
*turn unto the Lord: and all the kindreds of*
*the nations shall worship before thee (Ps. 22:27).*

It may not look like it now, but Christians belong to a winning cause. Someday their Lord will reign "from sea even to sea, and from the river even to the ends of the earth" (Zech. 9:10). "This gospel of the kingdom shall be preached in all the world for a witness unto all nations" (Matt. 24:14) when the angel of the judgment hour cries "to every nation, and kindred, and tongue, and people, saying with a loud voice, Fear God, and give glory to him" (Rev. 14:6, 7).

There is a definite prophecy that "it shall come to pass, that from one new moon to another, and from one sabbath to another, shall all flesh come to worship before me, saith the Lord" (Isa. 66:23). And in Psalm 72:11 we read: "All kings shall fall down before him: all nations shall serve him." When the King was born in Bethlehem of Judea, the angel said: "Thou . . . shalt call his name Jesus. . . . And the Lord God shall give unto him the throne of his father David: and he shall reign over the house of Jacob for ever; and of his kingdom there shall be no end" (Luke 1:31–33).

In this "house of Jacob" the overcomers will be gathered from all kindreds, all nations, all peoples, all tongues, over all the earth. He who was and is "the desire of all nations" (Haggai 2:7) has promised that the gospel of His worldwide kingdom shall be preached to all nations (Mark 13:10), and that those who believe shall be baptized and become one people through the "obedience to the faith among all nations" (Rom. 1:5). In Him all nations are to be blessed (Gal. 3:8). And to His city, the New Jerusalem, "the nations of them which are saved" shall enter in (Rev. 21:24).

MEDITATION PRAYER: *"All nations whom thou hast made shall come and worship before thee, O Lord; and shall glorify thy name"* (Ps. 86:9).

# JUNE 19

*Blessed are they that mourn: for
they shall be comforted (Matt. 5:4).*

We would think that being blessed would have nothing to do with mourning, but our infinitely wise Savior puts them together here in this beatitude. And as the preachers say: "What therefore God hath joined together, let not man put asunder" (Mark 10:9). When we mourn for our sins and the sins of others, we shall be blessed—not only in some future day, but here and now.

Henry Ward Beecher reminds us that sometimes when "men think that God is destroying them He is tuning them." George Romanes, the English scientist and great man of Oxford, lost his faith, and in the depths of his disbelief wrote: "When I think, as at times I must, of the hallowed glory of that Creator which once was mine, and then of the loneliness and barrenness of life as I now find it—at such times I feel the sharpest pangs of which my nature is susceptible." But he came back to faith at last, and strangely enough, it was through his own sufferings. When blindness came to his eyes, the light of faith flooded his heart.

The blessing of God's comfort comes through the blood of Jesus, through the power of the Holy Ghost. By the assurance that God will glorify Himself over all the sin of the world, we may know that we soon shall be freed from evil and dwell forever in His presence. Our Lord is "the God of all comfort" (2 Cor. 1:3). And His promise is that He will comfort us in all our trials, "that we may be able to comfort them which are in any trouble, by the comfort wherewith we ourselves are comforted of God" (verse 4).

MEDITATION PRAYER: *"Thou, which hast shewed me great and sore troubles, shalt quicken me again. . . . Thou shalt increase my greatness, and comfort me on every side" (Ps. 71:20, 21).*

# JUNE 20

*He shall send from heaven, and save me from the*
*reproach of him that would swallow me up. Selah.*
*God shall send forth his mercy and his truth (Ps. 57:3).*

David knew what he was talking about—his help was from God and not from human beings. These inspired words were written when he was fleeing from Saul. He said, "My soul is among lions" (verse 4), but he had no doubt of God's help. "He shall send from heaven, and save me. . . . God *shall* send forth his mercy and his truth."

We are told that Frederick Douglass, the great slave orator, once said in a mournful speech, when things looked dark for his race: "The white man is against us. Governments are against us. The spirit of the times is against us. I see no hope for the colored race. I am full of sadness." Just then a poor old woman in the audience rose and said, "Frederick, is God dead?"

Friend, it makes a difference when we count God in. He is the living God; He is not dead. To help us, He will send from heaven His angels, who excel in strength. He will remember us in our affliction, and in our trouble He will send forth His mercy, for His "mercy . . . endureth for ever" (Ps. 138:8). He will send forth His truth, and "his truth shall be . . . [our] shield and buckler" (Ps. 91:4). As light is the cure for darkness, so truth is the cure for falsehood. In times of danger and distress, the following prayer by an unknown author might well be ours:

> Grant me, O God, Thy merciful protection;
>> And in protection give me strength, I pray;
> And in my strength, O grant me wise discretion;
>> And in discretion, make me ever just;
> And with my justice may I mingle love;
>> And with my love, O God, the love of Thee;
> And with the love of Thee, the love of all.

MEDITATION PRAYER: *"Blessed be God, which hath not turned away my prayer, nor his mercy from me" (Ps. 66:20).*

# JUNE 21

*So shall they fear the name of the Lord from the west, and his glory from the rising of the sun. When the enemy shall come in like a flood, the Spirit of the Lord shall lift up a standard against him (Isa. 59:19).*

The time will come when "the glorious gospel of the blessed God" (1 Tim. 1:11) "shall be preached in all the world for a witness unto all nations" (Matt. 24:14), and people from the West and from the East shall fear Him. Every effort of the enemy to stop the work of God will be frustrated by the Spirit of the Lord. Read the Bible stories over again and notice how many times God's children were delivered by the power of God and not by the power of man—the three Hebrew worthies from the fire, Daniel from the den of lions, Joseph from prison, David from Goliath and from Saul, Jehoshaphat from the triple alliance, the apostle Peter from prison, the apostle Paul from the mobs, and many, many others.

Gideon learned that his help was from God and took no credit to himself, for he was only an instrument in God's hands. As John Ruskin has said: "There is but one way that man can ever help God—that is by letting God help him." And that is the way Gideon helped God, by permitting God to help him. If we *yield,* God will *wield.*

Let us always remember that it is "not by might, nor by power, but by my spirit, saith the Lord of hosts" (Zech. 4:6). James H. McConkey said that at one time he believed that a few men had a monopoly on the Holy Spirit. "But now," he said, "I know that the Holy Spirit has a monopoly on a few men." If our lives are surrendered to the Holy Spirit, He will lift up a standard against the enemy of our souls. Let us always remember that "the battle is the Lord's" (1 Sam. 17:47).

MEDITATION PRAYER: *"Deliver me from mine enemies, O my God: defend me from them that rise up against me" (Ps. 59:1).*

# JUNE 22

*Delight thyself also in the Lord; and he shall give thee the desires of thine heart (Ps. 37:4).*

It is natural for us to set up our desires and then to go about to secure them, forgetting that we should first seek the Lord and His righteousness, expecting that all these things will be added unto us (Matt. 6:33). God's way is just the opposite. He would have us seek Him first and delight ourselves in Him. Then that will have a transforming power upon us. When we delight ourselves in the Lord, He can give us the desires of our hearts, because they will be the right desires.

God often overrules in strange ways to bring these right desires to pass. For instance, Columbus, disheartened and discouraged, on his way back to France, stopped at a convent near Huelva. A monk heard his story, and he was the man who intervened in his behalf with Queen Isabella.

On his way to Strasbourg John Calvin found the regular road closed because of war, and was forced to pass through Geneva. There Farel with fiery eloquence demanded that he stay and lead the work of God.

Abraham Lincoln, in sorting over a barrel of rubbish, came upon a copy of Blackstone's *Commentaries*. That chance discovery awakened desires in his heart that changed the history of the world.

George Whitefield, unable to get along with his brother's wife, gave up his employment as bartender in the Bell Inn. Step by step he went to Oxford, where he came in contact with the Holy Club and became one of the world's greatest preachers. He said that the disagreement he had had with his sister-in-law was God's way of forcing him out of the business of drawing wine for drunkards, and into that of drawing water from the well of salvation for His spiritual Israel.

MEDITATION PRAYER: *"He will fulfil the desire of them that fear him: he also will hear their cry, and will save them" (Ps. 145:19).*

# JUNE 23

*For if, when we were enemies, we were reconciled to
God by the death of his Son, much more, being reconciled,
we shall be saved by his life (Rom. 5:10).*

It is reported that when Cecil Rhodes, the empire builder of South
Africa, lay dying, he said, "So much to do; so little done." He could
not say, as did our Savior at the climax of His career as He hung upon
the cross, "It is finished."

Reading the preceding verse with our promise text today, we see
the whole mediatorial work of Christ divided into two great stages—
the one already completed on the earth, the other in course of comple-
tion in heaven. Justification by His blood, reconciliation to God by the
death of His Son—this is the first phase. The second is salvation "from
wrath through him" (Rom. 5:9), salvation by His life. God performed
the first while we were yet enemies; much more will He perform the
second for His friends, the children of faith.

Our reconciliation was the reconciliation of enemies by the death
of Jesus. This is completed. Our salvation "from wrath through him,"
Christ's atoning work as our high priest in heaven, His work for us
through the Holy Spirit, shedding abroad His own life in our hearts, is
going on now. We read in Hebrews 7:25 that "he ever liveth to make
intercession for" us. Because of this, God's children on earth are spared
and blessed, and the image of God is being restored in them. They have
not only His example, which leads to salvation, but His personal presence through the Holy Spirit—"Christ in you, the hope of glory" (Col.
1:27). So when we follow Him, we "shall not walk in darkness, but
shall have the light of life" (John 8:12).

MEDITATION PRAYER: *"For with thee is the fountain of life:
in thy light shall we see light" (Ps. 36:9).*

# JUNE 24

*For with what judgment ye judge, ye shall*
*be judged: and with what measure ye mete,*
*it shall be measured to you again (Matt. 7:2).*

This promise of just judgment is really the complement of the golden rule: "Whatsoever ye would that men should do to you, do ye even so to them" (Matt. 7:12). Our text for today shows that we shall have done to us exactly what we have done to others.

False judgments have brought untold sorrow to the world. The Dakota Indians used to make the following prayer: "Great Spirit, help me never to judge another until I have walked two weeks in his moccasins."

Dwight Morrow put it in different words when, in giving a reason for his success in dealing with the people of the great republic of Mexico, he said, "I never judge a person until I discover what he would like to be as well as what he really is."

God understands our hearts; He knows what we would like to be; He knows what we are trying to do. He also knows our background and heredity, and takes all these things into consideration.

Our judgment of others may be unfair, because of our own twisted outlook, our inability to see things as they really are. A woman complained to a visiting friend that her next-door neighbor was a poor housekeeper. "Just look," she said, "at those clothes she has hung out on the line. See the black streaks on those sheets and pillowcases!" The friend stepped to the window and looked out. Then she raised the window and looked again. "It appears, my dear," she said, "that the clothes are perfectly clean, but that the streaks you see are on your own windowpane."

In our judgments let us be sure that the trouble is not in ourselves. In fact, we should be safer if we judged not, lest we be judged (Matt. 7:1). It is best to leave things in the hands of God.

MEDITATION PRAYER: *"Judge me, O God, and plead my cause . . . : O deliver me from the deceitful and unjust man" (Ps. 43:1).*

# JUNE 25

*I have set the Lord always before me: because he is at my right hand, I shall not be moved (Ps. 16:8).*

This is the way to live—with God always before us we shall have the noblest companionship, the holiest example, the sweetest consolation, and the mightiest influence."

Directly across the street from Bunhill Fields, one of London's most ancient cemeteries, is John Wesley's chapel, the house in which he lived and died, and his own tomb and monument. Just before his death, Wesley opened his eyes and exclaimed in a clear, strong voice to the young preachers who were standing around his bed, "The best of all is God is with us." Yes, my friends, that is the best of all. God is at our right hand; and, as the poet said: "Nearer than hands and feet."

We all need daily to practice the presence of God, and to remember those important and ever-true words, "Thou God seest me" (Gen. 16:13). And notice, this must all be by resolute act of will—"I have *set* the Lord always before me." It must be maintained as a settled, permanent thing. We do what we do, and we live as we live, in the presence of God. He is at our right hand, leading us, protecting us, guiding us.

In Burma may be seen the famous Sleeping Buddha, a gigantic image lying on its side with calm face, closed eyes, head resting on one hand, a gilded figure 30 feet long. There is no help here in trial, no tender bosom against which to lean in the hour of weakness or fear, no ear open to the cry of need. Buddha is asleep. Contrast this with Him who neither slumbers nor sleeps (Ps. 121:4), whose ear is always open to our cry. He is our heavenly Father, who says, "Fear thou not; for I am with thee: be not dismayed; for I am thy God" (Isa. 41:10). To His Israel of old He said: "Be strong and of a good courage, fear not, nor be afraid of them: for the Lord thy God, he it is that doth go with thee; he will not fail thee, nor forsake thee" (Deut. 31:6). And He says the same to us today.

MEDITATION PRAYER: *"My soul trusteth in thee: yea, in the shadow of thy wings will I make my refuge" (Ps. 57:1).*

# JUNE 26

*I said in mine heart, God shall judge the*
*righteous and the wicked: for there is a time there*
*for every purpose and for every work (Eccl. 3:17).*

Anyone who reads the Holy Scriptures will see that this is a moral universe and that all human beings are accountable to God. The Scripture says, "We shall all stand before the judgment seat of Christ" (Rom. 14:10), and, "Every one of us shall give account of himself to God" (verse 12). God "hath appointed a day, in the which he will judge the world" (Acts 17:31). The day is appointed. There is a time in God's plan for every purpose and for every work.

A young minister, after his first service in a new church, was confronted with an able young skeptic, Burt Olney. Olney said to him, "You did well, but I don't believe in the infallibility of the Bible."

" 'It is appointed unto men once to die, but after this the judgment' " (Heb. 9:27) was the young preacher's answer.

"I can prove that there is no such thing as judgment after death."

"But men do die," the pastor declared, "for 'it is appointed unto men once to die, but after this the judgment.' "

"That's no argument. Let's get down to facts and discuss the matter."

The pastor shook his head. "I am here to preach the Word of God."

Olney, annoyed, turned away with the remark "I don't believe you know enough of the Bible to argue about it."

"Perhaps you are right" was the calm rejoinder. "But please remember, 'it is appointed unto men once to die, but after this the judgment.' "

Those words rang in Olney's mind far into the night—"Judgment, judgment, judgment!" The next morning he called on the preacher. "I have spent a terrible night," he said. "The words of that scripture are burning their way into me; I can't get rid of them. What must I do to be saved?" When he left, he was a child of God.

MEDITATION PRAYER: *"Justice and judgment are the habitation of thy throne: mercy and truth shall go before thy face" (Ps. 89:14).*

# JUNE 27

*Whoso hearkeneth unto me shall dwell safely,*
*and shall be quiet from fear of evil (Prov. 1:33).*

There is a form of deafness known to the Greeks in which the sufferer is able to hear everything except words. And there is a spiritual disease in which disobedience can hear everything except God's Word.

If we wish to be safe, we must listen to God. How wonderful it is to be free from the tensions of life, conflict of mind, and confusion of heart! Fear is prevalent on every side today, but we can have peace of heart and quietude of mind if we will listen to God's voice and obey Him. Anyone who does obey God really listens, and one who does not obey does not listen.

"Sir," said the duke of Wellington to an officer of engineers who urged the impossibility of executing the direction he had just received, "I did not ask your opinion. I gave you my orders, and I expect them to be obeyed."

To some who believed on Him, Jesus said, "If ye continue in my word, then are ye my disciples indeed; and ye shall know the truth, and the truth shall make you free" (John 8:31, 32).

When God spoke great and mighty things to Daniel, He strengthened him. God's Word is food to the soul. "Thy words were found, and I did eat them; and thy word was unto me the joy and rejoicing of mine heart," declared the prophet Jeremiah (Jer. 15:16). It is our privilege to be like the boy Samuel, who said, "Speak, Lord; for thy servant heareth" (1 Sam. 3:9).

> Hear the words our Savior hath spoken,
>    Words of life, unfailing and true;
> Careless one, prayerless one, hear and remember,
>    Jesus says, "Blessed are they that do."
> —P. P. Bliss

MEDITATION PRAYER: *"With my whole heart have I sought thee: O let me not wander from thy commandments" (Ps. 119:10).*

184

# JUNE 28

*And thou, O tower of the flock, the strong hold of the daughter of Zion, unto thee shall it come, even the first dominion; the kingdom shall come to the daughter of Jerusalem (Micah 4:8).*

The first dominion, the dominion of this earth given to our father Adam, will be restored to a redeemed race. The time will come at last for "the redemption of the purchased possession" (Eph. 1:14). The earth, originally given to humans as their kingdom, betrayed by them into the hands of Satan, and long held by the mighty foe, will be brought back by the great plan of redemption in Christ. All that was lost in the first Adam will be restored in the Second Adam. All that was lost by sin will be restored through grace. "For thus saith the Lord that created the heavens; God himself that formed the earth and made it; he hath established it, he created it not in vain, he formed it to be inhabited" (Isa. 45:18). "The righteous shall inherit the land, and dwell therein for ever" (Ps. 37:29). Zion, the daughter of Jerusalem, received the first dominion. The church inherits the kingdom in Christ, the Tower of the flock. Have you found your refuge in Him? In the Scripture it is written, "The name of the Lord is a strong tower: the righteous runneth into it, and is safe" (Prov. 18:10).

There is a plant called samphire that grows only on cliffs near the sea, but always above the reach of the tide. Some shipwrecked sailors thrown ashore were struggling up a precipitous cliff. They were afraid that the advancing tide would overtake them, when one of them saw a luxuriant samphire plant. Instantly he raised a shout of joy: "We're safe, men; we're safe! Here is the samphire." True, the sea might come near and perhaps cast its spray upon them, but it would never reach them with its thundering waves. They were safe.

And so are we, if we are hidden in Christ. We may be in full sight of the world's storm, we may hear its roar and see its angry dashings, but we have a safe refuge.

MEDITATION PRAYER: *"Thou art my refuge and my portion in the land of the living" (Ps. 142:5).*

185

# JUNE 29

*And he saith unto him, Verily, verily, I say*
*unto you, Hereafter ye shall see heaven open, and the angels*
*of God ascending and descending upon the Son of man (John 1:51).*

This promise to Nathanael is a promise to all believers. Here we see the true meaning of Jacob's dream, when he saw vast shadowy stairs that seemed to lead from earth to the very gates of heaven. The Lord stood at the top of this ladder, and the angels passed up and down.

The mystic ladder of this dream represents Jesus, the only true mediator and medium of communion between earth and heaven, between God and humanity. He is the "new and living way" (Heb. 10:20). He says, "I am the way, the truth, and the life: no man cometh unto the Father, but by me" (John 14:6).

"Through Christ, earth is again linked with heaven. With His own merits, Christ has bridged the gulf which sin had made, so that the ministering angels can hold communion with man. Christ connects fallen man in his weakness and helplessness with the Source of infinite power" (*Steps to Christ,* p. 20).

Think of it—prayers ascending, answers coming down by way of Jesus, the Mediator. Think of this ladder coming right down into your house and mine, right by you as you read these lines. Heaven and earth will never be far apart again, for "God was in Christ, reconciling the world unto himself" (2 Cor. 5:19).

The phrase "Son of man" occurs 79 times in the Gospels and identifies our Savior with us, for He "was made in the likeness of men" (Phil. 2:7).

> Around our pillows golden ladders rise,
> And up and down the skies,
> With winged sandals shod,
> The angels come and go, the messengers of God!
> —R. H. Stoddard

MEDITATION PRAYER: *"Thy mercy, O Lord, is in the heavens; and thy faithfulness reacheth unto the clouds" (Ps. 36:5).*

# JUNE 30

*They shall not hurt nor destroy in all my holy mountain: for the earth shall be full of the knowledge of the Lord, as the waters cover the sea (Isa. 11:9).*

The twentieth century saw the greatest wars of all history. There has been unheard-of destruction, yet here is this promise, and it will certainly be fulfilled in God's own time and manner. But it will be only when all shall know of the Lord. However, we have the promise "They shall all know me, from the least of them unto the greatest" (Jer. 31:34).

"Fear not, little flock; for it is your Father's good pleasure to give you the kingdom" (Luke 12:32). And that kingdom shall fill the whole earth and shall have no end (Luke 1:33). "The greatness of the kingdom under the whole heaven, shall be given to the people of the saints of the most High" (Dan. 7:27). In the prophetic dream of the four-part image that pictured the world kingdoms, the fifth kingdom, which destroyed the image, was but a stone at first, cut out without hands, without any human intervention, but it became a great mountain and filled the whole earth (Dan. 2:34, 35). While the kingdom of God will sometime rule the world, it is already ruling the hearts of thousands. Jesus said, "The kingdom of God is within you" (Luke 17:21).

A Russian youth, having read the New Testament, became an objector to slaughter. Brought before a magistrate, he told him of the life that loves its enemies and does good to those who despitefully use it. "Yes," said the judge, "I understand; but you must be realistic. Those laws are the laws of the kingdom of God, and it has not come yet." The young man straightened and said, "Sir, I know that it has not come for you, nor for my country, nor for the world; but the kingdom of God has come for me, and I cannot go on living as if it had not." If we have been born into this kingdom of God, let us live as we were born to live.

MEDITATION PRAYER: *"That thy way may be known upon earth, thy saving health among all nations" (Ps. 67:2).*

# JULY 1

*Now the Lord had said unto Abram, Get thee out of thy country,*
*and from thy kindred, and from thy father's house, unto a land*
*that I will shew thee: and I will make of thee a great nation, and I*
*will bless thee, and make thy name great; and thou shalt be a blessing:*
*and I will bless them that bless thee, and curse him that curseth thee:*
*and in thee shall all families of the earth be blessed (Gen. 12:1-3).*

Abraham is one of the most renowned personages that the world
has ever known. Not only does he hold a conspicuous place in
the Holy Bible, but he is introduced by Muhammad into the Koran.
He is regarded by the Arabs as the father of their nation, and by the
Jews as the father of theirs. He is acknowledged also in India, Egypt,
Mesopotamia, and Damascus.

Think of the blessings he received from God. His believing poster-
ity has actually been multiplied as the stars of heaven; his venerable
name has been invested with immortal honor in the history of the
church; his natural descendants possessed Canaan for more than 14 centuries; and, above all, as his direct descendant according to the flesh, the
divine Savior appeared, who by His sufferings, death, resurrection, and
glory has brought redemption to a multitude that no man can number
(Rev. 7:9).

But notice, Abraham had to leave his own land, his friends and relatives, to go into a land he had never seen, and be a wanderer all the
days of his life. But he counted God's promises and blessing greater than
anything else on earth. That is why the promise to Abraham included
the greatest blessing of all, the coming Redeemer.

Not only were the Jews, Abraham's natural descendants, to be
blessed in him, but all the families of the earth. This blessing is for all
of God's children, for "if ye be Christ's, then are ye Abraham's seed,
and heirs according to the promise" (Gal. 3:29).

MEDITATION PRAYER: *"Let thy work appear unto thy ser-*
*vants, and thy glory unto their children" (Ps. 90:16).*

# JULY 2

*Which also said, Ye men of Galilee, why stand ye gazing up into heaven? this same Jesus, which is taken up from you into heaven, shall so come in like manner as ye have seen him go into heaven (Acts 1:11).*

We hear much of our Lord's first coming, but let us turn our thoughts today to the promise of His second coming. He *was* here in humiliation; He *is* here in the Spirit; He *shall be* here in glory. Jesus our Savior believed that He was coming back. He said, "I will come again" (John 14:3). The apostle Peter believed that He was coming back, for he said, "The chief Shepherd shall appear" (1 Peter 5:4). The apostle Paul believed that He was coming back, as we read in 1 Thessalonians 4:16: "The Lord himself shall descend from heaven."

In our promise for today we have the testimony of the holy angels, "This same Jesus . . . shall so come." He was taken up, and a cloud received Him out of sight. Of His second coming it is written, "Behold, he cometh with clouds; and every eye shall see him" (Rev. 1:7).

The Jacobites of Scotland in the old days never met one another on the mountain paths, never sat down to a council table, without lifting a cup to pledge the return of their king, Prince Charles. Finally he did come, but only to bring defeat, disaster, and suffering to Scotland. In every celebration of the Lord's Supper since that night in the upper room, followers of Christ have lifted the sacramental cup as a token of their faith in their King's return. "For as often as ye eat this bread, and drink this cup, ye do shew the Lord's death till he come" (1 Cor. 11:26). "Till he come"—those are the mystic words. And when He comes He will not bring pain, suffering, and disaster as did Prince Charles, but He will come in glory and power to set at liberty the captives of the grave, to wipe away tears from all eyes, and to set up a kingdom that shall have no end. "Even so, come, Lord Jesus."

MEDITATION PRAYER: *"O let the nations be glad and sing for joy: for thou shalt judge the people righteously, and govern the nations upon earth" (Ps. 67:4).*

# JULY 3

*I shall see him, but not now: I shall behold him,*
*but not nigh: there shall come a Star out of Jacob,*
*and a Sceptre shall rise out of Israel (Num. 24:17).*

These are the true words of a false prophet, false to himself and the principles of truth; but the Spirit of God came overwhelmingly upon him and he spoke the truth. He predicted that he would see the coming Redeemer, but he would not be near Him. He predicted the rise of the Star of Jacob, "the bright and morning star" (Rev. 22:16), even the Lord Jesus Christ. "A Sceptre shall rise out of Israel," he declared.

Jesus of Nazareth, King of the Jews, with a cross for a throne, came in fulfillment of divine prophecy; but in God's own time He will come as King of kings and Lord of lords, with a diadem of glory. How sad it is to have a part in the work and Word of God and then depart from it! We feel a little of it in the cry of Judas, "I have betrayed the innocent blood" (Matt. 27:4). We hear an echo of it in the words of Cain, "My punishment is greater than I can bear" (Gen. 4:13). Money isn't everything; in fact, it's nothing compared with eternal riches. Anyone who sells the hope of eternal life for any price that earth can offer sells out too cheap, and the one who exchanges the greatest treasures of earth for the true riches makes the best of bargains. Poor Balaam! He was one of those who, having eyes, saw not (Jer. 5:21). In his case gold hid God.

A man once visited Robert Hall, the great preacher, to take exception to some statement he had made in a sermon. It was evident that the man was in bondage to the love of money. Hall opened his Bible and, pointing to the word "God," asked, "Can you see that?"

"Certainly," replied the man.

Then the preacher took a gold coin and placed it over the word. "Can you see it now?" he asked. The man understood and, by God's grace, his spiritual sight was restored.

MEDITATION PRAYER: *"Help us, O God of our salvation, . . . and purge away our sins, for thy name's sake" (Ps. 79:9).*

# JULY 4

*He that believeth on the Son hath everlasting life:*
*and he that believeth not the Son shall not see life;*
*but the wrath of God abideth on him (John 3:36).*

Everlasting life is received by faith. God gave His Son that "whoso-ever believeth in him should . . . have everlasting life" (John 3:16). In John 1:12 we read, "As many as received him, to them gave he power to become the sons of God, even to them that believe on his name." By believing on His name—Jesus, or Savior—by accepting Him as our vicarious substitute upon the cross, we receive Him.

We have His own words, "I am the way, the truth, and the life" (John 14:6). Christ Himself is eternal life made manifest. "In him was life; and the life was the light of men" (John 1:4). "He that hath the Son hath life; and he that hath not the Son of God hath not life" (1 John 5:12). "And this is the record, that God hath given to us eternal life, and this life is in his Son" (verse 11). If we believe on Him, if true faith is ours, then we may know that we have eternal life (verse 13). This is the only way to really live; this is the true gospel. "For therein is the righteousness of God revealed from faith to faith: as it is written, The just shall live by faith" (Rom. 1:17). The revelation of eternal life in Jesus Christ is found in the Holy Scriptures.

H. Wheeler Robinson tells of the experience of a man who was both a skeptic and an anarchist. He entered a church in Paris and heard these words in song: "Lamb of God, who takest away the sins of the world." Pierced by a truth deeper than his own arguments, he ex-claimed: "O God, what a dream! If only He could!"

We may be sure that it is more than a dream. It is Christ's divine promise. But for unbelief there is no life, not even a sight of it. So let us believe, and Jesus receive, just now. "And this is life eternal, that they might know thee the only true God, and Jesus Christ, whom thou hast sent" (John 17:3).

MEDITATION PRAYER: *"Lord, I believe; help thou mine un-belief" (Mark 9:24).*

# JULY 5

*The righteous cry, and the Lord heareth,*
*and delivereth them out of all their troubles (Ps. 34:17).*

That's a plain, simple, and wonderful promise, isn't it? It's quite clear from this that the righteous will have trouble, and it will be so severe they will cry out. They will not only desire help, long for it, but will cry out for it.

We were fortunate in having a number of children in our home, but when they were little they got into trouble. If possible, they would run home to Mother or Father, get as close as possible to the source of help, and let their needs be known in loud voices. What a lesson for us! When we are in trouble, we should get close to the Lord and cry out to Him for help. He will hear us and deliver us from our troubles.

Sometimes our troubles come from our own sins. In such cases we must forsake our sins if we wish to be free from the trouble. Sometimes our troubles will last longer than we think they should, but when it is best for us, we shall be delivered out of them. By God's grace, let us not suffer from troubles before they arrive. Dean W. R. Inge has said, "Worry is interest paid on trouble before it comes due." And remember, it is those who cry out for help who will be heard.

> More things are wrought by prayer
> Than this world dreams of. Wherefore, let thy voice
> Rise like a fountain for me night and day.
> For what are men better than sheep or goats
> That nourish a blind life within the brain,
> If, knowing God, they lift not hands of prayer
> Both for themselves and those who call them friend?
> For so the whole round earth is every way
> Bound by gold chains about the feet of God.
> —Alfred, Lord Tennyson

MEDITATION PRAYER: *"O thou that hearest prayer, unto thee shall all flesh come"* (Ps. 65:2).

# JULY 6

*Trust in the Lord, and do good; so shalt thou dwell in the land, and verily thou shalt be fed (Ps. 37:3).*

What a beautiful promise regarding the "faith which worketh by love" (Gal. 5:6)! One thing is certain, we neither trust the Lord without doing, nor do we do without trusting. It is not ours to worry and do evil, but to trust and do good. We must have faith, and real faith works. "Faith, if it hath not works, is dead, being alone" (James 2:17). Works, holy works, are the fruit of faith; and "by their fruits ye shall know them" (Matt. 7:20). It is ours to trust and to do according to our trust.

A child once made a slip as she began to quote the twenty-third psalm. She said, "The Lord is my shepherd; that's all I want." Really, that is all we want, for with Him we have everything. Then the adversaries will not be able to root us out of Emmanuel's land, the providence of God, "the Canaan of His covenant love," as Spurgeon puts it.

But more than that, someday the whole earth will be given to God's people. "Blessed are the meek: for they shall inherit the earth" (Matt. 5:5). The Lord puts a "verily" in our promise text for today. In the Land of Promise, here and hereafter, His children shall be fed. They may not be fed by ravens or by an angel, by an Obadiah or by a widow, but "verily" they shall be fed.

> When we walk with the Lord
> In the light of His word,
> What a glory He sheds on our way!
> While we do His good will,
> He abides with us still,
> And with all who will trust and obey.
> —Rev. J. H. Sammis

MEDITATION PRAYER: *"In thee, O Lord, do I put my trust; let me never be ashamed: deliver me in thy righteousness" (Ps. 31:1).*

# JULY 7

*And the Spirit of the Lord will come upon thee,*
*and thou shalt prophesy with them, and shalt*
*be turned into another man (1 Sam. 10:6).*

The prophet Samuel had anointed Saul to be king over Israel. As soon as the ceremony was finished, he predicted by divine inspiration certain events to happen to Saul that very day. In verse 7 they are called "signs." They were proof that God had appointed him as leader of His people. The most important sign of all was that God would give him another heart and he would "be turned into another man."

Did these signs come to pass? Here are the words of verse 9: "And it was so, that when he had turned his back to go from Samuel, God gave him another heart: and all those signs came to pass that day." It was by the gift of another heart that Saul was turned into another man. This illustrates the need of every one of us. Jesus said to Nicodemus, "Except a man be born . . . of the Spirit, he cannot enter into the kingdom of God."

Why do we need this new birth? Because our natural heart "is enmity against God: for it is not subject to the law of God, neither indeed can be" (Rom. 8:7). We need a new birth, a new heart. We need to be born again, to be regenerated, for "the natural man receiveth not the things of the Spirit of God: . . . neither can he know them" (1 Cor. 2:14). This change is not wrought by any labors of our own, but entirely by the power of God. By earnest prayer, accompanied with complete dedication and surrender to God, the change will come, and several results will follow: first, an increase of spiritual understanding (Eph. 1:18); second, a change of heart (Jer. 31:33); third, a change of will (Heb. 13:20, 21); fourth, a new attitude toward sin (1 John 5:18); fifth, a new obedience (1 John 2:3); sixth, a separation from the world (verse 15); seventh, a new love for other people (1 John 3:14). Let us pray for this new birth.

MEDITATION PRAYER: *"Create in me a clean heart, O God; and renew a right spirit within me" (Ps. 51:10).*

# JULY 8

*If thou return to the Almighty, thou shalt be*
*built up, thou shalt put away iniquity*
*far from thy tabernacles (Job 22:23).*

Eliphaz, one of the counselors of Job, spoke a great truth here. It is really a summary of many other important scriptural passages. Has the power of sin pulled you down? Are you like a great ruin? Have your hopes and plans fallen about you in desolation? Was it your own sin and folly that brought you to this state of spiritual dilapidation? Right here in this text is a cure for such a condition.

The first thing to do is to return to the Lord. With deep repentance and sincere faith, turn back from the far country of backsliding and seek the Father's face in prayer. It is our duty to do it if we have wandered away from Him. It is our wisdom, too, to do it, because we cannot strive against God and still prosper. It is also to our immediate interest to return to God if we have wandered away from Him, because the chastisement that we have already suffered may be nothing compared with that which may still come. Remember, He is the Almighty One.

Here lies the Holy Book of God; take it up and read it quietly and alone, prayerfully, for yourself. There is the secret place of prayer; kneel before God, pour out your heart to Him, confess your sin, and He will graciously hear. "Turn, O backsliding children, saith the Lord; for I am married unto you" (Jer. 3:14). And here is the wonderful promise, "Thou shalt be built up." The ruins will be retrieved. Out of confusion we shall see beautiful symmetry; behind it all, the plan and work of God.

"Return unto thy rest, O my soul" is the meditation of the psalmist (Ps. 116:7). God is our rest. Let us return to Him, and we shall find rest. Let us "return unto the Lord, and he will have mercy upon . . . [us]; and to our God, for he will abundantly pardon" (Isa. 55:7).

MEDITATION PRAYER: *"Lord, be merciful unto me: heal my soul; for I have sinned against thee" (Ps. 41:4).*

# JULY 9

*Now if we be dead with Christ, we believe
that we shall also live with him (Rom. 6:8).*

This is another way of saying what the apostle also said in another place, "If one died for all, then were all dead" (2 Cor. 5:14). So it is declared that "the wages of sin is death; but the gift of God is eternal life through Jesus Christ our Lord" (Rom. 6:23). Our Savior has died for our sins. The wages of sin have already been exacted in our behalf, and we have actually died with Christ upon the cross. As Christ rose to live a new life, so we may rise again and live anew spiritually. "For if we have been planted together in the likeness of his death, we shall be also in the likeness of his resurrection" (Rom. 6:5).

This wonderful truth is beautifully symbolized in the believer's baptism. We die to the old life; we rise to the new. Now, with Christ, we are to live the true life of a Christian every day. We have been justified; we are being sanctified; we shall be glorified. "Your life is hid with Christ in God" (Col. 3:3), and "sin shall not have dominion over you: for ye are not under the law, but under grace" (Rom. 6:14). Our will is Christ's will. In us, by the Holy Spirit, He not only wills but does God's good pleasure (Phil. 2:13). We once served sin; we are now to serve righteousness. We have been born again, converted. As the apostle puts it: "I am crucified with Christ: nevertheless I live; yet not I, but Christ liveth in me: and the life which I now live in the flesh I live by the faith of the Son of God, who loved me, and gave himself for me" (Gal. 2:20).

The choice of this new life is ours in Christ. Shall we not choose it every day? Let us not forget the solemn words of Moses: "I call heaven and earth to record this day against you, that I have set before you life and death, blessing and cursing: therefore choose life, that both thou and thy seed may live" (Deut. 30:19).

MEDITATION PRAYER: *"Deal bountifully with thy servant, that I may live, and keep thy word" (Ps. 119:17).*

# JULY 10

*But upon mount Zion shall be deliverance,*
*and there shall be holiness; and the house of*
*Jacob shall possess their possessions (Obadiah 17).*

This promise was made particularly to God's people Israel, the descendants of Jacob, and refers to their holy city, Jerusalem. But in its larger sense it applies to all God's people, and will be fulfilled to the spiritual seed of Israel (Gal. 3:29).

God has promised His people deliverance from their enemies and from the enemies of all truth and righteousness. Not only that, but holiness; and finally the possession of the things that belong to them by inheritance. This threefold promise is ours today: deliverance, holiness, possession.

God's deliverance is often strange. Bishop Gobat, laboring among the tribes of the Druse Mountains, was invited to visit a certain chieftain. He had long desired to see him, hoping to influence him for good. But when the invitation came, he was ill. It was repeated, however, but again he was unable to accept for the same reason. When the third invitation came, he set out with a guide, but the guide lost the way. Soon after the way was found again, a hyena crossed the path and the superstitious guide would not go on. So the visit was given up, since the bishop had to sail for Malta the next day. Some time later he learned that by these means he had been kept from falling into the hands of enemies who had planned to murder him. Even the treacherous chieftain acknowledged, "That man must be the servant of God, for although I sent messenger after messenger to bring him, he was always hindered."

It is written that without holiness "no man shall see the Lord" (Heb. 12:14). Along with deliverance, holiness is given by God to those who are His own; and finally in the earth made new His people will "possess their possessions," for "the meek shall inherit the earth."

MEDITATION PRAYER: *"Save thy people, and bless thine inheritance: feed them also, and lift them up for ever" (Ps. 28:9).*

# JULY 11

*Be glad then, ye children of Zion, and rejoice in the Lord
your God: for he hath given you the former rain moderately,
and he will cause to come down for you the rain,
the former rain, and the latter rain in the first month (Joel 2:23).*

In the Scripture there are many symbols for the Holy Spirit: fire, which burns out uncleanness; water, which washes the soul; breath, which gives life; oil, which anoints for service; and others. Here the Holy Spirit is represented as gentle rain, which prepares the soil for planting; and the latter rain, which ripens the harvest.

Not long ago I visited the western state where I grew up as a boy. There had been a great drought, and the wheat harvest had failed. So it is in our lives and in the world harvest field. Without the showers from heaven, the blessed presence and power of the Holy Spirit, there can be no harvest, and our lives will be as dry as the hills of Gilboa without dew and rain (2 Sam. 1:21). Jesus said that the heavenly Father would "give the Holy Spirit to them that ask him" (Luke 11:13). Why, then, don't we ask for this blessed gift?

When the early disciples put away all differences and sought God in prayer, the day of Pentecost came and thousands were converted. The gospel was then carried to the very ends of the earth. The apostles claimed the power that Christ had promised. "Then it was that the Holy Spirit was poured out, and thousands were converted in a day. So it may be now. Instead of man's speculations, let the word of God be preached. Let Christians put away their dissensions, and give themselves to God for the saving of the lost. Let them in faith ask for the blessing, and it will come. The outpouring of the Spirit in apostolic days was the 'former rain,' and glorious was the result. But the 'latter rain' will be more abundant" (*The Desire of Ages,* p. 827).

MEDITATION PRAYER: *"Remember me, O Lord, with the favour that thou bearest unto thy people: O visit me with thy salvation"* (Ps. 106:4).

# JULY 12

*And in that day will I make a covenant for them with the beasts of the field, and with the fowls of heaven, and with the creeping things of the ground: and I will break the bow and the sword and the battle out of the earth, and will make them to lie down safely (Hosea 2:18).*

What a promise is this! The end of war. No more munition factories. No more inconceivable sums spent for military preparations. Peace even with the beasts of the earth, the fowls of heaven, and the creeping things on the ground. Real peace, world peace, eternal peace! But notice, it does not come from any association of nations. It does not come even from the will of people in their own works, but from God. "I will make a covenant," says the Lord. "I will break the bow and the sword and the battle out of the earth." To His followers Jesus says, "Peace I leave with you, my peace I give unto you" (John 14:27). It is by this miracle of inward peace—first, peace with God, and then peace with one another—that the lives of God's children are transformed, and through them the world. It is only when the entire world is filled with people who have peace in their own hearts that there will be peace in the world. "There is no peace, saith the Lord, unto the wicked" (Isa. 48:22).

In Kensington Garden, London, there is a picture of Waterloo a good while after the battle has passed. The grass and flowers have grown over the field. There is a dismounted cannon, and a lamb has come up from the pasture and lies sleeping at the very mouth of the cannon. So, when our souls stop warring with God, instead of the announcement "The wages of sin is death" come the words "My peace I give unto you." When sin is finally destroyed, war will be destroyed. Then Isaiah's dream of 2,500 years ago will come to pass, for "nation shall not lift up sword against nation, neither shall they learn war any more" (Isa. 2:4). May God hasten the day.

MEDITATION PRAYER: *"Surely the righteous shall give thanks unto thy name: the upright shall dwell in thy presence" (Ps. 140:13).*

# JULY 13

*And speak unto him, saying, Thus speaketh the Lord of hosts, saying, Behold the man whose name is The Branch; and he shall grow up out of his place, and he shall build the temple of the Lord (Zech. 6:12).*

Pilate unconsciously used these very words, "Behold the man!" (John 19:5). In this prophetic promise of Zechariah, Joshua, the high priest, is a remarkable living prophecy of the Messiah. A crown is placed upon his head; a crown of thorns was placed upon the head of Jesus. This shows that He was both king and priest of the royal line of David. The coming Messiah, or Christ, is here called "The Branch," as springing from the almost extinct royal line of David.

The promise is that "he shall grow up," or spring up, not only from His place (Bethlehem or Nazareth), but by His own divine power. His miraculous conception seems to be prefigured here. For 30 years He was practically unknown in an obscure village. He, the Messiah, who springs from such a humble origin, is to build the temple of the Lord. This He has done (1 Cor. 3:17; 2 Cor. 6:16). He is the foundation stone; in Him the whole temple fitly framed together literally grows (Eph. 2:20, 21). It is a living temple, the church of God, and every stone is a believer in Christ.

Savonarola was once preaching to a great multitude in Florence. Suddenly he cried aloud, "It is the Lord's will to give a new head to this city of Florence." Then he paused a moment, and all was perfect silence. The people were in suspense. Continuing, he said, "That new head is Christ. Christ seeks to become your king." At those words the vast audience sprang to their feet shouting, "Long live Jesus, King of Florence!"

While Jesus is rightful King, not only of Florence, but of every city in this world, and of all the world, He rules by His grace only in the hearts of those who acknowledge Him "both Lord and Christ."

MEDITATION PRAYER: *"Be thou exalted, O God, above the heavens: and thy glory above all the earth" (Ps. 108:5).*

# JULY 14

*He shall be great, and shall be called the Son of the Highest:*
*and the Lord God shall give unto him the throne of his*
*father David: and he shall reign over the house of Jacob for ever;*
*and of his kingdom there shall be no end (Luke 1:32, 33).*

These are the words of the holy angel Gabriel, "He shall be great." He had said these words also of John the Baptist, the forerunner of Jesus, but had added then, "in the sight of the Lord" (Luke 1:15). Now he omits this last phrase and adds, "[He] shall be called the Son of the Highest." Could there be any greater title than Son of the Most High? Our Savior is exalted above all the angel hosts, for "he hath by inheritance obtained a more excellent name than they" (Heb. 1:4). Through adoption we share with Him and become heirs of the kingdom.

When Prince Oscar Bernadotte, brother of the king of Sweden, a very sincere Christian, was asked to speak to a great crowd, he said: "What have you come out to see? Is it that you wish to see the son of a king? Look well at me then, for that I truly am—a son of the father of your country and a son of the King of kings."

And this King is to "reign over the house of Jacob for ever." Jacob stands for Israel, and his spiritual descendants include all those who believe. We see also that His kingdom is to be eternal. This is almost a direct quotation from Daniel 2:44: "And in the days of these kings shall the God of heaven set up a kingdom, which shall never be destroyed: and the kingdom shall not be left to other people, . . . and it shall stand for ever."

> Oh, that with yonder sacred throng
> We at His feet may fall,
> Join in the everlasting song,
> And crown Him Lord of all!
> —Edward Perronet

MEDITATION PRAYER: *"Thy throne, O God, is for ever and ever: the sceptre of thy kingdom is a right sceptre" (Ps. 45:6).*

# JULY 15

*He will fulfil the desire of them that fear him:*
*he also will hear their cry, and will save them (Ps. 145:19).*

When a student one day entered Pasteur's laboratory, he found the great scientist bent over his microscope. Not wishing to disturb him, the young man started to leave. Pasteur looked up, and the student said, "I thought you were praying." Turning again to his microscope, the great but humble man of science replied, "I was."

Prayer consists not only of words spoken, but of a constant attitude in the life of true Christians. Their desire is to glorify God and to enjoy Him forever. This desire is imparted by the Holy Spirit, therefore God will answer it. God-fearing people desire to be holy, to be useful to God, to be a blessing to others. They desire help in time of need, guidance in times of perplexity, deliverance in trouble. Sometimes these desires are so strong that they cry out in agony as a child might to its father or mother. Then the Lord hears and answers wondrously.

Like Daniel, we are to be people of desires, and God will help us to realize them. If we fear God, we have nothing else to fear, for then our salvation will be certain, and that will be our chief desire. The Lord will hear our cry and will save us. Let us often have this great threefold promise upon our tongues. It will bless us as long as we live.

> Prayer is the soul's sincere desire,
>     Unuttered or expressed;
> The motion of a hidden fire
>     That trembles in the breast.
>
> Prayer is the burden of a sigh,
>     The falling of a tear,
> The upward glancing of an eye
>     When none but God is near.
>                                    —James Montgomery

MEDITATION PRAYER: *"Thou openest thine hand, and satisfiest the desire of every living thing" (Ps. 145:16).*

# JULY 16

*The fear of man bringeth a snare: but whoso putteth his trust in the*
*Lord shall be safe (Prov. 29:25).*

Short's drugstore in Galveston, Texas, was open continuously day and night for 26 years. At the close of this period all their filled prescriptions were displayed, and above them was this sign: "Trusted 1 million times." No doubt there are individual Christians who could put up such a sign: "Trusted God 1 million times [or "2 million times," or "many million times"], and He has never failed."

Fear of other people brings a snare. "Put not your trust in princes, nor in the son of man, in whom there is no help. His breath goeth forth, he returneth to his earth; in that very day his thoughts perish" (Ps. 146:3, 4). Even the best of people are only human. Their lives are brief, and their strength is small. That is one reason it is unsafe to trust even in ourselves. As D. L. Moody said: "Trust in yourself, and you are doomed to disappointment. Trust in your friends, and they will die and leave you. Trust in money, and you may have it taken from you. Trust in reputation, and some slanderous tongue will blast it. But trust in God, and you are never to be confounded in time or eternity."

When the prodigal son came home to his father's house, he was safe and sound. The only place of safety today is the place of trust, of faith in God.

> Under His wings, O what precious enjoyment!
> There will I hide till life's trials are o'er;
> Sheltered, protected, no evil can harm me;
> Resting in Jesus I'm safe evermore.
> —W. O. Cushing

MEDITATION PRAYER: *"For thou art my hope, O Lord God: thou art my trust from my youth"* (Ps. 71:5).

# JULY 17

*I am the Lord thy God, which brought thee out of the land of Egypt: open thy mouth wide, and I will fill it (Ps. 81:10).*

Sometimes we see little boys or girls unwilling to open their mouths to receive needful food or medicine. It takes a lot of urging, coaxing, or even authority to get them open. But look at the little birds when their mother comes home with food. All you can see is a nestful of mouths wide open. "Open thy mouth wide," says the Lord, "and I will fill it." This should be a great encouragement to us to pray—yes, to request great blessings of God. Prayer should be just as natural with us as opening the mouth. Realizing that our deservings are so small, we often ask only small things of God. We should always be ready to ask great things and expect to receive them.

Notice the argument of the verse: God has already done great things for us, therefore He is ready to do still greater things. He invites us to ask for more—yes, to expect more.

There are three things that should make us open our mouths wide for God's blessings, to request God's blessings and to receive them: our great need, our great spiritual hunger, and the fear that we shall lose the blessing of heaven.

"Yes, we are praying for a revival," said a godly woman, "but we don't expect it."

> Guide me, O Thou great Jehovah!
>     Pilgrim through this barren land;
> I am weak, but Thou art mighty;
>     Hold me with Thy powerful hand.
> Bread of heaven, Bread of heaven,
>     Feed me till I want no more.
>                         —William Williams

MEDITATION PRAYER: *"Thy words were found, and I did eat them; and thy word was unto me the joy and rejoicing of mine heart" (Jer. 15:16).*

# JULY 18

*As one whom his mother comforteth, so will I comfort you; and ye shall be comforted in Jerusalem (Isa. 66:13).*

When Thomas Carlyle lay dying, he was asked if there was anything he wanted. Turning his face to the wall, the granite of his old Scotch heart broke up and he sobbed, "I want ma mither; I want ma mither!"

We can see how God is a father, but He comforts us as a mother also. Of all the comfort that a child loves best, it's Mother. One father can testify that, when for a good while the mother was away from home, the children would come to him with their little sorrows, accidents, aches, and pains; but just as soon as the mother returned, whenever they were hurt or had a childish heartbreak, they would run right past him, crying, "Where is Mother? Where is Mother?"

In this text God invites us to the unreserved confidence, to the holy familiarity, to the sacred rest, that His great father-mother heart longs to give. Sometimes we can respond only with sighs and sobs, but He does not despise them. He understands our tears and remembers that we are dust (Ps. 103:14). He can deal with our false and broken hearts much better than even our own mothers can.

Let us not try to bear our grief alone, but let us come to Him who is so gentle, so kind, so understanding. And let us invite others, that they too may be comforted with "the comfort wherewith we ourselves are comforted of God" (2 Cor. 1:4).

Why not more sermons from our pulpits, in our homes, in our lives, from Isaiah 40:1, 2: "Comfort ye, comfort ye my people, saith your God. Speak ye comfortably to Jerusalem, and cry unto her, that her warfare is accomplished, that her iniquity is pardoned"?

MEDITATION PRAYER: *"Let, I pray thee, thy merciful kindness be for my comfort, according to thy word unto thy servant" (Ps. 119:76).*

# JULY 19

*The backslider in heart shall be filled with his own ways:
and a good man shall be satisfied from himself (Prov. 14:14).*

That's the trouble with backsliding. That's why it's such a miserable condition. Nobody enjoys it. Backsliders are filled with their own ways. "The symptoms of spiritual decline," says Dr. Payson, "are like those which go with a decline of bodily health. First, loss of appetite for spiritual food, prayer, reading of the Scriptures, concern for others. When we see these symptoms we should be alarmed. Our spiritual health is in danger. We should go at once to the Great Physician for a cure."

On the other hand, there is much satisfaction in the service of God. Why do so many professed Christians look dissatisfied, gloomy, tense, and sad? If we are to be satisfied in the Lord's presence hereafter, why not be happy in His service now?

A wealthy woman, unfortunately deaf, made good use of her riches by providing for some excellent gospel services in a mission hall in London. On one occasion a well-known minister asked her, "What part do you take in this noble work?"

"Oh," she answered, "I smile them in, and I smile them out again."

It was not long before the minister saw the result of her sympathy, for great crowds gathered in the hall night after night and looked delighted to get a smile from her.

You know, friends, the bread of life and the water of life cannot be recommended to others by people who look as if the food and drink disagreed with them.

We are to be satisfied with the goodness of God's house (Ps. 65:4). Jesus was satisfied with the travail of His soul (Isa. 53:11). And when He dwells in our hearts by faith we should be satisfied, and happy, too.

MEDITATION PRAYER: *"O satisfy us early with thy mercy; that we may rejoice and be glad all our days" (Ps. 90:14).*

# JULY 20

*Blessed are the merciful: for they*
*shall obtain mercy (Matt. 5:7).*

Vou see, God will measure us with our own bushels, as someone has said. "He shall have judgment without mercy, that hath shewed no mercy" (James 2:13).

We must remember the two bears, *bear* and *forbear*. Surely we wish to be blessed and have mercy extended to us. If we fulfill the condition, we shall experience the beatitude. It is our privilege to be merciful as our Father in heaven is merciful (Luke 6:36). And this mercy is to be shown "with cheerfulness" (Rom. 12:8). In the parable of the good Samaritan the true neighbor was the one who showed mercy to a stranger.

Alexander Whyte, of Edinburgh, tells of an interview with a fine Christian man in his congregation who had given much for good causes and had helped many poor people in need. One day, after finishing some church business, he looked at the minister with earnest eyes and said, "Now, hae ye any word for an old sinner?"

"It took my breath away," said Whyte, "for I knew he was an old saint. But the paradox of grace is that the greatest saints feel themselves the greatest sinners. So I arose and held up my hand to him, and said, 'He delighteth in mercy' (Micah 7:18), and left the room. The next morning I received a letter from him. I have it in my desk. It read: 'Dear Friend: I will never doubt Him again. The sins of my youth— the sins of my youth. I was near the gates of hell, but that word of God comforted me, and I will never doubt Him again. I will never despair again. If the devil casts my sins in my teeth I will say, "Yes, it is all true, and you cannot tell the half of it, but I have to do with One who delighteth in mercy."'"

Whyte declared that that letter sanctified his desk.

MEDITATION PRAYER: *"For thou, Lord, art good, and ready to forgive; and plenteous in mercy unto all them that call upon thee"* (Ps. 86:5).

# JULY 21

*The righteous shall inherit the land,
and dwell therein for ever (Ps. 37:29).*

Notice, this is a double promise. First, "the righteous shall inherit the land"; second, they shall "dwell therein for ever." They do not buy it, discover it, merely take possession of it, claim it, see it, hope for it; but they *inherit* it, and their dwelling in it is never to be disturbed.

What is the land that they inherit? God promised Abraham the land of Canaan (Gen. 13:14-17), a land that He would afterward show him. But this land of Canaan was a type, a symbol, of the entire world, for we read in Romans 4:13 that the promise to Abraham was "that he should be the heir of the world," and that this promise came through faith. This promise was not only to Abraham and his seed, but to all those who are of faith through Christ. So the promise is by grace. "Therefore it is of faith, that it might be by grace; to the end the promise might be sure to all the seed; not to that only which is of the law, but to that also which is of the faith of Abraham; who is the father of us all" (Rom. 4:16).

So all Christians have inherited the right to a part of Abraham's farm, or to a part in all of it. They are heirs with Christ (Rom. 8:17) to the inheritance of the land, the entire world. With this promise we remember the words of Christ, "Blessed are the meek: for they shall inherit the earth" (Matt. 5:5). This is really a parallel to our promise text for today.

The usurper still claims authority in this world, but Jesus came that "he might destroy him that had the power of death, that is, the devil" (Heb. 2:14). The earth will be renewed and brought back to its Edenic beauty as the eternal home of the saved. It is by faith that we become citizens of God's spiritual kingdom now and are assured a place in His kingdom of glory soon to come.

MEDITATION PRAYER: *"Remember thy congregation, which thou hast purchased of old; the rod of thine inheritance, which thou hast redeemed" (Ps. 74:2).*

# JULY 22

*He, that being often reproved hardeneth*
*his neck, shall suddenly be destroyed,*
*and that without remedy (Prov. 29:1).*

This might be called a negative promise, a warning, but it is one to which we all need to take heed. God sends His warning to us again and again and again, sometimes by the direct reproof of a passage of Scripture, and sometimes through an impression by His Spirit, or by the word of a friend, by an accident, by an illness.

Those who reject or neglect all the divine reproofs so graciously sent in these various ways finally find themselves outside God's special protection; and sometimes even the strong words of God Himself are unavailing to win them back to righteousness. "I hewed them by the prophets; I have slain them by the words of my mouth," we read in Hosea 6:5. Those referred to would not turn to God. They hardened their necks against Him. Therefore, we read in verse 11, "he hath set an harvest" for them. And what a terrible harvest it is, for "their own doings have beset them" (Hosea 7:2). The harvest is terrible because the unrepentant heart reaps its own harvest, its own destruction, its own remediless end. "And he shall bring upon them their own iniquity, and shall cut them off in their own wickedness; yea, the Lord our God shall cut them off" (Ps. 94:23).

"Hardening of the neck" or its equivalent is a phrase used several times in the Scripture to represent stubbornness, deliberate rebellion against the Word and work of God. But there is a remedy for all those who will turn, all those who will listen to the Word of God. "I have no pleasure in the death of him that dieth, saith the Lord God: wherefore turn yourselves, and live ye" (Eze. 18:32).

Christ is the only remedy, Christ upon the cross, "that whosoever believeth in him should not perish, but have everlasting life" (John 3:16).

MEDITATION PRAYER: *"Turn us again, O God, and cause thy face to shine; and we shall be saved" (Ps. 80:3).*

# JULY 23

*Ask, and it shall be given you; seek, and ye shall find; knock, and it shall be opened unto you: for every one that asketh receiveth; and he that seeketh findeth; and to him that knocketh it shall be opened (Matt. 7:7, 8).*

It is just as simple as that—ask, seek, knock; and everyone who does so will receive. Find and face an open door. Why do we not ask more, seek more, knock more? It is because of our lack of faith. We do not believe that the answer will come; therefore it does not come. Or it may be that we are self-satisfied. "What is the use of praying?" asked Andrew Carnegie. "I already have everything I want. What more could I ask for?"

Our sins may inhibit the answer to our prayers. Or our prayers may not be answered because we pray a prayerless prayer. In a far-off land G. F. Pentecost met an educated man who was swinging a prayer wheel and repeating monotonous words. "What are you praying for?" he asked.

"Oh, nothing" was the reply.

"To whom are you praying?"

"Oh, nobody."

Let us remember the earnestness of the widow pleading before the judge for justice; of the housewife sweeping the house and seeking by candlelight for her lost coin; of the friend at midnight, pounding on the door, seeking bread for the late traveler.

Before musicians begin to play, they tune up their instruments. You sometimes wish that the operation could be dispensed with, but it cannot. Until the instruments have been tuned, there can be no harmony. So too we must be in tune with the Infinite and in the spirit of prayer if we would pray aright. Read the text again. It is a mighty threefold promise.

MEDITATION PRAYER: *"Let all those that seek thee rejoice and be glad in thee: and let such as love thy salvation say continually, Let God be magnified" (Ps. 70:4).*

210

# JULY 24

*But the people that do know their God*
*shall be strong, and do exploits (Dan. 11:32).*

Our strength comes from God. It is only when we know Him that we can be strong and in His strength do exploits. When the emperor of Germany dismissed his great counselor, Bismarck, the London publication *Punch* carried a cartoon by Tenniel. It represented Bismarck's leaving a great ocean liner while the emperor looked on, watching the departing guide with haughty self-satisfaction. The cartoon was entitled "Dropping the Pilot." J. H. Jollett, a well-known preacher of the 1800s, refers to this and says it portrays experiences in his own life. "But," he adds, "instead of a fallible statesman, I have dismissed the infallible God; I have dropped the Eternal Pilot. I have called it self-dependence, and with a great show of courtesy I have bowed the Lord out of the boat. Then I have taken the helm into my own hands, and steered by my own counsels, and the end has been sorrow and loss."

Have we not all done this at times? We bow the Lord out of our life, and then make wreckage of it. Trying to do exploits in such days as these, we must know God. "Trust ye in the Lord for ever: for in the Lord Jehovah is everlasting strength" (Isa. 26:4). We may be very weak. But we may "be strong in the Lord, and in the power of his might" (Eph. 6:10). Let us every day seek for—

> God's might to direct me,
> God's power to protect me,
> God's wisdom for learning,
> God's eye for discerning,
> God's ear for my hearing,
> God's Word for my clearing.

MEDITATION PRAYER: *"For thou art the God of my strength:*
*. . . why go I mourning because of the oppression of the enemy?" (Ps. 43:2).*

# JULY 25

*And it shall come to pass, that every
thing that liveth, which moveth, whithersoever
the rivers shall come, shall live (Eze. 47:9).*

Whatever this may mean in the future world, it certainly is true
of God's river of life now. Wherever it touches, there is life.
Ezekiel lived near the great Euphrates River and could see its life-giving
properties. Wherever its waters went, there was life.

It is written, "Except a man be born of water and of the Spirit, he
cannot enter into the kingdom of God" (John 3:5). And Jesus said to
the woman at the well, "Whosoever drinketh of this water shall thirst
again: but whosoever drinketh of the water that I shall give him shall
never thirst" (John 4:13, 14).

Are you really thirsty for spiritual things, for the water of life? Then
you are fortunate, for the promise is "I will give unto him that is athirst
of the fountain of the water of life freely" (Rev. 21:6). This is a part of
the joyful experience of salvation. "Behold, God is my salvation; I will
trust, and not be afraid. . . . Therefore with joy shall ye draw water out
of the wells of salvation" (Isa. 12:2, 3).

The Nile is one of the longest rivers of the world. For almost its entire
length it cuts through the most barren desert, yet when it pours into
the Mediterranean it is still a mighty stream. From the air one sees what
appears to be an endless green ribbon stretching out below. It is the
Nile valley watered by this life-giving, never-failing river.

The great river of God's mercy, love, and truth is flowing through
the desert of this world. Wherever it comes, there is life—life in it, life
with it, and life by it. Let us dwell by the river.

MEDITATION PRAYER: *"I stretch forth my hands unto thee:
my soul thirsteth after thee, as a thirsty land" (Ps. 143:6).*

# JULY 26

*But whosoever drinketh of the water that I shall give him shall never thirst; but the water that I shall give him shall be in him a well of water springing up into everlasting life (John 4:14).*

How well we know that all the waters of earth leave us thirsty in a short time. The water that Jesus gives quenches our soul thirst. Not only so, but it becomes in us a spring of life and blessing.

When Isaac redug the wells of Abraham his father, which had been filled with earth and debris by the Philistines, he found springing water, artesian water (Gen. 26:18, 19). Every Christian is an artesian well. But how many wells have been stopped by pleasures, sin, cares of this world! They may be completely hidden, or they may be so impure, so muddy and distasteful, that others are not blessed by them.

J. Frank Norris tells of an experience in his first pastorate. A deacon who had driven many a preacher out of the little church attempted the same thing on him. Norris went to visit the deacon. At first he was un-communicative and gruff, but after a while, through kind attention, he became friendly. They went out to the deacon's peach orchard and came to an old well. As they drew up the crystal, cold water and drank it together, the deacon told the story of the well. It had been made by his grandfather many, many years before, but had been filled up with all sorts of debris and entirely forgotten. During a great drought it was found and cleaned out, and became an unfailing supply to the people of the neighborhood. Now they were determined to keep it that way.

The young pastor put his arm around his friend and said, "Deacon, you're that well. Why don't you clean out the well?" There beside the well curb the two men prayed together, and the deacon did clean out the well and become a strong worker for Christ.

Let us by God's grace clean out the wells. Then the living water of His mercy will bless us, and through us, the world.

MEDITATION PRAYER: *"Give me this water, that I thirst not"* *(John 4:15).*

213

# JULY 27

*And I will make thee like the top of a rock: thou shalt*
*be a place to spread nets upon; thou shalt be built*
*no more: for I the Lord have spoken it (Eze. 26:14).*

Tyre was probably the greatest maritime city of antiquity. Its inhabitants, the Phoenicians, traded in all the known world. The
prophet speaks of all countries trading in its markets and contributing
to its wealth. Then from God comes a message of rebuke and a warning of coming judgment: "Behold, I am against thee, O Tyrus, and will
cause many nations to come up against thee. . . . And they shall destroy
the walls of Tyrus, and break down her towers: I will also scrape her
dust from her, and make her like the top of a rock. It shall be a place
for the spreading of nets in the midst of the sea: for I have spoken it,
saith the Lord. . . . And they shall lay thy stones and thy timber and thy
dust in the midst of the water" (Eze. 26:3-12).

This was all literally fulfilled. Alexander the Great besieged Tyre,
built a great mole from the mainland out to its rocky fortress, scraped
the very surface of the earth of the old city—rocks, timber, even dust—
and cast it into the sea, thus enabling his army of assault to reach the
supposedly impregnable city of the sea.

Those who visit Tyre today may see with their own eyes the fulfillment of this ancient prophecy. It is but a small village, rooted upon
the filled-in ground from Alexander's sea wall, and supported largely by
fishing. The glory of Tyre has vanished like a troubled dream. It has
sunk under the burden of prophecy. It is God's witness. Once a mighty
maritime city, ancient Tyre is no longer influential, and its rocky location is used for the drying of fishing nets. To us it says, "When God
speaks of nations or of individuals, He speaks the truth."

MEDITATION PRAYER: *"Thy testimonies are very sure: holi-*
*ness becometh thine house, O Lord, for ever" (Ps. 93:5).*

214

# JULY 28

*Then said I, Ah, Lord God! behold, I cannot speak:*
*for I am a child. But the Lord said unto me, Say not,*
*I am a child: for thou shalt go to all that I shall send thee,*
*and whatsoever I command thee thou shalt speak (Jer. 1:6, 7).*

All God's commandments are enablings. When Moses was called by God to lead His people out of Egypt, he protested that he was not a convincing speaker. The Lord answered, "Now therefore go, and I will be with thy mouth, and teach thee what thou shalt say" (Ex. 4:12). When we obey God, we shall have the strength to do what He bids us do.

In this command promise for today we too may share the experience of the young prophet Jeremiah. The Lord said to him, "Behold, I have put my words in thy mouth" (Jer. 1:9). As God's messengers we are to speak to lost people God's words, not our own. We are to preach His gospel, not mere human philosophy. "He that hath my word, let him speak my word, . . . saith the Lord" (Jer. 23:28). That is what Jesus did. He spoke the words of His Father.

A wayward young man ran away from home and was not heard of for years. Hearing of his father's death, he returned. The family assembled for the reading of the will, which, to the great surprise of all, told in detail of the waywardness of this son. In anger he arose, stamped out of the room, and was not heard of for three years. He was finally found, and informed that the will, after telling of his misdeeds, had bequeathed him $15,000. How much sorrow he would have been saved had he only listened to the entire will!

So it is with God's messages. They should all be spoken, all received, both the condemnation and the promises. It is true that the old Book says, "The wages of sin is death," but it says more. It continues, "but the gift of God is eternal life" (Rom. 6:23).

MEDITATION PRAYER: *"O Lord, open thou my lips; and my mouth shall shew forth thy praise" (Ps. 51:15).*

# JULY 29

*And it shall come to pass, that from one new moon
to another, and from one sabbath to another, shall all
flesh come to worship before me, saith the Lord (Isa. 66:23).*

In the nineteenth century a book appeared entitled *Looking Backward: 2000-1887.* It is an imaginary picture of the earth several centuries in the future, described by a man who lives still further in the future. Why not a good book called *Looking Further Forward*—way beyond the accomplishments of humanity, to the glorious future of God's promise? And what better text could there be for such a book than our promise text for today?

Life on that renewed earth, which will be the home of the redeemed of all ages, will be a social life, a busy life, a life of worship and praise to God. "From one new moon to another," that is, from month to month, there will be great gatherings of God's people. "And from one sabbath to another, shall all flesh come to worship before" God.

This eternal and wonderful home is for those of faith. It is for those who by grace are saved from the condemnation, the power, and at last the presence, of sin. This is the victory of the cross. Jesus died to redeem not only humanity but *"that* which was lost" (Matt. 18:11), which includes the lost world and lost nature itself. Even today "the whole creation groaneth and travaileth in pain together. Even we ourselves groan . . . waiting for the adoption, to wit, the redemption of our body" (Rom. 8:22, 23).

Let us be joyful in anticipation of it. "Look up, look up, and let your faith continually increase. Let this faith guide you along the narrow path that leads through the gates of the city into the great beyond, the wide, unbounded future of glory that is for the redeemed" (*Prophets and Kings,* p. 732).

MEDITATION PRAYER: *"O send out thy light and thy truth: let them lead me; let them bring me unto thy holy hill, and to thy tabernacles"* (Ps. 43:3).

# JULY 30

*Therefore with joy shall ye draw water*
*out of the wells of salvation (Isa. 12:3).*

It is this that made the future of Christianity," said Matthew Arnold: "its gladness, not its sorrow, its drawing from the spiritual world a source of joy so abundant that it ran over upon the material world and transfigured it."

Some contemporary described the secret of Dwight L. Moody's ministry in these words: "Moody was simply bubbling over with the glory of his message. He reveled in it. His joy was contagious. Men leaped out of the darkness into light and lived a Christian life from that hour."

The early believers received the word with joy (1 Thess. 1:6). It was for the joy set before Him that our Savior endured the cross (Heb. 12:2). And we are to serve God with joy and not with grief (Heb. 13:17). "Count it all joy when ye fall into divers temptations" (James 1:2). In spite of trials we look forward to the appearing of Jesus Christ "whom having not seen, ye love; in whom, though now ye see him not, yet believing, ye rejoice with joy unspeakable and full of glory" (1 Peter 1:8).

Joy is a fruit of the Spirit (Gal. 5:22). We are to pray with joy (Phil. 1:4). In fact, the kingdom of God itself is joy (Rom. 14:17). There is an old song that says, "Joy, joy, joy, there'll be joy by and by," but God's children are to have joy here and now. Wherever we are and whatever comes to us, it is our privilege to be joyful in the Lord (Isa. 61:10). Water from the wells of salvation is a joyous drink. How could one find salvation and not be happy? Through faith Christ dwells in the heart. The burden of sin is gone, and the witness of the Spirit declares that we are the children of God, that heaven is our home.

MEDITATION PRAYER: *"Restore unto me the joy of thy salvation; and uphold me with thy free spirit" (Ps. 51:12).*

# JULY 31

*And he said unto them, Go ye into all the world, and preach the gospel to every creature. He that believeth and is baptized shall be saved; but he that believeth not shall be damned (Mark 16:15, 16).*

A divine commission this. And notice, it is given to all believers, though spoken to the eleven, apparently in the upper room. Verse 17 makes it clear that it applies to "them that believe." Do we believe? Then the commission is to us.

The field is the world. The gospel has no barriers. It is to go to every creature—all races, all lands. The promise is to those who believe and are baptized. Salvation is assured to those who come by faith, and we are warned against the great sin of unbelief.

A prominent Christian merchant once rose in a missionary convention and told this experience: "I stood on the edge of one of the great provinces of China and said to my guide, 'How many men are there beyond us who have never heard the name of Jesus Christ?'

"'Thirty million,' he said, 'but we must go back. We are already in dangerous territory. We must go back at once.'

"As I stood there I heard the creaking of one of the primitive wagons of the region. The vehicle was drawn by a weather-beaten camel driven by a man in rags, and was loaded with cans of oil. There was also a crate of lamps marked 'Made in U.S.A.' You see, we could send them light for their homes, but not for their hearts."

Millions of dollars are being spent every year by business concerns to further their interests. Their representatives are found in all parts of the world, often risking their lives. Should not the representatives of the cross do as much to carry the life-giving gospel of the grace of God in Christ to earth's remotest bounds?

MEDITATION PRAYER: *"I will go in the strength of the Lord God: I will make mention of thy righteousness, even of thine only" (Ps. 71:16.).*

# AUGUST 1

*He that hath an ear, let him hear what the Spirit saith unto the churches; To him that overcometh will I give to eat of the tree of life, which is in the midst of the paradise of God (Rev. 2:7).*

Life to the Christian is a battle and a march, a battle and a march. John Bunyan called it "the holy war which rages in and around the city of Mansoul." By grace we may follow our conquering Leader at last into the very center of the Paradise of God, for there is the tree of life. Again we shall be where human beings once were, beyond the cherubim and the flaming sword, and there we may eat and live forever.

Some unknown writer put a lot of truth in a few words when they said, "If life is a comedy to him who thinks and a tragedy to him who feels, it's a victory to him who believes." Our victory is always in Christ. The apostle says, "Now thanks be unto God, which always causeth us to triumph in Christ" (2 Cor. 2:14). In Him our weakness is turned into strength, our defeat into victory.

A French business executive, permanently located in London, desired British citizenship. Many of his friends made light of his desire. "What difference does it make?" they asked. "You're a Frenchman. You have been here for years. Why become a British subject now?"

But he held to his purpose, and after a long time, by surmounting many problems, he finally received official notice of his citizenship. His friends gathered around him that day and said: "Do you feel any different now? You are the same man, in the same business, in the same city. Everything is just the same. Why have you gone to all this trouble? Really what difference does it make?"

The new British subject replied, "The difference is this: yesterday Waterloo was a defeat; today it's a victory!" And so it is with every true believer. "Faith is the victory . . . that overcomes the world."

MEDITATION PRAYER: *"Thanks be to God, which giveth us the victory through our Lord Jesus Christ" (1 Cor. 15:57).*

# AUGUST 2

*And he said, My presence shall go with
thee, and I will give thee rest (Ex. 33:14).*

This is a promise that includes all promises—"My presence shall go with thee." Here we have no continuing city. We just get our roots down and begin to relax when marching orders come. A change in work; another city, another state, another country—marching, marching, forever marching. But here is the promise: The Lord Himself will keep us company. His presence means His fellowship, His favor, His care, His mercy, every day. If God's presence is with us, everything in heaven and earth is ours. He who in His giving "spared not his own Son, . . . how shall he not with him also freely give us all things?" (Rom. 8:32).

We should learn to practice the presence of God. Edwin Booth once gave this crisp advice to a group of young actors: "A king sits in every audience. Play to the king." The King of kings stands in the midst of all the common things of life, and we should play to Him.

The wilderness journey was too much for Israel without God. With God nothing was too much for them. They could go forward in faith and perfect security and peace because the presence of God was with them, and we can have the same experience today.

An English cleric once said to a bright little girl in his church, "If you will tell me where God is, I will give you an orange."

"If you will tell me where He is not," promptly replied the child, "I will give you two oranges."

God's presence in the pillar of cloud and the pillar of fire led His people of old into the Promised Land, and He will lead us now.

MEDITATION PRAYER: *"Thou compassest my path and my lying down, and art acquainted with all my ways"* (Ps. 139:3).

# AUGUST 3

*Keep back thy servant also from presumptuous sins;*
*let them not have dominion over me: then shall I be upright,*
*and I shall be innocent from the great transgression (Ps. 19:13).*

Presumptuous sins are defiant sins, sins we commit with our eyes wide open, sins against light. Continuance in such sins finally brings a person into the condition known as "the great transgression," or the unpardonable sin.

There were some in Christ's day who attributed His mighty healing power to the devil, although they knew it was from God. Our Savior warned them of their danger, and said that God would forgive all manner of sin and blasphemy, but blasphemy against the Holy Ghost never has forgiveness (Matt. 12:31). In attributing the work of the Holy Spirit through Christ to the devil, they were knowingly sinning against light.

Let us not hold to sin in any form, but seek forgiveness at once, for "if we confess our sins, he is faithful and just to forgive us our sins, and to cleanse us from all unrighteousness" (1 John 1:9). God has promised to cast all our sins into the depths of the sea (Micah 7:19), to remove them from us as far as the east is from the west (Ps. 103:12), to put them behind His back (Isa. 38:17).

The ocean covers 71 percent of the earth's surface to an average depth of nearly 13,000 feet. Two of the deep spots are the one north of Puerto Rico, 30,200 feet; and the one east of the Philippines, about 34,000 feet. There is another great depth near the island of Guam, 35,600 feet. God uses the symbol of the depths of the sea for His pardon of our sins. There not even the penetrating cosmic rays can reach them, and they will be not only forgiven but forgotten. God Himself says, "I will remember their sin no more" (Jer. 31:34).

MEDITATION PRAYER: *"Who can understand his errors? cleanse thou me from secret faults" (Ps. 19:12).*

# AUGUST 4

*Yea, though I walk through the valley of the shadow*
*of death, I will fear no evil: for thou art with me;*
*thy rod and thy staff they comfort me (Ps. 23:4).*

How often has this precious promise strengthened Christians as they were finishing life's journey. The rod and staff of Holy Scripture were their stay. The presence of God was with them, and they were as unafraid as a child falling asleep on its mother's breast. All the promises of the heavenly Father were theirs, and His loving-kindness and tender mercy, which had followed them all the days of their life, were with them still.

This promise applies also to the dark valleys we meet in this life. In his *Pilgrim's Progress* John Bunyan puts the valley of the shadow into this pilgrimage long before the traveler passes through the river beyond which rise the celestial hills. Some of us have traversed dark and dreadful valleys many times and can bear witness that the Lord alone enabled us to come through safely.

Many believers have been pressed, oppressed, and depressed, but still have lived. David said, "He brought me up also out of an horrible pit, . . . and set my feet upon a rock" (Ps. 40:2). The shepherd's rod and staff were for the protection and care of the sheep. So will the Good Shepherd deliver us. Best of all, He will never leave us or forsake us, even in the dark valley. Sometimes the valley is darker than it needs to be because of our unnecessary fear. On the mantel in the ancient Hind's Hotel in Bray, England, is a legend all may read: "Fear knocked at the door. Faith answered. No one was there."

> Father, guide us on life's journey,
>    Be it day or night;
> In each valley of the shadow,
>    Find in Thee our light.

MEDITATION PRAYER: *"O Lord of hosts, blessed is the man that trusteth in thee"* (Ps. 84:12).

# AUGUST 5

*The Lord thy God will raise up unto thee a Prophet*
*from the midst of thee, of thy brethren, like unto me;*
*unto him ye shall hearken (Deut. 18:15).*

In these inspired words Moses, the servant of God, plainly and specifically prophesied of the Messiah to come. And God promised, "I . . . will put my words in his mouth; and he shall speak unto them all that I shall command him" (verse 18).

In fulfillment of this prophecy Jesus Christ came into this world as the Son of God, and took to Himself the divine name "I Am," for which attempts were made to stone Him.

His words were the words of God, which no one can neglect except at their own peril. He declared, "I and my Father are one" (John 10:30). The Temple officers who heard Him said, "Never man spake like this man" (John 7:46). "And all . . . wondered at the gracious words which proceeded out of his mouth" (Luke 4:22). He Himself said, "He that rejecteth me, and receiveth not my words, hath one that judgeth him: the word that I have spoken, the same shall judge him in the last day" (John 12:48). He declared that the heavenly Father had given Him a commandment, what He should say and what He should speak (verse 49). Jesus came in fulfillment of the prophecy made through Moses. He spoke the words of God. If we reject Him, we reject God Himself as well as His Son.

Solomon B. Freehof, distinguished Jewish preacher, said: "The consciousness of the presence of God has come to millions of men and women through Jesus. No Muslim ever sings, 'Muhammad, lover of my soul,' nor does any Jew say of Moses, the teacher, 'I need thee every hour.' He [Jesus] brought God near to men through His presence. He made the Divine personal for myriads of worshippers."

MEDITATION PRAYER: *"That men may know that thou, whose name alone is Jehovah, art the most high over all the earth" (Ps. 83:18).*

# AUGUST 6

*Whosoever therefore shall confess me before men, him will I confess also before my Father which is in heaven (Matt. 10:32).*

Let us never be ashamed to own our Lord. In one of D. L. Moody's meetings a little towheaded Norwegian boy who could hardly speak a word of English stood up and came to the front. Trembling and with tears trickling down his cheeks, he said, "If I tell the world about Jesus, He'll tell the Father about me." That was all he said, and all he needed to say. In fact, it was more than all the rest said that day. That's what it means to confess Him.

"Ye shall be [my] witnesses," said Jesus in Acts 1:8. In this world and in the great court of eternity we are to confess the Lord Jesus, and He will confess us before the Father. "I am not ashamed of the gospel of Christ," declared the apostle Paul in Romans 1:16, "for it is the power of God unto salvation." In other words, "It has done something for me. It has changed my life and the lives of others."

In a certain hospital a little fellow had a piece of bone removed from his arm. The operation was successful, and he recovered completely. On leaving the hospital he asked to see the doctor. "You wished to see me, Billy?" asked the surgeon.

The little fellow lifted up his hand and laid it on the doctor's shoulder—it was just as high as he could reach. With his face beaming, he said, "My mama will never hear the last about *you.*"

If we fully realize what Christ has done for us, we should say to Him, "My friends will never hear the last about You."

> Give us grace to follow fully
> Vanquishing our faithless shame,
> Feebly, it may be, but truly
> Witnessing for Thy dear name.
> —Frances R. Havergal

MEDITATION PRAYER: *"I will give thee thanks in the great congregation: I will praise thee among much people" (Ps. 35:18).*

# AUGUST 7

*Every place that the sole of your foot shall tread upon,*
*that have I given unto you, as I said unto Moses (Joshua 1:3).*

Joshua was leading the Israelites into the land of Canaan. Untrained and inexperienced, they were going up against fierce enemies behind great fortifications. God's promise was that every place on which their feet should tread would be theirs. God had given it to them. It was their country.

In our spiritual warfare God leads us into victories step by step. By His grace, through His strength, in His guidance, and at His command we must conquer our spiritual enemies. Then the Promised Land of glory will be ours. The life of the Christian should be a series of uninterrupted victories. There is no need for defeat. Clad in the scriptural armor, we are to go forward, ever forward in faith.

During one of Napoleon's early battles, his army was broken and ready to retreat. Escape was the only thought in the minds of the shattered ranks. The drummer boy was asked to beat a retreat. "I do not know how to beat a retreat," he said, "but I can beat a charge!" And he did. The disheartened, wavering men rallied, and with one magnificent thrust broke the power of the surprised enemy, cleared the field, and won the day.

The whole world belongs to God's children now, but after the second coming of Christ and the purification of this earth they will enter into their inheritance (Dan. 2:44), for the saints of the Most High shall possess the kingdom and shall dwell therein forever (Dan. 7:27).

Be of good courage, Christian, for you are in the battle for your soul. Even the battlefield itself belongs to you by God's promise. He who put "to flight the armies of the aliens" (Heb. 11:34) will put to flight all your spiritual enemies and give you victory in Christ.

MEDITATION PRAYER: *"Through thee will we push down our enemies: through thy name will we tread them under that rise up against us"* (Ps. 44:5).

# AUGUST 8

*Thy shoes shall be iron and brass; and as*
*thy days, so shall thy strength be (Deut. 33:25).*

God's children are princes of the royal blood. They are kings and
priests. Their strength shall be as their days, that is, in proportion
to the burden and stress of the day. Unexpected emergencies? Yes, and
unexpected strength. Long-drawn-out labors and sufferings? Yes, and
long-drawn-out strength and endurance to meet them.

Where does it all come from? From God. "The eternal God is thy
refuge, and underneath are the everlasting arms" (Deut. 33:27). No
matter how far down we may have sunk, lower still are the everlasting
arms, holding us, lifting us to the very heart of God.

A little lad trudged behind his father and his father's friend across a
field. They came to a drainage ditch, and the men went across it in their
stride. But the boy knew his limitations—the length of his legs. In a
voice that could not be denied, he cried, "Daddy, my legs are too
short." Instantly the father was by his side, lifting him over the ditch.

Often we find some problem too big for us, some ditch we cannot
cross alone. Then we find our heavenly Father more willing to help us
than we are to ask. When we seem to be going down in despair, suddenly we realize that underneath us are those everlasting arms.

Blind Milton spoke of that Glorious Presence, and John Henry
Newman sang:

> So long Thy power hath blest me, sure it still
>     Will lead me on
> O'er moor and fen, o'er crag and torrent, till
>     The night is gone.

MEDITATION PRAYER: *"When I said, My foot slippeth; thy*
*mercy, O Lord, held me up" (Ps. 94:18).*

226

# AUGUST 9

*Honour the Lord with thy substance, and with the firstfruits
of all thine increase: so shall thy barns be filled with plenty,
and thy presses shall burst out with new wine (Prov. 3:9, 10).*

Riches, gain, earnings, are really a crystallization of ourselves, our energies, our thoughts, our heartbeats. If we really honor the Lord ourselves, we shall honor Him with our increase.

Notice, the firstfruits are His. God is to be first and last and best in everything. There is much instruction in the inscription on an old Italian tombstone:

> What I gave away I saved;
> What I spent I used;
> What I kept I lost.

You see, giving to the Lord is but transporting our goods to a higher floor, which is the only place for safekeeping. We cannot place our gifts in the hand of God personally. Everything we give to God must be used for humanity. Christian stewardship is the practice of systematic, proportionate giving of time, abilities, material possessions, as a trust from God, to be used in His service here on earth.

Here is David Livingstone's testimony: "I will place no value on anything that I have or possess, except in relation to the kingdom of Christ. If anything that I have will advance that kingdom, it shall be given or kept, as by giving or keeping it I shall best promote the glory of Him to whom I owe all my hopes, both for time and eternity."

God gave His Son. The Son gave Himself. Let us be like those of old who "first gave their own selves to the Lord" (2 Cor. 8:5) and then honored Him with their substance in helping others who were in greater need than they themselves.

MEDITATION PRAYER: *"Thou, O God, hast prepared of thy goodness for the poor" (Ps. 68:10).*

# AUGUST 10

*For I know the thoughts that I think toward you, saith the*
*Lord, thoughts of peace, and not of evil, to give you an expected*
*end [or as the Revised Standard Version puts it, "a future and*
*a hope," or a happy future] (Jer. 29:11).*

No matter how things seem to us, God knows what He is doing. He knows what He has in mind. He knows that His thoughts toward us are good, and not evil, to give us a happy future. This is His expectation, and it should be ours. He is planning for it all the time.

Things may be going hard, but remember—

> . . . Behind the dim unknown,
> Standeth God within the shadow,
> keeping watch above His own.
> —James Russell Lowell

And He has promised with every trial to make a way of escape (1 Cor. 10:13). He has promised never to leave us, nor forsake us (Heb. 13:5).

Rowland Hill tells of a rich man and a poor man of his congregation. The wealthy man came to him with a sum of money that he wished to give to the poor brother, and he asked the pastor to give it as he thought best, either all at once or in small amounts. Mr. Hill sent the poor man a £5 note with the message "More to follow." Every few months a remittance was sent with the same notation, "More to follow." Now, that's grace. God's grace is like that—more to follow.

God's thoughts follow us all the time, and we are to have faith that "God's tomorrow will be better than today." His thoughts toward us are "thoughts of peace, and not of evil," to give us a happy future, an expected end.

MEDITATION PRAYER: *"I am poor and needy; yet the Lord thinketh upon me: thou art my help and my deliverer; make no tarrying, O my God" (Ps. 40:17).*

# AUGUST 11

*The meek will he guide in judgment:*
*and the meek will he teach his way (Ps. 25:9).*

This promise includes guiding and teaching; but meekness, a willingness to be guided and taught, is necessary if these two blessings are to be ours. Moses had to endure many hardships before he learned meekness. Then not only was he led by God but he was able to lead others.

The pillar of cloud by day and the pillar of fire by night not only went with the children of Israel but led them. But they had to be willing to be led before God worked this miracle for them. The star led the Wise Men to Christ, but they were willing to follow it.

To the extent that God's children are meek and teachable, to that extent will they be taught and guided. The proud learn little, for "pride goeth before destruction, and an haughty spirit before a fall" (Prov. 16:18). Meekness is revealed in different ways. We read of the meekness of love (1 Cor. 13:5, 7), of wisdom (James 3:13), of teaching (2 Tim. 2:25), of self-restraint (Ex. 23:4-9; Prov. 6:32), of long forbearing (Prov. 25:15). We have the examples of Joseph, Moses, David, and above all, of Jesus, who when reviled, upbraided not, and when crucified, prayed for His murderers.

We may know many things—the arts and sciences; but if we would know God's way, we must become as little children, listening to and obeying His will.

A missionary in Jamaica, examining some schoolchildren, asked the question "Who are the meek?" One boy answered, "Those who give soft answers to rough questions." We might add, Those also who are willing to learn from the rough teachers that God sometimes uses to guide and educate His saints. But the reward at last will be great, for it is written, "Blessed are the meek: for they shall inherit the earth" (Matt. 5:5).

MEDITATION PRAYER: *"Make me to understand the way of thy precepts: so shall I talk of thy wondrous works" (Ps. 119:27).*

# AUGUST 12

*The secret of the Lord is with them that fear him;
and he will shew them his covenant (Ps. 25:14).*

This promise does not mean that those who fear God will know all the secret things and mysteries of the universe to which He has given no key. Holy Scripture plainly declares that "the secret things belong unto the Lord our God" (Deut. 29:29). The meaning of this text is that the familiar intimacy of the Lord will be with His people. They will know Him as their heavenly Father and Friend.

When Bishop Watts Ditchfield was a small boy, he was visiting one day at the home of an old woman who asked him to read a motto on the wall, "Thou God seest me." Then she said: "When you are older, people will tell you that God is always watching to see when you do wrong, in order to punish you. But I do not want you to think of it in that way. Always remember that God loves you so much that He cannot take His eyes off you."

Jesus said to His disciples, "Henceforth I call you not servants; for the servant knoweth not what his lord doeth: but I have called you friends; for all things that I have heard of my Father I have made known unto you" (John 15:15). It is in the intimacy of friendship that God reveals His secret of salvation to His people. "If any man will do his will, he shall know of the doctrine, whether it be of God, or whether I speak of myself," said Jesus (John 7:17). Even the glorious gospel "is hid to them that are lost" (2 Cor. 4:3). They cannot see it. The secret of the Lord is not with them. But God promises to show His covenant to all who fear Him. His close relationship with His people is revealed especially in His communication to them by His Spirit of the covenant of salvation, which cannot be known by mere human reason, for "the Spirit itself beareth witness with our spirit, that we are the children of God" (Rom. 8:16).

MEDITATION PRAYER: *"Blessed is the people that know the joyful sound: they shall walk, O Lord, in the light of thy countenance" (Ps. 89:15).*

# AUGUST 13

*The steps of a good man are ordered by the Lord: and he
delighteth in his way. Though he fall, he shall not be utterly cast
down: for the Lord upholdeth him with his hand (Ps. 37:23, 24).*

The word here translated "a good man" is literally "a hero," "a
valiant man." As John Bunyan put it: "Mr. Valiant-for-the-truth."
God delights in his way. That's why he must prosper, even though he
goes through many trials, as did Joseph (Gen. 39:2-6, 21-23).

Notice, this promise does not assure a good person that they will
never fall, but that if they do, they will not be "utterly cast down." The
Lord will take them by the hand and raise them again. We have a beautiful picture of this in Matthew 14:31. Peter was sinking beneath the
angry waves, and Jesus stretched forth His hand to save him. Peter's
short prayer may often be ours, "Lord, save me."

The writer remembers receiving two terrific blows—one from
falling on the ice in learning to skate, the other from a senior minister
who gave some very hard, but much needed, rebuke. Both were hard
to endure, but were blessed in their outcome.

Stuart Hutchinson tells of his minister father, whose hobby was that
of a vinedresser. Late in the winter he would cut the vines until it
seemed that he would kill them, but when the next September came,
the heavy clusters of grapes proved he was right in what he did. On the
hill behind the house was a wild grapevine. One day Stuart said,
"Father, why don't you trim that vine?"

"Oh," he replied, "it isn't worth it."

Sometimes when God sends disappointments and trials we think
He doesn't love us; but remember, He is with us. When we fall we shall
not be utterly cast down, for the Lord will uphold us with His hand and
bring blessing out of the pain.

MEDITATION PRAYER: *"For thou hast delivered my soul from
death: wilt not thou deliver my feet from falling, that I may walk before God in
the light of the living?" (Ps. 56:13).*

231

# AUGUST 14

*I love them that love me; and those*
*that seek me early shall find me (Prov. 8:17).*

Remember this: heavenly wisdom loves its lovers and seeks its seekers. It has been said that one who seeks to be wise is already wise. If this is true of wisdom in general, certainly it must be true of the wisdom revealed in Jesus Christ, "who of God is made unto us wisdom, and righteousness, and sanctification, and redemption" (1 Cor. 1:30). The gospel story is God's saving wisdom. The apostle says that the preaching of Christ crucified is foolishness to some, "but unto them which are called, . . . [He is] the power of God, and the wisdom of God" (verse 24).

We do not need to go to any human philosopher for wisdom, for in Christ "are hid all the treasures of wisdom and knowledge" (Col. 2:3). And this wisdom is the true wisdom, which comes from above. It is our part, then, to seek this wisdom by seeking Christ, and by seeking Him early. In fact, we are to seek Him first, and the glorious reward is that we shall find Him. We should seek Him early in the day. Our very first thoughts on awakening should be of Him. We should seek Him by prayer and meditation and the study of His Word. We should seek Him early in life. We should teach our children the way to find the dear Savior, that their lives may be guided by His wisdom and love. Then in maturity and old age we should make Him first and last and best in everything. The great reward is that we shall find Him.

A Chinese Christian was explaining to some friends that "Jesus is the invisible God, and God is the visible Jesus." This is a unique way of saying, "He that hath seen me hath seen the Father" (John 14:9), and "I and my Father are one" (John 10:30). God is unseeable, unhearable, unknowable, and untouchable, except in Christ.

MEDITATION PRAYER: *"O God, thou art my God; early will I seek thee: my soul thirsteth for thee, my flesh longeth for thee in a dry and thirsty land, where no water is" (Ps. 63:1).*

# AUGUST 15

*And a man shall be as an hiding place from the wind,*
*and a covert from the tempest; as rivers of water in a dry place,*
*as the shadow of a great rock in a weary land (Isa. 32:2).*

Who could this man be but the Son of man, the "man of sorrows, and acquainted with grief" (Isa. 53:3), the Lord from heaven? Through His atoning sacrifice upon the cross He became a hiding place the just wrath of God against sin. In His care we escape the troubles of life and even the fear of death itself.

We once camped in the shadow of a gigantic rock in the midst of a Western desert. There, hidden in a grotto, was a great pool of cool, pure water. In our weary pilgrimage, Jesus is like a great rock bringing us shade and the water of life.

A party of travelers in North Africa was overtaken by a fierce simoom. The blinding sands rolled like an impenetrable cloud across the horizon and seemed to engulf the world. Just at that moment they came to a rude stone building that had been erected for the protection of desert travelers. They rushed into it, closed the door, and were safe.

Great storms of trouble are to sweep this earth in the final days of its history, yet in the darkness, the tempest, and the terror will be heard a voice saying, "Come, my people, enter thou into thy chambers, and shut thy doors about thee: hide thyself as it were for a little moment, until the indignation be overpast" (Isa. 26:20).

For every believer, Jesus, the Son of man, is the rock of refuge, the hiding place for the soul in trouble. He is—

> A shade by day, defense by night,
> A shelter in the time of storm;
> No fears alarm, no foes affright,
> A shelter in the time of storm.

MEDITATION PRAYER: *"Thou art my hiding place; thou shalt preserve me from trouble; thou shalt compass me about with songs of deliverance"* (Ps. 32:7).

# AUGUST 16

*Behold, the days come, saith the Lord, that I will raise unto David a righteous Branch, and a King shall reign and prosper, and shall execute judgment and justice in the earth. In his days Judah shall be saved, and Israel shall dwell safely: and this is his name whereby he shall be called, The Lord our righteousness (Jer. 23:5, 6).*

Jesus is the righteous branch. In His true name is His character, "The Lord our righteousness." No one will ever be saved in their own righteousness. It is all of God, for "their righteousness is of me, saith the Lord" (Isa. 54:17). "Abraham believed God, and it was counted unto him for righteousness" (Rom. 4:3). And that's how we are righteous—it's accounted to us.

People trusting to their own righteousness are like people seeking shelter under their own shadow. They may stoop even to the ground, but their shadow is still beneath them. When they flee to the shadow of a great rock or a widespreading tree, they find shelter from the noonday sun. So human merits are unavailing. Christ alone is able "to save them to the uttermost that come unto God by him" (Heb. 7:25).

Notice, His glorious name is "The Lord our righteousness." He is *our* righteousness, and there is only one way to receive it—by faith. "For therein is the righteousness of God revealed from faith to faith: as it is written, The just shall live by faith" (Rom. 1:17). The apostle Paul declares that this holy righteousness is "by faith of Jesus Christ . . . : whom God hath set forth to be a propitiation through faith in his blood, to declare his righteousness for the remission of sins that are past, through the forbearance of God" (Rom. 3:22-25). Let every believer speak His matchless worth and sound His glories forth.

MEDITATION PRAYER: *"According to thy name, O God, so is thy praise unto the ends of the earth: thy right hand is full of righteousness" (Ps. 48:10).*

# AUGUST 17

*Consider the lilies how they grow: they toil not, they spin not:
and yet I say unto you, that Solomon in all his glory was not arrayed
like one of these. If then God so clothe the grass, which is to day in
the field, and to morrow is cast into the oven; how much more
will he clothe you, O ye of little faith? (Luke 12:27, 28).*

Consider the lilies how they grow; the grass of the field, which is here for but a day. God gives beauty to nature, and will He not care for us? We need the faith of little children, who sing:

> He paints the lily of the field,
> Perfumes each lily bell;
> If He so loves the little flowers,
> I know He loves me well.
>
> —Maria Straub

Jesus revealed God as a father, and we are His children. He taught us to pray, "Our Father which art in heaven" (Matt. 6:9). "What man is there," said Jesus, "if his son ask bread, will he give him a stone? Or if he ask a fish, will he give him a serpent? If ye then, being evil, know how to give good gifts unto your children, how much more shall your Father which is in heaven give good things to them that ask him?" (Matt. 7:9-11). What is our trouble? Lack of faith. "According to your faith be it unto you" (Matt. 9:29).

In the days of the Reformation, Brentius of Württemberg, pursued by persecuting soldiers, hid in a hayloft, under the hay. The soldiers entered the place and ran their bayonets through the hay here and there without detecting him. Every day for 14 days a hen came and laid an egg within his reach. This was his only sustenance. When the supply ceased, he took it as a sign that it was safe for him to leave his hiding place. He found that the soldiers had just left town, and he was able to find safety.

MEDITATION PRAYER: *"Thou hast dealt well with thy servant, O Lord, according unto thy word" (Ps. 119:65).*

# AUGUST 18

*He that findeth his life shall lose it: and he that loseth his life for my sake shall find it (Matt. 10:39).*

This statement by our Savior is paradoxical and depends on the double sense attached to the word "life"—the natural and the spiritual, the temporal and the eternal. People who make this natural life and the things of time first will lose this life as well as the eternal. Those who sacrifice this life for the higher will have both.

It is difficult at times to give up things that we can see for things that we cannot see, but we must remember that "the things which are not seen are eternal" (2 Cor. 4:18). Moses was able to see the invisible, and he esteemed "the reproach of Christ greater riches than the treasures in Egypt: for he had respect unto the recompence of the reward" (Heb. 11:26). He made today secondary to tomorrow, time subservient to eternity.

Matthew left his counting table to follow Jesus. Peter and Andrew, James and John, left their fishing fleet to follow Christ. "He . . . that forsaketh not all that he hath . . . cannot be my disciple," said Jesus (Luke 14:33). Even life itself, with all its plans and hopes, must be given to Him to guide and to use.

The Indian maharaja, Dhuleep Singh, was presented to Queen Victoria just after the English had captured the great Koh-i-noor diamond. The gem was placed in his hand, and he held it for some time. Realizing that now it belonged to another by right of conquest, he said, "Madam, it gives me pleasure to place in your hands, as my sovereign, this treasure of my ancestors."

Have we made our great surrender to Christ? Have we placed in His hands that which we have inherited from our ancestors—the life that is His by right of the conquest of Calvary's cross?

MEDITATION PRAYER: *"Because thy lovingkindness is better than life, my lips shall praise thee" (Ps. 63:3).*

# AUGUST 19

*And thine ears shall hear a word behind thee,*
*saying, This is the way, walk ye in it, when ye turn*
*to the right hand, and when ye turn to the left (Isa. 30:21).*

This is a promise of divine guidance. Every new day is a road to travel; a path to walk, to run, possibly to climb. The promise is that when we turn off the path we shall hear a voice saying, "This is the way. Come back and walk in it."

A number of years ago a man was lost in the dense fog of the Welsh mountains and wandered about for two days and a night trying to find a way back to human habitation. He had never felt so lonely, so completely forsaken, so lost. Finally he heard someone say, "I wonder if he might have come this way." Then he realized that others were looking for him. There are many who have turned from the right way and are wandering about in the fog of broken hopes and shattered plans. They think they are utterly alone and forsaken. Then they hear a voice. Someone is seeking them, calling them back to the right way.

But there is something that we ourselves must do to find the right way. "Thus saith the Lord, Stand ye in the ways, and see, and ask for the old paths, where is the good way, and walk therein, and ye shall find rest for your souls" (Jer. 6:16). There are many ways, but only in the good way shall we find soul rest.

The psalmist must have known something of this cry of the soul for light when the path is dark. "Deep calleth unto deep," he says (Ps. 42:7). Out of the depths of humanity's need comes the cry for help, and out of the depths of God's love comes His answer: "This is the way, walk ye in it." It is the old way, "the way of holiness" (Isa. 35:8), "a new and living way" (Heb. 10:20), and those who walk in it are referred to as "those of the way."

MEDITATION PRAYER: *"Search me, O God, and know my heart: . . . and see if there be any wicked way in me, and lead me in the way everlasting" (Ps. 139:23, 24).*

# AUGUST 20

*Who delivered us from so great a death, and doth deliver:*
*in whom we trust that he will yet deliver us (2 Cor. 1:10).*

No wonder the great apostle had faith in his Savior—the One who had delivered, was delivering, and would deliver. That same trust may be ours. There are really three tenses to salvation. We have been saved, we are being saved, we shall be saved. Through our Savior's sacrificial atonement upon the cross we have been saved, justified from our sins. "By grace are ye saved through faith" (Eph. 2:8). Today we should be growing in grace and in the knowledge of the Lord (2 Peter 3:18). God works in us "both to will and to do of his good pleasure" (Phil. 2:13). In this sense we are being saved from sin day by day. In the fullest sense, which includes glorification, we are yet to be saved at the appearing of our Lord. This is for those "who are kept by the power of God through faith unto salvation ready to be revealed in the last time" (1 Peter 1:5). This is the end, or object, of our faith (verse 9). This is the salvation of which we are heirs (Heb. 1:14) and for which our Savior appears the second time (Heb. 9:28).

See this picture: A house is burning. In it is a very valuable violin, a Stradivarius. A music lover, knowing that it is there, rushes in at the risk of his life and saves it. That is salvation. But the violin is seriously damaged. It is taken to an expert, who with infinite care repairs it, for he knows its value. That also is salvation. The violin is saved from the fire and saved from its wounds. Now a great violinist takes it, tunes it, draws the bow over its strings, and it speaks to our hearts. That is the complete salvation of the violin, for it is restored to its intended usefulness.

Our threefold salvation is about to be accomplished in the second coming of Christ, the great Deliverer. Today and tomorrow and forever He is able to save us.

MEDITATION PRAYER: *"Let thy mercies come also unto me, O Lord, even thy salvation, according to thy word"* (Ps. 119:41).

# AUGUST 21

*The lip of truth shall be established for ever:*
*but a lying tongue is but for a moment (Prov. 12:19).*

The Hebrew word for "truth" signifies firmness; in Greek, that which cannot be hid, or which is unconcealed. Jesus reminds us, "He that doeth truth cometh to the light" (John 3:21). Truth may be suppressed for a time, but it cannot be buried forever. It is sure to have a resurrection. And the Hebrew derivation of the word "truth" reminds us of its indestructible firmness. "Heaven and earth shall pass away," Jesus said, "but my words shall not pass away" (Matt. 24:35).

Every motorist has had the experience of being attracted by the advertisements of hotels, motels, restaurants, etc., that are found to be entirely different from what they are represented to be.

What about the words of a Christian? What about the very profession of being a Christian? Are the goods as specified? Remember, truth wears well. Falsehood may triumph temporarily, but it is like Jonah's gourd, which grew up in the night and withered in the light of day. Truth—all kinds of truth—has time on its side, and will at last be vindicated.

Remember, the gospel is everlasting (Rev. 14:6) because it is the truth. It is based upon the unchanging will, word, and power of God. God is eternal, and so is truth. "His mercy is everlasting; and his truth endureth to all generations" (Ps. 100:5).

Let us always be careful, not primarily that we have truth on our side, but that we be on the side of truth.

> So let our lips and lives express
> The holy gospel we profess;
> So let our works and virtues shine,
> To prove the doctrine all divine.

MEDITATION PRAYER: *"For thy mercy is great above the heavens: and thy truth reacheth unto the clouds" (Ps. 108:4).*

# AUGUST 22

*He that hath clean hands, and a pure heart; who hath not lifted up his soul unto vanity, nor sworn deceitfully. He shall receive the blessing from the Lord, and righteousness from the God of his salvation (Ps. 24:4, 5).*

How a person lives is important. Notice—clean hands, pure heart, no foolish pride, no deceit, but truthfulness. The blessing of God will be on such a person.

But from whence do all these virtues come? Certainly not from the person's own heart. The answer is in the last phrase, "righteousness from the God of his salvation."

Righteousness by faith is the only righteousness a believer can have. It comes from God and is "by faith of Jesus Christ unto all and upon all them that believe" (Rom. 3:22).

"The righteousness by which we are justified is imputed; the righteousness by which we are sanctified is imparted. The first is our title to heaven, the second is our fitness for heaven" (Ellen G. White, in *Review and Herald,* June 4, 1895).

If one makes a profession of salvation but still lives the same old life of sin and defeat, their profession is worthless. "By their fruits ye shall know them" (Matt. 7:20). This is the old orchard test and the only true test. Righteousness in the heart will be revealed as righteousness in the outward life—clean living, pure thinking, simplicity, humbleness of spirit, truthfulness. On those who have these graces, the blessing of God descends and dwells.

It is for us to live out the life that God lives in us. When asked how long it took him to paint a certain picture, Joshua Reynolds replied, "All my life." We are all painters with the colors God gives us. May we always use them to His glory.

MEDITATION PRAYER: *"Open to me the gates of righteousness: I will go into them, and I will praise the Lord" (Ps. 118:19).*

# AUGUST 23

*Or let him take hold of my strength, that he*
*may make peace with me; and he shall*
*make peace with me (Isa. 27:5).*

On the cross God has already made peace with sinners, but all sinners have not made their peace with Him. "By His spotless life, His obedience, His death on the cross of Calvary, Christ interceded for the lost race. And now, not as a mere petitioner does the Captain of our salvation intercede for us, but as a Conqueror claiming His victory. His offering is complete, . . . wholly acceptable, and pardon covers all transgression" (*Christ's Object Lessons,* p. 156). Therefore we can come to God by Him without fear, for Christ pleads our cause, using the mighty arguments of Calvary.

It is Satan's special device to lead people into sin and then leave them in despair, fearing to ask for pardon. But God invites us to take hold of His strength. Jacob did this and wrestled with the angel until the break of day. When he discovered that he was contending with a divine personality, he clung on in faith, declaring, "I will not let thee go, except thou bless me" (Gen. 32:26). In his very weakness and surrender he found victory and peace, and his name was changed to Israel, or Overcomer.

Jesus said, "Peace I leave with you, my peace I give unto you: not as the world giveth, give I unto you. Let not your heart be troubled, neither let it be afraid" (John 14:27). If you are one of Christ's children, He has remembered you in His will. On the cross He willed His mother to John, His spirit back to His Father; but to His disciples, He willed His peace.

It is said that no one can make a will that lawyers cannot break, but we can challenge any of them to break Christ's will. No court can ever set it aside, and by faith we can claim it today.

MEDITATION PRAYER: *"Lord, thou wilt ordain peace for us: for thou also hast wrought all our works in us"* (Isa. 26:12).

# AUGUST 24

*Blessed are the meek: for they*
*shall inherit the earth (Matt. 5:5).*

By the universal voice of his army, Godfrey of Bouillon was saluted king of Jerusalem upon the capture of that city. A crown of gold was brought to him, but he set it aside, saying, "It is not fit for me, a mortal man and a sinner, to be crowned with gold in the city where Christ, the Son of God, was crowned with thorns."

"Meekness does not assert itself, because it has something better to assert," writes a contemporary. Jesus said, "If any man will come after me, let him deny himself" (Matt. 16:24). And He bids us, "Learn of me; for I am meek and lowly in heart" (Matt. 11:29). Jesus, the brightness of His Father's glory, "counted not the being on an equality with God a thing to be grasped, but emptied himself, taking the form of a servant" (Phil. 2:6, 7, ASV).

There was no bigotry in Him, no cold austerity. He who beholds Christ, "The Terrible Meek," as Charles Rann Kennedy calls Him, will yield self to the disposal of the Holy Spirit. The apostle Paul could say, "I am crucified with Christ: nevertheless I live; yet not I, but Christ liveth in me; and the life which I now live in the flesh I live by the faith of the Son of God, who loved me, and gave himself for me" (Gal. 2:20).

"It was through the desire for self-exaltation that sin entered into the world, and our first parents lost the dominion over this fair earth, their kingdom. It is through self-abnegation that Christ redeems what was lost. And He says we are to overcome as He did (Rev. 3:21). Through humility and self-surrender we may become heirs with Him, when the 'meek shall inherit the earth' (Ps. 37:11)" (*Thoughts From the Mount of Blessing,* p. 17).

MEDITATION PRAYER: *"For thou, O God, . . . hast given me the heritage of those that fear thy name" (Ps. 61:5).*

# AUGUST 25

*The wolf and the lamb shall feed together, and the lion shall eat straw like the bullock: and dust shall be the serpent's meat. They shall not hurt nor destroy in all my holy mountain, saith the Lord (Isa. 65:25).*

Conditions on earth are not like this today. In our world the wolf eats the lamb. The lion is a predator and feeds upon creatures less strong than itself—in fact, upon the bullock whenever it has the opportunity. The serpent acts with the nature of a serpent, and many die of snakebite every year. Hurt and destruction are worldwide, at times bursting out into desperate and terrible wars.

The time is coming when "the earth shall be full of the knowledge of the Lord, as the waters cover the sea," and that is why the Lord declares, "They shall not hurt nor destroy in all my holy mountain" (Isa. 11:9).

Hurt and destruction result from ignorance or an ignoring of the knowledge of God. The physical creation itself, and even the animal world, will be changed when human beings are immortalized and brought back to their Eden home.

"Blessed are the meek: for they shall inherit the earth" (Matt. 5:5). But today "the whole creation groaneth and travaileth in pain together," waiting "for the manifestation of the sons of God" (Rom. 8:22, 19). In the earth made new there will be perfect harmony between humans and their environment.

"To lick the dust," we are reminded by commentators, is figurative of the final, utter, and perpetual degradation of Satan and his emissaries (Isa. 49:23; Ps. 72:9). The reign of sin will then be over, and God will have a clean universe.

MEDITATION PRAYER: *"Then will I go unto the altar of God, unto God my exceeding joy: yea, upon the harp will I praise thee, O God my God" (Ps. 43:4).*

# AUGUST 26

*The Lord will strengthen him*
*upon the bed of languishing: thou wilt*
*make all his bed in his sickness (Ps. 41:3).*

Remember, this promise is made to the person who considers the poor, as we read in the first verse of this psalm. Am I one of these? If so, then I may take home this text as my own promise.

In the most ancient times it was the custom to exhibit the sick in public places so that benevolent persons, or those who had suffered from the same disease or had cared for such, might suggest a remedy. It was in this way, we are told, that the science of medicine had its beginning.

The sick must be helped by others. Disease brings that equality that death completes. Distinctions then are set aside. One person is not above another in the sickroom. There is no place for gaiety, human glory, or wit. Even the reason is sometimes clouded. Here the highest and brightest mortals find nothing left but weakness and pain.

How wonderful at such a time to have loving friends with their kind and tender ministrations, especially a Christian physician with a blessed ministry, than which there can be no greater comfort.

But above and beyond all this is the wonderful promise that God will be our nurse and attendant. How relaxing and restful it is to poor patients to have the bed remade, smoothed, and properly prepared for their aching body! Notice the promise that the Lord will "make all his bed in his sickness." Divine grace, divine love—these are the best stimulants and medicines. As someone has said: "There is no physician like the Lord, no tonic like His promise, no wine like His love."

But have we done our duty to the poor? If not, let us hasten about it, for we need this promise of God in our treasury.

MEDITATION PRAYER: *"This is my comfort in my affliction: for thy word hath quickened me" (Ps. 119:50).*

# AUGUST 27

*And there shall be signs in the sun, and in the moon, and in the stars; and upon the earth distress of nations, with perplexity; the sea and the waves roaring; men's hearts failing them for fear, and for looking after those things which are coming on the earth: for the powers of heaven shall be shaken. And then shall they see the Son of man coming in a cloud with power and great glory (Luke 21:25-27).*

These signs in the sun, moon, and stars have taken place. The great Dark Day occurred on May 19, 1780; the falling stars, on November 13, 1833. "Distress of nations" has been revealed in two world wars, and great preparations are being made for wars yet to come. Perplexity is with us—the distractions of nature, but above all, "men's hearts failing them for fear." There is a worldwide unease, a disease of heart and mind, an unutterable longing for eternal things, which can never be satisfied with any material pleasure or activity.

By their terrible discoveries people themselves have shaken the earth about them. Soon the heavens will be shaken, not by people, but by God. These signs of the times are all precursors of the coming of the Son of man. "Then shall they see the Son of man coming in the clouds" (Mark 13:26). He comes with power and glory.

A visitor to a certain home was told by the maid that the people she wished to see were gone, and it was not known when they would return. However, the caller noticed that the table was laid for dinner. Thinking that she had misunderstood, she queried, "So your mistress is coming home today?"

"I have not heard so," said the maid, "but as the time is uncertain, I keep everything ready each day." And that's how Christians ought to live—with everything ready each day, everything ready for their Master's return.

The signs of the times are in the skies and on the earth. Our Lord is coming, but we know not the hour.

MEDITATION PRAYER: *"Let all those that seek thee rejoice and be glad in thee" (Ps. 40:16).*

# AUGUST 28

*Verily, verily, I say unto you, The hour is coming,
and now is, when the dead shall hear the voice of the
Son of God: and they that hear shall live (John 5:25).*

When a preacher in a funeral sermon for a fellow minister said, "Our dear brother has departed, and we shall never look upon him again," an aged saint in the congregation exclaimed, "Thank God, that's a lie!" Yes, thank God, we may all say that such a statement is false, for the dead shall live.

Jesus is the prince of life. He is the life-giver. Our Savior had begun His ministry, and soon was to raise from the dead the daughter of Jairus, the widow's son, and Lazarus. We read His words in John 5:21: "For as the Father raiseth up the dead, and quickeneth them; even so the Son quickeneth whom he will."

At our Savior's second coming the righteous dead of all ages will rise in glory. "For the Lord himself shall descend from heaven with a shout, with the voice of the archangel, and with the trump of God: and the dead in Christ shall rise first" (1 Thess. 4:16). And they shall be changed, "in a moment, in the twinkling of an eye," from mortality to immortality (1 Cor. 15:52).

But there is another great promise in this text. The hour now is, Jesus said, when many who are dead in trespasses and sins shall hear the voice, the word, of the Son of God. They will believe it too and receive spiritual life through Him. So this also must be included in our promise text for today. It seems to be clearly indicated from the two preceding verses.

This is for us today and now. Speaking of the recorded miracles of Jesus, the apostle John says, "These are written, that ye might believe that Jesus is the Christ, the Son of God; and that believing ye might have life through his name" (John 20:31). Friend, is that eternal life yours by faith?

MEDITATION PRAYER: *"Thou shalt guide me with thy counsel, and afterward receive me to glory" (Ps. 73:24).*

# AUGUST 29

*Verily, verily, I say unto you, He that heareth my word, and believeth on him that sent me, hath everlasting life, and shall not come into condemnation; but is passed from death unto life (John 5:24).*

While in Cairo, William Jennings Bryan obtained a few grains of wheat that had slumbered for more than 30 centuries in an Egyptian tomb. He says: "As I looked at them, this thought came to my mind: If one of those grains had been planted on the banks of the Nile the year after it grew, and all of its lineal descendants had been planted and replanted from that time until now, its progeny would today be sufficiently numerous to feed the teeming millions of the world. An unbroken chain of life connects the earliest grains of wheat with the grains we sow and reap." This illustrates the Word of God revealed in Christ.

"The word of God is the seed. Every seed has in itself a germinating principle. In it the life of the plant is enfolded. So there is life in God's word. Christ says, 'The words that I speak unto you, they are Spirit, and they are life.' John 6:63. 'He that heareth My word, and believeth on Him that sent Me, hath everlasting life.' John 5:24. In every command and in every promise of the word of God is the power, the very life of God, by which the command may be fulfilled and the promise realized. He who by faith receives the word is receiving the very life and character of God" (*Christ's Object Lessons*, p. 38).

True belief is faith. "Faith cometh by hearing, and hearing by the word of God" (Rom. 10:17). The Word of God received in the heart is faith. By His grace we have "passed from death unto life." This everlasting life is for us here and now by faith in His Word. Let us claim God's promise and enter into this experience.

MEDITATION PRAYER: *"Uphold me according unto thy word, that I may live: and let me not be ashamed of my hope" (Ps. 119:116).*

# AUGUST 30

*There is therefore now no condemnation to
them which are in Christ Jesus, who walk
not after the flesh, but after the Spirit (Rom. 8:1).*

Christ is the city of refuge to every believer. "No power can take out of His hands the souls that go to Him for pardon" (*Patriarchs and Prophets,* p. 516). By faith, Christ's righteousness is their righteousness. They are "in Christ." Therefore it is written, "Who is he that condemneth? It is Christ that died, yea rather, that is risen again, who is even at the right hand of God, who also maketh intercession for us" (Rom. 8:34), that "we might have a strong consolation, who have fled for refuge to lay hold upon the hope set before us" (Heb. 6:18).

The very righteousness of the law itself is fulfilled in them. Christ dwells in their hearts by faith, and they in Him.

Seeking righteousness through his own works, the Saxon monk, Martin Luther, deeply impressed with the mighty words of Holy Scripture, seemed to hear in his heart a voice of thunder crying, "The just shall live by faith." These words seemed to follow him everywhere. From Wittenberg to Bologna to Rome, the voice grew more insistent until at last he turned from superstition to the gospel. It was in these words God then said, "Let there be light: and there was light" (Gen. 1:3). This was the birth of the Reformation. May it never die in the world or in our hearts.

"There is . . . no condemnation to them which are in Christ Jesus," because He was condemned in their place. Blessed deliverance! Wondrous message! This is their confidence and assurance as they go forth walking the path of obedience and living the life of trust.

MEDITATION PRAYER: *"Be thou my strong habitation, whereunto I may continually resort: thou hast given commandment to save me; for thou art my rock and my fortress" (Ps. 71:3).*

# AUGUST 31

*In the fear of the Lord is strong confidence:*
*and his children shall have a place of refuge (Prov. 14:26).*

Cities of refuge in ancient Israel were fortified strongholds. They were a symbol of the refuge provided by Christ to every believer. The "fear" of God is faith in Him and in all His Word, and His provision for us is our strong city. The one who fled to the city of refuge had to either stay there or fall prey to the avenger of blood. It is not enough that the sinner believe in Christ and come to Him for pardon. He must by faith and obedience abide in Him. "For if we sin wilfully after that we have received the knowledge of the truth, there remaineth no more sacrifice for sins, but a certain fearful looking for of judgment and fiery indignation" (Heb. 10:26, 27).

Driving over the Simplon Pass from Italy into Switzerland is a never-to-be-forgotten experience. A man was in a tunnel on this road when a great avalanche thundered down the mountainside, but he was perfectly safe because he was hidden inside the rocky heart of the mountain.

There are worse things than avalanches overhanging the path of each of us today—grief, pain, temptation, disappointment, trials, and loss. Where will we hide in the day of trouble? A child is frightened by a strange knock at the door. They run and bury their face in their mother's lap, and are safe. Even so, all believers find in God their safety. The fear of the Lord gives them "strong confidence" when they are troubled, tempted, worried, or in danger. They run to their city of refuge, to the Rock of defense. David said of the Lord, "Thou art my hiding place" (Ps. 119:114).

> O Rock divine, O Refuge dear,
>     A shelter in the time of storm;
> Be Thou our helper, ever near,
>     A shelter in the time of storm.
>                     —Vernon J. Chatsworth

MEDITATION PRAYER: *"Thou art my strong refuge" (Ps. 71:7).*

# SEPTEMBER 1

*And the ransomed of the Lord shall return, and come to Zion with songs and everlasting joy upon their heads: they shall obtain joy and gladness, and sorrow and sighing shall flee away (Isa. 35:10).*

The prophet caught the sound of music there, and song, such music and song as, save in the visions of God, no mortal ear has heard or mind conceived" (*Prophets and Kings*, p. 730). It's a song of salvation, for the ransomed sing it. It's a song of homecoming, for they are in Zion at last. It's a song of joy, for sorrow and sighing and every cause of them are forever gone. Your sorrow, friend, may be deep, inexpressible to others, but you shall have joy and gladness. Your sorrow will be gone. Your sighing will be gone. This is just as certain as tomorrow's sunrise, for both are based on God's promises.

The victors in the Olympic Games considered a crown of wild olive or laurel more honorable than a golden diadem. Think of the crown of these victors, the ransomed of the Lord. Their reward is eternal, a crown of everlasting joy, a crown that never fades, never grows heavy.

In spite of sorrow and sighing here in this old earth, we may look forward with optimism to the new earth with its joy and gladness, toward which God is constantly guiding our lives.

> My life is but the weaving
> > Between my God and me.
> I only choose the colors
> > He weaveth steadily.
> Sometimes He weaveth sorrow
> > And I in foolish pride,
> Forget He sees the upper
> > And I the under side.

And every day God is planning for us the great future, the joy, the gladness, which we may not now see.

MEDITATION PRAYER: *"Make me to hear joy and gladness; that the bones which thou hast broken may rejoice"* (Ps. 51:8).

# SEPTEMBER 2

*And as it is appointed unto men once to die, but after*
*this the judgment: so Christ was once offered to bear the*
*sins of many; and unto them that look for him shall he appear*
*the second time without sin unto salvation (Heb. 9:27, 28).*

That it is appointed unto human beings once to die is a fact of universal knowledge, and it is universally acknowledged. Unbelievers agree with Christians on this point: Everyone dies. But the next statement, "after this the judgment," we can know only from revelation. After death the next experience of every human being will be the judgment. Are we ready for it? We must face it. Yes, we must face Christ in judgment, for God "hath committed all judgment unto the Son" (John 5:22).

But here is another promise: Christ, who was once offered to bear the sins of humanity, will "appear the second time without sin unto salvation." This is the blessed hope. He who bore our sins upon the cross will again be manifested. He will come in power and glory as "King of kings, and Lord of lords" (Rev. 19:16). Those who have accepted His atoning sacrifice for sin upon the cross will behold Him with joy. They will "be changed, in a moment, in the twinkling of an eye, at the last trump" (1 Cor. 15:51, 52). They "shall be like him; for . . . [they] shall see him as he is" (1 John 3:2). But to those blinded by sin and their own selfishness, He will appear as the judge they cannot bear to see. Sir Walter Scott wrote of that time, that hour, that day:

> The day of wrath, that dreadful day,
> When heaven and earth shall pass away!
> What power shall be the sinner's stay?
> How shall he meet that dreadful day?

The way to meet it is in Christ, in the blessed hope. We must first look *to* Him, and then we shall look *for* Him. Life is a preparation for a greater life.

MEDITATION PRAYER: *"Thou satest in the throne judging right" (Ps. 9:4).*

# SEPTEMBER 3

*But he knoweth the way that I take: when he*
*hath tried me, I shall come forth as gold (Job 23:10).*

There are three wonderful parts to this promise: God knows our way, He will try us, and we shall come forth as gold. A patient who has confidence in a physician will willingly endure much suffering inflicted in order to be cured. If we settle it once and for all that God knows what He is doing and what is good for us, then we can endure the trial, realizing that His eye is watching over us.

Is it not written that God "shall sit as a refiner and purifier of silver" (Mal. 3:3)? Like a refiner of gold He watches the precious metal in the crucible. Hotter and hotter grows the fire. Clearer and more shining grows the metal. Bit by bit the dross is melted away and separated from the gold. At last refiners see their own image perfectly reflected in the pure molten mirror. Then it is taken from the fire to its proper use. How like the life of a Christian! How often the fires of tribulation, of test, of suffering, burn! Hotter and hotter they become until the children of God reflect the image of their Lord and come forth as gold.

God does not promise that we shall never be in trouble, but He does say of His child, "I will be with him in trouble" (Ps. 91:15). Joseph, the victim of injustice, with reputation blackened, was cast into an Egyptian prison, but the Lord was with him (Gen. 39:21). When the three young Hebrews were in the fiery furnace, "the form of the fourth . . . like the Son of God" was with them (Dan. 3:25).

So let us always remember that God knows the way we take. He steps unseen with us. In our trial He is with us, always with us.

"I don't know what is in the future," said a Salvation Army member, "but I know the Lord is in the future; and I know I am in the Lord."

What more than that do any of us need?

MEDITATION PRAYER: *"For thou, O God, hast proved us: thou hast tried us, as silver is tried" (Ps. 66:10).*

# SEPTEMBER 4

*Then Jesus beholding him loved him, and said unto him,*
*One thing thou lackest: go thy way, sell whatsoever thou*
*hast, and give to the poor, and thou shalt have treasure in*
*heaven: and come, take up the cross, and follow me (Mark 10:21).*

Just think what this young man had—youth, money, popularity, the special love of Christ. He was religious, he was moral. He was athletic, for he *ran* to Jesus. Yet he lacked one thing—the worship of the true God. He had an idol—his possessions.

Our Savior told him that if he would enter into life, he must keep the commandments (Matt. 19:17), and He quoted from the second table of the law, our duty to others. When He suggested that His inquirer sell all that he had and give to the poor, the young man went away *"very* sorrowful: for he was *very* rich" (Luke 18:23). He wouldn't make the sacrifice. He wouldn't give up his false god.

What a great worker for God this young man would have made with his talents and possessions. How much he could have done for the infant church and for the struggling cause of the gospel.

Bernard Palissy, who lived in the sixteenth century, experimented to recover the lost art of porcelain enamel, and in so doing was reduced to great financial distress. The world laughed at him, but at last he was certain that he had discovered the right formula. According to legend, he needed only a small piece of gold to mix with the other ingredients. But he was poor and had no gold. At last his wife came to his help, and by a beautiful act of loyalty and sacrifice showed that she believed in him. She took off her wedding ring and dropped it into the crucible. That was all that was needed to attain perfect success.

So our Savior asks us to sacrifice ourselves to Him and for Him, but many find it hard to do. Yet those who sacrifice what they treasure most will find that their loss is gain and that life thereafter is forever glorified.

MEDITATION PRAYER: *"I will freely sacrifice unto thee: I will praise thy name, O Lord; for it is good"* (Ps. 54:6).

# SEPTEMBER 5

*Be of good courage, and he shall strengthen your*
*heart, all ye that hope in the Lord (Ps. 31:24).*

The Bible is full of examples of courage—Abraham with his servants defeating the armies of the kings, Joshua invading Palestine, David meeting Goliath, Daniel in the lions' den, the three Hebrews in the fire, the apostles before the council, Stephen before his murderers, Paul before Nero, Jesus before Pilate.

If we use the courage we have, the Lord will give us more. He will strengthen us. If we are courageous in the Lord, we may expect that He will give us the help we need and will strengthen our hearts with faith and trust in Him.

When someone urged our Savior to flee from a certain place, saying, "Herod will kill thee," Jesus said, "Go ye, and tell that fox, Behold, I cast out devils, and I do cures to day and to morrow, and the third day I shall be perfected" (Luke 13:31, 32). What did He mean? He meant that God had given Him a work to do, and until that work was done, neither Herod, Pilate, Caesar, nor the devil himself could hurt Him.

And so all those who trust in the Lord and believe His Word need have no fear whatever when they are doing God's work and living the life God wants them to live.

Sir W. H. Russell, a war correspondent, speaks of the courage of General Gordon in the Crimean War. One day the Russians actually reached the English trench, and there stood General Gordon on the parapet with nothing but a stick in his hand, encouraging the soldiers to drive out the enemy.

"Gordon," his men cried, "come down! Come down!" But he took no notice. Then one of the soldiers was heard saying to his comrade: "It's all right—'e don't mind bein' killed; 'e's one of those Christians."

MEDITATION PRAYER: *"Let thy mercy, O Lord, be upon us, according as we hope in thee" (Ps. 33:22).*

# SEPTEMBER 6

*For thus saith the Lord God, the Holy One of Israel; In
returning and rest shall ye be saved; in quietness and in
confidence shall be your strength: and ye would not (Isa. 30:15).*

The children of Israel would not accept God's plan, but we may.
The worrying, fretting, questioning, tense, disturbed, troubled,
fearing mind is the curse of our day. Many are like swimmers going
down by struggling when they might float by faith. It is often well to
keep a quiet tongue, but how much better to have a quiet heart.
Remember the scripture that says, "Be still, and know that I am God:
. . . I will be exalted in the earth" (Ps. 46:10).

And confidence goes with quietness. During an earthquake the inhabitants of a small town were greatly disturbed and alarmed. At the
same time they were surprised to see the quietness and apparent calmness of an old woman who was well known among them. Someone
asked her if she wasn't afraid.

"No," said this mother in Israel. "I am happy to know that I have
a God who can shake the world."

Confidence is really faith and trust in God.

We may safely "trust . . . in the Lord for ever: for in the Lord
Jehovah is everlasting strength" (Isa. 26:4). Jesus said, "Heaven and
earth shall pass away, but my words shall not pass away" (Matt. 24:35).
That is our strength—confidence and faith in His strength.

Let us return to the old faith, the old trust, and find rest to our souls.

> I am resting, sweetly resting:
> 'Tis the safest place for me
> To be resting in the shadow
> Of the cross of Calvary.
>
> —F. E. Belden

MEDITATION PRAYER: *"By terrible things in righteousness
wilt thou answer us, O God of our salvation; who art the confidence of all the
ends of the earth, and of them that are afar off upon the sea" (Ps. 65:5).*

# SEPTEMBER 7

*For in the time of trouble he shall hide me in his*
*pavilion: in the secret of his tabernacle shall he*
*hide me; he shall set me up upon a rock (Ps. 27:5).*

There is no promise in the Bible that God's children will never have trouble, but here is a promise that in the time of trouble they may be hidden "in his pavilion: in the secret of his tabernacle." It is also promised in that great psalm of the time of trouble, the ninety-first: "He shall cover thee with his feathers, and under his wings shalt thou trust: his truth shall be thy shield and buckler" (verse 4).

Under His wings, what a refuge in sorrow!
How the heart yearningly turns to its rest!
Often when earth has no balm for my healing,
There I find comfort, and there I am blest.
—W. O. Cushing

God's providential protection is over His believers. They are hid under the shadow of His wings, in the secret of His tabernacle; but more, God will set their feet upon a rock. David experienced this, for he says of God: "He brought me up also out of an horrible pit, out of the miry clay, and set my feet upon a rock, and established my goings" (Ps. 40:2).

While under great mental depression a minister read this quotation from Luther: "I would run into the arms of Christ, though He stood with a drawn sword in His hand." He immediately thought of the words of Job, "Though he slay me, yet will I trust in him" (Job 13:15). His burden dropped, and he was filled with joy and peace in believing.

What we need today is adventuresome believing, trusting in times of trouble, standing upon the rock of absolute confidence in the Lord.

MEDITATION PRAYER: *"I will abide in thy tabernacle for ever: I will trust in the covert of thy wings" (Ps. 61:4).*

# SEPTEMBER 8

*And I heard a voice from heaven saying unto me, Write, Blessed are the dead which die in the Lord from henceforth: Yea, saith the Spirit, that they may rest from their labours; and their works do follow them (Rev. 14:13).*

To the people of God, death is but a momentary sleep from which they wake to life immortal. Longfellow said, "The grave itself is but a covered bridge leading from light to light, through a brief darkness."

Notice the three things promised to the dead in Christ: first, they are blessed; second, they rest from their labors and troubles; third, their works follow them. All who die in the Lord enter into blessedness. So if we live, we have the joy of God's service; if we die, we are blessed.

Those who die in the Lord find rest from labor—the hard labor, the unpaid labor that sometimes seems to be so useless, yet is not so in the Lord's sight.

But that isn't all—"their works do follow them." Drop a pebble into a pool, and the circling ripples reach out to all sides. Say a word, even think a thought, and its reverberations continue on and on into eternity. How much more, then, the works of God's children! Their deeds of kindness, their gifts of sacrifice, reach on to the eternity that awaits God's redeemed.

Notice also the word "henceforth"; that is, from the time the great threefold message of the preceding verses goes to the world. From the time that this message starts, those who die in the Lord are especially blessed. How wonderful it is to carry a message that blesses even those who die in it, as well as those who remain alive until the return of our Savior.

Someday soon it will be moving day for all of us—out of the palace, out of the beautiful home, out of the fine apartment, out of the tiny cabin, out of the attic, into "an house not made with hands, eternal in the heavens" (2 Cor. 5:1). Yes, it will be moving day.

MEDITATION PRAYER: *"How precious also are thy thoughts unto me, O God! how great is the sum of them!" (Ps. 139:17).*

# SEPTEMBER 9

*But they that wait upon the Lord shall renew their strength;*
*they shall mount up with wings as eagles; they shall run,*
*and not be weary; and they shall walk, and not faint (Isa. 40:31).*

They that wait upon the Lord are the servants of the Lord. They are to fly, and it takes strength to fly. In spiritual things not many of God's children "mount up with wings as eagles," but some do, and their strength is from God.

But here's a place for more of them, those who run in His service. Those who "wait upon the Lord . . . shall run, and not be weary." Obedience to the Word of God sustains us in the race of life. "I will run the way of thy commandments, when thou shalt enlarge my heart" (Ps. 119:32).

Most of us must walk, but that is the greatest accomplishment of all. The promise is "They shall walk, and not faint." The most difficult place in which to represent Christ is in the humdrum routine of everyday life. Those who mount up with wings as eagles have a great deal of encouragement and the thrill of accomplishment. They that run experience the speed, reach the goal, receive the applause of the onlookers. But they that walk—that's different! Someone has written a book entitled *Blessed Be Drudgery,* but about the only thing blessed in drudgery is that we may know the Blessed One, who will give us strength to walk and not faint.

Jesus did not ride on His missionary journeys. He walked the dusty roads of Palestine, and finally His feet were nailed to the cross. If He could walk and not faint, so by His strength can we. One step at a time, one step after another, and at last we reach the gate of the city. Among millions in this motorized age walking has become a lost art, and unfortunately it is becoming a lost art spiritually in many cases. Those who walk in the light of truth here will walk in the light of the Holy City (Rev. 21:24).

MEDITATION PRAYER: *"Cause me to know the way wherein I should walk; for I lift up my soul unto thee" (Ps. 143:8).*

# SEPTEMBER 10

*Because thou hast kept the word of my patience, I also will keep thee from the hour of temptation, which shall come upon all the world, to try them that dwell upon the earth (Rev. 3:10).*

Do we keep the word of His patience? And can we expect His keeping power in the hour of temptation, which is about to come upon all the world? In Revelation 14:12 we read: "Here is the patience of the saints: here are they that keep the commandments of God, and the faith of Jesus." The hour of temptation and trial is just before us.

In these days when the signs of the times proclaim that the coming of the Lord is near, this promise of the Savior is very dear, because the words of the next verse are: "Behold, I come quickly: hold that fast which thou hast, that no man take thy crown."

If we keep Christ's word, He will keep us. A man in a dream once saw himself in a glass cage surrounded by furious foes. They sought with all manner of weapons to destroy him, but their weapons could not pierce the glass wall, so he looked out upon them with safety. That is how it is with the Christian. Jesus said: "These things I have spoken unto you, that in me ye might have peace. In the world ye shall have tribulation: but be of good cheer; I have overcome the world" (John 16:33).

As the Israelites were safe in their houses under the mark of the blood when the destroying angel passed over, so God's people will be safe in this hour of trial and trouble that will come upon all the earth. The Lord's gracious invitation is: "Come, my people, enter thou into thy chambers, and shut thy doors about thee: hide thyself as it were for a little moment, until the indignation be overpast. For, behold, the Lord cometh out of his place to punish the inhabitants of the earth for their iniquity: the earth also shall disclose her blood, and shall no more cover her slain" (Isa. 26:20, 21). Those who have kept His word will be kept by the Word.

MEDITATION PRAYER: *"Thou art my hiding place and my shield: I hope in thy word" (Ps. 119:114).*

# SEPTEMBER 11

*Commit thy works unto the Lord, and*
*thy thoughts shall be established (Prov. 16:3).*

Committing our works, our doings, our plans—ourselves—once and for all to the hands of God takes away every cause for worry and concern. Our thoughts will be established, because we know that we belong to the Lord and He is watching over us, guiding us, sustaining us. The Scriptures declare: "As [a man] thinketh in his heart, so is he" (Prov. 23:7). And again: "Out of the . . . heart the mouth speaketh" (Matt. 12:34).

Someone has said, "Whatever is in the well of our thoughts will come up in the bucket of our speech." When our thoughts are established, our works will be guided. Everything, then, depends upon the committal of the life to God. Our thoughts' being established will react upon our works, so that altogether we shall be His. We must remember that thoughts are things, or at least become things.

The last words of Johann Herder, court preacher at Weimar and one of the most brilliant German authors, were: "Refresh me with a great thought."

After enumerating many excellent and praiseworthy things, the apostle commands, "Think on these things" (Phil. 4:8).

Charles Dickens based his lifework upon this principle: "Whatever I have tried to do in my life, I have tried with all my heart to do well. What I have devoted myself to, I have devoted myself to completely. Never to put one hand to anything on which I would not throw my whole self; never to affect depreciation of my work, whatever it was, I find now to have been golden rules."

When our works are committed to God, our thoughts will be established. We will do all that we have to do with our might, whether it be great things or small. Then life can be only a success. Have we committed our works to the Lord?

MEDITATION PRAYER: *"Let the beauty of the Lord our God be upon us: and establish thou the work of our hands" (Ps. 90:17).*

# SEPTEMBER 12

*Turn you to the strong hold, ye prisoners of hope: even to day do I declare that I will render double unto thee (Zech. 9:12).*

The prisoners of hope are to turn to their Stronghold. In times of distress and perplexity the unbelieving, who are not prisoners of hope, do not turn to the Stronghold. Their hearts fail them "for looking after those things which are coming on the earth" (Luke 21:26). Those who have not made God their refuge will not have Him for their consolation. Christ is our stronghold, and our hope is in Him. This promise is for those living in these last days.

In Micah 4:8 we read: "And thou, O tower of the flock, the strong hold of the daughter of Zion, unto thee shall it come, even the first dominion." The Babe of Bethlehem is to be the King of kings. The dominion lost in Adam is to be restored in Christ. The sufferings of God's people through all the ages will be rewarded double unto them in the eternal kingdom of heaven.

This promise text brings to mind the words of Jesus to the dying thief on the cross. When all had rejected or forsaken the Savior, this criminal called Him "Lord." Then, from the cross as from a throne, the Savior issued the decree of His kingdom that this trusting soul, who in the eleventh hour had thrown himself upon his dying Lord, should be with Him in Paradise. He will indeed be remembered when the Lord comes in His kingdom. And that decree was dated "today"—"Verily I say unto thee *today.*" So the cross dates every promise to the child of God and stamps it with authenticity.

God's children may be strangers in a foreign land, some of them even in the prisonhouse of death, but they are all prisoners of hope—"that blessed hope" (Titus 2:13).

MEDITATION PRAYER: *"My soul fainteth for thy salvation: but I hope in thy word" (Ps. 119:81).*

# SEPTEMBER 13

*He that covereth his sins shall not prosper: but whoso confesseth and forsaketh them shall have mercy (Prov. 28:13).*

This is the way of mercy—confession of sin, forsaking of sin. Those who cover their sins are tempted to falsify. They are guilty of hypocrisy in concealing or justifying their sins, or even in making a loud profession to compensate for them.

In confessing our sins we must be honest with the Lord. We must not only acknowledge our wrong but have a sense of its evil and deplore it. We must not blame others or even our own circumstances or weakness. Then we must forsake the evil thing and all places, companions, books, radio and television broadcasts, or whatever will lead us back into sin. Some confess but do not forsake their sin. It is still in them. And remember, we are not forgiven as payment for our confession or reformation, but only through the blood and grace of Christ.

A little girl playing in the park was frightened by a great dog that came bounding along, barking furiously. She burst out crying, and her mother could not pacify her. "See," said the mother, "the dog has stopped barking. Why don't you stop crying?"

The little girl looked around at the dog and, still sobbing, said, "Yes, Mama, but the bark is still in him."

Some earnestly try to reach the City of God, but hold on to some one sin. They are like some drunken sailors who, on a dark night, were returning to their ship. They got into their little boat, which was tied to the wharf, drew out the oars, and began to row. They rowed and rowed, but still their ship did not appear. At last the soberest of them discovered that they had not untied the mooring rope. God asks us not only to row but to cut loose from sin. Then, "if we confess our sins, he is faithful and just to forgive us our sins" (1 John 1:9).

MEDITATION PRAYER: *"Unto thee, O Lord, belongeth mercy: for thou renderest to every man according to his work" (Ps. 62:12).*

# SEPTEMBER 14

*Thy dead men shall live, together with my dead body shall they arise. Awake and sing, ye that dwell in dust: for thy dew is as the dew of herbs, and the earth shall cast out the dead (Isa. 26:19).*

This is the day of which the apostle Paul spoke, when "the Lord himself shall descend from heaven with a shout, with the voice of the archangel, and with the trump of God: and the dead in Christ shall rise first" (1 Thess. 4:16).

In our promise text death is pictured as a sleep, for the prophet says, *"Awake* and sing, ye that dwell in dust." The awakened saints, immortalized, will sing victory over death and the grave. When "this mortal shall have put on immortality," "in a moment, in the twinkling of an eye, at the last trump," "then shall be brought to pass the saying that is written, Death is swallowed up in victory" (1 Cor. 15:52, 54).

What a future this prophecy unrolls before us! Sometimes even Christians, speaking of a believer who has died, will say, "Our dear friend has gone to his final resting place." Let us never believe that for a moment! The grave is not the final resting place of any Christian. It is just the couch where they sleep through the night waiting for the resurrection morning, which has no shadow.

A converted Japanese artist said recently to a Christian worker, "I suppose the reason English artists put so much perspective into their drawings is that Christianity has given them a future, and the reason Oriental artists fail to do so is that Buddha and Confucius do not raise their eyes above the present."

So let us look forward in faith into "the great beyond, the wide, unbounded future of glory that is for the redeemed" (*Testimonies for the Church,* vol. 9, p. 288).

MEDITATION PRAYER: *"Consider and hear me, O Lord my God: lighten mine eyes, lest I sleep the sleep of death" (Ps. 13:3).*

# SEPTEMBER 15

*The Lord is nigh unto them that are of a broken heart;
and saveth such as be of a contrite spirit (Ps. 34:18).*

If we have not experienced that repentance which is not to be repented of, and have not with true humiliation of soul and brokenness of spirit confessed our sins, abhorring our iniquity, we have never truly sought for the forgiveness of sin" (*Steps to Christ,* p. 38).

The contrite soul is the repentant soul. In the following symbolic poem by Dante, he pictures the three steps of repentance: contrition, confession, satisfaction:

> Thither did we draw nigh, and that first stair
> Was of white marble, polished so and clean,
> It mirrored all my features as they were.
> The second, darker than dusk, perverse, was seen,
> Of stone all rugged, rough and coarse in grain,
> With many a crack, its length and breadth between.
> The third, which o'er the others towers amain,
> Appeared as if fiery porphyry,
> Like blood that gushes crimson from the vein.

Contrition, like the polished marble, reveals people to themselves, opens their eyes to their true condition, tears away their make-believe. The second step—"darker than dusk," and all rugged and coarse and cracked—represents confession, the tearing up of the roots of guilt and the spreading of the black iniquities before God. The third step, made of "fiery porphyry, like blood," is satisfaction, the offering up of self as a sacrifice and the receiving of Christ's atonement, thus cleansing the soul. Only when one takes these three steps can there be true repentance. The Lord is near to those who are brokenhearted because of their sins.

MEDITATION PRAYER: *"Against thee, thee only, have I sinned, and done this evil in thy sight: that thou mightest be justified when thou speakest, and be clear when thou judgest" (Ps. 51:4).*

# SEPTEMBER 16

*With my soul have I desired thee in the night; yea, with my spirit
within me will I seek thee early: for when thy judgments are in the
earth, the inhabitants of the world will learn righteousness (Isa. 26:9).*

In this promise is a warning to individuals and to the world. There are
those who seek God earnestly. When they awake in the night seasons
they pray and commune with Him. Early in the morning, and early in
life, they seek God in spirit. But there are thousands—yes, millions—
who never learn of His ways, never think of God, never desire to know
Him, until great judgments and afflictions suddenly face them and they
are overwhelmed.

So it was at the Flood, the destruction of Sodom and Gomorrah,
the captivity in Egypt, the overthrow of Jerusalem, the Babylonian captivity, the destruction of Jerusalem by the Romans, the persecutions
down through the ages, world wars, and confusion. When God's judgments are in the earth, the true child of God may be assured of His care
and protection. "He shall cover thee with his feathers, and under his
wings shalt thou trust: his truth shall be thy shield and buckler" (Ps.
91:4). Do we truly seek God? Do we long for communion with Him
day and night? He is not far from any of us.

For an orchestra to produce a perfect chord of music, it is necessary
that the instruments be attuned to one another. When, after perfect ad-
justment, the notes are struck, there is no jarring dissonance, but perfect harmony. So, before there can be harmonious living and true
communion with God, our wills must be attuned to His in loving du-
tifulness and submission.

> Our wills are ours, we know not how;
> Our wills are ours, to make them thine.
> —Alfred, Lord Tennyson

MEDITATION PRAYER: *"My mouth shall praise thee with joy-
ful lips: when I remember thee upon my bed, and meditate on thee in the night
watches" (Ps. 63:5, 6).*

# SEPTEMBER 17

*I will instruct thee and teach thee in the way which
thou shalt go: I will guide thee with mine eye (Ps. 32:8).*

This is a threefold promise direct from the mouth of the Lord: I will instruct thee; I will teach thee; I will guide thee. Christian workers are laborers together with God. Think of the wonderful privilege it is for them to be instructed by Him, to be taught by Him in their work, and to be guided by Him every day and every hour. When we walk humbly with God, we may ask Him to make our course of duty plain, and He will guide us with His eye.

A guide was conducting a group of tourists through Mammoth Cave, in Kentucky. When they reached the great room known as the Cathedral, he mounted the rock called the Pulpit and said he was going to preach a sermon. It was very short—just these five words: "Keep close to your guide."

The visitors soon found that it was a good sermon, for if they did not keep close to their guide they would be lost in the pits and defiles, or over the precipices. One cannot find their way through that dark cavern without a guide, but it is harder still to find one's way through the dark world without a guide—without the heavenly Guide, without His Word, which is a lamp unto our feet and a light unto our path (Ps. 119:105).

This divine guidance is not just for one day, but for all our days. "And the Lord shall guide thee continually" (Isa. 58:11). He will guide us into peace (Luke 1:79). He will guide us into truth (John 16:13). He will guide us on every side (2 Chron. 32:22).

Concerning our yesterdays, faith says, "Thou hast beset me behind"; concerning our tomorrows, "Thou hast beset me . . . before"; concerning today, "Thou hast . . . laid thine hand upon me" (Ps. 139:5). That's enough for us—to feel the presence of His guiding hand, our Instructor, our Teacher, our heavenly Guide.

MEDITATION PRAYER: *"For thou art my rock and my fortress; therefore for thy name's sake lead me, and guide me" (Ps. 31:3).*

266

# SEPTEMBER 18

*Let us therefore come boldly unto the throne of grace, that we may obtain mercy, and find grace to help in time of need (Heb. 4:16).*

The word "therefore" in our text refers to the preceding verses, which tell us that our Savior was tempted in all points like as we are, that He has gone into heaven, and appears there for us. "Therefore" we may "come boldly unto the throne of grace." In other words, our prayers may be based upon these facts.

That throne is not only a throne of majesty, power, righteousness, and glory but a throne of grace; and it is by grace through faith that we are saved (Eph. 2:8). Coming boldly to this throne, we obtain mercy and find grace in every time of need. It is the things we need that we are to receive, and we shall receive them when we need them—"in time of need." Nothing is too small, nothing too great. If we need something, we are to ask for it.

It is said that a man once asked Alexander the Great to give him some money, a portion for his daughter at her marriage. The king told him to go to his treasurer and demand it. He went and asked for an enormous amount. The treasurer was startled. He said that he could not give so much without a direct order from the king, and then he went at once to Alexander and told him that he thought a small part of the money should suffice.

"No," replied Alexander, "let him have it all. I like that man. He does me honor. He treats me like a king and proves by what he asks for that he believes me to be both rich and generous."

So let us go to the throne of grace *boldly*. Let us pray in a way that shows we have honorable views of our King's riches and bounty, and that we have faith in His promises.

MEDITATION PRAYER: *"Bow down thine ear, O Lord, hear me: for I am poor and needy" (Ps. 86:1).*

# SEPTEMBER 19

*The Lord will perfect that which concerneth me:*
*thy mercy, O Lord, endureth for ever: forsake not*
*the works of thine own hands (Ps. 138:8).*

Everything that concerns us concerns the Lord. "Nothing is too great for Him to bear. . . . Nothing that in any way concerns our peace is too small for Him to notice" (*Steps to Christ,* p. 100).

He does not begin a good work and then leave it unfinished. Our own evil hearts, the world, and the devil may attempt to hinder Him, but His work for us goes on day after day. By His providences, by His Holy Spirit, by His Holy Word, He is working out our eternal good. Of this we can be sure. As the apostle says: "Being confident of this very thing, that he which hath begun a good work in you will perform it ["will finish it," margin] until the day of Jesus Christ" (Phil. 1:6).

His mercy endures today and tomorrow and forever.

A mother seeking her son's pardon from Emperor Napoleon was told that since this was his second offense, justice demanded his death.

"But I don't ask for justice," she cried. "I plead for mercy."

"But," said the emperor, "he doesn't deserve mercy."

"Sire," replied the mother, "it wouldn't be mercy if he deserved it. Mercy is all I ask for."

"Well, then," said Napoleon, "I will have mercy." And the son was granted a pardon.

"It is of the Lord's mercies that we are not consumed, because his compassions fail not. They are new every morning: great is thy faithfulness" (Lam. 3:22, 23). We belong to Christ by creation and re-creation, so we can pray, "Forsake not the works of thine own hands."

MEDITATION PRAYER: *"Hear me, O Lord; for thy lovingkindness is good: turn unto me according to the multitude of thy tender mercies" (Ps. 69:16).*

# SEPTEMBER 20

*And the inhabitant shall not say, I am sick: the people
that dwell therein shall be forgiven their iniquity (Isa. 33:24).*

It was the entrance of sin into the world that brought sickness and death. When the last stain of sin is washed from the earth, there will be no more sickness, sorrow, heartbreak, or death. A troubled mind often leads to sickness. Dis-ease of mind and heart brings disease of body. And we are told that "a merry heart doeth good like a medicine" (Prov. 17:22). All true believers have discovered this. When the burden of sin is lifted from the heart by faith in Jesus Christ as our Redeemer, there is often a great increase in health of the body.

The time will come, as our promise declares, when in God's new earth the inhabitants will not say "I am sick," because there will be no sickness. Who are these people? Are they those who have never sinned? No, indeed. They are those who have been forgiven their iniquity. And that forgiveness is for us now, for "if we confess our sins, he is faithful and just to forgive us our sins" (1 John 1:9).

Years ago a man who was a very great sinner was executed in Ayr, Scotland, for his terrible wickedness. Those who knew him thought he had gone beyond the grace of God. While he was in prison he saw his own wickedness and, after great heart struggle, surrendered to God. When he came to the place of his execution, he could not refrain from crying out to the onlookers concerning his sense of pardon and the presence of God. "Oh, He is a great forgiver!" he said. "God is a great forgiver!" Then he added these words: "And now 'perfect love casteth out fear' [1 John 4:18]. I know that God has nothing to lay against me, for Jesus Christ has paid it all."

Because He is a great forgiver, in Him we have eternal hope.

MEDITATION PRAYER: *"If thou, Lord, shouldest mark iniquities, O Lord, who shall stand? But there is forgiveness with thee" (Ps. 130:3, 4).*

# SEPTEMBER 21

*And they shall see his face; and his name*
*shall be in their foreheads (Rev. 22:4).*

The words of our text remind us of 1 John 3:2: "Beloved, now are we the sons of God, and it doth not yet appear what we shall be: but we know that, when he shall appear, we shall be like him; for we shall see him as he is." Surely in His presence will be fullness of joy (Ps. 16:11).

Jesus spoke of the blessedness of the pure in heart, who will see God (Matt. 5:8). Moses asked to see the face of God, but this petition was not granted. It will at last be the privilege of every Christian to see the face of Him "whom having not seen, ye love" (1 Peter 1:8).

A young man fell in love with, and married, a young woman who was blind. For years they lived together happily. Finally a delicate operation was performed and she received her sight. His was the first face she ever saw. For some time she wanted to do nothing else but sit and look at him. "Is he as handsome as you had imagined?" someone asked.

"Oh, yes," she said. "I have imagined wonderful things of him. He has been so kind and his love has been so faithful. But he is far more handsome, far more noble, than I had ever dreamed."

What will it be to see the face of Christ? The redeemed will see Him because His name, His character, is written on their foreheads.

When the men of India visit a temple, they often emerge with the name of the god written across their forehead—Siva, Vishnu, or Kali. These names must be written by someone else, for the gods cannot write them. But the name on the foreheads of the saints mentioned in our text for today is written by the eternal God Himself. By His grace, may we bear that blessed name forever.

MEDITATION PRAYER: *"Thou, O Lord, art in the midst of us, and we are called by thy name; leave us not" (Jer. 14:9).*

# SEPTEMBER 22

*Bring my soul out of prison, that I may praise*
*thy name: the righteous shall compass me about;*
*for thou shalt deal bountifully with me (Ps. 142:7).*

A prison is a symbol of overwhelming trouble and affliction, even of the grave itself. Joseph was overwhelmed with trouble and was in prison literally, but the Lord brought him forth to be a ruler of the land. The Scripture declares, "The Lord looseth the prisoners" (Ps. 146:7). Through the Holy Spirit and the ministry of Noah in the days before the Flood, Christ preached to those in the prisonhouse of sin. Again He preached to them on the Sabbath day in Nazareth, where He had been brought up, as we read in the fourth chapter of Luke. Quoting from the sixty-first chapter of Isaiah, our Savior preached deliverance to the captives in the synagogue that day, and closing the book, He said to the congregation, "This day is this scripture fulfilled in your ears" (Luke 4:21).

So it may be with each of us this very day, September 22. We may be brought out of prison and praise God's name. We may receive His bountiful mercies and enjoy the fellowship of His children. How much more in heaven at last will the righteous gather as we praise the name of the Lord together!

There are many today who are at liberty physically, but their souls are in prison; they live in darkness and in chains.

When an ambassador for Queen Elizabeth I was being sent far away on some important and difficult business, he asked Her Majesty, "What will become of my own business and family?"

The queen replied, "You take care of my business, and I will take care of yours."

If we are doing God's work, He will certainly care for our interests. He will deal bountifully with us.

MEDITATION PRAYER: *"Let the sighing of the prisoner come before thee; according to the greatness of thy power preserve thou those that are appointed to die" (Ps. 79:11).*

271

# SEPTEMBER 23

*For this is the covenant that I will make with the house*
*of Israel after those days, saith the Lord; I will put my*
*laws into their mind, and write them in their hearts: and I will*
*be to them a God, and they shall be to me a people (Heb. 8:10).*

This is nothing less than the promise of the gospel. What we try to do and cannot do, God promises to do and does do for us. The natural human being "is not subject to the law of God, neither indeed can be" (Rom. 8:7). But God Himself writes His law in the heart. This is conversion and regeneration.

Every true believer is "the epistle of Christ . . . written not with ink, but with the Spirit of the living God; not in tables of stone, but in fleshy tables of the heart" (2 Cor. 3:3). The Spirit writes the law of God in the heart "that the righteousness of the law might be fulfilled in us, who walk not after the flesh, but after the Spirit" (Rom. 8:4). Such consecrated Christians are "in Christ," and Christ dwells in them by faith.

Campbell Morgan tells of visiting in a home in which he always smelled the strong fragrance of roses. One day he asked his host the reason for this. The reply was: "While in the Holy Land 10 years ago, I bought a small tube of attar of roses. It was wrapped in cotton wool and, as I was standing here unpacking it, I broke the bottle. I put the broken container, cotton wool, and all, into that vase on the mantel." There stood the beautiful vase, and as the lid was lifted, fragrance filled the room. The perfume had permeated the clay of the vase, and it was impossible for one entering the room not to be conscious of it.

If Christ is given preeminence in the life of a Christian, the fragrance of the Rose of Sharon will pervade, permeate, and bless the entire life, and others will be conscious of the presence of One unseen.

MEDITATION PRAYER: *"I have longed for thy salvation, O Lord; and thy law is my delight"* (Ps. 119:174).

# SEPTEMBER 24

*Verily I say unto you, Whosoever shall not receive the kingdom of God as a little child, he shall not enter therein (Mark 10:15).*

When Dwight L. Moody was in Scotland, a friend told him of a Scotch lass who came to the inquiry room as he was preaching. The minister there talked with her and said, "Young woman, you go home and read the fifty-third chapter of Isaiah."

The girl threw up her hands and said, "I cannot read; I cannot pray. Jesus, take me as I am."

"And," said the great evangelist, "she found what she desired."

In our text today Jesus says not merely "child," but "little child." We are to receive the kingdom of God as a little child would receive it—in sincerity, in complete faith and trust, and with humility. And how do we become as little children in the sense of this promise text? The answer is in Matthew 18:3, 4: "Verily I say unto you, Except ye be converted, and become as little children, ye shall not enter into the kingdom of heaven. Whosoever therefore shall humble himself as this little child, the same is greatest in the kingdom of heaven."

To have a part in Christ's kingdom one must become converted and live in humility, with victory over human pride.

> Lord, might I be but as a saw,
> A plane, a chisel in Thy hand.
> No, Lord, I take it back in awe;
> Such prayer for me is far too grand.
> I pray Thee, rather, let me lie
> As on Thy bench the favored wood;
> Thy saw, Thy plane, Thy chisel ply
> And work me into something good.
> —George Macdonald

MEDITATION PRAYER: *"Lord, my heart is not haughty, nor mine eyes lofty: neither do I exercise myself in great matters, or in things too high for me" (Ps. 131:1).*

# SEPTEMBER 25

*But the hour cometh, and now is, when the true*
*worshippers shall worship the Father in spirit and in truth:*
*for the Father seeketh such to worship him (John 4:23).*

These were the words of Jesus to the woman at the well and to all people everywhere. True worship is not merely in form; it must be in spirit and in truth. It was true in the time of our Savior's earthly life; it is true now; and it will be true until the end of time.

Religious forms of worship, the service of the mere natural human being, "cannot please God. But ye are not in the flesh, but in the Spirit, if so be that the Spirit of God dwell in you. Now if any man have not the Spirit of Christ, he is none of his" (Rom. 8:8, 9).

A missionary writer tells of one of the great temples in Japan where the worship consists of running around the sacred building 100 times and dropping a piece of wood in a box at each round. To some this may seem to be a very unspiritual worship, but what is the difference between that and going to church, sitting quietly listening to what the minister says, then going back home again, unless we go with the definite purpose to worship, unless we bow our hearts as well as our heads before God, unless we listen reverently, ready to obey the voice of God speaking to us from His Word, unless we commune with Him in prayer? How are we better than the earnest runner?

Our worship is to be in spirit and in truth, a spiritual worship and a true worship. It must be founded upon the Word of Him who said, "I am the way, the truth, and the life" (John 14:6). In reference to our worship of God, it would be well for us to pray, as did the psalmist, "Let the words of my mouth, and the meditation of my heart, be acceptable in thy sight, O Lord, my strength, and my redeemer" (Ps. 19:14).

MEDITATION PRAYER: *"I will praise thee, O Lord my God, with all my heart: and I will glorify thy name for evermore" (Ps. 86:12).*

# SEPTEMBER 26

*And the work of righteousness shall be peace; and the effect of righteousness quietness and assurance for ever (Isa. 32:17).*

The effect of unrighteousness is just the opposite—trouble, turmoil, restlessness, sleeplessness, worry, dis-ease of soul. "The wicked are like the troubled sea, when it cannot rest, whose waters cast up mire and dirt" (Isa. 57:20).

The grace of God reconciles the soul to Himself, "quiets the strife of human passion, and in His love the heart is at rest" (*The Desire of Ages,* p. 336). "Being justified by faith, we have peace with God through our Lord Jesus Christ" (Rom. 5:1).

In our day scuba diving has become popular. Its devotees tell us that while the surface of the sea may be lashed with storms, a few fathoms down it is always quiet and calm, and everything is at peace.

In the midst of World War II a European Christian remarked, "On the surface there is storm, but 20 fathoms down there is quiet and calm." So the righteousness of Christ, received by faith, brings peace to the person who is no longer at war with God, and that peace brings assurance.

Passing a crowd on his way to church in London one day, Lord Guthrie heard a layperson addressing the people. He was saying, "I have not been to college, but I have been to Calvary." That day Lord Guthrie heard Canon Liddon, James Oswald Dykes, and C. H. Spurgeon speak. After a lapse of many years he said he could not remember one single sentence of those celebrated preachers that day, but that he had never forgotten the words of the earnest layperson who had the assurance in his heart: "I know whom I have believed, and am persuaded that he is able to keep that which I have committed unto him against that day" (2 Tim. 1:12).

MEDITATION PRAYER: *"Now the God of peace . . . make you perfect in every good work to do his will . . . through Jesus Christ" (Heb. 13:20, 21).*

# SEPTEMBER 27

*Then said Jesus unto them again, Verily, verily, I say unto you, I am the door of the sheep. . . . I am the door: by me if any man enter in, he shall be saved, and shall go in and out, and find pasture (John 10:7-9).*

Christ is the door to the fold of God. Through this door all His children, from the earliest times, have found entrance. In Jesus, as shown in types, as shadowed in symbols, as manifested in the revelation of the prophets, as unveiled in the lessons given to His disciples, and in the miracles wrought for the sons of men, they have beheld 'the Lamb of God, which taketh away the sin of the world' (John 1:29), and through Him they are brought within the fold of His grace. Many have come presenting other objects for the faith of the world; ceremonies and systems have been devised by which men hope to receive justification and peace with God, and thus find entrance to His fold. But the only door is Christ, and all who have interposed something to take the place of Christ, all who have tried to enter the fold in some other way, are thieves and robbers" (*The Desire of Ages,* pp. 477, 478).

A door shuts in and shuts out. Those who enter by Christ, the door, find salvation. They find the more abundant, eternal life.

In the days of George Whitefield, Lady Hamilton once asked the duchess of Buckingham to come and hear the great preacher. The proud duchess refused to go, saying, "It is monstrous to be told that you have a heart as sinful as the most common wretch that crawls." To find salvation we must come to Christ as sinners. "And thou shalt call his name Jesus: for he shall save his people from their sins" (Matt. 1:21).

MEDITATION PRAYER: *"My mouth shall shew forth thy righteousness and thy salvation all the day" (Ps. 71:15).*

# SEPTEMBER 28

*Marvel not at this: for the hour is coming, in the which all that are in the graves shall hear his voice, and shall come forth; they that have done good, unto the resurrection of life; and they that have done evil, unto the resurrection of damnation (John 5:28, 29).*

Three things are here promised: first, the resurrection of all the dead; second, a resurrection of life; third, a resurrection of damnation, or judgment.

All who are in their graves will come forth in one or the other of these resurrections. The apostle Paul mentions them as the resurrection of the just and of the unjust (Acts 24:15). And in 1 Thessalonians 4:16 we read: "For the Lord himself shall descend from heaven with a shout, with the voice of the archangel, and with the trump of God: and the dead in Christ shall rise first."

In the twentieth chapter of Revelation these two resurrections are clearly described as being a thousand years apart. The first resurrection is of the righteous. "On such the second death hath no power, but they shall be priests of God and of Christ, and shall reign with him a thousand years" (Rev. 20:6). In verse 5 we read, "But the rest of the dead lived not again until the thousand years were finished." Some say that death ends all, but it doesn't. We must all rise. We must all stand before the judgment bar of God (Rom. 14:10). We must all meet the deeds done in the body.

In his funeral oration at his brother's grave, Robert Ingersoll, the acknowledged skeptic, gave utterance to these words: "In the night of death Hope sees a star, and listening Love can hear the rustle of a wing." Beautiful sentiment, sentiment of faith! But where did he get it? Certainly not from the gardens of infidelity and doubt. As McCaughtry says: "This is a rose plucked from the garden where Christ slept and rose again."

MEDITATION PRAYER: *"Let the wickedness of the wicked come to an end; but establish the just; for the righteous God trieth the heart and reins" (Ps. 7:9).*

# SEPTEMBER 29

*For, behold, I create new heavens and a new earth: and the former shall not be remembered, nor come into mind (Isa. 65:17).*

The margin reads, "Come upon the heart." In the new earth the events of life in the former earth condition will not be remembered to come upon the heart; that is, to cause sadness, sorrow, disappointment, worry, or heartache. But we shall certainly remember the way in which the Lord has led us through His loving providence and great mercy.

We shall remember the story of the cross and our redemption. Those who sing the new song before the throne will say, "Thou art worthy . . . : for thou wast slain, and hast redeemed us to God by thy blood out of every kindred, and tongue, and people, and nation" (Rev. 5:9).

In that blessed land we shall see things as God sees them. What now appears to us to be merely a chain of meaningless and even cruel events will then appear in all its harmony as the providence of God leading on to our eternal joy. "And God shall wipe away all tears from their eyes; and there shall be no more death, neither sorrow, nor crying, neither shall there be any more pain: for the former things are passed away" (Rev. 21:4). There will be no sorrow there, for Christ is there. In the language of Bonar's sweet hymn:

> Christ Himself the living splendor,
> Christ the sunlight, mild and tender;
> Praises to the Lamb we render;
> Ah, 'tis heaven at last!

> Broken death's dread bands that bound us,
> Life and victory around us;
> Christ the King Himself hath crowned us;
> Ah, 'tis heaven at last!

MEDITATION PRAYER: *"Sing unto the Lord, O ye saints of his, and give thanks at the remembrance of his holiness" (Ps. 30:4).*

# SEPTEMBER 30

*And it shall come to pass, that before they call,*
*I will answer; and while they are yet speaking,*
*I will hear (Isa. 65:24).*

According to its placement in a passage dealing with the new-earth state yet to come, this promise will have special application there; but it applies here, too, for our God is a prayer-hearing and a prayer-answering God. Foreseeing our needs and our prayers regarding those needs, the heavenly Father arranges His providences so that before the need actually arises He has supplied it, before the terrible trial assails us He has prepared deliverance. This is because He knows everything in the future as well as in the past. He foresees our need, and His answer is really there before our prayer is made.

God is in heaven, and we are on earth; yet by His Spirit He is everywhere present. While we are praying, He is answering. While we are speaking, He is hearing. Our prayers may be so short and so intense in time of danger that we can hardly remember a word of them. We think of the prayer of Peter, "Lord, save me." We may pray that same prayer without actually using the words. How wonderful that while we are speaking He hears, and before we call He is preparing deliverance. "Call upon me in the day of trouble: I will deliver thee" is His word (Ps. 50:15).

Years ago a boy in church opened his eyes during prayer. All heads were bowed. He looked at the minister. He saw his lips moving and heard the words. *How foolish,* he thought, *for anyone to imagine that those words could be heard beyond these walls.* Today that boy is a man and owns a radio. He listens to stations thousands of miles away and thinks of people speaking into a microphone, addressing invisible audiences on other continents. He thinks of an instrument sensitive enough to pick up voices among the stars. Now prayer seems to him the most natural thing in the world. "O thou that hearest prayer, unto thee shall all flesh come" (Ps. 65:2).

MEDITATION PRAYER: *"Hear my prayer, O Lord, and let my cry come unto thee" (Ps. 102:1).*

# OCTOBER 1

*This book of the law shall not depart out of thy mouth; but thou shalt meditate therein day and night, that thou mayest observe to do according to all that is written therein: for then thou shalt make thy way prosperous, and then thou shalt have good success (Joshua 1:8).*

It is natural to want success, to be prosperous. And here is the formula: The law of God in the mouth, in the mind, in the heart, revealed in obedience. This is the way to have not only success but *good* success.

The entire universe—the solar system, galaxies, planets, plant life, animal life, even human beings, all that we know and see about us—obeys physical law. This law is the law of God. Broken law always brings its penalty. "The wages of sin is death" (Rom. 6:23). In the spiritual world, obedience to the law of God is necessary to spiritual life. While we are saved by grace through faith (Eph. 2:8), this faith leads to obedience. It is the faith that works by love (Gal. 5:6). It is actually the righteousness of the law that is "fulfilled in us, who walk not after the flesh, but after the Spirit" (Rom. 8:4).

David declares by inspiration: "Blessed is the man that walketh not in the counsel of the ungodly. . . . But his delight is in the law of the Lord; and in his law doth he meditate day and night. . . . And whatsoever he doeth shall prosper" (Ps. 1:1-3). True belief leads to obedience and to blessing. The obedient life is a successful life.

Some time ago a United Press dispatch reported that at the University of California termites had eaten through a large stack of pamphlets entitled *Control of Termites*. This shows that information alone is not enough. There must be a practical application.

Speaking to His disciples regarding the things He had taught, Jesus said, "If ye know these things, happy are ye if ye do them" (John 13:17).

MEDITATION PRAYER: *"Then shall I not be ashamed, when I have respect unto all thy commandments" (Ps. 119:6).*

# OCTOBER 2

*The Lord shall count, when he writeth up*
*the people, that this man was born there (Ps. 87:6).*

Read the two verses preceding: "I will make mention of Rahab and Babylon to them that know me: behold Philistia, and Tyre, with Ethiopia; this man was born there. And of Zion it shall be said, This and that man was born in her: and the highest himself shall establish her."

It was Oliver Wendell Holmes who said, "We are omnibuses in which our ancestors ride." So God takes note of our environment and our inheritance. He knows all about us. God knows all about our bloodstream, and our thought stream, too, and He makes allowance for all these things. That's why the Scripture declares that He is no respecter of persons. God, and God alone, knows how to balance the inheritance of the chromosomes and the intricate influences of environment. Someone has well said that He is too wise to make a mistake and too good to be unkind in His dealing with us. The most important question for each of us is Have I been born again? (1 Peter 1:23). God knows the answer to this question, too.

A young conscript on the battlefield of Europe was confronted with his first cavalry charge. A mounted officer was about to dispatch him with one sweep of his sword, when suddenly he recognized him as the son of one of his best friends. Instantly he changed the pitch of the blade, and slapped the young man across the back with the broad side of his sword. The officer had recognized the lad's heritage, remembered whose son he was and where he was born, and acted accordingly. Will not our Savior, who knows all about us and loves us still, do the same? His records are more accurate than those of the county courthouse. Someday the Lord will count when He writes up the people. It is our privilege to know now that our names are written in the book of life (Phil. 4:3).

MEDITATION PRAYER: *"Judge me, O Lord my God, according to thy righteousness" (Ps. 35:24).*

# OCTOBER 3

*And they shall put my name upon the children*
*of Israel; and I will bless them (Num. 6:27).*

It would be well to memorize the beautiful Aaronic blessing in the three verses preceding: "The Lord bless thee, and keep thee: the Lord make his face shine upon thee, and be gracious unto thee: the Lord lift up his countenance upon thee, and give thee peace." Israel was the people of God. They were called by His name and were to represent Him to the world.

Israel was blessed as a nation as long as they walked in the path of obedience. The same is true of God's spiritual Israel today. The Lord led Israel through the wilderness because His name was upon them. And His true children can say, "He leadeth me in the paths of righteousness for his name's sake" (Ps. 23:3).

The wise man once exclaimed, "The name of the Lord is a strong tower: the righteous runneth into it, and is safe" (Prov. 18:10). Christian believers today carry the very name of Christ. They are followers of Jesus. Those who have kept His Word and not denied His name (Rev. 3:8) have this promise: "I also will keep thee from the hour of temptation, which shall come upon all the world, to try them that dwell upon the earth" (Rev. 3:10). And of each overcomer God declares, "I will write upon him the name of my God" (verse 12).

> Take the name of Jesus with you,
>> Child of sorrow and of woe;
> It will joy and comfort give you,
>> Take it, then, where'er you go.
>> —Lillian Baxter

MEDITATION PRAYER: *"I will declare thy name unto my brethren: in the midst of the congregation will I praise thee" (Ps. 22:22).*

# OCTOBER 4

*For he shall give his angels charge over thee,*
*to keep thee in all thy ways (Ps. 91:11).*

This is a wonderful promise text, even if the devil did try to twist it once to his own use (Luke 4:10). The whole angelic host is commissioned "to minister for them who shall be heirs of salvation" (Heb. 1:14; cf. Gen. 28:12; Ps. 34:7; John 1:51).

To the Christian the ways of sin are not "thy ways." "Thy ways" are the paths of duty, as wise old Adam Clarke reminds us. We are to keep to our own ways, not those of the flesh, the world, and the devil. We are to keep to the ways that God has appointed for us, and there He has promised to care for us. When Satan quoted this verse and the next to our Savior, he left out "in all thy ways." He was urging Christ to go another way, the way of pride and sin.

A timid young minister had preached his first sermon on angels and thought he had made a failure. A few days later a frail old woman said to him: "I have been afraid for years, living alone away out there on the edge of town. But since hearing your sermon, I have no more fear. I just think of that text, 'The angel of the Lord encampeth round about them that fear him, and delivereth them'" (Ps. 34:7).

We read of the guardian angels too: "Take heed that ye despise not one of these little ones; for I say unto you, That in heaven their angels do always behold the face of my Father which is in heaven" (Matt. 18:10). The angel of the Lord delivered the apostle Peter from prison the night before his expected execution. An angel appeared to Paul at night on a stormy sea. An angel strengthened our Savior in the Garden of Gethsemane. And when He comes in glory, all the holy angels will be with Him (Matt. 16:27).

MEDITATION PRAYER: *"For thou art great, and doest wondrous things: thou art God alone" (Ps. 86:10).*

# OCTOBER 5

*The Lord shall fight for you, and ye shall hold your peace (Ex. 14:14).*

The Israelites in attempting to leave Egypt were caught in the wilderness, with the Egyptians behind them and the Red Sea before them. An unarmed multitude at the mercy of the crack troops of Egypt, they blamed Moses for their dilemma. "Fear ye not, stand still," said that man of God, "and see the salvation of the Lord, which He will shew to you to day: for the Egyptians whom ye have seen to day, ye shall see them again no more for ever. The Lord shall fight for you, and ye shall hold your peace" (Ex. 14:13, 14).

That is a good suggestion. Often the Lord can do much more for us when we hold our peace. We need to stand still and see God work. As we read the rest of the wonderful story, we see the waters congealed in the heart of the seas, a nation of slaves marching to liberty on dry land, and the destruction of the hosts of Pharaoh. In the midst of the turmoil, conflict, threats, and roar of the enemy, it is good for us to remember the words "Be still, and know that I am God: . . . I will be exalted in the earth" (Ps. 46:10).

Our victory today is not in weapons, but in faith. "This is the victory that overcometh the world, even our faith" (1 John 5:4). It is when we hold our peace that God can speak to us and to others. "For thus saith the Lord God, the Holy One of Israel; In returning and rest shall ye be saved; in quietness and in confidence shall be your strength" (Isa. 30:15). When God fights our battles, there is always victory and the assurance of real peace. "And the peace of God, which passeth all understanding, shall keep your hearts and minds through Christ Jesus" (Phil. 4:7). The word "keep" here might be translated "garrison." God garrisons the hearts of His people when the battle is over. Then our peace is forever sure.

MEDITATION PRAYER: *"I will extol thee, O Lord; for thou hast lifted me up, and hast not made my foes to rejoice over me" (Ps. 30:1).*

# OCTOBER 6

*For his anger endureth but a moment; in his*
*favour is life: weeping may endure for a night,*
*but joy cometh in the morning (Ps. 30:5).*

Let us remember that the brevity of God's anger here is a sign of His mercy. Our Father is a God who is ready to pardon the iniquity and to pass by "the transgression of the remnant of his heritage" (Micah 7:18). The afflictions that He permits are in some way for our good. As someone has said, "Tears clear the eyes for the sight of God and His grace." Even then He keeps a record of our grief, for it is written by the psalmist: "Put thou my tears into thy bottle: are they not in thy book?" (Ps. 56:8).

For all believers, the way into light leads through darkness, and often the darkest hour is just before the dawn. But every night is followed by a morning, every sunset by the light of day. The last night the children of Israel spent in Egypt was a dark night, but the morning found them on their way to the Promised Land. It was a dark night for the disciples and all the world when Jesus lay in the tomb, but it was followed by the light of the glorious resurrection morning, and that light has been shining around the world to this very day.

> When it is night, with shadows deep and still,
>     And all the cloudy flags of day are furled,
> However dark the hour, remember, friend,
>     It's always morning somewhere in the world.
>
> In the soul's night, when every star is gone,
>     And love's bright chalice into fragments hurled,
> Ah, heart, know this: The sun will rise again;
>     It's always morning somewhere in the world.

MEDITATION PRAYER: *"Yea, the darkness hideth not from thee; but the night shineth as the day: the darkness and the light are both alike to thee" (Ps. 139:12).*

# OCTOBER 7

*For this shall every one that is godly pray unto thee
in a time when thou mayest be found: surely in the floods
of great waters they shall not come nigh unto him (Ps. 32:6).*

Today is the day when the Lord may be found, for it is written: "Now is the accepted time; behold, now is the day of salvation" (2 Cor. 6:2). That is why we are to seek the Lord while He may be found, and call upon Him while He is near (Isa. 55:6). We all need to listen to the warning of the apostle: "Take heed, brethren, lest there be in any of you an evil heart of unbelief, in departing from the living God. But exhort one another daily, while it is called To day; lest any of you be hardened through the deceitfulness of sin" (Heb. 3:12, 13).

If we keep on praying terms with God during fair weather, we shall be safe in the big rains. In the great floods of trouble that are coming upon the world, God's care for His children will be sure, though we may not know the manner of His deliverance.

Near Port Royal, Jamaica, there is a tomb with this epitaph: "Here lieth the body of Louis Caldy, Esq., native of Mont Pelier, France. He was swallowed up by the earthquake at this place in 1692, but by the great providence of God was, by a second shock, flung into the sea, where he continued swimming until rescued by a boat, and lived forty years afterward."

God's care is over us, even when we do not see it in such startling ways. John Greenleaf Whittier wrote:

> Yet, in the maddening maze of things,
>     And tossed by storm and flood,
> To one fixed trust my spirit clings;
>     I know that God is good!

MEDITATION PRAYER: *"The floods have lifted up, O Lord, the floods have lifted up their voice; the floods lift up their waves. The Lord on high is mightier than the noise of many waters, yea, than the mighty waves of the sea" (Ps. 93:3, 4).*

# OCTOBER 8

*Observe and hear all these words which I command thee, that it may go well with thee, and with thy children after thee for ever, when thou doest that which is good and right in the sight of the Lord thy God (Deut. 12:28).*

Charles Spurgeon once said: "Though salvation is not by the works of the law, yet the blessings which are promised to obedience are not denied to the faithful servants of God. The curses our Lord took away when He was made a curse for us, but no clause of blessing has been abrogated."

We are not to pick and choose what we shall obey of God's Word, for "all these words which I command thee" are for us to observe and obey. All the iniquity of the fathers may have an effect upon the children of the third and fourth generations of them that hate God, still He says that He will show mercy unto thousands of them that love Him and keep His commandments (Ex. 20:5, 6). Of the holy angels it is written that they "do his commandments, hearkening unto the voice of his word" (Ps. 103:20). How much more should we!

A teacher was explaining to her class the work of God's holy angels. The text under consideration was Psalm 103:21: "Bless ye the Lord, all ye his hosts; ye ministers of his, that do his pleasure." "How do the angels carry out God's will?" she asked. Many answers followed. One said, "They do it directly." Another said, "They do it with all their hearts." A third added, "They do it well." After a while a quiet little girl said, "They do it without asking any questions."

May our obedience be like that before the world, and especially before our children. Then, by God's grace, it shall go well with us and with them.

MEDITATION PRAYER: *"Teach me to do thy will; for thou art my God: thy spirit is good; lead me into the land of uprightness" (Ps. 143:10).*

# OCTOBER 9

*Be still, and know that I am God: I will be exalted*
*among the heathen, I will be exalted in the earth (Ps. 46:10).*

We must individually hear Him speaking to the heart. When every other voice is hushed, and in quietness we wait before Him, the silence of the soul makes more distinct the voice of God. He bids us, 'Be still, and know that I am God' (Ps. 46:10). Here alone can true rest be found. . . . Amid the hurrying throng, and the strain of life's intense activities, the soul that is thus refreshed will be surrounded with an atmosphere of light and peace" (*The Desire of Ages*, p. 363).

Four-year-old Bobby was attending the Sabbath school class for little people. He sat quietly, not saying a word, but simply looking on. The teacher wondered why, but said nothing. Later Bobby's mother came for him. When they were getting ready to leave, the teacher asked why the little fellow had not joined in the singing that morning. At first he said nothing. Then his mother, thinking that perhaps he had not been cooperative, exclaimed, "Why, Bobby, what was the matter?"

Slowly the little boy replied, "Somebody has to listen." As it is written, "A little child shall lead them" (Isa. 11:6). In quiet reverence Bobby had worshipped. So we too, even in the rush and crush of modern life, may find "the peace of God, which passeth all understanding" (Phil. 4:7) in the quiet moment spent in meditation and prayer.

The nations may forget God; the world may seem to be under the control of evil powers; but remember this, you who love the Lord, He will yet be exalted in the earth.

> We bless Thee for Thy peace, O God,
>     Deep as the soundless sea,
> Which falls like sunshine on the road
>     Of those who trust in Thee.

MEDITATION PRAYER: *"Thou shalt arise, and have mercy upon Zion: for the time to favour her, yea, the set time, is come"* (Ps. 102:13).

# OCTOBER 10

*For thus saith the high and lofty One that inhabiteth eternity, whose name is Holy; I dwell in the high and holy place, with him also that is of a contrite and humble spirit, to revive the spirit of the humble, and to revive the heart of the contrite ones (Isa. 57:15).*

D avid knew this, for he said, "Though the Lord be high, yet hath he respect unto the lowly" (Ps. 138:6).

We are told that the star nearest to the earth is so far away that it would take light from this star, traveling at the inconceivable speed of more than 186,000 miles a second, four years to reach the earth. The North Star is more than 300 light-years away. The great constellation of Orion is from 500 to 600 light-years away. And now it is announced from the great Palomar Observatory that stars have been photographed so far away that it would take hundreds of millions years for their light to reach this earth. This is beyond our human comprehension, and we wonder if people actually know it to be a fact. The vastness of the universe staggers our imagination, but it gives us just a little suggestion of the might and power of our God.

> I sing the mighty power of God,
>     That made the mountains rise,
> That spread the flowing seas abroad,
>     And built the lofty skies;
> I sing the wisdom that ordained
>     The sun to rule the day;
> The moon shines full at His command,
>     And all the stars obey.

> —Isaac Watts

But here is a divine revelation that the God of infinite space and infinite duration, who dwells in "light which no man can approach unto" (1 Tim. 6:16), also dwells with those who are humble and contrite, to revive them and strengthen them for life's pilgrimage. How beautiful, how wonderful, to know that the Creator and Sustainer of the universe is our God and Friend.

MEDITATION PRAYER: *"What is man, that thou art mindful of him? and the son of man, that thou visitest him?" (Ps. 8:4).*

# OCTOBER 11

*All that the Father giveth me shall*
*come to me; and him that cometh to me*
*I will in no wise cast out (John 6:37).*

And the reason for our Savior's statement comes in the next words: "For I came down from heaven, not to do mine own will, but the will of him that sent me. And this is the Father's will which hath sent me, that of all which he hath given me I should lose nothing, but should raise it up again at the last day. And this is the will of him that sent me, that every one which seeth the Son, and believeth on him, may have everlasting life" (verses 38-40).

The "coming" ones in the last part of our promise text are the "given" ones in the first. Although they are given by God to His Son, they are spoken of as coming; that is, by their voluntary advances to Him and acceptance of Him—"him that cometh to me"—"whosoever will" (Rev. 22:17). So the door is wide open. Notice, there must be not only *willing* but *coming*. Our Savior came down from heaven, not to do His own will, but to carry out the great plan in reference to the divine and human side of salvation.

An evangelist working in the oil fields of California encouraged the young people and children to read the New Testament. In each Testament was a blank page on which to inscribe their names. After they had finished reading the Holy Word, they were encouraged to write under their names a brief statement of their acceptance of Christ as their Savior, if they could do it sincerely. One very small boy wrote in a scrawling hand, "I *expect* Jesus." And, after all, accepting Jesus is really expecting Him to be the center of our lives and to guide us to the end, not only while reading our Bibles, but in every act of life. Jesus accepted His mission from the Father, and *expected* much from God. Our success as Christians will be in proportion to our acceptance and expectation.

MEDITATION PRAYER: *"My lips shall greatly rejoice when I sing unto thee; and my soul, which thou hast redeemed" (Ps. 71:23).*

# OCTOBER 12

*And he said unto me, Thou must prophesy*
*again before many peoples, and nations,*
*and tongues, and kings (Rev. 10:11).*

A worldwide message, like fire, like a rainbow, like the sun, but "clothed with a cloud"; a message declaring that time should be no longer; a message from a little book that had been closed but that was now open—evidently the book of Daniel. "And I took the little book out of the angel's hand, and ate it up; and it was in my mouth sweet as honey: and as soon as I had eaten it, my belly was bitter" (Rev. 10:10). What a picture of the Great Disappointment that followed the Advent movement of the early 1840s! Sweet anticipation, bitter reality. So it was with the first disciples. They expected our Savior to become king of Israel, but instead, the cross was His throne. After that first disappointment they had a worldwide work to do, scattering the gospel throughout the earth.

And now there is another work to do. "Thou must prophesy again before many peoples, and nations, and tongues, and kings." This is a worldwide work preparatory to the coming of the Lord in power and glory to bring an end to sin, pain, and death. "Go ye into all the world" is His command, "and preach the gospel to every creature" (Mark 16:15). Our Savior also declared, "This gospel of the kingdom shall be preached in all the world for a witness unto all nations; and then shall the end come" (Matt. 24:14).

The need for Christian missions is greater than ever before. Millions have never heard the story of Jesus. We have the gospel, and it is our duty to take it to others until the work is done.

Upon the tomb of David Livingstone in Westminster Abbey is this inscription, "Other sheep I have, which are not of this fold" (John 10:16). It is for these other sheep that the call must still go out, that we must "prophesy again" to many nations, and tongues, and kings.

MEDITATION PRAYER: *"I will praise thee, O Lord, among the people: and I will sing praises unto thee among the nations" (Ps. 108:3).*

# OCTOBER 13

*Behold, the eye of the Lord is upon them that fear him,*
*upon them that hope in his mercy; to deliver their soul*
*from death, and to keep them alive in famine (Ps. 33:18, 19).*

At the battle of Prestonpans, the Highland chief of the noble house of M'Gregor fell wounded by two bullets. The clan wavered and gave the enemy an advantage. Seeing this, the old chieftain raised himself up and, with blood gushing from his wounds, cried: "I am not dead, my children. I am looking to see you do your duty." At these words his brave Highlanders rushed anew into the conflict.

But our battle is against evil. It is unto life, not unto death. And our Chieftain is not dead or dying, but alive forevermore. Because He ever liveth, "he is able also to save them to the uttermost that come unto God by him" (Heb. 7:25). It is plainly stated in Psalm 34:15, 16: "The eyes of the Lord are upon the righteous, and his ears are open unto their cry. The face of the Lord is against them that do evil, to cut off the remembrance of them from the earth."

How often are we aware of God's watchcare over us! There are places in our wilderness of wandering where we might say, as did one of old, "Thou God seest me" (Gen. 16:13).

> Why should I feel discouraged,
>     Why should the shadows come,
> Why should my heart be lonely
>     And long for heaven and home,
> When Jesus is my portion?
>     My constant friend is He:
> His eye is on the sparrow,
>     And I know He watches me.
> —Mrs. C. D. Martin

MEDITATION PRAYER: *"For thou hast made him most blessed for ever: thou hast made him exceeding glad with thy countenance" (Ps. 21:6).*

# OCTOBER 14

**_Say not thou, I will recompense evil; but wait_**
**_on the Lord, and he shall save thee (Prov. 20:22)._**

Yes, evils and injustices will come to us at the hands of others. And when they do, shall we say, "I will give him as good as he sends"? No. Let anger cool down. We should say nothing, do nothing, to avenge ourselves. Let us follow the example of Hezekiah, who spread Rabshakeh's letter before the Lord, and pray unto the Lord, as he did (2 Kings 19:14-19). This will greatly relieve the burdened mind.

The apostolic command is: "Recompense to no man evil for evil" (Rom. 12:17). And the words of Jesus are: "I say unto you, That ye resist not evil: but whosoever shall smite thee on thy right cheek, turn to him the other also. . . . Love your enemies, bless them that curse you, do good to them that hate you, and pray for them which despitefully use you, and persecute you; that ye may be the children of your Father which is in heaven" (Matt. 5:39-45). _hard to do many times_

When we do not know what to do, let us follow the advice of today's promise, _"Wait on the Lord, and he shall save thee."_

A small boy hailed his playmate next door and started to run out for the usual morning play together when an older member of the family said teasingly: "Are you going to play with him again? I thought that you quarreled yesterday and were never going to have anything more to do with each other. You have a funny memory!"

Jimmy looked surprised for a moment. Then, with a satisfied smile, he said as he hurried away, "Oh, Roland and me is good forgetters."

And so should we all be—and good forgivers, too, trusting in the Lord.

MEDITATION PRAYER: _"Thou hast seen it; for thou beholdest mischief and spite, to requite it with thy hand" (Ps. 10:14)._

# OCTOBER 15

*And this is the will of him that sent me, that every one which seeth the Son, and believeth on him, may have everlasting life: and I will raise him up at the last day (John 6:40).*

It is the will of God that all who see His Son as the Savior and believe on Him may have everlasting life. The promise of Jesus is clear: "I will raise him up at the last day."

A minister passing the corner of Fourth Avenue and Jefferson Street in Louisville, Kentucky, one cold November morning saw a man who had been placed on the sidewalk in front of a building in order that he might receive alms from passersby. Both his arms were gone, and he had no legs. His face was marked with the miseries of many winters, but his eyes were very bright. His head was bare, for his hat was pinned to his ragged clothing to receive the proffered coins. The minister asked the poor man if he didn't wish to be moved inside the building to get out of the cold. But one standing by said, "He cannot hear." Then he wrote his question on a piece of paper: "May I move you to a warm place?" The onlooker said, "He cannot read; neither can he speak." But, looking into the man's eyes, the minister seemed to read there these words: "O man, please give me something with which to get bread and a warm place to stay." That look was rewarded, for help was extended immediately.

But there is a more important look than that. God says, "Look unto me, and be ye saved, all the ends of the earth: for I am God, and there is none else" (Isa. 45:22). This is the look that God must see in the spiritual eye of every lost soul.

With the eye of faith we must see the Son, and believing on Him, receive everlasting life. This is the definite promise of our Savior: "I will raise him up at the last day." Seeing is believing, and believing is receiving everlasting life.

MEDITATION PRAYER: *"In his favour is life: weeping may endure for a night, but joy cometh in the morning" (Ps. 30:5).*

# OCTOBER 16

*After those days, saith the Lord, I will put my law in their inward parts, and write it in their hearts; and will be their God, and they shall be my people. And they shall teach no more every man his neighbour, . . . saying, Know the Lord; for they shall all know me, from the least of them unto the greatest of them, saith the Lord: for I will forgive their iniquity, and I will remember their sin no more (Jer. 31:33, 34).*

This is God doing what we cannot do ourselves. This is righteousness by faith. What the law could not do, because it was weak through the flesh (Rom. 8:3), God does through His Holy Spirit, writing His law in the hearts of believers, so that Christ really lives in them by faith, and His will is their will. Then we know God as the God of grace, passing by our transgressions, separating our sins from us as far as the east is from the west, hiding them behind His back, and blotting them out as a thick cloud. He forgives our iniquities, for it is written, "If we confess our sins, he is faithful and just to forgive us our sins, and to cleanse us from all unrighteousness" (1 John 1:9).

Not only so, but the promise goes further still: "I will remember their sin no more." Can God forget? He says He will forget our sins, and He means what He says. So the Lord completely obliterates the iniquity of His people. This is God's act of oblivion. This is the forgiving Father receiving back into His home and into His heart the prodigal child. When God forgives, He forgets. Why? Because "Christ died for our sins according to the scriptures" (1 Cor. 15:3).

> Forgiven, forgotten, all cleansed in the blood,
>   My sins are remembered no more;
> Atoned for by Jesus in Calvary's flood,
>   My sins are remembered no more.

MEDITATION PRAYER: *"Hide thy face from my sins, and blot out all mine iniquities" (Ps. 51:9).*

295

# OCTOBER 17

*Restore unto me the joy of thy salvation; and uphold me with
thy free spirit. Then will I teach transgressors thy ways;
and sinners shall be converted unto thee (Ps. 51:12, 13).*

This is really a promise of what God will do through all of us who have the joy of salvation and who are upheld by His Spirit. This psalm is David's cry for forgiveness and mercy after his great sin. Listen to his plea: "Hide thy face from my sins, and blot out all mine iniquities. Create in me a clean heart, O God; and renew a right spirit within me. Cast me not away from thy presence; and take not thy holy spirit from me" (verses 9-11). Then he prays that the joy of salvation shall be restored to him, that he may be upheld by God's free spirit. When this happens, he says, "Then will I teach transgressors thy ways; and sinners shall be converted unto thee."

This is the only real preparation for soul winning. Soul winners must themselves be won to Christ. They must be forgiven. They must have the joy of salvation. They must have the witness of the Spirit in their own heart that they are chidlren of God (Rom. 8:16).

One night in Paris, Paganini played before a great audience. As he was tuning his violin one of the strings broke. Disappointment swept over the audience. As the artist played, a second string snapped. Although the audience was annoyed, he continued to play until a third string broke. The listeners were disgusted. Quietly Paganini said, "Ladies and gentlemen, you now hear one string and Paganini." Then he began to bring such music out of that one string that the audience leaned forward that they might not miss a note. He sat down to wild applause, because he had brought so much out of so little. One string and Paganini—one surrendered soul and God. The Holy Spirit will take our little and do tremendous exploits for God when we are surrendered to His touch.

MEDITATION PRAYER: *"Thy God hath commanded thy strength: strengthen, O God, that which thou hast wrought for us" (Ps. 68:28).*

# OCTOBER 18

*Wherefore he is able also to save them to the uttermost that come unto God by him, seeing he ever liveth to make intercession for them (Heb. 7:25).*

What Christ is able to do for us, He will do for us. This is a promise not only of His power but of His willingness to save all who believe. Because He is a priest forever, He is able to save forever. But to be saved forever, we must "come unto God by him." Jesus said, "I am the way, the truth, and the life" (John 14:6). "There is none other name under heaven given among men, whereby we must be saved" (Acts 4:12). We must accept Him as our personal Savior from sin, as having died for us, as having paid the price of our redemption. He who offered one sacrifice for sins forever now appears in the presence of God for us (Heb. 9:24), our Interceder and High Priest.

When Dr. Philip Doddridge lived at Northampton, a poor man was condemned to death for sheep stealing. The laws were very cruel in those days. Dr. Doddridge thought there was little proof of the man's guilt, and he also believed in the Great Book, which teaches that a human being is better than a sheep. He tried every way he could to get the sentence reprieved, but was unsuccessful. On the road to his execution the convict asked to stop opposite Dr. Doddridge's house. Kneeling down, he said: "God bless you, Dr. Doddridge. Every vein in my heart loves you. Every drop of my blood loves you, for you tried to save every drop of it."

There was a man! What love he had for the intercessor who had failed. But our Savior has succeeded, and what a price He has paid! Why should not every one of us who rejoices in their blood-bought salvation say: "Every vein in my heart loves Thee, O Christ. Every drop of my blood loves Thee, for Thou hast died to save me, and dost live to intercede for me"?

MEDITATION PRAYER: *"Save us, O Lord our God, and gather us from among the heathen, to give thanks unto thy holy name, and to triumph in thy praise" (Ps. 106:47).*

# OCTOBER 19

*But love ye your enemies, and do good, and lend, hoping for nothing again; and your reward shall be great, and ye shall be the children of the Highest: for he is kind unto the unthankful and to the evil (Luke 6:35).*

God is good to all, and if we are His children we are good to all. It is those who are not working for a reward who will receive a reward.

When, at Worms, Luther was forsaken and dispirited, suddenly a servant entered his hotel room bearing a refreshing drink, the offering of Duke Erich of Brunswick, a powerful ruler belonging to the pope's party. As the Reformer, touched by this act of kindness, drank, he said, "As on this day Duke Erich has remembered me, may the Lord Jesus Christ remember him in the hour of his last struggle."

The servant took the message to his master, and in the hour of his death the aged duke recalled Luther's words. Addressing the young man who stood at his bedside, he said, "Take the Bible and read to me." The dying man took comfort as the youth read the words of Christ: "Whosoever shall give to drink . . . a cup of cold water only . . . , verily I say unto you, he shall in no wise lose his reward" (Matt. 10:42).

Love is the one final, irresistible force in the world. God, who loved the unlovely in us, desires to love the unlovely through us as we reflect His love to others.

> For the love of God is broader
> Than the measure of man's mind,
> And the heart of the Eternal
> Is most wonderfully kind.
> —Frederick W. Faber

MEDITATION PRAYER: *"It is a good thing to give thanks unto the Lord, . . . to shew forth thy lovingkindness in the morning, and thy faithfulness every night" (Ps. 92:1, 2).*

# OCTOBER 20

*Be not afraid of sudden fear, neither of the desolation of*
*the wicked, when it cometh. For the Lord shall be thy confidence,*
*and shall keep thy foot from being taken (Prov. 3:25, 26).*

It has been said that we should be far more shocked at the sin that deserves hell than at the hell that comes out of sin. Punishment that often follows sin in this world is really a preserving salt that saves society from destruction. We read in Isaiah 26:9 that when God's judgments are in the earth, "the inhabitants of the world will learn righteousness." God's people are not to be alarmed or to fear, whatever may come on the earth. "Fear thou not; for I am with thee: be not dismayed; for I am thy God" is a divine command (Isa. 41:10).

Events for which we are unprepared may happen suddenly, but we are always to be prepared for God's care and protection. "He shall cover thee with his feathers, and under his wings shalt thou trust" (Ps. 91:4). World events and threats that cause men's hearts to fail them "for fear, and for looking after those things which are coming on the earth" should not frighten God's children, but only cause them to look up, knowing that their redemption draws nigh (Luke 21:26, 28).

The Baptist pioneer in Germany, Pastor Oncken, suffered much in fines and imprisonment for the truth's sake. He was once threatened by the burgomaster of Amberg, who held up his finger and said: "Do you see that finger? So long as that can move, I will put you down."

Oncken replied: "I see your finger, but I see also an arm which you do not see. So long as that is stretched out, you cannot put me down."

And that is the promise: "The Lord shall be thy confidence." May He be our confidence always.

MEDITATION PRAYER: *"In thee, O Lord, do I put my trust:*
*let me never be put to confusion" (Ps. 71:1).*

# OCTOBER 21

*But they which shall be accounted worthy to obtain that world, and the resurrection from the dead, neither marry, nor are given in marriage: neither can they die any more: for they are equal unto the angels; and are the children of God, being the children of the resurrection (Luke 20:35, 36).*

The "children of this world," mentioned in verse 34 of this chapter, are men and women in their present state of mortality, procreation being necessary to restore the loss caused by death; but in the world to come there will be no more death.

"Those who . . . are 'accounted worthy,' will have a part in the resurrection of the just. Jesus said . . . that 'they that have done good' shall come forth 'unto the resurrection of life' (John 5:29). . . . All who have truly repented of sin, and by faith claimed the blood of Christ as their atoning sacrifice, have had pardon entered against their names in the books of heaven" (*The Great Controversy,* pp. 482, 483). They have become partakers of the righteousness of Christ, and so are accounted worthy.

Michael Faraday, while showing a friend his laboratory, handed him a beautiful silver cup that he had received as a prize. Suddenly it slipped from the visitor's hand and dropped into a vat of acid, where, to his horror, it melted away like a snowflake. The scientist calmed his friend, and stepping to a shelf, picked up a small piece of mineral and dropped it into the acid. The silver immediately began to be precipitated at the bottom of the vat, where it was collected. "I will send it back to the manufacturers," he said, "and have it recast." And so he did, into a more beautiful vase than before.

So our Creator, in the plenitude of His power and wisdom, will bring forth the bodies of His redeemed—changed, new, immortalized, fashioned like unto His own glorious body—"the children of the resurrection."

MEDITATION PRAYER: *"Into thine hand I commit my spirit: thou hast redeemed me, O Lord God of truth" (Ps. 31:5).*

# OCTOBER 22

*Call unto me, and I will answer thee, and shew thee*
*great and mighty things, which thou knowest not (Jer. 33:3).*

God encourages prayer. He commands prayer. Our minds are brought into harmony with God by prayer, but this is not all—God answers prayer. His promise is "I will answer thee"; and every true prayer, prayed according to the will of God, is answered. Jesus said, "Ask, and ye shall receive" (John 16:24). In James 4:2 we are told, "Ye have not, because ye ask not."

For God to say Yes to our prayers, there must be a full surrender to His will (Ps. 37:4). His words must abide in us so that we shall ask according to His Word (John 15:7). We must have the leadership, the guidance, of the Holy Spirit (Rom. 8:26, 27). And we must pray in the name of Jesus (John 14:13, 14).

Prayer is asking, seeking, knocking. The answer to prayer is receiving, finding, going through an opened door. Many of God's answers will surprise us. There are great things in store for us.

The missionaries who went to the island of Tahiti worked for 16 years without a single convert. The mission society in England seriously considered abandoning the field, but a few saw that the failure lay in their unbelief. They called a special season of prayer for God's blessing on that island far away, then sent letters of reassurance to the weary workers there. On the ocean those letters crossed others from the missionaries telling of the entire overthrow of idolatry. What seemed to be an invincible fortress of evil had suddenly collapsed before the new Pentecost. "Before they call, I will answer; and while they are yet speaking, I will hear" (Isa. 65:24).

MEDITATION PRAYER: *"For in thee, O Lord, do I hope: thou wilt hear, O Lord my God" (Ps. 38:15).*

*He shall call upon me, and I will answer him: I will be with him in trouble; I will deliver him, and honour him. With long life will I satisfy him, and shew him my salvation (Ps. 91:15, 16).*

Here we have a sixfold promise to those who pray: I will answer him, I will be with him, I will deliver him, I will honor him, I will satisfy him, I will show him my salvation. What more could one want?

Again in our promise today it is plainly stated that God's children will call upon Him; they will pray, and the Lord will be with them in trouble. The deliverance is certain, and honor will come to them. They will be satisfied with long life—eternal life. And they will see God's everlasting salvation (Isa. 45:17).

God's dealings with us may seem strange at times, and we may not see how He is working out the answers to our prayers.

There is an old Hebrew story of a rabbi journeying on muleback through wild country, his only companion a rooster, whose shrill crowing woke him at sunrise for his devotions. He came to a village and sought shelter, but the inhabitants would not take him in. He found a cave where he spent the night. During the night a wolf killed his rooster and a lion devoured his mule. Early in the morning he went into the village and, to his surprise, found no one alive in the whole town. A band of robbers had plundered the place and killed all the people. "Now," he said, "I understand. If they had received me, I too would have been killed. Had not my mule been killed, its noise would have revealed my hiding place. God has been good to me."

Let us wait on the Lord to fulfill His promises in His own way and in His own time. "I waited patiently for the Lord; and he inclined unto me, and heard my cry" (Ps. 40:1).

MEDITATION PRAYER: *"Bow down thine ear to me; deliver me speedily: be thou my strong rock, for an house of defence to save me" (Ps. 31:2).*

# OCTOBER 24

*Look unto me, and be ye saved,*
*all the ends of the earth: for I am God,*
*and there is none else (Isa. 45:22).*

Charles Spurgeon calls this a promise of promises. He says that it lies at the very foundation of our spiritual life. Salvation comes through a look, the look of faith, unto Him who is "a just God and a Saviour" (Isa. 45:21).

A heavy snowstorm forced young Spurgeon to seek refuge in a little Methodist chapel on an obscure street. He wanted salvation, but did not know how to find it. There was no minister present that day, but a layman came into the pulpit, opened his Bible, and read these words: "Look unto me, and be ye saved, all the ends of the earth." Fixing his eyes on Spurgeon as though he knew him personally, he said, "Young man, you are in trouble, and you will never get out of it unless you look to Christ." Then he lifted up his hands and cried, "Look, look, look! It is only a look."

That young man later became one of the world's greatest preachers, and he said: "I saw at once the way of salvation—I looked. I had been waiting to do 50 things, but when I heard that word 'Look,' I saw at once the way of salvation."

When Moses lifted up the brazen serpent in the wilderness, those who looked were healed (Num. 21:8, 9). "And as Moses lifted up the serpent in the wilderness, even so must the Son of man be lifted up: that whosoever believeth in him should not perish, but have eternal life" (John 3:14, 15).

> In a look there's life for thee,
> In a look at Calvary;
> Blessed thought, salvation free,
> By a look at Calvary.

—F. E. Belden

MEDITATION PRAYER: *"Unto thee lift I up mine eyes, O thou that dwellest in the heavens" (Ps. 123:1).*

# OCTOBER 25

*Because he hath set his love upon me, therefore will I deliver him:*
*I will set him on high, because he hath known my name (Ps. 91:14).*

Where is *our* love set—upon God, or upon ourselves? Do we know His name, or are we strangers to Him? He is revealed in Jesus Christ as love and salvation. "Thou shalt call his name Jesus: for he shall save his people from their sins" (Matt. 1:21).

Christ Himself says, "And thou shalt love the Lord thy God with all thy heart, and with all thy soul, and with all thy mind, and with all thy strength: this is the first commandment" (Mark 12:30). If we have set our love upon God, He will be the center of our life. God is love, and as we see His love displayed in the natural world and in the salvation revealed in Christ, we exclaim, "Behold, what manner of love" (1 John 3:1), and "we love him, because he first loved us" (1 John 4:19). Love begets love.

An American minister, visiting Robert MacCheyne's historic church in Dundee, Scotland, asked an old parishioner if he remembered the great preacher. Yes, he remembered MacCheyne well. "Can you recall any of his texts?" He could not. "Can you remember anything he said in his sermons?" He could recall nothing. "There is only one thing I remember, one thing I will never forget," he said. "I was just a little boy standing at the roadside one day when Mr. MacCheyne came along. He stopped and came over to me and said: 'Jamie, I'm going in to see your wee sister. She's dying; and, my boy, I must have you for Jesus. I cannot allow you to go on outside God's kingdom.' He had his hand on my head, and I have never forgotten the trembling of his fingers." No wonder that boy gave his heart to Christ. What blessing such a trembling touch of love would bring to many a child!

MEDITATION PRAYER: *"Let them also that love thy name be joyful in thee" (Ps. 5:11).*

# OCTOBER 26

*Jesus said unto her, I am the resurrection, and the life: he that believeth in me, though he were dead, yet shall he live: and whosoever liveth and believeth in me shall never die (John 11:25, 26).*

These words comforted Martha, who had just lost her brother, and they have comforted the children of God down through the weary centuries to this very day. It is written, "Because I live, ye shall live also" (John 14:19). Can we imagine the world's great philosopher's saying, "I am the resurrection, and the life"? Could Socrates say it, or Plato, or Aristotle? Could any of the great teachers or leaders of this world say it? Yet Jesus could say it, and it was the truth. Only He could proclaim over the rent sepulcher, "I am the resurrection, and the life."

Our Lord declared, "He that believeth on the Son hath everlasting life" (John 3:36). The believer may fall asleep in what we call death, but it is not eternal death. As it was said of Lazarus, it may be said also of the believer, "He sleepeth." And someday our Savior will come, as He said, to "awake him out of sleep" (John 11:11).

While R. W. Dale was once building a sermon on the subject "The Empty Tomb of Christ," the thought of the risen Lord broke upon him in a new revelation. "Christ is alive," he said to himself. "Alive now, today, just as certainly as I am! He is alive this very minute, and alive forevermore." At first it seemed hardly true. Then it came with a sudden burst of glory—Christ is now living! "I must get this across to my people," he said. "I must preach it in every sermon."

Why shouldn't this wonderful thought grip our hearts every day? "I am he that liveth, and was dead; and, behold, I am alive for evermore" (Rev. 1:18). "And whosoever liveth and believeth in me shall never die."

MEDITATION PRAYER: *"O Lord, thou hast brought up my soul from the grave: thou hast kept me alive, that I should not go down to the pit" (Ps. 30:3).*

# OCTOBER 27

*Commit thy way unto the Lord; trust also in him; and he shall bring it to pass. And he shall bring forth thy righteousness as light, and thy judgment as the noonday (Ps. 37:5, 6).*

In Hebrew this thought is "Roll thy way upon the Lord," as of one rolling off from their own shoulders a burden they cannot carry, to the shoulders of another, who is able to bear it. "Casting all your care upon him; for he careth for you" (1 Peter 5:7). "Thy way," of course, means "thy doings," "thy understandings," "thy plans," or, as in Proverbs 16:3, "thy works."

A certain poor woman applied to the sultan of Turkey for compensation for the loss of her property. "How did you lose it?" he inquired.

"I fell asleep, and robbers came and stole it."

"But why did you fall asleep?"

"I fell asleep because I believed that you were awake" was the astonishing reply.

The sultan was so pleased with her trust in him that he made compensation for her loss. We can trust God with all our affairs, for He is always awake. He neither slumbers nor sleeps (Ps. 121:3). Let us commit our way to Him, "and he shall bring it to pass."

The afflictions and troubles that now seem to cast a shadow over the righteous will in the end be the evidence that they are the children of God, as in the case of Job and others. Jesus seemed to be forsaken on the cross, and His righteous cause seemed to be forever lost; but at His resurrection He was "declared to be the Son of God with power" (Rom. 1:4).

Leave your vindication in the hands of God, and trust Him. Someday it will be as clear as noonday that you are His servant.

MEDITATION PRAYER: *"Preserve my soul; . . . O thou my God, save thy servant that trusteth in thee" (Ps. 86:2).*

# OCTOBER 28

*Now the just shall live by faith: but if*
*any man draw back, my soul shall have*
*no pleasure in him (Heb. 10:38).*

Martin Luther declared that there are two kinds of faith: first, believing about God and believing that what He says is true, which is really a form of knowledge; and second, believing in God, which means that we put our trust in Him and give ourselves up to His will. Such faith throws itself upon God, whether in life or in death, and that is necessary in the life of every Christian. Such faith comes from hearing—that is, accepting—the Word of God (Rom. 10:17). The just, or righteous, person remains just, or righteous, by faith. It is Christ's righteousness, God's justice, that is theirs. It is through faith that we share the righteousness of Christ, the power of Christ, the resurrection of Christ, the glory of Christ.

A poet and an artist were once examining a painting by Poussin depicting the healing of the two blind men. The poet mentioned several remarkable things about the painting. The artist seemed unsatisfied and pointed out something else. He said, "Do you see that discarded cane lying there by the steps of the house?"

"Yes."

"What does it mean?"

"Why, on those steps the blind man sat with his cane in his hand; but when he heard that Christ had come, he was so sure that he would be healed that he dropped his cane and rushed into the presence of the Lord. Isn't that a wonderful conception of faith?"

And it was. Too often we hold on to the old canes and crutches of self-help and of righteousness that we have done, instead of looking wholly to Jesus. "This is the victory that overcometh the world, even our faith" (1 John 5:4).

MEDITATION PRAYER: *"I will praise thee for ever, because thou hast done it" (Ps. 52:9).*

# OCTOBER 29

*But in the days of the voice of the seventh angel, when he shall begin to sound, the mystery of God should be finished, as he hath declared to his servants the prophets (Rev. 10:7).*

The seventh trumpet covers events in the final years of the gospel dispensation to the beginning of the eternal world. In the early days of the sounding of the seventh angel the mystery of God is to be finished. What is the mystery of God? The apostle Paul declares in Galatians 1:11, 12 that "the gospel which was preached of me is not after man. For I neither received it of man, neither was I taught it, but by the revelation of Jesus Christ." So the mystery came to him by revelation, and the gospel came by revelation. It is quite clear that the mystery of God is the gospel.

The prophets of the Old Testament and the apostles of the New predicted and proclaimed it. The startling promise here is that it shall be finished. Then a decree will go forth: "He that is righteous, let him be righteous still: and he that is holy, let him be holy still. And, behold, I come quickly" (Rev. 22:11, 12). Then the number of the elect will have been made up, probation will end, and our Savior will come.

Has the gospel finished its gracious work in our hearts? Have we responded to it? If not, why not? "Now is the accepted time; . . . now is the day of salvation" (2 Cor. 6:2). "Come; for all things are now ready" (Luke 14:17).

Out in the wasteland of Arizona a kind man would light a lantern every night and hang it outside his cabin near the only well of good water for many a desert mile. Remember, friends, God's lantern is the cross. It shines across the deserts of this life, and in the darkest hours it shines the brightest. The time to turn to it is now, before life is gone.

MEDITATION PRAYER: *"But as for me, my prayer is unto thee, O Lord, in an acceptable time" (Ps. 69:13).*

# OCTOBER 30

*And at that time shall Michael stand up, the great prince which standeth for the children of thy people: and there shall be a time of trouble, such as never was since there was a nation even to that same time: and at that time thy people shall be delivered, every one that shall be found written in the book (Dan. 12:1).*

Three things are promised here: the standing up of Michael, the time of trouble, the deliverance of God's people. Our Savior now appears in the presence of God for us (Heb. 9:24), but someday He will cease His intercessory work, stand up, and begin to reign as King of kings. Then probation will close, and the final time of trouble will occur. But the blessed promise is: "At that time thy people shall be delivered, every one that shall be found written in the book," the book of life spoken of by the apostle Paul in Philippians 4:3. In the darkest hour of trouble the Lord Himself will come.

One night a young woman came to Charles Berry, a liberal preacher of England, and said, "My mother is dying. I want you to come and get her in." He went and talked to the poor gasping woman about having a good record. She said, "But that's not for the likes of me." He told her of God's love, but she said, "It's not for the likes of me." He told her to forget the past and throw herself upon the mercy of God. But that did not help. The poor soul was desperate, and so was the minister. All he could think of was the hymn "There Is a Fountain Filled With Blood," and as he began to sing it, light came into the woman's face. The dying mother could grasp that, and she accepted Christ as her Savior. The next morning he told his congregation, "I got her in, all right; but I did something more—I got myself in too."

May we all be safe inside the fold when Michael stands up.

MEDITATION PRAYER: *"That thy beloved may be delivered: save with thy right hand, and answer me" (Ps. 108:6).*

# OCTOBER 31

*Therefore the redeemed of the Lord shall return, and come with singing unto Zion; and everlasting joy shall be upon their head: they shall obtain gladness and joy; and sorrow and mourning shall flee away (Isa. 51:11).*

This is the final return of Israel, the true believers of all ages, to God's eternal Zion. Their joy is everlasting, and sorrow and mourning shall flee away because their cause is forever gone. "God shall wipe away all tears from their eyes; and there shall be no more death, neither sorrow, nor crying, neither shall there be any more pain: for the former things are passed away" (Rev. 21:4).

Those who possess that land are the redeemed. That is the important part of this promise text—we must be redeemed by our Near Kinsman, He who "took not on him the nature of angels; but . . . the seed of Abraham," that He might "be made like unto his brethren" (Heb. 2:16, 17). He who was not only the Son of God but the Son of man took our place upon the cross. He died for us, and in Him we are redeemed if we will accept it.

Luther once imagined Satan coming to him with a long list and saying, "These are your sins. How dare you hope for heaven?" But he noticed that the devil was holding his hand over the bottom of the list. "Take away your hand," said Luther. And there he saw written, "The blood of Jesus Christ . . . cleanseth us from all sin" (1 John 1:7). So the Reformer took hope; and so may we, for we are "not redeemed with corruptible things, as silver and gold, . . . but with the precious blood of Christ" (1 Peter 1:18, 19).

> Redeemed! how I love to proclaim it!
> Redeemed by the blood of the Lamb;
> Redeemed through His infinite mercy,
> His child, and forever, I am.
> —Fanny J. Crosby

MEDITATION PRAYER: *"Redeem Israel, O God, out of all his troubles" (Ps. 25:22).*

# NOVEMBER 1

*Great peace have they which love thy law:*
*and nothing shall offend them (Ps. 119:165).*

In a stricter sense the Ten Commandments, and, in a wider sense, all the Word of God, are the true basis of soul peace.

When, on one of his voyages, Columbus came to the mouth of the Orinoco River, one of his sailors said they had found an island. The explorer replied, "No such river as that flows from an island. That mighty torrent must drain a continent."

So it is with the law of God. It came from no finite source. It sprang from the depths of infinite wisdom, love, and grace; and its sources are inexhaustible. It brings help for all our needs. Through the Word of God the Holy Spirit acts as Comforter.

Those who love the law of the Lord will not be lifted up by prosperity or cast down by adversity. Their faith in God's Word will dispel all objections. Even when they meet some great mystery of faith, they will not say, "This is an hard saying; who can hear it?" (John 6:60), as did some of old time, but they will accept the Holy Word without question. They will never take offense at the Lord's ways, because they love the Lord's Word.

A Japanese student endeavoring to describe one of his friends to an American said, pointing to a Bible lying nearby, "He believes this Book very much!" Could our friends describe us in that way?

"The law of the Lord is perfect, converting the soul: the testimony of the Lord is sure, making wise the simple" (Ps. 19:7).

> My blest Redeemer and my Lord,
> I read my duty in Thy Word;
> But in Thy life the law appears,
> Drawn out in living characters.
> —Isaac Watts

MEDITATION PRAYER: *"I will delight myself in thy commandments, which I have loved" (Ps. 119:47).*

# NOVEMBER 2

*Blessed is the man that endureth temptation: for when he is tried, he shall receive the crown of life, which the Lord hath promised to them that love him (James 1:12).*

Blessed in temptation—strange, but true! He "that endureth temptation," not he who succumbs to it. "When he is tried"—then by faith he receives the crown of life in fulfillment of God's promise. Why? Because he loves God.

Those who love God will endure temptation. "Love is the fulfilling of the law" (Rom. 13:10). No one with their natural eyesight can actually see blessing while they are enduring trial. But when the furnace test is over, they will come forth with the divine mark of approval, "the crown of life." That is the reward—the crown of life; not mere existence, but eternal life. They will be rewarded also with holiness, happiness, righteousness, joy, and the witness of the Spirit in their heart. "And this is life eternal, that they might know thee the only true God, and Jesus Christ, whom thou hast sent" (John 17:3). Do we truly know and love our Lord?

A young Chinese father had named his son Moo Dee. When the pastor called, he asked why such a name, for he had never heard it before. The father answered: "I have heard of your man of God, Moody. In our dialect *moo* means 'love,' and *Dee,* 'God.' I would have my child love God too."

To love God is to know Him, for "God is love" (1 John 4:8).

> God is love; His mercy brightens
> All the path in which we rove;
> Bliss He wakes, and woe He lightens:
> God is wisdom, God is love.
>
> —J. Bowring

MEDITATION PRAYER: *"All this is come upon us; yet have we not forgotten thee, neither have we dealt falsely in thy covenant" (Ps. 44:17).*

# NOVEMBER 3

*Call upon me in the day of trouble: I will deliver thee,*
*and thou shalt glorify me (Ps. 50:15).*

Again and again God urges us to call upon Him, but this is an urgent occasion—the day of trouble, when it is dark at noon and the sky gets blacker every hour. In such an emergency the Lord invites us to lay our case before Him, and He reassures us, "I will deliver thee." Then we are to glorify Him.

Let us never forget that the Lord is our strength, our fortress, and our refuge in the day of affliction (Jer. 16:19). He is the "God of all comfort; who comforteth us in all our tribulation" (2 Cor. 1:3, 4).

Christian biography testifies to God's deliverance of His servants. As a child, John Wesley was delivered from a burning house. Under his portrait there is a house in flames with the inscription "Was not this a brand plucked from the burning?" (See Zech. 3:2.) Thomas Guthrie had a miraculous escape on the cliffs of Arbroath. John Knox was delivered in arising from his chair a second or two before it was shattered by a bullet. John Howard escaped the hand of an assassin, and George Washington had a similar experience at White Plains. David Livingstone sometimes met with as many as three hairbreadth escapes in a single day. Some of us count our burdens more than our blessings, but let us think of God's many deliverances and say, "Bless the Lord, O my soul, and forget not all his benefits" (Ps. 103:2).

When the storm is raging, or a dark mood is upon us, let us look at the beautiful Jesus. Let us say, "Christ, the Son of God, loves me, and He died to save me." Then we shall praise Him as did Charles Kingsley, who wrote, "Must we not thank, and thank forever, and toil, and toil forever, for Him?"

MEDITATION PRAYER: *"But do thou for me, O God the Lord, for thy name's sake: because thy mercy is good, deliver thou me" (Ps. 109:21).*

# NOVEMBER 4

*Because thou hast made the Lord, which is my refuge, even the most High, thy habitation; there shall no evil befall thee, neither shall any plague come nigh thy dwelling (Ps. 91:9, 10).*

When the 10 strokes of God were falling upon old Egypt land, no harm came to anyone in a dwelling marked with the blood sign over the door on that terrible night of the firstborn. "When I see the blood, I will pass over you" was the promise (Ex. 12:13). So in the latter days of earth, during the seven last plagues, no plague shall come nigh the dwelling of one of God's children.

In ancient Israel those who fled to the city of refuge to escape the avenger's blood must, for their own safety, remain there until the death of the high priest. His death meant life to them. So it is with the followers of the religion of Jesus Christ. Christ, our high priest, has died for us, and we are safe only "under the blood."

It is those who make the Most High not only their refuge but their habitation who have this promise. They are the ones who dwell in God. They know that "the name of the Lord is a strong tower: the righteous runneth into it, and is safe" (Prov. 18:10).

From the beginning of time, people of faith have really dwelt in God. "Lord, thou hast been our dwelling place in all generations. Before the mountains were brought forth, or ever thou hadst formed the earth and the world, even from everlasting to everlasting, thou art God" (Ps. 90:1, 2). It is the person who dwells in the secret place of the Most High who abides under the shadow of the Almighty (Ps. 91:1). And to all such, these words of Moses apply: "The eternal God is thy refuge, and underneath are the everlasting arms" (Deut. 33:27).

MEDITATION PRAYER: *"Give us help from trouble: for vain is the help of man" (Ps. 108:12).*

# NOVEMBER 5

*For as in Adam all die, even so in Christ shall all be made alive.*
*But every man in his own order: Christ the firstfruits;*
*afterward they that are Christ's at his coming (1 Cor. 15:22, 23).*

All sinned in Adam; all rise in Christ. "But every man in his own order." As Hugh Fausset reminds us, the Greek here uses the figure of troops, "each in his own regiment." All will arise, but all will not be saved. Each will have their proper place—Christ first (Col. 1:18); after Him, those who are Christ's, at His coming. "For the Lord himself shall descend from heaven . . . : and the dead in Christ shall rise first" (1 Thess. 4:16). This is the first resurrection, the resurrection unto life. "Blessed and holy is he that hath part in the first resurrection" (Rev. 20:6). "Then cometh the end" (1 Cor. 15:24), with the resurrection of "the rest of the dead," which live "not again until the thousand years [are] finished"—the wicked (Rev. 20:5).

It is those who are Christ's who obtain the resurrection from the dead in the highest sense. As surely as our Savior rose from the dead, so shall all those who are His. Jesus said, "Every one which seeth the Son, and believeth on him, may have everlasting life: and I will raise him up at the last day" (John 6:40).

An Army chaplain tells of having bivouacked with his brigade, each soldier wrapped in his blanket with nothing over him but the cold, cloudy sky. During the night snow fell. Early in the morning the chaplain looked out over the field and saw long rows of little mounds like new graves all covered with snow. Suddenly reveille sounded. There was a stir and a shaking of snow as hundreds of men stood up in momentary amazement at the sight. So will it be at the last trump, when those in Christ arise.

MEDITATION PRAYER: *"Return, O Lord, deliver my soul: oh save me for thy mercies' sake. For in death there is no remembrance of thee: in the grave who shall give thee thanks?" (Ps. 6:4, 5).*

315

# NOVEMBER 6

*For if we have been planted together in the likeness of his death, we shall be also in the likeness of his resurrection (Rom. 6:5).*

Our Savior died upon the cross, was buried in Joseph's new tomb, and rose again victorious over death. In baptism we are planted together with Him in the likeness of His death, and rise again in the likeness of His resurrection. This shows (1) that we have faith in His death and resurrection for us; (2) that our old man of sin is dead and buried, and we rise to live a new life; (3) that we believe that if we are taken by death we shall rise again in the first resurrection and live eternally with our Lord. "Therefore we are buried with him by baptism into death: that like as Christ was raised up from the dead by the glory of the Father, even so we also should walk in newness of life" (Rom. 6:4).

When we see the meaning of baptism, there is no doubt as to its form. We read of the baptism of the chancellor of Ethiopia by Philip: "And he commanded the chariot to stand still: and they went down both into the water, both Philip and the eunuch; and he baptized him" (Acts 8:38). Our Savior was baptized in the Jordan, not because He was a sinner, but that He might "fulfill all righteousness," and also be our example. There is "one Lord, one faith, one baptism" (Eph. 4:5).

A minister went to what is said to be the tomb of Jesus in Jerusalem, and lay down in it. He felt that he had been buried with Christ, but he was really buried with Him when he went with Him into the watery grave of baptism.

Thus through the emblematic grave
The glorious suffering Savior trod;
Thou art our Pattern, through the wave
We follow Thee, blest Son of God.
—S. F. Smith

MEDITATION PRAYER: *"For thy lovingkindness is before mine eyes: and I have walked in thy truth" (Ps. 26:3).*

# NOVEMBER 7

*So shall my word be that goeth forth out of my mouth: it shall
not return unto me void, but it shall accomplish that which I please,
and it shall prosper in the thing whereto I sent it (Isa. 55:11).*

As the rain and snow falling upon the earth make possible the
production of food for human bodies, so shall the Word of God
bring forth spiritual food to the hearts of those who feed upon it. God's
Word always accomplishes the purpose for which He sends it. It never
returns void, but always laden with a harvest. It is sure to accomplish
*that* which He pleases, and it prospers in *the thing* whereto He sends it.

God sends His Word on definite errands. "He sendeth forth his
commandment upon earth: his word runneth very swiftly" (Ps.
147:15). The entire process of nature "is turned round about by his
counsels: that they may do whatsoever he commandeth them upon the
face of the world in the earth" (Job 37:12). And in the affairs of humanity His Word accomplishes His purpose and does not return void.

A little girl unwittingly expressed a great truth when she said, "I tell
you, the Bible does not end in Timothy; it ends in revolutions." Of
course, she meant Revelation; but, as Toyohiko Kagawa once said:
"When you start a Bible movement it means revolution, a quiet revolution against darkness and crime."

The Word of God changes civilizations and nations by changing
hearts. Every regenerated believer is born again "by the word of God,
which liveth and abideth for ever" (1 Peter 1:23).

> 'Tis a pearl of price exceeding
> All the gems in ocean found;
> And, its sacred precepts heeding,
> So shall you in grace abound.

MEDITATION PRAYER: *"Stablish thy word unto thy servant,
who is devoted to thy fear" (Ps. 119:38).*

# NOVEMBER 8

*And they shall be mine, saith the Lord of hosts, in that*
*day when I make up my jewels; and I will spare them,*
*as a man spareth his own son that serveth him (Mal. 3:17).*

In connection with this we should read the preceding verse: "Then they that feared the Lord spake often one to another: and the Lord hearkened, and heard it, and a book of remembrance was written before him for them that feared the Lord, and that thought upon his name."

In the great Peace Tower of the Parliament buildings in Ottawa, Canada, there is a beautiful room lined with slabs of stone on which are carved the great battles of the First World War, in which the Canadian Army took part. In the center of the room is a white marble altar on which rests the open Book of Remembrance containing the names of those who gave their lives in their country's service. Every day a page is turned, exposing new names to the visitor's view.

Our God has a book of remembrance of those who converse about Him. He listens to their talk and records it. Is the Lord pleased with our conversation? Those who please Him in this way are said to be His jewels. "They shall be mine," He says, "when I make up my jewels; and I will spare them." He who has bought us, sought us, and wrought in us His own image will spare us in that day.

In the National Gallery of London one may see the famous painting of two Roman women in the home of Cornelia, the mother of the Gracchi. The visitor has been exhibiting her jewels, and now says to Cornelia, "Show me your jewels." Just at that moment her two boys enter the room. Clasping them to her, Cornelia replies, "These are my jewels."

Those who think about God and talk about Him are His jewels. Of all such it is said, "Thou shalt also be a crown of glory in the hand of the Lord, and a royal diadem in the hand of thy God" (Isa. 62:3).

MEDITATION PRAYER: *"And my tongue shall speak of thy righteousness and of thy praise all the day long" (Ps. 35:28).*

# NOVEMBER 9

*But I say unto you, I will not drink henceforth of this*
*fruit of the vine, until that day when I drink it new*
*with you in my Father's kingdom (Matt. 26:29).*

This was our Savior's promise of reunion, as He celebrated the Last Supper with His disciples. The Passover wine used by our Lord was the pure juice of the grape. The prophet Isaiah refers to it when he speaks of "the new wine . . . in the cluster" (Isa. 65:8). Here it represents Christ's "blood of the new testament, which is shed for many for the remission of sins" (Matt. 26:28). By this expression "new testament," or covenant, our Lord means the reconciliation that God has established between Himself and humankind by the atoning sacrifice of His Son upon the cross.

From what our Lord says here it is clear that the Communion itself is a pledge to all true Christians of the joy that awaits them in the kingdom of glory. Their spiritual enjoyments here are great, but to be with the Lord Himself will be "far better" (Phil. 1:23).

On a cupboard shelf in the humble cottage of a poor Highland widow was an old cracked cup covered with a glass globe. Years before on a hot day a carriage had stopped at her door, and the woman inside had asked for a drink of water, which was given to her in this very cup. Imagine the widow's astonishment when she learned that the one who had used that cup was Queen Victoria. Her lips had touched it and made it an object of priceless value to the widow.

The cup that our Master used at the Last Supper has become to all true disciples a symbol of His undying love and sacrifice. As the cup on the widow's shelf reminded her of the queen's visit, so the cup in the Communion service reminds us of our Savior's sacrifice and of His promise, "I [will] drink it new with you in my Father's kingdom."

MEDITATION PRAYER: *"I will sing praise to thy name, O thou most High" (Ps. 9:2).*

# NOVEMBER 10

*For the Lord God will help me; therefore shall I not*
*be confounded: therefore have I set my face like a flint,*
*and I know that I shall not be ashamed (Isa. 50:7).*

These are prophetically the words of Christ, who would suffer as our sin-bearing substitute. The Son of God, who was also the Son of man, was treated with all the malignity of evil people and demons. In those times of terrible persecution and suffering His heart trusted in God; yet, in His humanity, at the climax of His crucifixion He cried, "My God, my God, why hast thou forsaken me?" (Matt. 27:46). But in it all He said, "I shall not be confounded." He set His face like a flint to accomplish the salvation of humanity, and in it He was not ashamed. Those who are guided by the Lord will find blessing even in calamity. "Behold, happy is the man whom God correcteth: therefore despise not thou the chastening of the Almighty" (Job 5:17). Out of the evil, God can and will bring good.

A man had a very rare plant in a flowerpot, close to a pool of water. Although he tended it carefully, it barely kept alive. One day in his absence a careless boy knocked it over, breaking the pot and toppling the plant into the water. When the owner returned weeks later, he noticed the luxuriant growth of an unknown plant coming out of the water. Later he learned that the plant that had languished so in the pot was a water plant. So it is many times with starving, thirsting souls. What seems to be a calamity, a great, unmitigated sorrow permitted by what seems to them to be a callous Providence, is really a blessing in disguise—something that beautifies the character and brings out strength and patience and understanding never known before.

Those who meet disaster and sorrow in true faith are able to say with the psalmist, "I know, O Lord, that thy judgments are right, and that thou in faithfulness hast afflicted me" (Ps. 119:75).

MEDITATION PRAYER: *"It is good for me that I have been afflicted; that I might learn thy statutes" (Ps. 119:71).*

# NOVEMBER 11

*Cast thy burden upon the Lord, and he shall sustain thee: he shall never suffer the righteous to be moved (Ps. 55:22).*

We are not to lay our burden down and pick it up again, but to roll it on the Lord and leave it there. It may be a heavy burden, but He is omnipotent. Do not try to bear your burden alone; it is too heavy, it is too much for you. Remember, "he shall sustain thee." He accepts us in Christ as righteous, and He will never suffer us to be moved from our standing before Him. "O Lord, my strength, and my fortress, and my refuge in the day of affliction," prayed His servant Jeremiah (Jer. 16:19).

Some of the most beautiful characters of earth have been afflicted in their bodies and have borne agonies for years. One such was Nathaniel Kendrick, the founder of Colgate University. He was paralyzed in the prime of life and lay in bed for many years, unable to move. Then it seemed that the majesty of his Christian faith shone forth with power. Once his son said to him, "Father, I have never loved you as I do now. Oh, if I could only bear your pain for you!"

The reply was: "No, son, I have not one pain to spare. He who allows me to suffer loves me even more than you do and knows just what is best for me. I sometimes think this is the happiest period of my life. His mercies to me are so great."

> All thy griefs by Him are ordered,
> Needful is each one for thee;
> Every tear by Him is counted,
> One too much there cannot be.
>
> And if, whilst they fall so thickly,
> Thou canst own His way is right,
> Then each bitter tear of anguish
> Precious is in Jesus' sight.

MEDITATION PRAYER: *"In the day of my trouble I will call upon thee: for thou wilt answer me"* (Ps. 86:7).

# NOVEMBER 12

*When thou passest through the waters, I will be
with thee; and through the rivers, they shall not overflow
thee: when thou walkest through the fire, thou shalt not be
burned; neither shall the flame kindle upon thee (Isa. 43:2).*

There is no bridge or ferry—we must pass through the deep waters;
but the Lord Himself says, "I will be with thee." Enemies may
surround us, persecutions and cruel mockings be as a fiery furnace.
What shall we do? Walk through them, for "the form of the fourth"
(Dan. 3:25) will be by our side, and there shall not be even the smell of
fire upon us. Such is the security of heaven-born, heaven-bound pilgrims. The flood cannot drown them, nor the fire burn them.

> And he walks with me, and He talks with me,
> And He tells me I am His own.
> —C. Austin Miles

A minister sat down at the bedside of an aged Christian. Pointing
to a chair on the other side of the bed facing at such an angle as to suggest that another visitor had just left, he said, "I see I am not your first
visitor today."

"Ah," said the afflicted one, "I'll tell you about that chair. Years ago
I found it impossible to pray. Often I would fall asleep on my knees,
and if I kept awake, my thoughts would wander. I spoke to a minister
about it, and he told me to sit down with a chair opposite me and think
of the Lord Jesus as sitting in it; and then to talk to Him as to a friend,
face to face. I have been doing that ever since, and He has become very
real to me. That is why the chair stands like that by my bed." Later that
week the good man died with his hand resting on the chair reserved for
the Lord.

Our Savior has promised, "I will never leave thee, nor forsake
thee" (Heb. 13:5).

MEDITATION PRAYER: *"O God, be not far from me: O my
God, make haste for my help" (Ps. 71:12).*

# NOVEMBER 13

*I will heal their backsliding, I will love them freely:*
*for mine anger is turned away from him (Hosea 14:4).*

With this, we place Jeremiah 3:22: "Return, ye backsliding children, and I will heal your backslidings." The response follows: "Behold, we come unto thee; for thou art the Lord our God." The third chapter of Jeremiah might be entitled "Hope for Backsliders." In the twelfth and thirteenth verses we read: "Return, thou backsliding Israel, saith the Lord; and I will not cause mine anger to fall upon you: for I am merciful, saith the Lord, and I will not keep anger for ever. Only acknowledge thine iniquity, that thou hast transgressed against the Lord thy God." Then we come to the great climax in verse 14: "Turn, O backsliding children, saith the Lord; for I am married unto you: and I will take you one of a city, and two of a family, and I will bring you to Zion."

Hope for backsliders? There is no doubt about it. Let all such, both outside church fellowship and in the church, return to God without delay.

An officer in the Indian Army had raised a tiger cub as a pet, and it seemed perfectly docile. One day as the officer was sleeping in his chair the tiger began licking his hand. As he continued to lick, blood appeared from an abrasion. Immediately the tiger's wild nature was aroused and he attacked his master, who barely escaped death. Although the animal seemed tame and domesticated, the tiger nature was still in him.

Some Christians who have been regenerated have backslidden. To all such, the Lord says, "Remember therefore from whence thou art fallen, and repent, and do the first works" (Rev. 2:5). The call to backsliders is the call to repentance and obedience. God will heal the sickness of backsliding. He will love us freely.

MEDITATION PRAYER: *"Let me not be ashamed, O Lord; for I have called upon thee" (Ps. 31:17).*

# NOVEMBER 14

*And it shall come to pass, that whosoever shall call on the*
*name of the Lord shall be delivered: for in mount Zion*
*and in Jerusalem shall be deliverance, as the Lord hath said,*
*and in the remnant whom the Lord shall call (Joel 2:32).*

Whosoever" is a big word, a wide word. As the old-time evangelists used to say: "'Whosoever' means me." With such a promise as this, why do we not call on the Lord? We have His royal "shall" to make it certain. From any situation, habit, sin, or condemnation there is deliverance in God. The crowd may not find it, but some will. It is "in the remnant whom the Lord shall call." Those whom the Lord calls are to call upon Him.

A cashier in a New York bank, a very faithful Christian, could not make his account balance by many thousands of dollars. He had never used a dollar of the bank's funds, nor could he find any error in his accounts. The next day the bank examiner was to look over his books, and he would be declared a defaulter. Early that morning he went to the director's office alone and, in great agony of spirit, pleaded with God for one hour. Suddenly calm came to his troubled heart. As though led by an invisible hand, he went from his knees to the safe. There he noticed a blotter marking a place in one of the account books. Opening its pages, he found items that had not been posted and that made his account balance exactly. That providential discovery vindicated his honesty and showed the faithfulness of God, who said, "Call upon me in the day of trouble: I will deliver thee" (Ps. 50:15). God's deliverance from sin as well as from trouble is in this promise.

> O Lord, because of our great need,
> A vast and mighty sum,
> We bow and for Thy mercy plead,
> Come, great Deliverer, come!

MEDITATION PRAYER: *"Thou hast enlarged me when I was in distress; have mercy upon me, and hear my prayer" (Ps. 4:1).*

# NOVEMBER 15

*And all things, whatsoever ye shall ask in*
*prayer, believing, ye shall receive (Matt. 21:22).*

True Christians will live so near the Lord that what they pray for will be the will of God. "The Lord is nigh unto all them that call upon him, to all that call upon him in truth" (Ps. 145:18). "Ye shall seek me, and find me, when ye shall search for me with all your heart" (Jer. 29:13). "Without faith it is impossible to please him: for he that cometh to God must believe that he is, and that he is a rewarder of them that diligently seek him" (Heb. 11:6).

When J. Hudson Taylor, the famous missionary, first went to China in a sailing vessel, the ship was becalmed near some cannibal islands. Slowly it drifted toward the shore, where savages were eagerly anticipating a feast. The captain went to Mr. Taylor and begged him to pray to God for help. Mr. Taylor said, "I will, provided you set the sails to catch the breeze." But the captain did not want to become a laughingstock by unfurling his sails in a dead calm. However, Mr. Taylor would not pray until the sails were up. As they drifted nearer and nearer to the shore the captain was desperate, so up went the sails.

While Mr. Taylor was engaged in prayer, there came a knock at his stateroom door. It was the captain. "Stop praying," he said, "stop praying. There is more wind than we can manage." They had drifted within a hundred yards of the shore when a strong wind had suddenly struck the sails. J. Hudson Taylor really knew God in prayer. It was true of him that "faith sees the heavenly legions, where doubt sees nought but foes."

"Men ought always to pray, and not to faint" (Luke 18:1). "Therefore I say unto you, What things soever ye desire, when ye pray, believe that ye receive them, and ye shall have them" (Mark 11:24).

MEDITATION PRAYER: *"I cried to thee, O Lord; and unto the Lord I made supplication" (Ps. 30:8).*

# NOVEMBER 16

*And the streets of the city shall be full of boys
and girls playing in the streets thereof (Zech. 8:5).*

What a sign of peace and prosperity is this—city streets filled with boys and girls at play! Nothing more wonderful can happen to a family than the birth of a child. A young minister, filled with joy and wonder at the birth of his first child, telegraphed the glad news to his parents. His preacher father replied with Psalm 127:3-5: "Lo, children are an heritage of the Lord. . . . As arrows are in the hand of a mighty man; so are children of the youth. Happy is the man that hath his quiver full of them."

"Why do you bow to that newsboy?" President Garfield was asked by a friend.

"Because," the president answered, "no one knows what's buttoned up in that boy's jacket."

Whenever we look into the eyes of a child we are beholding the face of tomorrow, and possibly the face of greatness. Who knows but that it may be a young John Knox, a John or Charles Wesley, a George Whitefield; or a Florence Nightingale, a Clara Barton, a Helen Keller? Jesus said, "Suffer little children to come unto me, . . . for of such is the kingdom of God" (Luke 18:16). On this basis, as Bishop William Taylor used to say, "there are no heathen children. They are not such until misled by the influences that surround them."

The deacons of the church had asked the pastor to resign. "We love you," they said, "but there hasn't been a convert this year."

"Oh, yes," said the pastor. "You forgot little Bobby. Of course, he's very young, and I don't suppose it's right to count him."

Years later when Robert Moffat came back from his great missionary work in Africa, the king of England arose and bared his head in his presence. Let us take an interest in the boys and girls playing in our streets, that we may see them later in the streets of a brighter city.

MEDITATION PRAYER: *"Out of the mouth of babes and sucklings hast thou ordained strength" (Ps. 8:2).*

# NOVEMBER 17

*They that sow in tears shall reap in joy. He that goeth forth and weepeth, bearing precious seed, shall doubtless come again with rejoicing, bringing his sheaves with him (Ps. 126:5, 6).*

Some seed needs to be watered with tears, so weeping times are good sowing times. Through our tears we may not see the harvest, but it will come, and we shall reap in joy if we faint not.

If we carry forth precious seed for sowing, there is no doubt that we shall return, bringing in our sheaves. Each of us is a sower going forth to sow. Some of our sowing is of good seed; some, evil. Which shall it be today? It is the "precious seed," the good seed, that brings forth fruit for the kingdom of God and enables us to reap with joy and come with rejoicing, bearing our sheaves.

Many a minister has been forced, for the profit of the flock, to sow the precious seed with tears. "Six weeks of painful, dangerous sickness did more for me than six months in a theological seminary," said a very successful minister.

The model minister of Christ in Rome wrote to his son Timothy: "Therefore I endure all things for the elect's sakes, that they may also obtain the salvation which is in Christ Jesus" (2 Tim. 2:10).

> He that goeth forth with weeping,
>     Bearing precious seed in love,
> Never tiring, never sleeping,
>     Findeth mercy from above.
>
> Sow thy seed, be never weary,
>     Let no fears thy soul annoy;
> Be the prospect ne'er so dreary,
>     Thou shalt reap the fruits of joy.
>                 —Thomas Hastings

MEDITATION PRAYER: *"That I may publish with the voice of thanksgiving, and tell of all thy wondrous works" (Ps. 26:7).*

# NOVEMBER 18

*Rejoice not against me, O mine enemy: when I fall, I shall arise; when I sit in darkness, the Lord shall be a light unto me (Micah 7:8).*

The basis for this promise is found in the verse preceding: "I will look unto the Lord; I will wait for the God of my salvation: my God will hear me." It is when we have faith in God, trustingly wait for the fulfillment of His promises, and seek Him earnestly in prayer that we can be sure of rising when we fall and finding light in dark places. "Nothing is apparently more helpless, yet really more invincible, than the soul that feels its nothingness and relies wholly on the merits of the Savior. By prayer, by the study of His Word, by faith in His abiding presence, the weakest of human beings may live in contact with the living Christ, and He will hold them by a hand that will never let go. These precious words every soul that abides in Christ may make his own" (*The Ministry of Healing*, p. 182).

In Psalm 112:4 we read, "Unto the upright there ariseth light in the darkness." We may find ourselves in some dark dungeon experience, but however dark it may be, the Lord will be our light.

When one of the Reformers had acquitted himself in public disputation as a credit to his Master's cause, a friend asked to see the notes he had been observed to write, supposing that he had taken down the arguments of his opponent and sketched the substance of his own reply. The friend was surprised to find that the notes consisted of this petition: "More light, Lord! More light, Lord!"

> The Lord is my light; then why should I fear?
> By day and by night His presence is near;
> He is my salvation from sorrow and sin;
> This blessed persuasion the Spirit brings in.
> —James Nicholson

MEDITATION PRAYER: *"Bless the Lord, O my soul. O Lord my God, thou art very great. . . . Who coverest thyself with light as with a garment"* (Ps. 104:1, 2).

# NOVEMBER 19

*For as the lightning cometh out of the east, and shineth even unto the west; so shall also the coming of the Son of man be (Matt. 24:27).*

The return of Christ will be universally known, witnessed by the whole world. "They shall see the Son of man coming in the clouds of heaven with power and great glory" (Matt. 24:30). He is not to appear secretly in some desert place, or privately in the secret chambers. He comes with all the holy angels. Suddenly the heavens will be filled with glory, then "a shout, . . . the voice of the archangel, and . . . the trump of God" (1 Thess. 4:16).

William M. Dyke, blinded by an accident when 10 years of age, won university honors, also a beautiful bride whom he had never seen. Just before his marriage he submitted to an eye operation, and the climax came on the day of his wedding. The bride entered the church, leaning on the arm of her aged father, Admiral Cave. There stood her future husband and his father and the great oculist, who was cutting away the last bandage. A beam of rose-colored light from a window fell across his face, but he didn't seem to see it, as with a cry of joy he sprang forward to meet his bride. "At last! At last!" he cried, as he gazed for the first time upon her face. What a meeting! But how much greater will be the joy of the redeemed as they are presented in the presence of His glory and see their blessed Redeemer for the first time face to face.

> O soon I shall gaze upon the face of Him,
> Pierced to redeem me from the curse of sin,
> And praise Him forever with the glad new hymn;
> I shall be satisfied then.
>
> —Horatius Bonar

MEDITATION PRAYER: *"Blessed is the man whom thou choosest, and causest to approach unto thee, that he may dwell in thy courts: we shall be satisfied with the goodness of thy house, even of thy holy temple" (Ps. 65:4).*

# NOVEMBER 20

*And this gospel of the kingdom shall be preached*
*in all the world for a witness unto all nations;*
*and then shall the end come (Matt. 24:14).*

Modern methods of transportation and communication have made it possible for gospel messengers and the gospel message to go quickly to earth's remotest bounds. The everlasting gospel will be preached for a witness, a testimony, to every nation, kindred, tongue, and people (Rev. 14:6). Then, just as certainly as the gospel preaching goes to the world, "shall the end come."

The apostolic preaching of the gospel, as it went out from old Jerusalem to the civilized world of that time (Rom. 10:18; Col. 1:6, 23), was followed by the destruction of Jerusalem as a symbol of the world itself. When the gospel witness goes forth again, this time to all the world, the end of the world or age will come, and the kingdom of glory will be set up. The Lord shall reign "from sea even to sea, and from the river even to the ends of the earth" (Zech. 9:10).

What preachers we should be in such an hour as this! Someone asked an old Scotch woman what she thought of Robert Murray McCheyne's preaching. She hesitated a moment, then replied, "He preaches as if he was a-dyin' to have you saved." And so should we preach, for "the Lord is at hand" (Phil. 4:5).

> Long they've toiled within the harvest,
>     Sown the precious seed with tears;
> Soon they'll drop their heavy burdens
>     In the glad millennial years;
> They will share the bliss of heaven,
>     Nevermore to sigh or moan;
> Starry crowns will then be given,
>     When the King shall claim His own.
>                                   —L. D. Santee

MEDITATION PRAYER: *"They shall speak of the glory of thy kingdom, and talk of thy power"* (Ps. 145:11).

# NOVEMBER 21

*When my father and my mother forsake me,*
*then the Lord will take me up (Ps. 27:10).*

Davids father and mother were unable to shelter him, for they were forced into exile. Our parents may be able to care for us for a time, but the Lord will care for us at all times and for eternity.

Jesus was speaking of children when He said, "In heaven their angels do always behold the face of my Father. . . . It is not the will of your Father which is in heaven, that one of these little ones should perish" (Matt. 18:10-14).

Many years ago a company of slaves were sold at auction in Nigeria. Just one little boy was left on the auction block. He presented such a miserable appearance that people laughed at the suggestion of buying him. Finally, however, someone purchased him for a roll of tobacco, and with the rest of the slaves he had to march to the coast. There he was put in the hold of a ship bound for America. On the high seas the ship was captured by the British, who took the slaves to Freetown, in Sierra Leone, and set them at liberty. The little boy was taken in by some missionaries.

Many years later there was an interesting service at St. Paul's Cathedral in London. In the presence of the great of the earth this little boy, now grown, was consecrated as the first bishop of Nigeria. So the lonely little slave, whose parents could not or would not help him, became Bishop Samuel Crowther, and his name is still revered as a true hero of the cross.

The great father heart of God yearns over His little ones, and of them it is written, "He shall cover thee with his feathers, and under his wings shalt thou trust" (Ps. 91:4).

MEDITATION PRAYER: *"The poor committeth himself unto thee; thou art the helper of the fatherless" (Ps. 10:14).*

# NOVEMBER 22

*And even to your old age I am he; and even to hoar hairs will I carry you: I have made, and I will bear; even I will carry, and will deliver you (Isa. 46:4).*

In contrast to the idols, which need to be borne by others, the Lord bears His people in safety from birth to old age. He likens Himself to a nurse, tenderly carrying a child. Notice His multiple promise: I will bear, I will carry, I will deliver. We grow old, but God is still the I AM, the unchangeable Lord of heaven and earth. We may become a burden to others and to ourselves, but He will care for us. He who has carried us as lambs in His bosom will not forsake us when we are old.

"I am on the bright side of 70," said the aged man of God. "Bright side, because nearer to everlasting glory."

The apostle who wrote, "Being such an one as Paul the aged" (Philemon 9), also testified, "Notwithstanding the Lord stood with me, and strengthened me" (2 Tim. 4:17). Though everyone forsook him before the bloodthirsty emperor of Rome, the Lord did not.

Notice that the promise "I will carry you" is doubled in our text. And we need this double promise when physical weakness and afflictions come upon us, that we may keep not only in the path of righteousness but in the way of joyfulness as we grow old.

> Lord, keep me joyful in the way,
>     Until the story's told;
> And as I walk with slower step,
>     Grow sweeter growing old.
>
> May each new day that dawns for me,
>     More of Thy grace unfold;
> Until the last and best of life
>     Is sweeter growing old.

MEDITATION PRAYER: *"Now also when I am old and gray-headed, O God, forsake me not; until I have shewed thy strength unto this generation, and thy power to every one that is to come" (Ps. 71:18).*

# NOVEMBER 23

*For the mountains shall depart, and the hills be removed; but my kindness shall not depart from thee, neither shall the covenant of my peace be removed, saith the Lord that hath mercy on thee (Isa. 54:10).*

God's covenant is God's promise. It is a covenant of peace, and a promise of mercy and kindness. The mountains are still here, and the hills are still here. That is certain evidence that His kindness, peace, and mercy have not departed from us. The author of all the promises of the Bible is "the same yesterday, and to day, and for ever" (Heb. 13:8). He says, "Behold, I have graven thee upon the palms of my hands; thy walls are continually before me" (Isa. 49:16). He never forgets us.

Sometime ago a certain printer in an Eastern city of the United States sent out an impressive trademark. It was a circle within which is his name with the words "I never disappoint." So it is with God's promises; He never disappoints.

It is true that "the heavens shall vanish away like smoke, and the earth shall wax old like a garment," but our God's "righteousness shall not be abolished" (Isa. 51:6).

A well-known organization has advertised itself as "strong as the Rock of Gibralter," but even that great fortress may fall. "Therefore will not we fear, though the earth be removed, and though the mountains be carried into the midst of the sea. . . . The Lord of hosts is with us; the God of Jacob is our refuge" (Ps. 46:2-7).

> When all Thy mercies, O my God!
> My rising soul surveys,
> Transported with the view, I'm lost
> In wonder, love, and praise.
> —Joseph Addison

MEDITATION PRAYER: *"For thy mercy is great unto the heavens, and thy truth unto the clouds" (Ps. 57:10).*

# NOVEMBER 24

*Then shall the dust return to the earth*
*as it was: and the spirit shall return*
*unto God who gave it (Eccl. 12:7).*

This is the reversal of the Genesis story, where we read: "God formed man of the dust of the ground, and breathed into his nostrils the breath of life; and man became a living soul" (Gen. 2:7). When we come to the end of life's journey, the dust returns to the earth as it was; and the spirit, or breath of life, returns unto God who gave it. Our personality, our life, our eternal destiny, are safe there.

So, Christian, "set your affection on things above, not on things on the earth. For ye are dead, and your life is hid with Christ in God. When Christ, who is our life, shall appear, then shall ye also appear with him in glory" (Col. 3:2-4). Our true citizenship is in heaven, "from whence also we look for the Savior, the Lord Jesus Christ: who shall change our vile body ["the body of our humiliation," ARV], that it may be fashioned like unto his glorious body" (Phil. 3:20, 21).

An eaglet was caught and raised with the chickens, so the great bird had no sense of his power of flight. With the other birds, he was always looking down to the ground for food. The owner decided to teach the eagle to fly, so lifted him up in his hands, but as soon as he was released he fell to the ground. Then he threw the bird above his head, but his fall was all the more severe. After many trials the eagle was put up on a fence and held there for a moment. He lifted his head, and catching a glimpse of the sun, suddenly pushed out one wing, then the other. With a shriek and a bound he rose from the fence. In another moment he began to soar, higher and higher, until soon he was lost from sight in the blazing light of the sun.

True, we are children of earth now, but through Christ our Savior, heaven is our home.

MEDITATION PRAYER: *"My soul shall be satisfied as with marrow and fatness; and my mouth shall praise thee with joyful lips" (Ps. 63:5).*

# NOVEMBER 25

*Verily, verily, I say unto you,*
*If a man keep my saying,*
*he shall never see death (John 8:51).*

To every believer Christ is "the resurrection, and the life" (John 11:25). "I am come," said Jesus, "that they might have life, and that they might have it more abundantly" (John 10:10). "Whoso eateth my flesh, and drinketh my blood, hath eternal life; and I will raise him up at the last day" (John 6:54). "To the believer, death is but a small matter. Christ speaks of it as if it were of little moment. 'If a man keep my saying, he shall never see death,' 'he shall never taste of death.' To the Christian, death is but a sleep, a moment of silence and darkness. The life is hid with Christ in God" (*The Desire of Ages,* p. 787). Jesus said, "Our friend Lazarus sleepeth; but I go, that I may awake him out of sleep" (John 11:11).

"For we know," says the apostle, "that if our earthly house of this tabernacle were dissolved, we have a building of God, an house not made with hands, eternal in the heavens" (2 Cor. 5:1). And our desire is "not . . . that we would be unclothed, but clothed upon, that mortality might be swallowed up of life. . . . Knowing that, whilst we are at home in the body, we are absent from the Lord: (for we walk by faith, not by sight:) . . . willing rather to be absent from the body, and to be present with the Lord. Wherefore we labour, that, whether present or absent, we may be accepted of him" (verses 4-9).

When death had brought grief to the home of Thomas Carlyle, a friend opened the Bible and read the words of Jesus: "Let not your heart be troubled. . . . In my Father's house are many mansions" (John 14:1, 2).

"Aye," muttered Carlyle, "if you were God, you had a right to say that. But if you were only a man, what do you know any more than the rest of us?" And that's the truth. But He is God, and He does know.

MEDITATION PRAYER: *"Lord, what is man, that thou takest knowledge of him! or the son of man, that thou makest account of him!"* *(Ps. 144:3).*

# NOVEMBER 26

*Peace I leave with you, my peace I give unto you:*
*not as the world giveth, give I unto you. Let not your*
*heart be troubled, neither let it be afraid (John 14:27).*

Shortly before His crucifixion our Savior bequeathed this legacy of peace to His disciples. "This peace is not the peace that comes through conformity to the world. Christ never purchased peace by compromise with evil. The peace that Christ left His disciples is internal rather than external, and was ever to remain with His witnesses through strife and contention" (*The Acts of the Apostles,* p. 84).

He was the Prince of Peace, but His coming brought many contentions into the world. Those who opposed His teachings would bring controversy and bitter trouble to His followers, and He warns His people, "In the world ye shall have tribulation" (John 16:33). "They shall lay their hands on you, and persecute you. . . . And ye shall be betrayed" (Luke 21:12-16). But of every tempest-tossed and tried servant of His, Jesus says, "I will love him, and will manifest myself to him" (John 14:21). Nothing or no one can take this peace from that person's heart. "Let not your heart be troubled: ye believe in God, believe also in me" (John 14:1). Faith in Christ brings peace. In fact, "He is our peace" (Eph. 2:14).

A bricklayer had fallen from a great height and was lying fatally injured. He was approached by a minister from the neighborhood, whose first words were: "My dear friend, I am afraid you are dying. I urge you to make your peace with God at once."

"Make my peace with God!" exclaimed the injured man. "Why, that was made 1,900 years ago when my Savior died upon the cross. Christ is my peace, and has been ever since I knew Him."

And so is He our peace, today and tomorrow and forever.

MEDITATION PRAYER: *"My heart is fixed, O God, my heart is fixed: I will sing and give praise"* (Ps. 57:7).

# NOVEMBER 27

*No weapon that is formed against thee shall prosper;*
*and every tongue that shall rise against thee in judgment*
*thou shalt condemn. This is the heritage of the servants of the*
*Lord, and their righteousness is of me, saith the Lord (Isa. 54:17).*

There may be great activity in the arsenal of evil, forging weapons against the saints, but on every product of these flaming foundries is this inscription: "It shall not prosper."

A company of Scottish Covenanters in the old days of persecution were pursued by their persecutors. They were entirely exhausted. Reaching a little hill that separated them from their enemies, their leader said, "Let us pray here, for if the Lord hear not our prayer and save us, we are all dead men." Then he prayed, "Twine them about the hill, O Lord, and cast the lap of Thy cloak over poor old Saunders and these poor things." Before he had done speaking, a mist rose up about the hill and wrapped the devoted little band about like the very cloak of the Lord, for which he had prayed. In vain their enemies sought them, and while they were wearying themselves to find them, an order came calling them away in an opposite direction.

In the end, the weapon formed against God's children will not prosper. He will break it or dull its edge.

Now we hear another hubbub—slander, libel, falsehood, ridicule, insinuation. These things may condemn us for a moment, but we shall condemn them at last and forever. God's promise is: "Thou shalt hide them in the secret of thy presence from the pride of man: thou shalt keep them secretly in a pavilion from the strife of tongues" (Ps. 31:20). This is the heritage of God's servants. Why? Because their "righteousness is of me, saith the Lord." This righteousness is ours by faith (Rom. 3:22). It is a gift (Rom. 5:17). "Clad in the armor of Christ's righteousness, the church is to enter upon her final conflict" (*Prophets and Kings*, p. 725).

MEDITATION PRAYER: *"I will offer to thee the sacrifice of thanksgiving, and will call upon the name of the Lord" (Ps. 116:17).*

# NOVEMBER 28

*He that dwelleth in the secret place of the most High*
*shall abide under the shadow of the Almighty (Ps. 91:1).*

Shortly after the Civil War in the United States, two Americans were crossing the Atlantic and heard a third man with an exceedingly rich tenor voice singing on deck in the moonlight, "Jesus, Lover of My Soul." When the music ceased, one of the men turned to the singer and asked if he had been in the Civil War. He said that he had been a Confederate soldier. Then he was asked if he was at such a place on such a night.

"Yes," he said, "and a curious thing happened that night. I was on sentry duty on the edge of a dark wood. The night was cold, and I was lonely and not a little frightened, because the enemy was close. I was homesick and miserable, too. About midnight, when everything was still, I began to feel unusually depressed and frightened, so I began to sing this hymn softly, 'Jesus, Lover of My Soul.' When I came to the verse, 'All my trust on Thee is stayed, all my help from thee I bring; cover my defenseless head with the shadow of Thy wing,' a strange peace came over me, and I was no longer afraid."

"Now," said the first man, "listen to my story. I was a Union soldier with a party of sharpshooters and scouts in those woods that very night. We saw you outlined against the sky. My men focused their rifles on you, when suddenly you sang those words, 'Cover my defenseless head with the shadow of Thy wing.' We listened. I said, 'Boys, put down your rifles. We can't shoot now.'"

We are not merely to flee to God's secret place, but to abide there. "For in the time of trouble he shall hide me in his pavilion: in the secret of his tabernacle shall he hide me" (Ps. 27:5). In harmony with this promise our prayer may be, "Keep me as the apple of the eye, hide me under the shadow of thy wings" (Ps. 17:8).

MEDITATION PRAYER: *"Because thou hast been my help, therefore in the shadow of thy wings will I rejoice" (Ps. 63:7).*

# NOVEMBER 29

*And the Lord shall guide thee continually, and satisfy thy soul in drought, and make fat thy bones: and thou shalt be like a watered garden, and like a spring of water, whose waters fail not (Isa. 58:11).*

What wonderful promises for the spiritual life as well as the material do we find here! Guidance, satisfaction, health—the whole life, like a watered garden, blooming even in the heat of summer and bringing forth fruit in season.

"On the last day, the great day of the feast, Jesus stood and cried, saying, If any man thirst, let him come unto me and drink. He that believeth on me, as the scripture hath said, from within him shall flow rivers of living water" (John 7:37, 38, ARV). Believers are like artesian wells, life-giving and never-failing in every desert way.

Deep in the Mammoth Cave of Kentucky is a bronze tablet that reads: "Out of the lowest depths there is a path to the loftiest heights." And nearby stands a guide ready to show the reader the way out. In Christ we have a guide who will show us the way out of all life's difficulties.

> He leadeth me! O blessed thought!
> O words with heavenly comfort fraught!
> Whate'er I do, where'er I be,
> Still 'tis God's hand that leadeth me.
>
> Lord, I would clasp my hand in Thine,
> Nor ever murmur nor repine;
> Content, whatever lot I see,
> Since 'tis my God that leadeth me.
> —J. H. Gilmore

MEDITATION PRAYER: *"From the end of the earth will I cry unto thee, when my heart is overwhelmed: lead me to the rock that is higher than I" (Ps. 61:2).*

# NOVEMBER 30

*I am the living bread which came down from heaven: if any man eat of this bread, he shall live for ever: and the bread that I will give is my flesh, which I will give for the life of the world (John 6:51).*

The promise here is twofold: If anyone eats this bread they will live forever, and Christ will give this bread for the life of the world. He Himself is the living bread, "the bread of life" (John 6:48).

How may we eat this living bread? What did our Savior mean when He identified the living bread with His own flesh? He said: "Except ye eat the flesh of the Son of man, and drink his blood, ye have no life in you. Whoso eateth my flesh, and drinketh my blood, hath eternal life; and I will raise him up at the last day. For my flesh is meat indeed, and my blood is drink indeed" (verses 53–55).

Some of His disciples, hearing these words, said, "This is an hard saying; who can hear it?" (verse 60). And they "went back, and walked no more with him" (verse 66). But Christ explained the meaning of these words in the sixty-third verse: "The flesh profiteth nothing: the words that I speak unto you, they are spirit, and they are life." The apostle Peter so understood our Savior, for we find him asking, "Lord, to whom shall we go? thou hast the words of eternal life" (verse 68).

The Arabs have great respect for wheat in any form. When a morsel of bread falls to the ground, they will gather it up in their right hand, touch it to their forehead, and place it in a recess or on a wall where the birds may find it, for they say, "We must not tread underfoot the gift of God."

When a person has once tasted the bread of life, they have no more desire for the husks of Egypt, for "the weak and beggarly elements" of the world (Gal. 4:9). Have we eaten of the fruits and bread of the kingdom of grace? It's a sad day when the hunger for them is lost. May we all pray, "Lord, evermore give us this bread" (John 6:34).

MEDITATION PRAYER: *"Whom have I in heaven but thee? and there is none upon earth that I desire beside thee" (Ps. 73:25).*

# DECEMBER 1

*And this is the promise that he hath*
*promised us, even eternal life (1 John 2:25).*

This is a promise of promises and should be understood in the light of the preceding verse: "Let that therefore abide in you, which ye have heard from the beginning. If that which ye have heard from the beginning shall remain in you, ye also shall continue in the Son, and in the Father."

From the beginning of the gospel, salvation through the blood of Christ, which cleanses from all sin, was promised (1 John 1:7-9). We abide in Christ when His words abide in us, and so Christ dwells in our hearts by faith (Eph. 3:17). The result of all this is "fruit unto holiness, and the end everlasting life" (Rom. 6:22). For "the gift of God is eternal life through Jesus Christ our Lord" (verse 23). And again, in 1 John 5:11 we read that "God hath given to us eternal life, and this life is in his Son." "For as the Father hath life in himself; so hath he given to the Son to have life in himself" (John 5:26). He says, "Because I live, ye shall live also" (John 14:19). This eternal life, which we have now by faith, includes immortality bestowed at the second coming of Christ. "And this is life eternal, that they might know thee the only true God, and Jesus Christ, whom thou hast sent" (John 17:3).

Remember, friend, "your life is hid with Christ in God," but "when Christ, who is our life, shall appear, then shall ye also appear with him in glory" (Col. 3:3, 4). Eternal life is ours by faith now. Therefore, let us be happy.

"A little faith will bring your soul to heaven," said Dwight L. Moody, "but a lot of faith will bring heaven to your soul."

MEDITATION PRAYER: *"I will also praise thee with the psaltery, even thy truth, O my God: unto thee will I sing with the harp, O thou Holy One of Israel" (Ps. 71:22).*

# DECEMBER 2

*But my God shall supply all your need*
*according to his riches in glory*
*by Christ Jesus (Phil. 4:19).*

There are two handles by which we may take hold of our tomor-
rows: anxiety and faith. Which shall it be? Here is God's promise,
Heaven's checkbook—all our needs are to be supplied, according to
His riches. Not necessarily our wants and desires, but our needs.

Think of Pastor Harms with his little church of poor peasants at
Hermannsburg supporting 357 missionaries in 30 years. When asked
how they did it, his reply was that they depended upon the divine draft,
"My God shall supply all your need according to his riches in glory."

Frank Lloyd Wright undertook the "impossible" task of building
the immense Imperial Hotel in Tokyo, Japan, a land of terrible earth-
quakes. Eight feet below the surface of the earth he found a 60-foot bed
of soft mud. After four years of work amid ridicule and jeers, he was
successful in floating his great structure upon this strange foundation.
There it was, perfectly balanced. Soon the worst earthquake in 52 years
shook down many houses and buildings nearby, but amid the ruins the
Imperial Hotel stood. It could adjust itself to the tremors of the earth.

When we place ourselves in the hands of God, we are safe in all
life's crises and storms. God specializes in crises. The apostle Paul was
sure that the Lord would supply all the needs of the Philippians, and we
can be sure that He will supply ours, too. The God of the early church
is our God today. His riches of grace are large, but what shall we say of
His riches in glory?

"I believe in faith as much as anyone," says one, "but you must
have the money in the bank." We agree, if it is God's bank, supplying
God's people by Christ Jesus.

MEDITATION PRAYER: *"O continue thy lovingkindness unto*
*them that know thee; and thy righteousness to the upright in heart" (Ps. 36:10).*

# DECEMBER 3

*Many are the afflictions of the righteous: but the Lord delivereth him out of them all (Ps. 34:19).*

God does not promise that His people will not have trouble. He does not say that they will never be afflicted, but He promises to bring them out of all their afflictions. In some cases this deliverance may not be completed in this life. God did not keep the worthies out of the fire, but "the form of the fourth" was with them. He did not keep Daniel out of the lions' den, but His angel delivered him there. He did not keep the apostle Paul out of the storm, but His angel was with him in the storm. Of the apostle Peter, bound with two chains in the innermost prison, it is written: "Behold, the angel of the Lord came upon him, and a light shined in the prison" (Acts 12:7).

It is indeed true that "many are the afflictions of the righteous," but "the righteous cry, and the Lord heareth, and delivereth them out of all their troubles" (Ps. 34:17). The Scriptures declare that "man is born unto trouble, as the sparks fly upward" (Job 5:7). But there is something more to it than this. As Edward Judson, son of Adoniram Judson, has said: "Suffering and success go together. If you are succeeding without suffering, it is because others before you have suffered. If you are suffering without succeeding, it is that others after you may succeed."

It was in the very midst of the storm when, to the disciples in the little boat, everything seemed lost, that Jesus appeared walking on the water and said, "It is I; be not afraid" (Matt. 14:27).

> When waves of trouble round me swell,
>   My soul is not dismayed;
> I hear a voice I know full well—
>   "'Tis I; be not afraid."
>
> —C. Elliott

MEDITATION PRAYER: *"Be pleased, O Lord, to deliver me: Lord, make haste to help me" (Ps. 40:13).*

# DECEMBER 4

*He will turn again, he will have compassion upon us;*
*he will subdue our iniquities; and thou wilt cast all*
*their sins into the depths of the sea (Micah 7:19).*

With this we should read the preceding verse: "Who is a God like unto thee, that pardoneth iniquity, and passeth by the transgression of the remnant of his heritage? he retaineth not his anger for ever, because he delighteth in mercy." Then follows our promise text.

Notice that these two verses form a prayer and meditation combined. First the prophet prays to God, then seems to meditate in his own heart concerning God's mercy and compassion and forgiveness. Then again he prays, "And thou wilt cast all their sins into the depths of the sea." It would be well to memorize both these verses—a wonderful prayer, a wonderful meditation.

To while away a few minutes in a physician's waiting room, an earnest Christian man picked up a scientific volume and began to read. Suddenly he cried out, "Praise the Lord!"

The doctor, who was nearby, said, "What have you found now to praise God about?"

"It says here that a scientific expedition has just discovered a spot in the Pacific Ocean more than 35,000 feet deep. Why shouldn't I praise the Lord? Thirty-five thousand feet of water over my sins! For He shall 'cast all their sins into the depths of the sea.'"

But, after all, this is only a beautiful figure to describe the eternal separation of sin from the repentant soul, for there is something more effective than 35,000 feet of water over our sins. Our Savior's blood has covered them. He "died for our sins according to the scriptures" (1 Cor. 15:3).

MEDITATION PRAYER: *"Remember not the sins of my youth, nor my transgressions: according to thy mercy remember thou me for thy goodness' sake, O Lord" (Ps. 25:7).*

# DECEMBER 5

*Awake, O sword, against my shepherd, and against the man that is my fellow, saith the Lord of hosts: smite the shepherd, and the sheep shall be scattered: and I will turn mine hand upon the little ones (Zech. 13:7).*

Our Savior declared that this prophecy referred to Himself (Matt. 26:31, 32). In the determinate council of God, Jesus was smitten for our sins. He who came to be a blessing to the world received a sword stroke of death, even while bestowing that blessing upon humanity. Sin is so terrible in God's sight that He "spared not his own Son, but delivered him up for us all" (Rom. 8:32).

The wicked of this earth are often unconsciously made to be the sword of God's will (Ps. 17:13). Jesus was put to death by wicked people, who unconsciously fulfilled Zechariah's prophecy.

The sword was to awake "against the man that is my fellow," my equal, or my nearest kin. In John 10:30 we find the words of Jesus, "I and my Father are one." Our promise text declares that He who should die on the cross as a man was also divine. And the Father Himself addressed Jesus as "God" (Heb. 1:8).

At our Savior's crucifixion His disciples were scattered, and then in A.D. 70 the Jewish nation was scattered at the destruction of their city. The promise comes, "I will turn mine hand upon the little ones"—that is, I will intervene in their favor. The humble followers of Christ to the end of time are sustained, comforted, and delivered. After His crucifixion His followers were comforted by His resurrection, and at the time of the destruction of Jerusalem they were delivered. As someone has said: "The hand of Jehovah was turned in wrath upon the Shepherd, that His hand might be turned in grace on the little ones."

MEDITATION PRAYER: *"My soul followeth hard after thee: thy right hand upholdeth me" (Ps. 63:8).*

# DECEMBER 6

*And it shall come to pass afterward, that I will pour out my spirit upon all flesh; and your sons and your daughters shall prophesy, your old men shall dream dreams, your young men shall see visions (Joel 2:28).*

Reading beyond our promise text, we find the prophecy of great signs and wonders in heaven and earth, the coming of the great and terrible day of the Lord, and the promise of final deliverance to all who call upon the name of the Lord.

The prophecy of the great outpouring of the Holy Spirit was not completely fulfilled on the day of Pentecost, but continues through the gospel dispensation and will have its final climax just before the coming of Christ. It is fulfilled, not only in the gift of prophecy and the other gifts that Jesus promised to the church, but also in a great baptism of the Holy Spirit to empower God's people for their final work on earth in preparation for their Lord's return.

Dr. Fisher once wrote to his friend, Lord Eldon, then in government service, asking a special favor. The answer was: "Dear Fisher: I cannot today give you the preferment for which you asked. I remain, Your sincere friend, Eldon. (Turn over.)" Then on the other side were these words: "I gave it to you yesterday."

So God answers the prayer of His children for the baptism of the Holy Spirit.

"From the day of Pentecost to the present time, the Comforter has been sent to all who have yielded themselves fully to the Lord and to His service." "But near the close of earth's harvest, a special bestowal of spiritual grace is promised to prepare the church for the coming of the Son of man. . . . It is for this added power that Christians are to send their petitions to the Lord of the harvest" (*The Acts of the Apostles,* pp. 49, 55). For this power let us daily pray.

MEDITATION PRAYER: *"In the day when I cried thou answeredst me, and strengthenedst me with strength in my soul" (Ps. 138:3).*

# DECEMBER 7

*So then faith cometh by hearing,*
*and hearing by the word of God (Rom. 10:17).*

The way to increase faith is to feed upon the Word of God. The Holy Scripture received into the heart actually becomes faith. In one of Martin Luther's spiritual conflicts he seemed to hear the devil ask him if he felt that his sins were forgiven. "No," said the great Reformer, "but I know that they are forgiven, because God says so in His Word."

The apostle Paul did not say, "Believe on the Lord Jesus Christ and thou shalt *feel* saved," but "Believe on the Lord Jesus Christ, and thou shalt *be* saved" (Acts 16:31). The Philippian jailer heard the word of God and believed; so did the Ethiopian chancellor. The father of the afflicted boy heard the word and cried, "Lord, I believe; help thou mine unbelief" (Mark 9:24). On the day of Pentecost 3,000 sinners heard the word and believed; and millions since that day have heard and believed. Yes, "faith cometh by hearing."

The captain of the old ironclad *Merrimac* was a skeptic. One day in the Pennsylvania Soldiers' Home, where he was staying, the chaplain challenged him to read the Bible and mark in red anything that he didn't believe, and to begin with the Gospel of John. With a glitter in his eye the old captain accepted the challenge. Whenever the chaplain would ask him if he had marked anything yet, he would only smile. Several days later the chaplain stepped into his room and found him dead. The Bible lay open on his bed, and the chaplain began looking for red marks. He found nothing until he came to John 3:16. Beside that verse he found these words written in red: "I have cast my anchor in a safe harbor, thank God!"

If we will but honestly hear the Word of God, faith will come. It will grow, and it will lead us into this safe harbor too.

MEDITATION PRAYER: *"I rejoice at thy word, as one that findeth great spoil" (Ps. 119:162).*

# DECEMBER 8

*That if thou shalt confess with thy mouth the Lord Jesus,*
*and shalt believe in thine heart that God hath raised*
*him from the dead, thou shalt be saved (Rom. 10:9).*

Have I avowed the belief of my heart with the words of my mouth? At the beginning of the Reformation, Martin of Basel was afraid to confess Christ openly, so he wrote on a leaf of parchment: "O most merciful Christ, I know that I can be saved only by the merit of Thy blood. Holy Jesus, I acknowledge Thy sufferings for me. I love Thee! I love Thee!" Then he removed a stone from the wall of his room and hid it there. It was not discovered for more than 100 years.

About the same time Martin Luther found the truth in Christ and said, "My Lord has confessed me before men; I will not shrink from confessing Him before kings." And the mighty Reformation followed. The whole world knows of Martin Luther, but who has ever heard of Martin of Basel? Jesus said, "Whosoever therefore shall confess me before men, him will I confess also before my Father which is in heaven" (Matt. 10:32).

When Victorinus was asked to join the church, he said, "What? Do walls make a Christian?"

"No" was the reply. "But he who is ashamed of Me, of him too will I be ashamed before My Father."

The apostle Paul insists upon a lip confession of the Lord. And notice, his words are very plain as to the result: "Thou shalt be saved." But to experience the beatitude of heaven, we must be saved from the guilt of sin, from the power of sin, from the punishment of sin, and finally from the very presence of sin.

Our Savior Himself "before Pontius Pilate witnessed a good confession" (1 Tim. 6:13). So it is our privilege to witness for Him at every suitable opportunity.

MEDITATION PRAYER: *"I will speak of thy testimonies also before kings, and will not be ashamed" (Ps. 119:46).*

# DECEMBER 9

*Fear thou not; for I am with thee: be not dismayed; for I am thy God: I will strengthen thee; yea, I will help thee; yea, I will uphold thee with the right hand of my righteousness (Isa. 41:10).*

God commands us not to fear and reminds us that He is with us. We are not to be dismayed, for He is our God. This should really be enough, but there follows the beautiful threefold promise: "I will strengthen thee; . . . help thee; . . . uphold thee."

Our strength may be nothing, but God's strength is omnipotent. "Trust ye in the Lord for ever: for in the Lord Jehovah is everlasting strength" (Isa. 26:4). And the promise is "I will help thee." His strength within us is supplemented by His help without, for He is "a very present help in trouble" (Ps. 46:1). We may say, "The Lord is my helper, and I will not fear what man shall do unto me" (Heb. 13:6), for day by day our "help cometh from the Lord, which made heaven and earth" (Ps. 121:2). And then, beyond all that, we have God's hand to lean upon—yes, His *right* hand.

A minister tells of his little girl's coming to his study and finding the door closed. With her tiny hand she could not grasp the doorknob firmly enough to open it. But suddenly the door opened from the inside, and she ran in crying, "Oh, Daddy, I opened the door all by myself." Of course, it was her father's hand that had done it. So God helps us when we do our best, and in His strength we are strong.

> Like as a father, constant is He,
> God in compassion regardeth our plea;
> In need He cometh, precious His promise:
> Father in heaven forever to be.
> —F. E. Belden

MEDITATION PRAYER: *"Blessed be the Lord my strength, . . . my goodness, and my fortress; my high tower, and my deliverer: my shield, and he in whom I trust" (Ps. 144:1, 2).*

# DECEMBER 10

*Henceforth there is laid up for me a crown of righteousness, which the Lord, the righteous judge, shall give me at that day: and not to me only, but unto all them also that love his appearing (2 Tim. 4:8).*

On one occasion when Father Taylor, the evangelical preacher, was preaching from this text, "I have fought a good fight, I have finished my course, I have kept the faith: henceforth there is laid up for me a crown of righteousness," he suddenly stopped, and looking up to heaven, cried out with a loud voice, "Paul, are there any more crowns there?" Then, turning to the congregation, he said: "Yes, friends, there are many more crowns left. They have not all been taken. Blessed be God, there is one for me, and one for all of you who love the appearing of our Lord Jesus Christ."

The apostle in chains had appeared before an unrighteous judge who had condemned him unjustly, but he knew that someday the righteous judge, even the Lord Jesus Christ, would give him his true reward—a crown of righteousness, and not to him only, but to all those who love our Lord's appearing.

The Mamertine Prison, in which the apostle may have written this last letter of his, is still damp, cold, and dreary; but the light of this wonderful promise has lit the hearts of millions through the darkest valleys of life, and will continue to illuminate the world to the end of time.

> The Lord is my light, my all and in all;
> There is in His sight no darkness at all;
> He is my Redeemer, my Savior and King;
> With saints and with angels His praises I sing.
> —James Nicholson

MEDITATION PRAYER: *"And as for me, thou upholdest me in thine integrity, and settest me before thy face for ever" (Ps. 41:12).*

# DECEMBER 11

*Lift up your eyes to the heavens, and look upon the
earth beneath: for the heavens shall vanish away like smoke,
and the earth shall wax old like a garment, and they that dwell
therein shall die in like manner: but my salvation shall be for
ever, and my righteousness shall not be abolished (Isa. 51:6).*

During the French Revolution the Vendean revolutionist Jeanbon St. Andre said to a Vendean peasant, "I will have all your churches pulled down, so that you will no longer have anything to remind you of your old superstition."

"But," said the peasant, "you will leave us the stars."

Even the constellations of the heavens, which seem to us so fixed, will change in the course of ages. The atmospheric heavens will "pass away with a great noise" (2 Peter 3:10), the earth shall wax old and be changed; but God's salvation is forever. His righteousness will never be abolished. He is "the same yesterday, and to day, and for ever" (Heb. 13:8). We can depend upon His Word, too, for we read in Psalm 119:89, "For ever, O Lord, thy word is settled in heaven." The universe itself may change its form and pass away, but God will not change. Because "I change not; therefore ye sons of Jacob are not consumed" (Mal. 3:6).

> The stars shine over the ocean,
>     The stars shine over the lea,
> The stars look up at the mighty God,
>     The stars look down on me.
>
> The stars will shine a million years,
>     For a million years and a day,
> But God and I will live and love
>     When the stars are passed away.

MEDITATION PRAYER: *"They [the heavens] shall perish, but thou shalt endure: yea, all of them shall wax old like a garment; as a vesture shalt thou change them, and they shall be changed" (Ps. 102:26).*

# DECEMBER 12

*Blessed and holy is he that hath part in the first resurrection: on such the second death hath no power, but they shall be priests of God and of Christ, and shall reign with him a thousand years (Rev. 20:6).*

All those who have died since the beginning of time will rise at last. "For as in Adam all die, even so in Christ shall all be made alive. But every man in his own order: Christ the firstfruits; afterward they that are Christ's at his coming" (1 Cor. 15:22, 23). "This is the first resurrection" (Rev. 20:5), the resurrection of the "blessed and holy." A thousand years later the rest of the dead rise to judgment and the second death. Between these two resurrections is the millennium, the thousand years of prophecy during which the blessed and holy are priests of God and of Christ, and reign with Him. Where will we be during the millennium—with Christ, in the heavenly place; or upon this earth, which will be waste and void?

In the beginning, before the face of nature was marred by sin, God said of this world that it was very good. If that was true of this earth, what will heaven be like? A small girl looked up wondering into the star-studded sky and exclaimed, "If the wrong side of heaven looks like that, what must the right side be like?" And so say we.

As travelers often study the language of countries to which they expect to go, let us study the language of heaven, the language of faith, the language of love.

> Let us learn the language of that home
> Whilst here on earth we be,
> Lest our poor hearts for want of words,
> Be dumb in that high company.

MEDITATION PRAYER: *"They shall abundantly utter the memory of thy great goodness, and shall sing of thy righteousness" (Ps. 145:7).*

# DECEMBER 13

*I the Lord have called thee in righteousness, and will*
*hold thine hand, and will keep thee, and give thee for a*
*covenant of the people, for a light of the Gentiles (Isa. 42:6).*

This passage is like a High Sierra range with four glorious snow-clad peaks of promise that reflect God's promise in four words—*call, hold, keep, give*. God calls His children, He holds them, He keeps them, and He gives them.

When Staupitz commanded Martin Luther to ascend the pulpit and preach, the modest professor put up 15 arguments, or pretexts, with which to excuse himself. Staupitz persisted.

"Ah, worthy doctor," said Martin, "it would be the death of me."

"What then?" was the response. "Be it so in God's name."

Luther then ascended the pulpit in the old wooden chapel, which was propped up on all sides to keep it from falling, and there commenced the Reformation by preaching. The mighty results that followed proved the call to have been from God.

God calls all believers to His service. They are all to be workers for Him. "Go ye into all the world, and preach the gospel" (Mark 16:15) was said to all Christ's disciples. He holds the hands of those He calls and leads them through every dark place and into the right fields of labor. He keeps them as "a wall . . . on their right hand, and on their left" (Ex. 14:22) when they cannot keep themselves. Then, to bless others, He gives them His covenant, His promise, as a light to the nations.

> Are you Christ's light bearer? of His joy a sharer?
> Is this dark world fairer for your cheering ray?
> Is your beacon lighted, guiding souls benighted
> To the land of perfect day?
> —Priscilla J. Owens

MEDITATION PRAYER: *"Therefore will I give thanks unto thee, O Lord, among the heathen, and sing praises unto thy name" (Ps. 18:49).*

# DECEMBER 14

*For our conversation is in heaven; from whence also we look for the Saviour, the Lord Jesus Christ: who shall change our vile body, that it may be fashioned like unto his glorious body, according to the working whereby he is able even to subdue all things unto himself (Phil. 3:20, 21).*

Sickness, physical disabilities, the burdens of age come upon us, and then we know that this body is indeed "the body of our humiliation," as one translation puts it. In the body, temptations of the flesh afflict us, and we know that the word "vile" is not too strong. Our bodies humble us; they link us even with the dust. But our Savior has promised to change it all.

The apostle Paul says that our conversation, our citizenship, is in heaven, from whence we look for our Savior to appear. A day of change is coming—no more aching brows, swollen limbs, failing hearts. It is coming—the day of immortal youth, when even these bodies of ours shall suddenly be changed, "like unto his glorious body." What a promise! What a hope!

An old English soldier was relating how one of his companions had lost both legs in the Crimean War. The day came when the soldiers were to appear before the queen for their medals. "Someone pinned one on me," said the soldier, "but when the queen saw the legless man being carried on a stretcher, she took his medal in her own hands and pinned it on him, exclaiming, 'My brave soldier! My brave soldier!' And as she bent over him, her tears fell upon his face. My friend never mentioned the medal afterward, but he would always say, 'Boys, I looked into the face of the queen, and that was reward enough for me.'" And so it will be with God's children when they look into the face of their Savior. Then "we shall be like him; for we shall see him as he is" (1 John 3:2).

MEDITATION PRAYER: *"All thy works shall praise thee, O Lord; and thy saints shall bless thee" (Ps. 145:10).*

# DECEMBER 15

*For we must all appear before the judgment seat of Christ;*
*that every one may receive the things done in his body, according*
*to that he hath done, whether it be good or bad (2 Cor. 5:10).*

All human beings must appear in judgment. But to the Christian what a glorious consideration—our Redeemer is to be our judge! "The Father . . . hath committed all judgment unto the Son" (John 5:22). He who died for us passes final sentence as to the reward for our works.

When Dr. Channing was 10 years old, he heard Dr. Hopkins preach a mighty sermon on the subject of the judgment. He was deeply impressed and expected his father to speak to him about his soul's salvation. But not a word was said. On reaching home, the father sat down to read. Dr. Channing says: "I made up my mind that my father did not believe one word of what he had heard. He was not alarmed, so why should I be? I dismissed the whole subject from my thoughts." Could it be that the father's thoughtlessness drove his son into the ranks of unbelief regarding evangelical Bible doctrines? In view of the solemn and certain fact that everyone must stand before the judgment seat of Christ, shall we not speak of it to our children and friends?

All our works must be wrought in Christ. He is the sure and only foundation. "Now if any man build upon this foundation gold, silver, precious stones, wood, hay, stubble; every man's work shall be made manifest: for the day shall declare it, because it shall be revealed by fire; and the fire shall try every man's work of what sort it is. If any man's work abide which he hath built thereupon, he shall receive a reward. If any man's work shall be burned, he shall suffer loss: but he himself shall be saved; yet so as by fire" (1 Cor. 3:12-15). Are we preparing here for our appearance there?

MEDITATION PRAYER: *"Thou didst cause judgment to be heard from heaven; the earth feared, and was still" (Ps. 76:8).*

# DECEMBER 16

*But the salvation of the righteous is of the Lord: he is their strength in the time of trouble. And the Lord shall help them, and deliver them: he shall deliver them from the wicked, and save them, because they trust in him (Ps. 37:39, 40).*

The Old Testament and the New Testament are in perfect harmony on this subject. Our salvation does not come from humans, but from the Lord, and it is by faith that we will be saved, because we trust in Him. We read in Ephesians 2:8: "For by grace are ye saved through faith; and that not of yourselves: it is the gift of God." From the beginning of the world until today it has always been true that it is not by any works of righteousness we have done but through His mercy that He saves us (Titus 3:5).

A man who seemed to be going blind and had only $100 to his name went to a great eye specialist. "I am not sure whether you can pay my fee," said the doctor. "I never perform an operation for less than $500."

"Then I must go blind and remain so," said the poor man.

"You cannot come up to my terms, and I cannot go down to yours. But there is another way," suggested the specialist. "I can perform the operation free."

And so it is that we come to the Great Physician and say:

> Nothing in my hand I bring,
> Simply to Thy cross I cling.
> —Augustus M. Toplady

Notice what the Lord will do for His people. He will be their strength in time of trouble; He will help them, deliver them, and save them. What wonderful words of encouragement! He who has brought us salvation will be our guide through life. No real harm can come to us while we abide in Him and He abides with us.

MEDITATION PRAYER: *"But I am poor and needy: make haste unto me, O God: thou art my help and my deliverer; O Lord, make no tarrying" (Ps. 70:5).*

# DECEMBER 17

*If we confess our sins, he is faithful and just to forgive us our sins, and to cleanse us from all unrighteousness (1 John 1:9).*

This is one of the great promises and one needed by everybody, for "all have sinned, and come short of the glory of God" (Rom. 3:23), and "the wages of sin is death" (Rom. 6:23). This is one of the absolutely necessary steps toward heaven—confession of sin. Read the connection here. It is the Lord who forgives our sins, the Lord who cleanses us from all unrighteousness. And He is faithful. He will not forget one sin; He will not overlook one. Every sin will be cleansed, every one will be forgiven. His death was an atoning sacrifice "for the sins of the whole world" (1 John 2:2).

Not only is He faithful, but He is just. If we confess our sins and accept Christ as our Redeemer, it would be unjust on God's part not to forgive us, since Jesus has died for our sins—every one of them. The debt has been canceled on the cross. It cannot be collected now.

Political offenders are sometimes given what is called an amnesty. That means, literally, a "not remembering." This is exactly what the Lord grants to everyone who comes to Him through His Son Jesus Christ. No matter what the offense or offenses may be, our God, who is ready to pardon, says, "Their sins and iniquities will I remember no more" (Heb. 10:17).

Not only does our God forgive, but He cleanses from all unrighteousness. The life of the Christian is to be like His every day. Deliverance from the condemnation of sin is justification, and deliverance from the power of sin is sanctification. Someday He will deliver from the presence of sin, and that will be glorification. Until that day let us lean upon this wonderful promise.

MEDITATION PRAYER: *"Iniquities prevail against me: as for our transgressions, thou shalt purge them away" (Ps. 65:3).*

# DECEMBER 18

*And the peace of God, which passeth all understanding,*
*shall keep your hearts and minds through Christ Jesus (Phil. 4:7).*

P hilippi was a military colony, an outpost of the Roman Empire. In his Epistle to the Philippians the apostle uses several military terms. One such is found in our promise verse for today.

In the phrase "shall keep your hearts," Paul used a Greek word meaning "guard," or "garrison," as a well-protected stronghold. In Isaiah 26:1-3 it is written: "We have a strong city; salvation will God appoint for walls and bulwarks. Open ye the gates, that the righteous nation which keepeth the truth may enter in. Thou wilt keep him in perfect peace, whose mind is stayed on thee: because he trusteth in thee."

God's truth, God's salvation, God's peace, are the gates, walls, and bulwarks protecting His people. Yes, what a mighty fortress is the peace of God! It passes all understanding. We cannot analyze it. The greatest student of mind therapy cannot lay it out on the table for mental dissection. It is not arrived at by mental gymnastics. It is not a result of psychiatric therapies or yoga philosophies. It is the peace of God. It is the peace that Jesus knew and offered to His followers. "Peace I leave with you, my peace I give unto you: not as the world giveth, give I unto you. Let not your heart be troubled, neither let it be afraid" (John 14:27). Our emotions as well as our intellect will be garrisoned by this peace "through Christ Jesus."

> Peace, peace, sweet peace,
> Wonderful gift from above;
> Oh, wonderful, wonderful peace,
> Sweet peace, the gift of God's love.
> —P. P. Bilhorn

MEDITATION PRAYER: *"The Lord lift up his countenance upon thee, and give thee peace" (Num. 6:26).*

# DECEMBER 19

*And there shall be no more curse: but the throne of God and of the Lamb shall be in it; and his servants shall serve him (Rev. 22:3).*

In the very beginning of this world, sin brought a curse upon the earth (Gen. 3:17). "The wages of sin is death" (Rom. 6:23). The curse that followed sin has affected the entire human race. In the verse preceding our promise text, we are told that the tree of life will bear a different fruit every month there by the river of life. Had the first Adam been permitted to eat of this tree after he sinned, he would have lived forever in his fallen state, and that would have been the greatest curse of all.

We are told that God will dwell here in this earth made new, for "the throne of God and of the Lamb shall be in it." He can dwell only where there is no curse or sin, which is the cause of the curse. It is the Lamb, and He alone, who "hath redeemed us from the curse . . . , being made a curse for us: for it is written, Cursed is every one that hangeth on a tree" (Gal. 3:13).

The curse of sin and death comes upon all those who disobey God's law of righteousness. And all have sinned; therefore, all have been under the curse. Jesus, who knew no sin, was made sin for us "that we might be made the righteousness of God in him" (2 Cor. 5:21). In that curseless land of blessing, God's servants will truly serve Him. Here we serve God by helping others, but there we shall serve Him directly.

Kepler, the astronomer, looking up from his mathematical computations, once said, "I think Thy thoughts after Thee, O God." May this be our service here and before the throne.

MEDITATION PRAYER: *"O Lord, how great are thy works! and thy thoughts are very deep" (Ps. 92:5).*

# DECEMBER 20

*But if we walk in the light, as he is in the light,*
*we have fellowship one with another, and the blood of*
*Jesus Christ his Son cleanseth us from all sin (1 John 1:7).*

What a promise this is! If we walk in the light as it is revealed in Christ, we have Christian fellowship and cleansing from all sin through His blood.

Hemeralopia is a peculiar disease of the eye, causing a defect of vision so that objects can be seen only at night. Are not some Christians afflicted with a sort of spiritual hemeralopia? They desire just a little light. The bright sunshine of a holy, consecrated life pains their weak eyes. They walk in some light, but not in the light as Christ is in the light.

It is the obedient whom the blood of Christ cleanses from all sin. The person who knowingly rejects light cannot plead this promise.

"What is the blood of Christ?" asked Livingstone in that last solitary month of his African wanderings. "It is Himself. It is the inherent and everlasting mercy of God, made apparent to human eyes and ears. The everlasting love, disclosed by our Lord's life and death. It shows that God forgives because He loves to forgive."

As we pray, we look up into a face of forgiveness, a face marked with lines of suffering endured for our sakes. "Ye were not redeemed with corruptible things, as silver and gold, . . . but with the precious blood of Christ" (1 Peter 1:18, 19).

> Thy love, O Christ, arisen,
> Yearns to reach all souls in prison:
> Now beneath the shame and loss
> Sinks the plummet of Thy cross.
> Never yet abyss was found
> Deeper than Thy grace can sound.

MEDITATION PRAYER: *"Make thy face to shine upon thy servant: save me for thy mercies' sake" (Ps. 31:16).*

# DECEMBER 21

*And there shall be no night there; and they need no candle,
neither light of the sun; for the Lord God giveth them light:
and they shall reign for ever and ever (Rev. 22:5).*

In the city of God 'there shall be no night.' None will need or desire repose. There will be no weariness in doing the will of God and offering praise to His name. We shall ever feel the freshness of the morning and shall ever be far from its close. . . . The glory of God and the Lamb floods the Holy City with unfading light. The redeemed walk in the sunless glory of perpetual day" (*The Great Controversy*, p. 676).

The light of that city is divine, "for the glory of God did lighten it, and the Lamb is the light thereof. And the nations of them which are saved shall walk in the light of it" (Rev. 21:23, 24). If we follow Him who is the light of life here, we shall walk with Him in eternal light there.

Those who come out of the darkness of sin into the light of the gospel will reign here in the light the Lord God shall give.

John Newton, who came out of the depths of sin and degradation to be a noble minister of God, said there will be three wonders he will see in the light of heaven. The first wonder will be to see so many people there whom he did not expect to see. The second wonder will be to miss many people whom he did expect to see. The third and greatest wonder of all will be to find himself there. God grant that we may all share that wonder too in the city of light eternal.

> So at last we see in heaven's bright morning
> The face of Him who brought our soul from night;
> And in the pure glory of that fair dawning,
> All shadows end in His eternal light.

MEDITATION PRAYER: *"Every day will I bless thee; and I will praise thy name for ever and ever"* (Ps. 145:2).

# DECEMBER 22

*Then the eyes of the blind shall be opened, and the ears
of the deaf shall be unstopped. Then shall the lame man leap
as an hart, and the tongue of the dumb sing: for in the wilderness
shall waters break out, and streams in the desert (Isa. 35:5, 6).*

The blind, the deaf, the lame, the dumb—how wonderfully Jesus healed them all, and how the water of life did flow when He was on earth! But how much more extensively and literally will all of this great promise be fulfilled in the new earth and in the New Jerusalem now above, "which is the mother of us all" (Gal. 4:26). Some eyes that have never had one glimpse of the beauties of this earth, or of its sorrowful, sordid scenes either, will open wide in astonishment at the glory of Emmanuel's land. The ears of those who have never heard their names spoken by human lips will thrill to the music of angels and the voice of Christ. Limbs paralyzed through long years of suffering will leap for joy in the abundance of immortal health. Tongues that have never formed an articulate word will help fill the chorus of redemption's song. What a hope, what joy, what a land, what a Savior!

Jesus said, "Blessed are the meek: for they shall inherit the earth" (Matt. 5:5). And with the apostle Peter we too "look for new heavens and a new earth, wherein dwelleth righteousness" (2 Peter 3:13). So this is a real promise for real people of a real home in a real land—the land, as someone has said, "where dreams come true."

But how shall we find that land? When asked the way to heaven, Bishop Wilberforce once said, "Take the first turn to the right and go straight forward." And to this land our Savior Himself is "the way" (John 14:6).

MEDITATION PRAYER: *"To the end that my glory may sing praise to thee, and not be silent. O Lord my God, I will give thanks unto thee for ever" (Ps. 30:12).*

# DECEMBER 23

*And God shall wipe away all tears from their eyes; and there shall be no more death, neither sorrow, nor crying, neither shall there be any more pain: for the former things are passed away (Rev. 21:4).*

No more tears, death, sorrow, crying, pain. Who would not wish to live in such a land? All these things are among the former things. Now they are passed away. How? Through a change in civilization? Through great wisdom, culture, education? Through human effort? No, never! By the power of God. *"God* shall wipe away all tears from their eyes." So, friend, read His promise through your tears and have faith in God.

> Have faith in God to bring the end of tears,
> Have faith in God; no death, no pain, no fears.
> Have faith in God through the eternal years.
> Have faith, dear friend, in God.

After his dream of the City of God, John Bunyan wrote: "Now, just as the gates were opened to let in the men, I looked in after them, and behold, the City shone like the sun; the streets also were paved with gold; and in them walked many men, with crowns on their heads, palms in their hands, and golden harps, to sing praises withal. They were also of them that had wings, and they answered one another without intermission, saying, Holy, holy, holy is the Lord. And after that they shut up the gates: which when I had seen, I wished myself among them."

And so do we all. May the Good Shepherd lead every one of us to that city at last.

MEDITATION PRAYER: *"For thou, Lord, hast made me glad through thy work: I will triumph in the works of thy hands" (Ps. 92:4).*

# DECEMBER 24

*Therefore the Lord himself shall give you*
*a sign; Behold, a virgin shall conceive, and bear*
*a son, and shall call his name Immanuel (Isa. 7:14).*

Who is this Son of the "sign," the virgin-born? Isaiah tells us, "Immanuel." Thus nearly seven centuries before the angel announced His birth to the wondering shepherds in the starlit fields of Judea, a gospel prophet announced the coming of the Holy Child.

To Joseph, the espoused husband of the virgin Mary, the angel said: "Take unto thee Mary thy wife: for that which is conceived in her is of the Holy Ghost. And she shall bring forth a son, and thou shalt call his name Jesus: for he shall save his people from their sins. Now all this was done, that it might be fulfilled which was spoken of the Lord by the prophet, saying, Behold, a virgin shall be with child, and shall bring forth a son, and they shall call his name Emmanuel, which being interpreted is, God with us" (Matt. 1:20-23).

All this was done to save us who are alive today and all others who have ever lived or ever will live. "From the days of eternity the Lord Jesus Christ was one with the Father. . . . To this sin-darkened earth He came to reveal the light of God's love" (*The Desire of Ages,* p. 19).

"He says, 'A body hast thou prepared me.' . . . His divinity was veiled with humanity—the invisible glory in the visible human form. . . . So Christ was to come in 'the body of our humiliation' (Phil. 3:21, RV), 'in the likeness of men.' . . . Yet He was the incarnate God, the light of heaven and earth. . . . So Christ set up His tabernacle in the midst of our human encampment. . . . 'The Word became flesh, and tabernacled among us (and we beheld His glory, glory as of the Only Begotten from the Father), full of grace and truth' (John 1:14, RV, margin). . . . By His humanity, Christ touched humanity; by His divinity, He lays hold upon the throne of God" (*ibid.,* pp. 23, 24). This is the Incarnation; this is our Savior.

MEDITATION PRAYER: *"I will extol thee, my God, O king; and I will bless thy name for ever and ever" (Ps. 145:1).*

# DECEMBER 25

*For unto us a child is born, unto us a son is given: and the government shall be upon his shoulder: and his name shall be called Wonderful, Counsellor, The mighty God, The everlasting Father, The Prince of Peace (Isa. 9:6).*

Who is this Child of Bethlehem, cradled in a manger? The angels will tell you, He is the "Saviour, which is Christ the Lord" (Luke 2:11). Adam will tell you, The Seed of the woman that shall bruise the serpent's head. Ask Abraham, and he will tell you, He is King of Salem, King of Peace. Jacob will tell you, He is Shiloh of the tribe of Judah. Isaiah will tell you, He is Immanuel, God with us. Jeremiah will tell you that He is "the Lord our Righteousness" (Jer. 23:6). Daniel will tell you, He is the Messiah, the Anointed One. Hosea will tell you, He is "the Lord God of hosts" (Hosea 12:5). John the Baptist will tell you, He is "the Lamb of God" (John 1:29). Ask Nathanael, and he will tell you, He is the "Son of God; . . . the King of Israel" (verse 49). And God Himself proclaimed from heaven, "This is my beloved Son, in whom I am well pleased" (Matt. 3:17). "Unto the Son he saith, Thy throne, O God, is for ever and ever" (Heb. 1:8). Ask the powers of darkness, and they will acknowledge Him as "the Holy One of God" (Mark 1:24). And so may we well say, "This is Jesus, the Christ, our Savior, and the Redeemer of the world."

> Incarnate God, laid in a manger,
>> Born Son of man for death and pain;
> Thy virgin mother, O tiny Stranger,
>> The sword must pierce to seal our gain.
>
> The star ablaze, its radiance stealing
>> O'er shepherd hills, from heaven above;
> We see the Wise Men, reverent, kneeling,
>> And we, with them, O King of Love.

MEDITATION PRAYER: *"Let the people praise thee, O God; let all the people praise thee" (Ps. 67:5).*

# DECEMBER 26

*And when the chief Shepherd shall appear, ye shall receive a crown of glory that fadeth not away (1 Peter 5:4).*

In this the two apostles are in perfect harmony, for Paul declares in 2 Timothy 4:1 that the Lord Jesus Christ shall judge the living and the dead at His appearing, and adds in verse 8: "Henceforth there is laid up for me a crown of righteousness, which the Lord, the righteous judge, shall give me at that day: and not to me only, but unto all them also that love his appearing." This is the crowning time, at "his appearing."

Everything depends upon His appearing, His return. We are to love His appearing. We are to look for the glorious appearing (Titus 2:13). He who appeared in the presence of God as our high priest will appear the second time without sin unto salvation to them that look for him (Heb. 9:24, 28). Are we looking for Him? When the Chief Shepherd appears, the undershepherds will find their reward, and the sheep their eternal home.

Dean Farrar relates that Queen Victoria, after hearing one of her chaplains preach at Windsor on the second advent of Christ, spoke to the dean about it and said, "O how I wish the Lord would come during my lifetime."

"Why does Your Majesty feel this very earnest desire?" asked the great preacher.

With her countenance illuminated with deep emotion the queen replied, "Because I should so love to lay my crown at His feet."

> And when I shall see His glory face to face,
> Hear His glad welcome, feel His fond embrace,
> And feast on the fulness of His heavenly grace,
> I shall be satisfied then.
>
> —Horatius Bonar

MEDITATION PRAYER: *"The king shall joy in thy strength, O Lord; and in thy salvation how greatly shall he rejoice!" (Ps. 21:1).*

# DECEMBER 27

*Beloved, now are we the sons of God, and it doth not yet appear what we shall be: but we know that, when he shall appear, we shall be like him; for we shall see him as he is (1 John 3:2).*

By repentance toward God and faith in Christ, the fallen children of humanity may once more become the children of God. Our Savior has opened the way so that the most sinful, needy, oppressed, and despised may become a part of the heavenly family.

Jesus taught us, when we pray, to say, "Our Father." He is eager to welcome us as His children. "We have an Advocate in the heavens, and whoever accepts Him as a personal Savior, is not left an orphan, to bear the burden of his own sins" (*Thoughts From the Mount of Blessing,* p. 104). "Beloved, now are we the sons of God." "And if children, then heirs; heirs of God, and joint-heirs with Christ; if so be that we suffer with him, that we may be also glorified together" (Rom. 8:17).

The glory that is waiting for God's children has not yet appeared. It appears when Christ appears. "For our light affliction, which is but for a moment, worketh for us a far more exceeding and eternal weight of glory" (2 Cor. 4:17). "For I reckon," says the apostle, "that the sufferings of this present time are not worthy to be compared with the glory which shall be revealed in us" (Rom. 8:18).

As we become more and more like Christ by beholding Him spiritually now, so shall we be like Him in glory, for by beholding we become changed (2 Cor. 3:18).

Back in the days of slavery a visitor once watched a group of slaves slouching and shuffling off to their work. One tall, broad-shouldered fellow walked by, head erect, with a steady gait. "How's that?" the visitor asked. "Oh, he's the son of an African king" was the reply. "And he never forgets it." Let us not forget that we are sons and daughters of the King of kings.

MEDITATION PRAYER: *"Thou art my God, and I will praise thee: thou art my God, I will exalt thee" (Ps. 118:28).*

# DECEMBER 28

*For the Lord himself shall descend from heaven with a shout, with the voice of the archangel, and with the trump of God: and the dead in Christ shall rise first: then we which are alive and remain shall be caught up together with them in the clouds, to meet the Lord in the air: and so shall we ever be with the Lord. Wherefore comfort one another with these words (1 Thess. 4:16–18).*

This is the first resurrection, the resurrection of the just, the resurrection to life. The living saints will then be caught up with those who have just been raised from the dead to meet the Lord in the air. This is translation. It is then that we shall be changed from mortality to immortality. "Then shall be brought to pass the saying that is written, Death is swallowed up in victory" (1 Cor. 15:54). To God's children this is the end of the former things and the beginning of the new. Therefore let us "comfort one another with these words."

Dr. A. T. Pierson relates that the telegram announcing the death of his friend, Dr. A. J. Gordon, came at 3:00 in the morning. Being unable to sleep, he scanned the entire New Testament to see what it said about death. He noticed that after the resurrection of Jesus the apostles seldom used the word "death" to express the close of a Christian's life, but "sleep." What a comfort it is to think of our loved ones as being asleep in Christ, instead of having ceased to be. We look forward to the morning.

> When I shall awake in that fair morn of morns,
> After whose dawning never night returns,
> And with whose bright glory day eternal burns,
> I shall be satisfied then.
>
> —Horatius Bonar

MEDITATION PRAYER: *"In God we boast all the day long, and praise thy name for ever" (Ps. 44:8).*

# DECEMBER 29

*And he that sat upon the throne said, Behold,*
*I make all things new. And he said unto me, Write:*
*for these words are true and faithful (Rev. 21:5).*

Certainly all things need making new. It is about time for the old vesture to be rolled up and the new creation to put on its beautiful garments. Only the Lord who made all things in the beginning can make them new. It takes as great power to make a new world out of an evil one as it does to make one out of nothing. And our Jesus is able to do it. He has been making saints out of sinners. Soon He shall change the body of our humiliation, that it may be like unto His glorious body (Phil. 3:21, ARV). He came "to save *that* which was lost" (Luke 19:10) as well as *those* who were lost. And this new earth will become the eternal home of God's redeemed. "Blessed are the meek: for they shall inherit the earth" (Matt. 5:5).

The New Jerusalem, with its holy inhabitants, will descend from God out of heaven (Rev. 21:2) to become the capital of this earth renewed. All things will be new—new heavens, a new earth, a new immortal race. There will be new work—"they shall build houses, and inhabit them" (Isa. 65:21); new relationships—"God himself shall be with them, and be their God" (Rev. 21:3); new contact with nature—"the wolf . . . shall dwell with the lamb, and the leopard shall lie down with the kid; and the calf and the young lion and the fatling together; and a little child shall lead them" (Isa. 11:6); a new security—"there shall be no more death, neither sorrow, nor crying, neither shall there be any more pain" (Rev. 21:4). And this is a certified promise, for He who inspired it said, "Write: for these words are true and faithful" (verse 5).

MEDITATION PRAYER: *"Among the gods there is none like unto thee, O Lord; neither are there any works like unto thy works" (Ps. 86:8).*

# DECEMBER 30

*For the earth shall be filled with the knowledge of the glory of the Lord, as the waters cover the sea (Hab. 2:14).*

Stand on the seashore and look at the endless expanse, float over it, fly over it, and it seems to cover the entire earth as it did at the world's first dawn. Lord Byron wrote:

> Time writes no wrinkle on thine azure brow;
> Such as creation's dawn beheld, thou rollest now.

As the waters once covered the earth in darkness, so the knowledge of the glory of the Lord shall cover the earth with light and joy.

The margin of our text pictures that future even more wonderfully—"For the earth shall be filled by knowing the glory of the Lord." "The people that dwell therein shall be forgiven their iniquity" (Isa. 33:24). They shall know the glory of the Lord in forgiveness. They shall know that glory of the Lord in fulfilling His promises, for they have come from earthly wanderings to celestial homes, from dens and prisons to joys and mansions, out from iron doors and in through pearly gates. They are home at last, and home forever. Then shall their peace be as a river, and their righteousness as the waves of the sea (Isa. 48:18). Peace, righteousness, knowledge—worldwide and forever!

It is those who have this true knowledge of God who are the real optimists. They are looking forward to something better than this world has ever known. Then, and then only, will the blessed ones be able truly to sing, "As it was in the beginning, is now, and ever shall be, world without end. Amen."

> Thus the vision of God's future—
> All the world in Christ is blest;
> Something higher than the highest,
> Something better than the best.

MEDITATION PRAYER: *"I will speak of the glorious honour of thy majesty, and of thy wondrous works"* (Ps. 145:5).

# DECEMBER 31

*He which testifieth these things saith, Surely I come quickly. Amen. Even so, come, Lord Jesus (Rev. 22:20).*

This is a wonderful text with which to end the year. It contains the last promise and the last prayer in the Bible, and the prayer is in response to the promise. Before we begin another year let us look at this promise and allow it to sink deep into our hearts. These are the very words of Jesus, and He emphasizes the surety of His coming. "Surely I come," He says. Not only so, but "I come quickly." May the response of every one of our hearts be "Even so, surely and quickly, come, Lord Jesus!" This has been the prayer of the church in all its pilgrimage.

We should be ready for His coming (Matt. 24:44). We should be watching for His coming (Luke 12:37). We should earnestly desire His coming (2 Peter 3:12, 13). We should pray for our Lord's coming (Rev. 22:20). We should preach the Second Coming (1 Thess. 4:16–18).

The last act of Horatius Bonar before lying down to sleep each night was to draw aside the curtain, look up into the heavens, and say, "Perhaps tonight, Lord." In the morning his first act was to raise the blind, and looking out upon the dawn, say, "Perhaps today, Lord."

Has it been a long time? To us the exhortation is: "The Lord direct your hearts into . . . the patient waiting for Christ" (2 Thess. 3:5). May the words continue to echo in our hearts: "The Lord is at hand, the time is short."

> He is coming, O my spirit,
> With His everlasting peace,
> With His blessedness immortal and complete.
> He is coming, O my spirit,
> And His coming brings release,
> I listen for the coming of His feet.

MEDITATION PRAYER: *"Blessed be the Lord God of Israel from everlasting, and to everlasting. Amen, and Amen" (Ps. 41:13).*